Around & About
South-West Wales

Around & About South-West Wales

by

Graham Roberts

Logaston Press

LOGASTON PRESS
Little Logaston Woonton Almeley
Herefordshire HR3 6QH
logastonpress.co.uk

First published by Logaston Press 2007
Copyright © Graham Roberts 2007

ISBN 978 1904396 74 1

Set in Times by Logaston Press
and printed in Great Britain by
The Cromwell Press Ltd., Trowbridge

This book is dedicated in all humility to the memory of Wynford Vaughan-Thomas, CBE (1908-1987), an iconic Welshman who was born in Swansea. He attended the Grammar School there, where the English Master was the father of Dylan Thomas, and after Oxford returned to Wales as Keeper of Manuscripts and Records of the National Library at Aberystwyth before joining BBC (Wales). During the war he became a distinguished BBC War Correspondent, broad-casting most memorably from an RAF Lancaster during a bombing raid over Berlin, and from the Anzio Beachhead. Afterwards he travelled worldwide but his heart was clearly in Wales and in 1967 he returned as a Director of Harlech TV (now ITV Wales) and was appointed Director of Programmes.

His many books on Wales and the Welsh countryside (to some of which I am indebted here) stemmed from a variety of travels through his native land, on a bicycle, on horseback, and on foot – on two occasions by walking over the high mountains all the way between the coasts of south and north Wales. As President of the Council for the Protection of Rural Wales it was quite fitting that he should officially open the Pembrokeshire Coast Path on 16 May 1970.

Wynford Vaughan-Thomas died at his home in Fishguard in 1987.

Contents

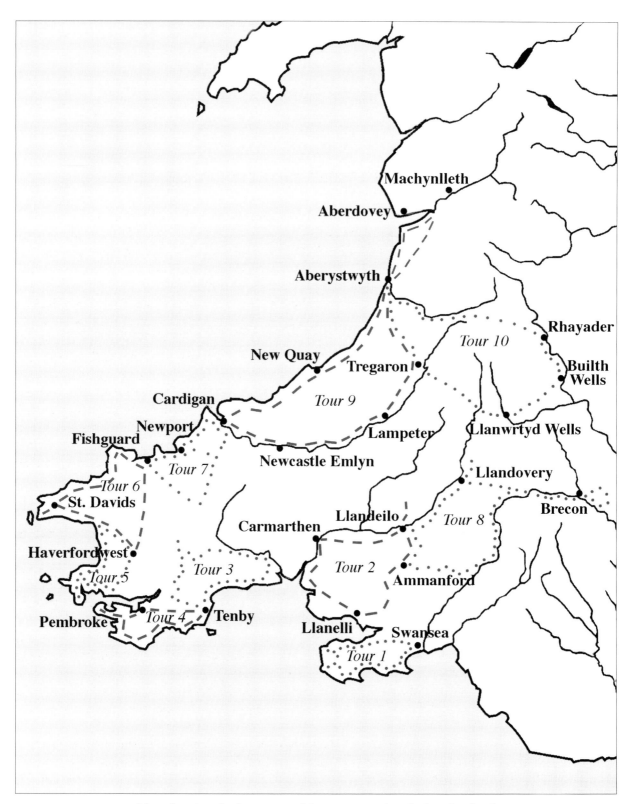

Map showing the locations of the ten tours detailed in this book

Preface and Acknowledgements

In my early days I did not stray far from north Wales or what was then Caernarvonshire until towards the end of the war, when the Army beckoned. Then came college, where part of the curriculum took us on land surveying and mapping practice to a camping field near Aberystwyth. It was below Constitution Hill and this allowed nostalgic views across Cardigan Bay towards the distant mountains of the Lleyn peninsula and Bardsey Island, the scene of a subsequent blissful time spent among Manx Shearwaters and other unfamiliar birds, Atlantic grey seals, 'twitchers', lighthouse keepers, a lone farm family — and Shades of 20,000 'saints'. But while we wielded theodolites, levels and measuring chains close to the shore, it never occurred to us that the grey-blue seas, where dolphins were to be seen leaping above the waves, actually covered a drowned expanse of once fertile land and tall forest that reached out to the west for over 7 miles between Bardsey and the Teifi estuary. There was little if any mention at that time of 'climate change', 'global warming' or of the rises in average temperatures during post glacial times that had produced a great thaw to raise sea levels and inundate such coastal areas just 5,000 years or so ago, (and which, by just another 100 years from now, are predicted to have resulted in more severe flooding, erosion, changed coastlines and vanished beaches in west Wales, especially in Gower and along Pembrokeshire shores). And yet even the past history of Cantre'r Gwaelod, 'The Hundred in the Deep' of Cardigan Bay, could be regarded as quite recent and modest compared with the great Welsh mountain-building epoch of between 400 million and 570 million years ago, or those of the violent earth movements that caused the rock upheavals, acute folding and other spectacular effects exposed along the coast paths of Pembrokeshire.

Later on, after moving close to the Welsh border at Hereford, conveniently half way between my former home and that of Wendy, my wife, in south Wales, there were many opportunities for us to explore and discover the natural and man-made wonders to our west and south. There were the Brecon Beacons, the 'Lakeland' of mid Wales produced by the great Elan valley reservoirs and, down the Vale of Rheidol Steam Railway line the golden sands of Cardigan Bay. Swansea was not very far away, where Wendy's father, widely known there as 'J.H.', had been manager of the Midland Bank, Wind Street Branch. During the war he spent hours on the roof with stirrup pump and sand bucket, defiantly guarding his domain as he fire-watched with high explosive and incendiary bombs falling all about him. The sturdy bank miraculously survived, very close to where most of the other town centre buildings were reduced to rubble. Afterwards taken over and then closed down from offices in Hong Kong and Shanghai, it still retains its bold façade, fine solid floors and deep-lustred hardwood furnishing and fittings after a 'makeover' into one of Wind Street's body of 'theme' pubs. Were it possible, 'J.H.' might now be even less favourably struck by the planning approach and brutal architecture of the rebuilt town centre, but doubtless far more in favour of the more recent 'Maritime Quarter' taking the place of the old South Dock which the German bombers largely missed, as well as other great improvements all along the fine sweep of Swansea Bay towards The Mumbles.

Apart from the many more holiday-makers, their cars and soaring house prices there has not been any drastic change across to the west since then, or on the Gower peninsula where Wendy has happy memories of her cycling trips after the lifting of wartime access restrictions, especially those of Langland Bay where, after our wedding at St. Paul's Church, Sketty, we had the reception.

Since then we have returned many times with family and friends to the Gower beaches and cliff-tops, while there have also been holidays and outings in Pembrokeshire, Ceredigion, Powys and West Glamorgan. Away from the coast there are the wild and beautiful Preseli hills where we have marvelled at how, and why, 3,500 years ago huge 4-ton bluestone blocks were moved across almost 200 miles of land and water to Stonehenge on Salisbury Plain. After bracing walks along the National Trail around Dinas Island, we have keenly indulged in the fresh crab salads and other temptations at The Old Sailors Inn above Pwllgwaelod beach on Fishguard Bay. Their cheese-board carried the locally produced farm fare that we watched being made at Llangloffan — equally likely to be on offer on the menu at the centuries-old Sloop Inn by the magical small harbour of Porthgain. At the end of the day there has been evensong in the quiet of St. Davids Cathedral, before settling in for the night at our hotel overlooking St. Brides Bay and Skomer Island.

There has as well been much to do and see at Tenby and all along the coast through Manorbier, Stackpole and Barafundle, the two Freshwater beaches to Angle and the busy Irish Sea entrance to Milford Haven waterway, and eastwards by Saundersfoot, Amroth and Pendine to Laugharne, the final home and resting place of Dylan Thomas.

After all our travels we came to think that there was little that we had not covered in south-west Wales — until I began to explore and research more closely for this book. This showed how much we had really missed out or failed to appreciate, back for me to 1947 on the shore of the Cardigan Bay 'Hundred in the Deep'. The exercise has since been a rewarding experience, greatly backed up by Wendy's role in driving us along anything from dual-carriageway roads to the very narrow sort with grass growing down the middle, and also by her own recollections of earlier days in Swansea and Gower. Almost everywhere has been packed with places and features of great interest, style, beauty and enjoyment and I hope that readers will be able to share in some or all of the selection I have described and illustrated — and that they will be prompted to explore further for themselves, for there is much else to see.

But although the area is not really vast, it has not been possible for me alone to muster all the facts and figures needed within the scope of this book and, as is usual on holiday I have followed directions from guidebooks and leaflets to be found at Tourist Information Centres, churches, castles, abbeys and other ancient monuments, as well as a range of other sources that have included the services of the National Library of Wales. I have quoted many of these in the text, where it will be realised how I respect the series published by Cadw and by the custodians of other great historic buildings not managed for the State. I have also been able to learn of directions to follow or places to research from writers who have covered the ground in the past. They include recent contributors to the Pevsner 'Buildings of Wales' Series, Phil Carradice, John Davies and Sybil Edwards, while outstanding before them were William Condry, Maxwell Fraser, Alun Llewelyn, Ronald Lockley and Wynford Vaughan-Thomas — and all the way back to Daniel Defoe in the 18th century and Gerald of Wales, Giraldus Cambrensis, born in 1154 and raised at Manorbier Castle. The works of these, and hopefully all the others, are set out in the 'List of References and for Further Reading' at p.ADD, while I also appreciate assistance with some of the history from Ted Gundry in Anglesey.

A great deal would also have been missed without the range of Ordnance Survey maps available in the *Explorer* and *Landranger* series, and although a good Road Atlas can be very useful, these sheets are almost indispensable for any real exploration and discovery and I have quoted *Landranger* map numbers in the introduction to each tour.

Most of the photographs in the book are my own, but I am grateful to the following for help with or permission to use photographs: Malcolm Thurlby pp.79 and 160; Chris Musson p.161; George Nash p.162; Wendy Roberts p.252; Jane Gobourn pp.132, 141, 144, 158, 197 (both), 198, 215, 219 (all), 222 and 228; Peter Roberts p.104; the Eppynt Hill & Beulah Speckled Face Sheep Society p.244; and to Katy Shoesmith for the map-work.

Also I especially wish to thank Andy Johnson of Logaston for the benefit of his design and editing expertise and for much encouragement.

Any map of Wales, and places mentioned in the text, will contain Welsh names, and in the hope that it will add to understanding of the terrain, I have included a glossary of some of the words that are most likely to be encountered as place names and their meanings. As a variety of perhaps unfamiliar names and terms arise throughout the journeys, there is also a short general glossary which I hope will assist.

Swansea

The first people to recognise the potential of the natural harbour at the mouth of the River Tawe were Scandinavian raiders who were scouring the Bristol Channel a thousand years ago. It is thought that one of these, known as Sveinn or Swayne, was attracted by quite a large island, or Old Norse *ey* that then divided the river close to its mouth and he adopted it to set up a trading station. From the 12th century onwards it acquired a variety of names such as Sweyne's Ey, and eventually became Swansea, while to the Welsh it was Abertawe (*aber* here on the coast meaning estuary), as known to Giraldus Cambrensis (*c*.1125–1223). This was after the arrival of the Normans, who regarded the location not only as of great commercial but also strategic value. By 1116, on a site later known as The Old Castle, they had built an earth and timber motte and bailey fortification as the nucleus of a first settlement. A stone built castle followed in *c*.1300, immediately to the south-west, and murage grants indicate that the medieval borough which became established to the north and east of it, in an L-shaped cluster of buildings, was protected by a defensive wall.

The streets within followed the grain of the river valley from the mouth of the Tawe, while outside the walls, and served by the Strand, the town quay and ferry formed part of a significant trading post from very early days. After a turbulent phase lasting through the 12th and 13th centuries, Swansea settled down to become the chief port and market centre for the neighbouring Gower peninsula and Vale of Glamorgan. The Cambrian Pottery, the first and most famous of Swansea's potteries, was founded at the Strand in 1764 (and continued until 1870) but by the end of the 18th century much wider prospects were beginning to open up.

The use of coal at Swansea was first recorded in 1249 and by the 16th century there was an export trade that provided the main basis for the local economy. By 1724, just prior to the dawning of the Industrial Revolution, Daniel Defoe (1660–1731), describing 'Swanzey' as a considerable town for trade with a good harbour, observed 'a very great trade for coals, and culm [small coal used for igniting lime kilns], which they export to all parts of Somerset, Devon and Cornwall, and also to Ireland itself; so that one sometimes sees a hundred sail of ships at a time loading coal here; which greatly enriches the country and particularly this town of Swanzey which is really a very thriving place'. Then, towards the end of the century, a fashion for swimming in the sea had arrived and Swansea was being presented as 'The Brighton of Wales', with fine sands and bathing facilities. Furthermore Walter Savage Landor (1775–1864), a leading poet, playwright and essayist, likened the magnificent curved sweep of Swansea Bay to the Bay of Naples and invalids were arriving there to take the waters at St. Helens (now known rather more for great cricket and rugby). By the summer of 1804, when the population had increased from a steady 2,000 to more than 6,000, Swansea's *The Cambrian* — the first weekly newspaper to be published in Wales — reported that: 'Swansea is very full — genteel company and families are almost daily arriving at this resort of fashion. The promenade on The Burrows displayed an assemblage of beauty and elegance fascinating beyond description'. The town would probably have consolidated its role as a busy harbour with the pleasures of a charming holiday resort, but for the presence of easily worked, high quality coal closely accessible to the ocean port, and the emergence of new metallurgical industries calling especially for plenty of copper. The ore was shipped to the Tawe from Cornwall, Parys Mountain in Anglesey and carried round the Horn from South America in specially built clippers. The first copper works entered production at Landore as far back as 1717 and, following construction of the Swansea Canal in 1798, copper and lead smelting had started to spread up the Tawe Valley. By 1860 there were 12 further smelters, located on both sides of the river, and their output combined to make Swansea the largest copper-smelting region in the world, employing some 10,000 people. Victorian Swansea became 'Copperopulis' and had also turned to zinc for galvanising iron, to Siemens steel as a base for the tinplate produced for use as food and drink containers, together with a range of chemicals. The chances of Swansea becoming 'The Brighton of Wales' during the 19th century had literally gone up in smoke and that lustre instead went to Aberystwyth (pp.201-204). The many sailing ships waiting to load coal at the riverside wharves, seen by Defoe early in the 18th century, produced a need to enlarge the harbour and, combined with the growth of Port Talbot, this activity had a further bearing on the appeal of Swansea Bay as a holiday resort. The main period of wet dock construction took place between 1850 and 1920, starting with the enclosure of a part of the River Tawe to create the North Dock, substituting the New Cut which flowed direct to the sea. The dock opened in 1852, to be followed in 1859 by the South Dock, but after about a century they both were obsolete and after 1930 North Dock became the first to be filled in. On the eastern side of the river, the Prince of Wales' Dock was opened in 1881 and extended in 1898, while the King's Dock was constructed on the foreshore and bed of Swansea Bay in 1909. Connected by a passage to the Prince of Wales' Dock, it was extended in 1920 to create Queen's Dock and this was developed for oil tanker traffic in association with the Llandarcy refinery that operated from 1922.

A rail network was well established by then, the South Wales Railway (later GWR) having arrived from Chepstow in 1850. Close to the South Dock, the Llanelli Railway (later LNWR and LMS) opened Victoria Station in 1867. Trains to and from Llanelli and Shrewsbury travelled along a high embankment extending half way to Mumbles at Blackpill, on a route that was badly located close to the shoreline. It was not the first commercial passenger railway to travel that way, for Swansea claims the very first service in the world, and one that did not seriously blight or screen the foreshore or coastal landscape.

The first regular passenger railway in the world

After coal, the next important natural resource of the area was carboniferous limestone, present over much of Gower where the magnificent south coast cliff scenery displays some of the finest sections in Britain. In former times the beauty of the coastline was rather less appreciated than now and the cliffs were extensively quarried for the limestone to be burnt in kilns, such as those still to be seen for example at Parkmill, Green Cwm and Lunnon. Before the days of superphosphate and other 'artificials' the slaked lime was mostly used to promote fertility and for 'sweetening' the soil of local Gower fields, but at suitable anchorages boats called to take loads across the Bristol Channel to Devon and Somerset. Signs remain to be seen of the limestone trade carried out from Swansea Bay and the village of Mumbles, whence as well as uses for agriculture, limewash, building construction and industry the stone was dressed for the building of private houses, public buildings and engineering works such as the harbour walls. Transport over the five miles distance was not however easy or safe, especially across the sands, and in 1803 plans were drawn up for either a canal or tramroad to be constructed around the bay between the Swansea Canal at the Culm Wharfs along the Strand and a field opposite Oystermouth Castle. The industrial tramroad option was adopted and built at a cost of £9,000 by Spring 1806, using horse-drawn wagons to convey the limestone. But from 25 March 1807, fare-paying passengers were also carried, and they enjoyed a service that would continue, with short breaks, until the line closed in 1960. And so the Swansea and Mumbles

Railway became the first regular passenger-carrying railway in the world: the Stockton and Darlington line for horse drawn trains was laid out in 1825 and George Stephenson launched the Liverpool to Manchester passenger service with steam trains in 1830. Competition from the adjacent new turnpike road stifled the Mumbles Railway passenger service soon afterwards, but it restarted in 1860 and in 1877 steam traction took over with saddle tank engines bearing names that included *Crumlyn, Swansea* and *Hampshire*. Their range was extended to reach the **Mumbles Pier** when it opened in 1898 and they continued to pull open-topped coaches for the 5-mile journey until 1929. Electrification was then introduced, using 13 smoother running and more comfortable tramcars, some with covered top decks. All were controlled by a reliable signalling system in place of the former token arrangement and by 1953 the railway is said to have carried as many as 3,150,000 people. There were great celebrations the following year to mark the 150th anniversary, but despite everything the decision was taken in 1958 to close the railway. This was 'in favour of a more modern system of transport' said the Deputy Mayor of Swansea at the inevitable Guildhall luncheon. There were mixed emotions around the Bay, for some were in agreement with the closure while others thought it quite wrong: some people still do. The day after the ceremonial last train ran on 5 January 1960 an advertisement by demolition contractors appeared in *The Times* inviting bids for souvenirs. Before long there was little left to see of the Mumbles Railway, apart from an electricity substation at Blackpill and the cab sawn from tramcar number 7. This is now displayed at the Maritime and Industrial Museum (below) and some visitors, perhaps with the popular trams still running along Blackpool promenade in mind, imagine what a great attraction a tramway between the modern city centre, Oystermouth and Mumbles Pier could be. Instead, in common with initiatives pursued through much of Swansea since 1960, opportunities have been taken to enhance the foreshore and promenade alongside the line of the former track-bed and tram stations.

Regeneration

From the eastern approach alongside the docks the second city of Wales can be seen as not presenting the finest planned townscape in the Principality. Describing Swansea where he lived during his childhood and youth, Dylan Thomas (1914–1953) spoke in his *Reminiscences of Childhood* in 1943 about 'an ugly, lovely town … crawling, sprawling, slummed, unplanned, jerry-villa'd, and smug suburbed by the side of a long and splendid-curving shore'. The renowned BBC war correspondent, commentator, author and much else, Wynford Vaughan-Thomas (1908–1987), a friend and fellow stalwart of the Edwardian Uplands suburb, later wrote of the rambling, unplanned, smokily-romantic Swansea, quoting Dylan Thomas as saying that it 'has got as many layers as an onion and each one reduces you to tears!'. He continued: 'Our town was never planned, it was sprayed over the landscape with a Flit gun. Tall Victorian houses on the lower slopes of Town Hill [where he lived] look out on the wondrous architectural mix-up spread below. The builders of Swansea were masters of the art of surrealist juxtaposition'. Such sentiments came from two most loyal and devoted sons of Swansea, but despite it all there had been enough previous vision and planning for their 'lovely town' to have been separated into three crucially distinct zones: the industrial area behind Townhill and Kilvey Hill in the Lower Tawe valley; the dockland and commercial areas; and the residential neighbourhoods on the seven hills of the town and along the lower ground closer to the shoreline.

The industrial area

The considerable industrialisation that developed in the Lower Swansea Valley during the 18th century expanded further still during the 19th and by its close Swansea had become a leading metallurgical centre. Much secondary industry and employment was also generated — but all at great cost to the environment. A local rhyme from *c*.1890 paints the picture:

It came to pass in days of yore
The Devil chanced upon Landore
Quoth he: 'By all this fume and stink
I can't be far from home, I think'.

This was by no means all that was to be suffered, however, for not only could the fumes and stink hang over much of Swansea, especially when the sulphurous wind came from the east, but the smelting processes left an all too solid mass of barren toxic slags and furnace waste in the Valley (the extraction of 1 ton of copper, for example, could typically produce residue from some 13 tons of ore and 18 tons of coal). But by early in the 20th century the industrial heyday was over and several external factors gradually produced a decline in demand and production. By mid-century the Lower Swansea Valley was just left as a vast dump, comprising more than 7 million tons of slag and furnace waste, spread out in heaps of more than 60 feet in height, some of them even visible from the town centre. The devastation was spread over an area of 700 acres — and twice as much again was heavily blighted and eroded. This huge part of Swansea was regarded as the biggest industrial wasteland in Great Britain, if not in the whole of Europe.

Almost all the land was owned by private individuals or companies and few had made any more effort than their reckless predecessors to respect the environment or attempt ways to bring it back to life. And so 'The Lower Swansea Valley Project' began — with a detailed study by departments of the University College (now University of Wales), Swansea between 1960 and 1966 to establish the physical character and problems of the valley floor and the social and economic situation there. The project area was shaped like an inverted triangle, with the port at the apex and the A48 as its base, and it extended over 1,174 acres.

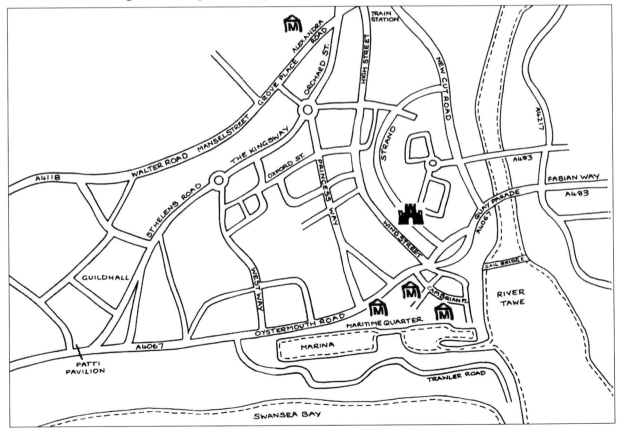

Plan of Swansea

Some 31% of this area comprised tips and derelict buildings, 32% wasteland and marsh, 17% operational industry and there was a residue of cleared sites, railways, tracks and the river and canal. There were also 41 disused mine shafts. The Final Report in 1967 recommended that all the derelict areas should be acquired by Swansea Council, in order that they could be reclaimed as a whole. Since then, the Authority has been joined in its efforts by many bodies and individuals, so far achieving land levelling, clearance of toxic pollutants to restore trees to the valley, a flood prevention scheme with a lake, new roads and river crossing, the Swansea Enterprise Park, Business Village and industrial estates and recreational areas which include the Swansea Sports Stadium at Morfa and a riverside cycling trail. At Morriston, further to the north-west along the A48 is the 20-storey Government office block housing the national Driver and Vehicle Licensing Agency (DVLA).

Dockland and the commercial area

The transformation that began in the Lower Swansea Valley during the 1960s extended to the North and South Dock areas and the town centre. The North Dock had been filled in from the 1930s and by the late 1980s work could begin on the Parc Tawe retail development, between the Strand and the river. Covering an area that was once occupied by the River Tawe, there are now familiar multiple stores, as well as a 10-screen cinema and a Megabowl ten-pin bowling alley. Rather different is the huge pyramidal '**Plantasia**' glasshouse containing more than 5,000 plants from the tropical regions of the world. There are different zones that, between March and September provide a controlled humid climate for butterflies. The tropical zone features a section of rainforest and there is an arid zone for cacti and other such plants that are able to flourish where there is less than 25cm of rain a year. Of particular interest among the different birds, insects, fish and reptiles are endangered species of very lively Cotton-top Tamarin monkeys. Below New Cut Bridge and across the A4067 Quay Parade, further downstream, the former Weaver's Dock basin, once served from the North Dock, has been filled for occupation by Sainsbury's supermarket and car park. (Until it was demolished with some difficulty in 1983, Weaver's Flour Mill of 1898 was a formidable landmark, quite famous among civil engineers as Britain's first ever multi-storey, reinforced-concrete framed building).

Between Oystermouth Road, the sea and the Tawe estuary, part of the South Dock occupied the fashionable Burrows, but from 1859 this select area assumed a quite different role in support of Swansea's fishing industry. In all, the South Dock wharves could accommodate some 40 deep-sea steam trawling vessels, along with a spacious market and services that included an ice factory. But after serving for 110 years, in 1969 the dock closed and was being filled in until, in the mid-1970s, ideas started to form that required some of the infill to be moved again. This was to allow for the launch of a project that would bring much credit and acclaim for the then newly elevated (in 1969) City of Swansea.

Centred on a yacht and small boat marina for some 500 vessels and surrounded by modern flats and a range of other attractive buildings, it warranted more than just a workaday name, and so it became known as '**The Maritime Quarter**'. Completed in 1989, some of

Swansea Marina

the former buildings were re-used as part of the design, when the red brick Pump House became a restaurant. The former Coast Lines warehouse was converted into an **Industrial and Maritime Museum** and recent work of renovation extends to the creation of a waterfront terrace overlooking the group of historic ships moored alongside the Museum Quay. These include the *Olga*, a Bristol Channel pilot cutter from 1909, the *Helwick*, a 1937 lightship and *Canning*, a steam tug built in 1954. These can be seen from the new Marriott hotel that overlooks the marina from the Mumbles end, in a fine setting close to the bay. It provides 122 guest bedrooms, 7 meeting

Cambrian Place in the Maritime Quarter

rooms, a restaurant and a free gymnasium, and an indoor swimming pool — for those perhaps not prepared to brave the nearby sea.

Water levels for the boats within the marina are controlled at mid-tidal depth by the Tawe Barrage, completed in 1992. It soon required modifications to correct de-oxygenation problems and they now account for columns of bubbles that help to mix the sea and fresh water in the interests of upstream river fish and other wildlife.

Statue of Dylan Thomas

More than 5 hectares of the historic core of Georgian, Victorian and Edwardian buildings in the Maritime Quarter, including Cambrian Place, have been declared as a Conservation Area by Swansea Council and buildings that survived the wartime bombing have been converted into flats, with new ones added. Leaving only the façade, the former early 19th century Assembly Rooms have been adapted for a housing association development, and all in all the Quarter must accommodate more than 1,000 homes of different kinds. There are also workshops, a restaurant and shops, and the old telephone exchange in Pier Street has been converted into an Environment Centre — the first in Wales.

As this is Swansea, there is inevitably a strong Dylan Thomas element and in a former garage this is represented by the **Dylan Thomas Theatre**, Gloucester Place, and what was once the 19th-century Guildhall in Somerset Place, and in danger of demolition, was refurbished to become **The Dylan Thomas Centre and National Literature Centre for Wales**. With a theatre, galleries, a restaurant, book and craft shops, it was officially opened by former U.S. President Jimmy Carter in 1995 as a venue for talks, readings, plays, films and exhibitions and the annual Dylan Thomas Festival. Among the pieces of sculpture and carved stone panels that have been commissioned for 'architectural enhancement' of the Quarter there is a statue in Abernethy Square of Captain Cat, the blind sea captain from *Under Milk Wood*, and of the poet himself — seated close to the theatre on a stone plinth in Dylan Thomas Square. The chair is thought to be a good likeness — but not so the image of the poet, which is felt locally not to resemble him at all: some wags have called it 'A Portrait of the Artist as Someone Else'! As there is so much emphasis on his connection with Swansea, it would probably be better if the bronze were not placed in quite such a focal position.

Dylan Thomas

Dylan Marlais Thomas was born on 27 October 1914 at 5 Cwmdonkin Drive in the hilly Swansea suburb known as the Uplands and he lived there throughout his childhood and adolescence. Leaving Swansea Grammar School in Heathfield, Mount Pleasant (where his father was senior English master) at 16½, he obtained a job as a cub reporter with the *South Wales Daily Post* (now *Evening Post*). He had been writing poetry long before then and was to describe his times as a schoolboy and young teenager in Wales in his collection of short semi-autobiographical stories, *Portrait of the Artist as a Young Dog*. Published in 1940, this has been widely regarded as one of the best examples of poetry in prose in modern literature. In his 1943 BBC broadcast, *Reminiscences of Childhood*, he recalled that 'this sea town was my world', a

Statue of Captain Cat

heartfelt devotion that showed in a great deal of his material, such as *Memories of Christmas*, *The Hunchback in the Park* — and *Return Journey*, movingly written in 1947 after he had walked around the town centre to take in the consequences of the heavy wartime bombing. It also had a great effect on his output of poetry, some two-thirds of which had already been written during his late teens before it became necessary for him to seek essential London literary and publishing contacts — an experience which he came to regard as 'capital punishment'. His first departure was in 1933, and at the end of the following year an initial collection of 18 poems was published. It gained immediate acclaim and a prize and was followed in 1936 by another set of 25 poems. By then Dylan had met in a London pub his future wife, a model and mistress of the Welsh painter, Augustus John. Caitlin Macnamara married Dylan at Penzance Registry Office in 1937 and during an often tempestuous relationship they were to produce three children, the first in 1939 after they had started to move away from London to Laugharne in Carmarthenshire (see pp.77-78). During most of the 1940s their time was divided between the two and, for a while New Quay in Cardiganshire. Dylan made his first radio broadcast on the BBC Welsh Service in 1937 and he subsequently wrote, narrated or took part in numerous productions — oddly seldom being heard on the national wavelengths. He served

Dylan Thomas's birthplace
at 5 Cwmdonkin Drive, Swansea

as a scriptwriter for war-time documentaries and with film companies until, in 1949, he and his family settled in the Boat House at Laugharne. They were never well off, and early in 1950 Dylan sailed off on the *Queen Elizabeth* for his first tour of the USA and Canada to raise funds through 39 readings and lectures. Two other lucrative visits took place in 1952 and at the end of that year he published his *Collected Poems 1934–1952*, dedicated to Caitlin. They were termed: 'most of the poems I have written, and all, up to the present year, that I wish to preserve'. In an introductory Note in November 1952 he wrote: 'These poems, with all their crudities, doubts, and confusions, are written for the love of Man and in praise of God'. It has since been said that many of them 'belong to the permanent body of any poetry'.

Sadly, in less than 12 months after their publication, he was dead. His final public engagement took place in October 1953 during a fourth American tour, when he collapsed on 5 November at the Chelsea Hotel in New York, died in hospital four days later and was buried back at Laugharne on 25 November. He had written much of *Under Milk Wood, a Play for Voices* there but was not to hear the first BBC broadcast performance of this, his most widely known composition. It famously took place two months later on 25 January 1954 and involved a distinguished all Welsh cast, with Richard Burton opening as First Voice.

Dylan Thomas had lived his short 39 years outrageously, was often a self indulgent womaniser, philanderer, heavy drinker and much else, but his long-term friend and former neighbour Wynford Vaughan-Thomas knew much more of the better side of the person whom he and many others regarded as 'the greatest lyric poet of our time'. In 1981 he wrote of his last picture of him — on the balcony of the Boat House:

> I could see him as the Reverend Eli Jenkins. And surely the Reverend's evening prayer in *Under Milk Wood* says everything that should be said in memory of that rare, eloquent and wayward genius who was Dylan Thomas:
>
> > We are not wholly bad or good
> > Who live our lives under Milk Wood
> > And Thou, I know, will be the first
> > To see our best side not our worst

During the following year a plaque in his memory was unveiled in Poets' Corner, Westminster Abbey, and after her death in Italy in 1994 Caitlin was buried with him at Laugharne.

Opposite the Dylan Thomas Centre and beyond the public pay and display car park, the spectacular Sail Bridge, one of two new footbridges, crosses to the sprawling dockland on the other side of the Tawe. This is now the commercial Port of Swansea, actively being transformed from its 19th and early 20th century uses to provide for those called for in the 21st. These already include housing and hotel accommodation, tourism, building and technology, car showrooms, a McDonalds eatery and the longer established dock facilities for the Swansea-Cork car ferry.

The 'SA1 Swansea Waterfront' project to the east of the river will form the newest addition to the Maritime Quarter. It is being designed to regenerate this historic part of Swansea across 40 hectares of dockland, providing 200,000 square metres of new accommodation and, again, rejuvenating historic buildings. Intended to be set out around a series of tree-lined streets and squares, it will be bordered by a further riverside promenade.

Down the side of the Dylan Thomas Centre in the opposite direction, Somerset Place heads towards the city centre and at the junction with Adelaide Street meets the flank frontage of the very handsome 5-star Morgans 20 bedroom hotel. Listed at Grade II*, this dates from 1902 when it was built to house, obviously in great style, the Swansea Harbour Trust, which was the authority responsible for managing the thriving maritime trade of the town. Behind a dignified classical façade across to the left, **Swansea**

Swansea Museum

*The Swansea Harbour Trust building,
now Morgans Hotel*

Museum in Victoria Road was founded in 1835, became the Royal Institution of South Wales and is the earliest museum in the Principality. It displays items of local history, art and archaeology, has a unique collection of Swansea porcelain and pottery and fine examples of maritime art. It is sited where Oystermouth Road begins at the junction with Cambrian Place, and just before the closed 1970s Leisure Centre on the former LMS Victoria Station site a short way beyond, is the new **National Waterfront Museum**. This opened in October 2005 and within 15 galleries, and with the aid of up-to-the-minute forms of interpretation, it tells a full story of Welsh industrial and maritime history, culture and achievement.

At the junction of Somerset Place with the A4067 Quay Parade, a pedestrian subway connects the Maritime Quarter with the southern end of the commercial city centre at Wind (pronounced as wine) Street. With Castle Street and High Street to the north it runs parallel with the River Tawe and once led

towards the fashionable Burrows by the bay as one of Swansea's most prestigious thoroughfares, becoming a commercial nucleus of the town during the Victorian era and afterwards. In pride of place, in the centre of the road near the upper end on a dais, was a huge monument to Sir Henry Hussey Vivian, 1st Baron Swansea of Singleton, the industrialist who was responsible for so much of the local wealth and prosperity. This has gone now, but there is still a mixture of imposing Georgian, Victorian and other buildings to serve as a reminder of the appearance of the commercial town

Wind Street

during its 19th-century heyday. But the banks, businesses, hotel, theatre, Head Post Office, and Lord Swansea, have long since moved away and, intended by planners in 1997 to change from retail and banking uses into an attractive licensed café and restaurant quarter. Instead with a string of trendy bars and theme catering establishments, Wind Street has at times become more of what has been locally described as 'a booze boulevard' and 'an area of intensive drinking'.

The remarkable thing is that so much of the street has survived the intense Luftwaffe bombing of the 1940s, for the vast and famous Ben Evans department store that stood at the northern end, just beyond the surviving Midland Bank, was one of nearly 400 shops and more than 100 offices that were destroyed. The first raids occurred over the docks in July 1940, followed by what was the first major raid over Britain on 1 September — but the worst was to come during a three days blitz on the 19, 20 and 21 February, 1941. The entire town centre from Castle Street westwards beyond Union Street, amounting to over 40 acres, was flattened by many hundreds of high-explosive bombs and what are thought to have been more than 56,000 incendiaries. By the third day the impression was that the whole town was on fire and, according to the head of the police fire brigade, so much water was taken from the North Dock that the level dropped by 11 feet! Later he recalled: 'We were glad to see the tide coming in'. Extensive damage was caused at Mayhill, Town Hill, Brynmill, Manselton, Mount Pleasant, Brynhyfryd and St. Thomas and records show that during 72 hours of absolute horror, 227 people, including 37 children, were killed, nearly 400 injured to varying extents and thousands were made homeless. Throughout the war, air raid fatalities in Swansea reached 387, with 412 other people suffering serious injury: certainly no-where else in Wales suffered as badly. In 1967 Dylan Thomas undertook a survey of the shops that were lost in High Street, Temple Street, College Street and other parts of the town centre and many featured in his radio broadcast and short story: *Return Journey*. He would have seen the roofless shell of St. Mary's Parish Church that stands on the site of the original medieval foundation. Successive re-buildings had only left the Herbert Chapel, part of a 15th-century structure, by 1941 and then this was also lost during the blitz. The present church on St. Mary's Square was rebuilt from 1954 to designs by the Sir Percy Thomas Partnership and re-consecrated in 1959. It is in the diocese of Swansea and Brecon and thought by some to be the cathedral, especially since Swansea was declared a city in 1969. However since the Church in Wales came into being following the disestablishment in 1920, the cathedral has actually been located since 1923 at St. John's, Brecon.

In medieval times it was common for the **market** of a town, and often an associated market cross, to be set up near the church. This pattern will be found elsewhere during the travels described in this book and Swansea's original market and cross were in Cross Street (now part of Princess Way), between St. Mary's and Castle Square. Subsequent markets became established in 1652 and 1774, and then in 1830 the present 2-acre site in Oxford Street was adopted. In 1897 this, then the largest market in Wales, was provided with a grand new hall covered by a glass-covered, iron-framed dome, impressive twin towered entrance and façade that dominated the Oxford Street frontage and indeed much of the town centre. But all that too was reduced to rubble during the 1941 raid and there are still Swansea people who can remember the terrific sound as the massive roof collapsed. After the site was cleared a temporary open-air market was soon built up — in some places temporary stalls were produced from packing cases that had been used to ship wartime aircraft through the docks. Then in 1960 a new and spacious building opened and beneath a curved roof some 100 stalls each day (except on Sundays), within a truly lively market atmosphere, offer a tempting range of fresh food, and very much else. Notable specialities are locally caught fish, much of it brought in fresh by anglers or from day boats, fruit and vegetable produce from Gower and the Glamorgan countryside, Welsh cakes cooked before you on the stalls, Penclawdd cockles gathered from the Loughor Estuary — and laver bread. This forgivably selective local delicacy is made from laver, a seaweed collected from rocky shores west of Swansea. After washing, it is boiled for several hours into the dark gelatinous pulp on offer, when it can be mixed with oatmeal, formed into cakes, fried and served with bacon.

But while the church and market were rebuilt during the 1950s where they stood, this was not the case for the flattened shops, pubs, offices and other commercial buildings, or the pattern of ancient streets within the former town centre. Instead the new roadways were to include wide boulevards such as Kingsway, which opened in 1950, Princess Way and others. A massive redevelopment programme commenced at that time when brute concrete was the leading flavour among architects and builders. As at other heavily bombed towns, their efforts were also influenced by the theories and techniques of the Swiss architect and town planner, Le Corbusier (1887–1965). The outcome for Swansea during the 1950s and '60s was a dismal town centre complex of flat-topped 'shoe box'-type buildings, while casualties such as the impressive and hugely popular Ben Evans department store of the 1890s were not replaced in any way to restore some character or charm to the area, so that where 'Ben's' had been along Castle Bailey Street became part of Castle Gardens. Renamed Castle Square, these were later remodelled and landscaped for £1.5 million to become 'a more fitting focal point for the city centre', specially featuring a cascade with a sculptured leaf of stained glass relating to a teenage poem by Dylan Thomas and a fountain (as well as an ideal surface for young skateboarders to show off their skills — despite the bye-laws and thousands of studs and metal plates that have been expensively added to put them off!).

Facing the Square from the east are the ruins of the early 1330s castle, with Bishop Henry de Gower's fine arcaded parapet, completely dwarfed from the Strand by a vast British Telecom tower block.

Occupying much of the frontage on the opposite side of the open space is an un-enthralling 1950s block that was first taken by Boot's the Chemists. They left to become a 'magnet store' at the nearby 1970s Quadrant Shopping Centre and were followed at this hub of Swansea's city centre by McDonald's.

The closing decades of the 20th century have seen the City and County of Swansea, its population nearing 250,000, experiencing a positive renaissance while serving as a marketing, distributive, administration, cultural and academic centre for a population of well over half a million in south and west Wales. Great numbers of these people, and others, also relish the much longer-standing contrasts and delights of the Gower peninsula and there must be many therefore who naturally look towards Swansea for their main shopping requirements. These have increasingly been met since the early 1970s by stores and supermarkets in the heart of the city and the Quadrant and St David's shopping centres. With full weather protection and bright décor, like most such precincts in other towns they cater for what has been termed 'The

Castle Square (above) with a detail of Bishop de Gower's arcaded parapet on the castle (below)

Great Shopping Experience' — to be enjoyed with a host of familiar High Street names that are there 'to make shopping a Pleasure'. For the disabled, this is assisted by special access arrangements, toilets and a Shopmobility service providing a choice of wheelchairs. There is direct access to multi-storey car parking and a bus station serving all local and surrounding areas, with the Tourist Information Centre in Plymouth Street at its north end and the rear of the enlarged and refurbished late-Victorian **Grand Theatre**, Singleton Street, in view beyond.

Before the last war, the equivalent shopping parade for the people of Swansea and its catchment was based on Wind Street, Castle Street and High Street. During the air raids many commercial buildings were destroyed or badly damaged — one side of Castle Street being totally lost. Afterwards some businesses never re-opened, and recent competition from modern town centre and fringe area shopping malls, especially the **Parc Fforestfach** and **Morfa Shopping Park** with their easy access and free parking, the internet and other forms of retailing have left Castle Street and High Street in a sadly run-down state. In a nation-wide 'shake-up' by House of Fraser, it was made worse by the closure in January 2005 of the upmarket David Evans department store — after 140 years of trading. By then up to 50 shops in and near the city centre were boarded up, closing down or advertised for letting in buildings that had once contributed great tone and character to the city. Many others were tenanted by bargain basement and discount stores, while other streets in the city centre that were developed during the 1950s and '60s were also being described as drab and in a tired looking state. Most are in urgent need of an overhaul if the image of Swansea is not to suffer permanent damage. Announcement during 2005 of a £3.5 million 'makeover' grant, possibly towards the cost of upgrading some shop-fronts, street furniture and of a general 'smartening up', should be a start — but is regarded by some critics as really little more than a 'drop in the ocean'.

Swansea – West

Three main thoroughfares lead from the city centre axis through the western residential suburbs towards the Mumbles. The route to the north at Alexandra Road starts opposite the main line High Street train station, as the A4118 and soon leads to the **Glynn Vivian Art Gallery** on the right. Opened in 1911, based on a bequest by Richard Glynn Vivian (1835–1910) of Sketty Hall , a member of the wealthy copper dynasty, it is one of the finest buildings in Swansea. Housing works by artists who include Barbara Hepworth, Augustus John, Ceri Richards and others of comparable stature, it also exhibits permanent displays of 19th-century paintings, Tompion clocks and European, oriental and local ceramics. These include world-renowned and collectible pottery and porcelain of the highly famed 18th- and 19th-century Swansea and Nantgarw factories. To complement the works of the old masters and 20th-century artists there is a modern wing with an Exhibitions Programme and this provides an overview embracing the work of today's artists. Directly across the road the elegant **Central Library** building dates from 1888.

Until the 1941 blitz there was a Goat Street in central Swansea and the choice of name might have been an allusion to the mountainous gradients of many of the residential streets to the

The Glynn Vivian Art Gallery

north and west. Clifton Hill, at the first right turn after the Art Gallery, is one example where the slope must equal those in the Rhondda Valley where one prominent writer observed that 'many who watched the first cars struggling to climb them were convinced that Henry Ford had backed a loser'! Constitution Hill, also to the right after the A4118 becomes Grove Place, De La Beche Street, Mansel Street and then Walter Road, rises at another staggering rate. It is where, in 1901, one early 'loser' appears to have been a funicular tramway that was withdrawn after barely three years of no doubt strenuous service. After passing St. James's Church on the right, Walter Road continues to Uplands Crescent and the local shopping centre. Again to the right, Mirador Crescent is where, at No. 22, Dylan Thomas attended his dame school during the 1920s — and the literary tourist might also like to know that Eaton Crescent (formerly Eaton Grove), off the opposite side of the main road, is where his close friend, the future classical scholar and lyric poet, Vernon Watkins (1906–1967), lived between 1913 and 1923. They were both life-long friends of another talented figure, Daniel Jones (1912–1993), a musician and composer who would dedicate one of his future 13 symphonies to Dylan. He lived within their walking range at Eversley Road at the approach to St. Paul's Church, Sketty. Before the war, all three used to meet regularly at the Kardomah Café in Castle Street, along with Alfred Janes. He was another of 'the boys' who drank countless cups of coffee there and the artist who was to paint their portrait that is now on permanent display at The Glynn Vivian Art Gallery (as also is that of Dylan's wife, Caitlin Thomas, by Augustus John).

Back at The Uplands, the next right turning after Mirador Crescent is Uplands Crescent and this joins Cwmdonkin Drive as it climbs steeply towards No. 5, the birthplace of Swansea's most celebrated son and cult figure. It is where he lived throughout his childhood and teenage years, and perhaps a more agreeable approach is to continue slightly further along Uplands Crescent before turning right into Glanmor Road. Then another right turn is required to enter Park Drive — a cul de sac that passes the foot of Westfa Road to reach the principal entrance of **Cwmdonkin Park**.

Cwmdonkin Park

Not far along the path, opposite a bowling green, tennis courts, pavilion and shelter such as they would have been in his day, there is a memorial to Dylan Thomas. Dedicated in 1963 on the 10th anniversary of his death, it is set in a water garden in the form of an irregular block of blue pennant stone from the local Cwmrhydyceirw quarry. It is inscribed with lines from the ending of his poem *Fern Hill*:

Oh as I was young and easy in the mercy of his means
Time held me green and dying
Though I sang in my chains like the sea

The Thomas house is semi-detached and was newly built in 1914 at a time when the Edwardian Uplands suburb was spreading away from the industrial pollution over to the east with the growth of mechanised road transport. Number 5 is at a point where it is possible to share the view residents would have had over the Uplands rooftops to Swansea Bay and the Mumbles.

The former Coast Lines warehouse,
now an industrial and maritime museum

A fitting exhibit in the National Waterfront Museum
overlooking the refurbished Pump House

Back near the town centre the A4067 Quay Parade is sign-posted westwards to Gower, Mumbles and Sketty, passing the Swansea Museum to become Oystermouth Road. Just beyond the new **National Waterfront Museum** on the left, the **Swansea Leisure Centre** is expected to re-open in late 2007 after major refurbishment. It is followed on the left by Bathurst Street, leading to the Marriott Hotel, Trawler Road and the Maritime Quarter. The vast early 1980s **County Hall** is nearby on the left opposite the Swansea Prison, dating from 1825 with subsequent extensions. Behind it is Vetch Field in Sandfields, the 93-year old football ground home of Swansea City F.C. where the last ball was kicked in May 2005. Newly promoted 'Swans' started their League One season at the new stadium at Morfa in Landore, where a symbolic strip of Vetch turf was inserted into the pitch, hopefully to pacify the spirits of departed fans whose ashes had been buried beneath the old ground! Swansea R.F.C., the 'Ospreys', also performed well during the 2004/5 Season in becoming Celtic League Champions, and they too transferred to the new **Morfa Stadium**. Further along towards the Mumbles is **Victoria Park**, opened in 1887 to mark the Queen's Golden Jubilee and later reduced in size to accommodate the **Guildhall and Law Courts**. The Guildhall was built during the inter-war depression period as an unemployment relief project. Designed in Portland Stone by Sir Percy Thomas, it opened in 1934 with a tall white clock tower that serves as a landmark across many miles. It houses the **Brangwyn Hall**, named to honour Sir Frank Brangwyn, R.A. (1867–1956) who painted the hall's cycle of 17 panels depicting the British Empire of around 1900. Originally the murals were intended for the House of Lords in London, but were rejected, reportedly because their Lordships considered that the colours were too bright and vivid. The local civic fathers, however, were more than happy to have them fitted into their new Guildhall near the sea-front and they now add further brilliance to the annual Swansea Festival of Music and the Arts as well as to many other major concerts and events. That north side of the road was connected from 1914 by an arched steel footbridge which crossed to the Sands over the Oystermouth Road, Mumbles Railway track and main LNWR railway lines at the Slip. Close to Swansea Bay Station and with various forms of merry entertainment, this was for many years a favourite meeting place for hordes of local people and the **Slip Bridge** continued in service after they moved away, until in 2003 it was found to be unsafe. After being hoisted from its steps and supports to a temporary home at the Swansea Bay Recreation Ground on Mumbles Road for renovation and painting, it took on a new role along the promenade and cycle path that follows the magnificent sweep of Swansea Bay between the Maritime Quarter and Mumbles.

The home of Swansea Cricket and Football Club

At the western end of Victoria Park, the **Patti Pavilion** now looks neglected and the worse for wear and maybe one day Madame Adelina will return to haunt those responsible! Nevertheless, since 1919 it has served Swansea for many years as a splendid venue for the Welsh National Opera, concerts, dances, variety shows — even as an exams hall for the University.

Across Gorse Lane, the **St. Helens** home ground of Swansea Cricket and Football Club is well known to fans who still recall past glories, such as when Wilf Wooller led Glamorgan to their first county cricket championship in 1948, when Don Shepherd captained the side that beat Australia in 1968, to be followed by Tony Lewis a year later, along with the famous victory against the 'All Blacks' rugby team in 1935 and many 1990s Heineken League title successes.

On the opposite side of what has now become Mumbles Road, a sequence of memorials begins with one to Swansea Jack, a retriever who was awarded the animals' V.C. after saving 27 people from drowning during the 1930s. Swansea men who were killed during the Anglo-Boer Wars between 1900 and 1902 are commemorated a few yards further along the Esplanade and there is then the Swansea War Memorial, dedicated to those who died during the two World Wars.

The promenade continues to the **municipal golf-course** at Ashleigh Road to reach the **Blackpill Lido** and then goes on towards Oystermouth and The Mumbles, while the Swansea Bike Path turns away to cross the main road at the paddling pool, swings and other child-friendly attractions. It then follows the route of the former LMS Central Wales line through **Clyne Country Park** towards Gowerton. The disused ground along the shoreline from the Maritime Quarter previously occupied by this service, and also that bequeathed by the Mumbles Railway, has been well used and landscaped in creating a pleasurable and safe seafront. This contributes towards the reputation of Swansea as being so well provided with open spaces, parks, gardens and recreation grounds, the oldest at **Brynmill** first enjoyed in the 1840s..

The Vivians were regarded as the 'Copper Kings' of Swansea during the 19th century, and in 1847 John Henry Vivian (1785–1855), the fabulously wealthy and influential master of the Hafod Copperworks, purchased property for his eldest son, Henry Hussey Vivian (1821–1894) and his wife just to the west of Brynmill, yet further along the road to the Mumbles. Jessie Vivian tragically died soon after giving birth to their son and **St. Paul's Church** was erected in Sketty as her memorial, to the design of the eminent Henry Woodyer, in 1850. It adjoins **Singleton Park**, which the Vivians assembled from some 12 farms to produce the 250-acre Singleton Estate and John Henry Vivian substantially enlarged Marino, his mansion there. He named the majestic result Singleton Abbey, after the Norman De Sengleton family from Sussex, and one of its special features was a splendid walled garden, planned and planted out by Sarah, his wife, to serve the family needs of fresh fruit, vegetables and flowers.

Henry Hussey Vivian remarried twice, was created a baronet in 1882 and became the 1st Baron Swansea of Singleton a year later. But his heir, the 2nd Lord Swansea, does not seem to have inherited his devotion for Singleton and in 1920 Singleton Abbey and the Estate went on the market and was acquired by Swansea Council for use as a public park and amenity.

Swansea University College was founded that year and was greatly assisted in its early days when the Council refurbished and handed over Singleton Abbey for use as the college administrative headquarters, conveyed nearly 50 acres of surrounding land and another area for playing fields at no cost, and made a grant of £50,000 — a gift then valued in total at about £100,000. On 19 July 1920, King George V laid the foundation stone of the proposed buildings and presented the College Charter to the first President. The initial college session began that October with 89 students, eight of them women, and including many ex-servicemen. By the start of the Second World War the roll had reached 488, it then dropped to 305 but by 1963 there were over 2000 full-time students and in 1970 around 3,500. The increasing numbers that were enrolling during the 1960s meant a period of hectic construction works, as is evident from the characteristic architecture of that period, and by 2005 many more glass and concrete buildings and land had been added in order to accommodate the staff and around 12,000 students of what had become the **University of Wales, Swansea**.

Within the campus, the **Taliesin Arts Centre** is open to the public and offers cinema, an average of ten visiting exhibitions per year and live dance, drama, jazz and world music performances. The **Ceri Richards Gallery** largely exhibits the work of Welsh artists and has art and potting studios, while an extension to the Arts Centre houses the **Egypt Centre**. This is home to the largest collection of Egyptian artefacts outside the British Museum and is said to display more than 3,500 objects dating from 100,000 BC to AD 500 — mostly collected by the pharmacist Sir Henry Wellcome (1853–1936).

Seen at its best in August, the Vivians' walled garden is now occupied by the **Singleton Botanical Gardens,** usually approached from the main Sketty Road park entrance (see below). Inside the gate and wall, interest is at once stirred by two fine herbaceous borders with well-balanced plant combinations, ranged alongside the path that leads towards an eye-catching system of display beds and an allotment style vegetable garden. There are a rose terrace and herb and bog gardens, with divided glasshouses that contain plants from the main temperate zones of the world, hot desert regions, the tropics and some species that yield material of economic value, such as sugar, olives, rice, coffee and coconut. The displays and collections attract some 100,000 visitors a year and in 2004/5 helped to earn one of only eight annual Green Flag Awards for the whole of Wales. (These form part of the National Standard for Parks and Open Spaces in the country and are managed by the Civic Trust). Elsewhere in the park, **The Ornamental Gardens** feature magnolias, camellias and an internationally famous rhododendron collection in which the Vivians also had a significant hand, as well as an archery lawn and rock, bog and winter gardens.

Singleton Park otherwise provides an impression of broad open space, broken here and there by mature trees and, at one point, by a mock 'Swiss Cottage'. It makes a first rate venue for the Swansea County Show, attracting around 25,000 visitors each Spring Bank

The mock Swiss cottage in Singleton Park

Sketty Hall

Holiday as the biggest two day event held in Wales.

Richard Glynn Vivian (1835–1910) was the 4th son of John Henry Vivian and inherited a quarter share in Vivian and Sons, who operated the largest copper works in Swansea. But he took no part in running the business and a preference for art collecting and travel instead took him all over the world. Eventually, in 1898, he returned to Swansea and bought **Sketty Hall**, a Georgian mansion adjoining Singleton Park and devoted much of his time to refurbishment and the redesign of the gardens. Towards the end of his days he offered to leave his art collection to the people of Swansea, and cover the cost of a gallery to house it. The Council accepted, after overcoming worries about future running costs, and the striking Italian-style Glynn Vivian Art Gallery in Alexandra Road (above) is now one of the city's major attractions. Sketty Hall is now owned by the University and is open to the public as a restaurant, business and hotel training centre and for conferences, weddings and other functions. The formal Italian Gardens adjoin Singleton Park and there is a further park access just down Sketty Lane on the way to Singleton Hospital and to the new Wales National Pool Swansea.

The A4067 Mumbles Road continues westward between the King George V playing field on the right and Ashleigh Road Golf Course on the seaward side to the left to arrive at Blackpill, the Clyne Country Park and car park. This is close to the Woodman pub and the main entrance to **Clyne Gardens**. About 48 acres in area, these are widely regarded as among the finest in the Principality and in 2004/5 ranked with Singleton Botanic Gardens (above) as holders of one of the eight Green Flag Awards granted in Wales. There are said to be about 2,000 different types of plants there, including 800 rhododendrons — many of them unique to the Gardens and contributing to the Gardens' position as holders of the National Collection — which they also possess for their range of enkianthus and pieris plants. To the left of the entrance, the 'church border', of spring-flowering rhododendrons, azaleas and drifts of wild garlic, is so named because of its proximity to Clyne Chapel. It was opened in 1908 and in a private vault are the remains of William Graham Vivian, his sister, Dulcie Charlotte Vivian (d.1921) and their nephew, Admiral Algernon Walker-Heneage-Vivian (d.1952). Each in turn had taken a leading role in the evolution of Clyne since William Graham Vivian (1827–1912), the second son of J.H. Vivian had started the process in 1860. Inspired by Joseph Hooker, the famous botanist of the time,

A classic view of the Mumbles along the road from Swansea

he began to experiment with the ornamental planting of rhododendrons — greatly assisted by the acid soil, high rainfall and mild climate of the locality. Dulcie carried on with the plantings after he died and in 1921 Algernon, having retired from the Royal Navy to rejoin the board of the copper company of Vivian and Sons, and also inheriting the estate, took full advantage of the gardens' growing conditions in applying his keen interest in horticulture and the environment. Rapidly becoming expert in rhododendron cultivation and hybridisation, and sponsoring many renowned professional plant-hunters to collect seeds of the plants of China, Tibet and Burma, he had the greatest influence on the garden as it can now be seen. Death duties forced the sale of the estate upon his death in 1952 and Swansea Corporation compulsorily purchased the Castle and Gardens, transforming them to a public garden during the two subsequent years.

Nowadays, after the entrance lodge, church border and azalea garden, come the 'Admiral's Tower', built in 1928, and a lower valley that is well suited for large-leafed rhododendrons, then the 'Crossroads' and Bog Garden. This is where many visitors are impressed by what they regard as 'Giant Rhubarb', but which actually is a colony of *Gunnera Manicata*, a native of southern Brazil — with huge leaves of 2.5m x 2.5m on 2m high stalks. The Japanese Bridge and Top Pond have an oriental flavour and then there are the main field, the Bluebell Wood and Gazebo. Clyne Castle, gothic mansion of the Vivians from 1860 until 1952, is now separately occupied and enclosed since Swansea Corporation sold the building and its immediate curtilage to the then rapidly expanding University College of Swansea in 1955.

The Mumbles

Mumbles is strictly the rather odd name of the two detached limestone islets off the headland at the southern end of Swansea Bay and, although not everyone agrees, their rounded appearance has prompted acceptance of its derivation from the Romano-British *mammulae* 'the breasts'. The area that forms the western suburb of Swansea is generally regarded however as extending from Blackpill through Oystermouth to Southend, Mumbles Head, Bracelet and Limeslade Bays. From Blackpill, Mumbles Road shadows the promenade that started at the Swansea Maritime Quarter, as it continues past Oystermouth to Southend to the seaward side of numerous hotels, pubs, guest-houses, restaurants and some small car parks. There is a rather larger car park signposted to the right at the former Clement's Quarry, just before the junction with the B4593 Newton Road, a busy shopping street. The first turning from it to the right is Castle Avenue, and this ends at the entrance to the grounds of **Oystermouth Castle,** perched high on a hill.

Despite extensive damage during an outbreak of warfare at the end of the 13th century, much of the masonry of the castle gateway keep and curtain walls is still fairly intact, thanks to prompt repair works. Some of the other best work was added in the early 14th century and it can be seen in the tall chapel tower, with its great buttresses and delicate window tracery, built when the castle had become more of a residence than the stronghold it had been for the two previous centuries. The elevated setting affords some of the best views across **Swansea Bay**, and between the 17th and early 20th centuries it would no doubt have been possible to pick out up to 200 oyster ketches and skiffs on the moorings at Oystermouth during the

Oystermouth Castle

season from September to early March. Tragically they must all have departed soon after dredging came to an abrupt end during 1920/21, when all the oysters became diseased — and when the fishermen probably had to rely instead on their other employment in the dusty limestone quarries. The castle grounds are well used and most suitable for events such as the open-air plays performed during the Ostreme Festival. These are likely to be from standard versions — and not 'bowdlerised', or expurgated, according to the practice of Thomas Bowdler (1754–1825), who edited the *Family Shakespeare* of 1818 to omit 'those words and expressions which cannot with propriety be read aloud in a family'. He lived for a while at Brynmill and, having bequeathed his name to an entry in most good English dictionaries, he now rests in Oystermouth churchyard.

The road continues through Southend and popular yachting and water skiing stretches, where developments at the Knab Rock have produced new car parking and launching facilities. A one-way drive leads to the car park at the former terminus of the Mumbles Railway and **Mumbles Pier**. From its opening in 1898, huge crowds would arrive there on the train, perhaps to catch a White Funnel paddle steamer for Ilfracombe in Devon, be entertained by the band or simply stroll at the seaside and along the 800 feet-long pier. Soon after the First World War this was extended to one side for the Mumbles lifeboat service.

The Mumbles Road continues above through a cutting made in the limestone headland in 1887 to allow access to Bracelet and Limeslade Bays, or down a steep hill and steps to the pier and to the two Mumbles. A warning tower has stood on the outer islet since 1794 and in 1860 defence batteries were added to the south and east when a French attack was feared. Both islands may be reached for about three hours when the tide is out and it is possible to see Bob's Cave, just below the now defunct lighthouse. (This cave floods at high tide and great care is needed in view of the speed of the tidal race between the mainland and the islands.)

Bracelet Bay is the first of the limestone bays along the south coast after Swansea Bay and, like **Limeslade Bay**, which comes next, is pebbly with some sand when the tide is out. Between them is Tutt Hill and the coastguard station and major maritime co-ordination centre. This is where Mumbles Road ends, with the benefit of extensive car parks and the bus terminus, a restaurant, play area and toilets, but from Limeslade a fairly gentle path continues on to **Rotherslade** and **Langland Bay** for those wishing to ease their legs into action along the first of many spectacular Gower cliff walks.

To reach these bays by road, return to Oystermouth village and turn left at the mini roundabout at the White Rose pub onto the B4593 Newton Road. At the top of the rise turn left into Langland Road to follow the signs for Caswell and Langland where there are spacious car parks. To join the Gower tour, return to Oystermouth, turn left back along the bay road to Blackpill and turn left onto the B4436 Mayals Road and the signs for South Gower, Bishopston and Pennard.

Poised on the hill above Langland Bay beneath prominent French-style towers is a huge mock gothic Victorian pile that started as a summer residence for one of the Crawshay dynasty of Merthyr Tydfil iron-masters. Typically, it became known as Langland Castle and was afterwards enlarged and converted into the Langland Castle Hotel – and then the first Langland Bay Hotel. Now it is a convalescent home and the more recent Langland Bay Hotel, adapted from the original coachman's quarters and outbuildings (and once an idyllic venue for wedding receptions), has made way for the modern Crawshay Court apartments. Down below at the western end of the promenade, the small Hole in the Wall ice cream and beach-goods shop was once the pump house for supplying seawater for hotel guests' saltwater baths!

The next bay along, **Caswell Bay** has firm sands and limestone cliffs on each side, those on the east having interesting rock layers that tilt steeply upwards as a result of earth movement of some 280 million years ago — an example of many such 'upfolds' that show along the southern coast of Gower.

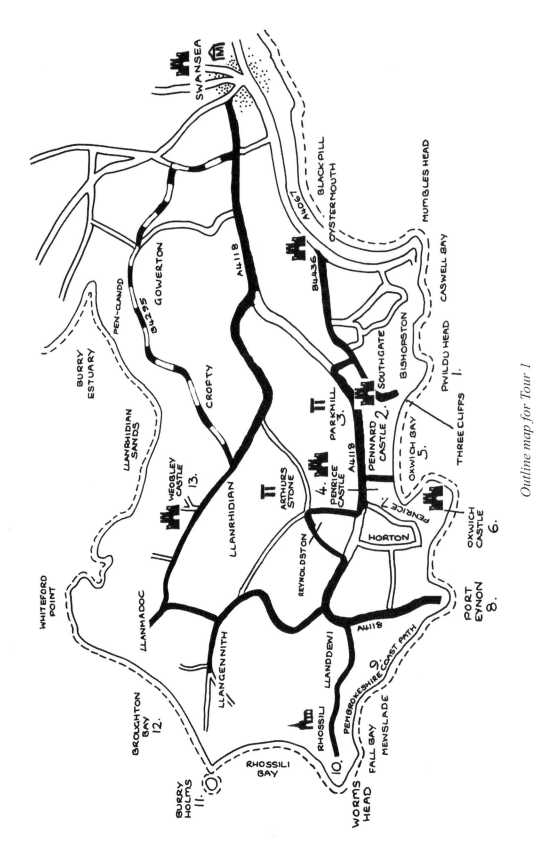

Outline map for Tour 1

The numbers 1 to 13 relate to the boxed information given within the tour

Tour 1   Gower

This tour includes a variety of bays, castles, prehistoric sites, small villages and their churches and open countryside. The roads on Gower are generally well surfaced, but even the one and only A class road can be quite narrow in places. The B roads are about the same, but the unclassified through and minor roads can reduce to single-lane width where there is a need to keep an eye out for passing places along the way — remembering with good grace, when facing the need to reverse, that the people who live and work there often have to do it all the time. This is all in the nature and charm of the place and it will not change, so there are times during the summer months when the roads and car parks become very badly choked with vehicles. Some, therefore, prefer Gower during the spring and autumn, and there are even those who obtain a thrill in the depths of winter, from witnessing the ferocity of the seas around its coast. The distance is 25 miles following the main circuit without dropping down to any of the bays. (OS Landranger 159)

Gower

Heading out into the Bristol Channel, this enchanting peninsula to the west of Swansea is known in Welsh as Gwyr, maybe because of its slightly curved shape, and it is therefore rather a sore point with the residents that it is often called *The* Gower. Extending for some 18 miles from east to west and between 3 and 8 miles wide, it largely takes the form of an undulating plateau or platform that is raised from about 200 to 300 feet above sea level. This is underlain by carboniferous limestone and has a number of Old Red Sandstone ridges that rise by up to over 600 feet — the highest of them being Rhossili Down, Llanmadog Hill and Cefn Bryn, which separates South Gower from North. The coastline varies from steep rugged limestone cliffs and sandy bays and coves between The Mumbles and Worm's Head, the unforgettable 3-mile sweep of unbroken sand below Rhossili Down, the Whiteford Sands, dunes and burrows to the west, and the marsh landscape of tidal sandflats, winding creeks and salt pans that face the Burry estuary to the north. In all there are 135 acres of Heritage Coast, while 20% of the peninsula is common land that is being considered as one of the Special Areas of Conservation under European legislation. The consequent range of sea and land habitats has led to the creation of three National Nature Reserves, while Glamorgan Wildlife Trust owns and manages many other reserves and there are numerous Sites of Special Scientific Interest (SSSIs). It is no wonder therefore that in 1956 Gower was the first place in Britain to achieve status as an Area of Outstanding Natural Beauty (AONB) under The National Parks and Access to the Countryside Act, 1949.

The National Trust owns about 5,500 acres of the land, including three-quarters of the coastline — amounting to some 26 miles, while its operations also involve the management and conservation of many archaeological sites and monuments that extend from Iron Age forts to a Second World War radar station. For their part, Cadw protect, conserve and manage several ancient monuments, castles and other buildings among the wealth of historic remains that scatter the landscape. Active also is the Gower Society, dedicated to playing its part in preserving the character and natural beauty of the peninsula and there are other voluntary and statutory organisations, including the local authority, that also strive to share in this common aim. But as in the countryside anywhere, crucial to all that is achieved towards the beautification and protection of Gower is the role and support of the working farmers, smallholders, tenants, graziers, commoners and many other local people. Ever concerned about the impact on their surroundings of ruinous commercialisation, they must still be able to make their livelihood on the peninsula, however cherished it is by so many other interests.

This route starts on the A4067 alongside Swansea Bay which it follows until Black Pill is reached where you follow a well signed right turn for South Gower, Bishopston and Pennard at traffic lights into the B4436 Mayals Road. Mayals Road leads up to Clyne Common, where far ahead there is a first sighting of Cefn Bryn hill and the white buildings of Swansea Airport in the distance over to the right. Until Oxwich Bay is reached, about 7 miles further on, all access to beaches will have to be on foot, and after passing the sign on the left for Murton and Caswell, certainly one of the most rewarding walks to one of the best begins a little further along to the left at Bishopston.

1. Bishopston Valley, Brandy Cove, Pwll Du Bay — and smuggling

Down a steep lane at the road junction for Bishopston, the site of St. Teilo's Church is one of the earliest historic settlements in Wales and thought to date from AD 480, while the present building and its battlemented tower originate from the 12th and early 13th centuries. The stone font is just as old, while a fine 15th-century oak hammer-beam roof is now visible following works to the ceiling in 1927. The church is at the head of the narrow, rugged and wooded Bishopston Valley that descends for 2½ miles to Pwll Du Bay, watered by the stream from Barland Common.

St. Teilo's Church, Bishopston

This can disappear into a 'sink' and after running underground below Guzzles Hole it then re-appears to follow the surface before being dammed by the Black Pool (Pwll Du) at the rear of the stony beach and seeping through to the sands. Some of the woodland originated just after the last Ice Age, much of it over 500 years ago, and it is typical of the tree growth that once covered Gower. The valley has been owned and managed by the National Trust since 1954 and the trees have been conserved in ways that enhance habitats for the birds, insects, fungi and plants. Ramparts of the Hanging Cliff Iron Age fort and the remains of Longash silver-lead mine overlook the valley to the left and there are several small quarries and limekilns on the way to the hugely scarred cliffs at Pwll Du. These quarries operated until the early 20th century supplying great quantities of limestone for building and agriculture, collected by sometimes up to 30 small sailing boats at a time, mostly from north Devon. The stone waste was washed and rounded by the action of the sea over subsequent years to form the high ridge at the back of the storm beach. Surviving behind it still is a building that until the 1940s was the 18th-century Beaufort Inn, one of five inns that once served to slake the valley quarrymen's and boatmen's thirsts — as well as those of other less law-abiding regulars!

There are several footpaths in the valley, but depending on the season and weather some can be rather muddy and challenging along the 2½ mile hike to the bay, and one locally received recommendation is for a detour along the village road through Bishopston, passing between The Valley and The Joiners pubs and the local shops to the post office and Bishopston Stores at the sharp left hand Pyle Corner before Pyle Road. To the right here Pwll Du Lane and Brandy Cove Road begin as residential streets — but then continue as footpaths onwards and downwards to the seashore.

During the 18th and early part of the 19th centuries this coastline from Caswell and Brandy Cove towards Pennard was much favoured by smugglers, not just of brandy but also gin, tea, tobacco and other goods bearing high customs duty. These were imported, or 'run', at Pwll Du, which is still one of the most secluded coves on the coast, and the 'stuff' was carried by packhorse for part of the way up the valley before the turn into what is still known as Smugglers' Lane. This supposedly led to secret cellars at Great Highway and Little Highway Farms — and the buildings, if not the cellars, still remain off the Pennard to Southgate road.

To the west of the bay, Pwll Du Head is, at 300 feet, the highest headland on the coast. This was not lost on Iron Age inhabitants, who built the most easterly of a series of promontory forts there. Below the summit to the south-east, **Graves End** marks the burial place of a 'cargo' of at least 68 press-gang victims, some say in irons, who were drowned in the holds when the Admiralty tender *Caesar* was driven into the cliffs in 1760.

After leaving Bishopston, the B4436 descends steeply into the valley at Kittle Hill and rises under a canopy of trees to reach **Kittle** village, a later Beaufort Arms on the right and then a sign for Pennard. Shortly afterwards it turns at right angles to the right, but this tour continues straight ahead, following the Pennard and Southgate sign. Immediately to the right is St. Mary's Church, Pennard, which is a source of some mystery for there are remains of another parish church close to **Pennard Castle**. This was covered by wind-blown sand and abandoned in the 16th century and yet St. Mary's could have

St. Mary's Church, Pennard

had its origins in the 13th, as is suggested by early 13th-century dogtooth mouldings above a window. So which building was first, and did some parts of St. Mary's, such also as the sturdy beam that supports the west gallery, come from the buried church by the castle? The font was formerly an ancient water stoup with a carved Jacobean cover and there are hefty wooden dog rails to protect the sanctuary. A tablet on the nave wall bears the words: 'Death cannot steal the light which love has kindled nor the years change it' to commemorate the lyric poet Vernon Watkins (1906–1967, see p.13), who came to live, and died, at West Cliff. The links and Clubhouse of Pennard Golf Club soon appear on the right and a drive down the village street, keeping an eye open for the commoners' jaywalking ponies and cattle, ends at the bus terminus and car park (NT) close to the cliff top at Southgate.

Pobbles Beach and Three Cliffs Bay from Pennard Cliffs

The spectacular **Pennard Cliffs** (NT) extend from Pwll Du Head to Three Cliffs, over to the west, and they form part of common land where local farmers exercise ancient rights to graze their stock. The limestone contains caves of all sizes and close to the car park, **Minchin Hole** is the largest so far to have revealed bones of animals that roamed here when sea levels were much lower than now, when Stone Age Man hunted the valley between today's Gower and Somerset. Bones of reindeer, mammoth, cave bear and wolf have been found from when the climate was much

Gower Plant Life

There are more than 1,000 different plant species that are native or naturalised in the diverse local environments of Gower. They are to be found on the cliffs, sand dunes, pebble and sandy beaches, woodland, moorland, heath, farmland, freshwater and estuarial habitats and are conditioned by an equal number of local variations, involving climate, soil type, slope and ground stability and the degree of human and animal interference. A prominent and economically important consequence of the combination of generally mild weather with few late frosts, rather high humidity and fairly even annual rainfall of the area is that much of the land is good for the cultivation of early potatoes. Factors such as these have resulted in the varied range of plant and plant communities that can be seen in the Bishopston Valley, while the exposed limestone rock along the south Gower coast is where some really outstanding plants are to be found. Pennard Cliffs and the stretches of coastline extending westwards towards Worm's Head are especially noted among botanists and plant lovers for the Yellow Whitlow Grass (*Draba Aizoides*), an Alpine species that is found nowhere else nearer than the Belgian Ardennes and the Cote d'Or near Dijon, save in the joints and crevices of Pennard Castle — where the attractive spikes of yellow saxifrage-like flowers are at their best in March and April. In the sand dunes at Three Cliffs Bay, among colourful orchids and bloody cranesbill is to be found the rare Isle of Man cabbage, and in the grassland, ledges and crevices from Port Eynon towards Worm's Head there are further plants of considerable rarity and outstanding interest. Not everything is so exotic or difficult to find, for in May the cliffs are bright with flowers such as the yellow spring cinquefoil, patches of spring squill and other plants that only flourish in completely exposed situations. They would not tolerate the dappled shade around Parkmill for example, where vast areas of woodland are blanketed with strong smelling wild garlic, wood anemone and bluebell. On the coast nearby, the dunes of Penmaen and Nicholaston Burrows support a rich growth of lime-loving species and varieties of orchids, and further to the west among the luxuriant aquatic flora of the National Nature Reserve at Oxwich Marsh are strikingly beautiful yellow-flowered fringed water lilies. As for the acres of commons of the peninsula, they support most heathland species, and in wetter spots during the summer display silky heads of cotton grass, while in the salt marshes to the north, sea lavender provides a carpet of lilac blue flowers and there are good stands of marsh mallow.

One important aspect of the wide appeal of Gower is the rich floral tapestry that is created, season after season, by these and so many other different plants, all amazingly concentrated within an area that is hardly 18 miles long by not more than 8 miles wide.

colder, and hyaena, lion, rhinoceros and elephant that were here when it became warmer. There is also evidence of human occupation of the cave during the more recent Roman period and into the Dark Ages. Half a mile to the east, **Bacon Hole** also contained bones of a wide variety of exotic animals, and most of those recovered at Pennard and elsewhere in Gower are now housed in the Swansea Museum.

Paths along East Cliff lead to the Iron Age fort and descend to Bishopston Valley and Pwll Du Bay, while in the opposite direction towards West Cliff. Others head towards the first of three breaks in the continuity of limestone cliffs from Mumbles Head, at the dunes of **Penmaen**. **Pobbles** and **Three Cliffs** beaches appear far below and to the right there are some of the holes of Pennard golf links, Pennard Castle and the site of the adjacent old church. There are ways down through the sand to them all, made easier in some places with timber-slatted steps and walkways — which also help to reduce the erosion that would otherwise be caused by countless scrambling feet! In some parts they also lead past wild plants, some of which are not likely to be seen anywhere else in Britain.

Every approach to **Pennard Castle** has to be on foot, and the most favoured way extends from the Pennard Cliff path and along the boundary of the golf links (but also see the entry on Parkmill that follows shortly).

After leaving **Southgate** and **Pennard** to return to the B4436, turn left at the church to follow the signs for Port Eynon, Parkmill and the Heritage Centre and arrive at a T-junction with the A4118 from Swansea and Upper Killay. (This road has passed the B4271 North Gower road junction and the entrance

2. Pennard Castle

Although there is not now much of it left, the castle poised high up on its steep limestone crag above Pennard Pill and the sandy burrows, if not the most interesting, still manages from a distance to look the most imposing of all those on Gower. It began as a ringwork fort during the 12th century, complementing that on the promontory across the bay at Penmaen Burrows. Both were replaced with local limestone and sandstone structures by the Normans during their period of military consolidation in the late 13th century

Pennard Castle and Pill

— and it is these that have partly survived at Pennard. In the event nature, rather than any human action, played the principal part in their destiny and that of the neighbouring small settlement and church, for there were soon unforeseen problems with sand blow and the force of the south-westerly winds. Strong gales produced gradual encroachment during the 14th and 15th centuries and these are thought to have culminated in a mighty sandstorm in 1607. Except for this, Pennard Castle does not appear to have featured in history to any extent. Nowadays the courtyard curtain wall overlooking the valley is still in a good state, almost to battlement level, while outside it a later projecting square building also stands. There are substantial remains of a twin-towered gatehouse, but the southern curtain wall on the windward side has collapsed and remains that were excavated in 1961 have been reburied. There are also signs of a rectangular stone hall and its subdivisions within the courtyard area, and they too await future research and attention.

to **Swansea Airport,** a former RAF fighter station at Fairwood Common. It is now possible to have short trial flying lessons in 2-seater Cessna 152 and 4-seater Koliber and Grumman Tiger light aircraft from there, when needless to say the aerial views of Gower are truly stunning.)

Turn left on the A4118 to follow the sign for Parkmill, Penmaen and Oxwich, soon to face the lodge of the late 18th-century Kilvrough Manor, a recreational centre for young Oxfordshire people. The estate is bounded by a very high, somewhat leaning, wall close alongside the A4118, making the road seem even

The Gower Heritage Centre

narrower than it often is, before it starts to descend past the Gower Inn on the right to reach the extended village of **Parkmill** and Three Cliffs Bay Car Park. An 800-year-old water-powered corn and saw mill has survived there and is restored as the centrepiece of **The Gower Heritage Centre**. Although especially child-friendly, this also educates visitors of all ages with displays of local trades and handicrafts that have been employed in creating the rural history and heritage of Gower.

---

3. Parkmill

The steep, narrow road flanking Shepherds General Store, a popular pull-in and top-up place for holidaymakers, leads sharply up to Lunnon and then Ilston at the top of the cwm, or valley. St. Illtud's Church is thought to have origins in a 6th-century monastic cell.

A stream, locally known for some reason as the Killy Willy, flows down Ilston Cwm through the woods heading for Parkmill and the sea. After joining a brook falling from the Spring at Kitten Well it accompanies one of Gower's finest walks. Starting from the left hand side of the road, this first passes marshy ground that in May can be yellow with marsh marigolds, then followed by purple loosestrife and meadow sweet. Soon the woodland is left behind and the valley bottom widens to produce open grazing for wild ponies and cattle on the left and dense trees and shrubs of Northill Wood on the right of the path. High up on the left, the ruins of Pennard Castle come into view and the stream broadens at a point where 18th-century engravings showed ships at anchor. Movement of sand into the Pennard Valley has since stopped that practice, and areas of grassy saltmarsh and other habitats now make for the delight of botanists instead. Except during high tides, the stream can be crossed by stepping-stones that lead towards the foot of Pennard Burrows and pathways up to the castle ruins and to the cliffs. Then it winds its way in a deep channel in the sand towards the Three Cliffs and the sea, creating just one of the hazards that explain why Three Cliffs Bay is regarded as so unsafe for bathing.

Back at the start of the path at Parkmill, a bridleway climbs steeply up to the right through the wild garlic of Northill Wood, to emerge into the open between narrowly spaced high hedges, rich with the different plant varieties that denote their great age. It enters a lane to rejoin the A4118 near Penmaen Church and it is hard to believe that, until relatively recent times, this was the only surface route to and from West Gower beyond!

At the brown sign for the Heritage Centre and Parc-Le-Breos House on the right hand side of the road at Parkmill, a lane leads into Parkwood and a Forestry Commission car park near Kithen Well

Parc le Breos burial chamber

Disused limekiln

Spring and the lush valley of **Green Cwm**. A short distance up the drive there is what is popularly known as **Giant's Grave**, or **Parc le Breos.** The Information Plaque announces: 'Park Le Bruce Burial Chamber. Erected in the Neolithic Age 3000–1900 BC for the communal burial of the dead'. Originally covered by a large mound of stones as a chambered tomb, recent excavations and research have suggested that no fewer than 40 people were buried there, including one infant, seven children, and adults ranging between 25 and 60 years old. There is a disused limekiln close by, and about two hundred yards further north a footpath leads up the eastern side of the valley to a cave known as **Cathole,** in a high rock face among the trees. Flint blades discovered there have indicated that it was occupied by hunters towards the end of the last Ice Age, perhaps around 12,000 BC. Bone analysis of the people buried long after them, at Park le Breos, indicates that they too enjoyed a diet that was rich in protein.

Through woodland glades carpeted with wild flowers further beyond the car park is Parc-le-Breos House, a 19th-century hunting lodge. Set in 70 acres of what was once the deer park of William de Braose, Lord of Gower, it offers farmhouse accommodation and meals, riding holidays — even purpose-built kennels for visitors' pets.

The A4118 at Parkmill is nearly at sea level, but by the time it has ascended the 'new' Penmaen Road as far as the crossroad at Penmaen Green and St. John the Baptist's Church it is some 250 feet higher. The minor road to the right curves back as a crescent, passing the rear of the prominent Three Cliffs Care Home, formerly the workhouse, while a track breaks off upwards to the right, taking The Gower Way along the rounded central ridge of **Cefn Bryn**. It reaches almost 620 feet above sea level, the second highest point in Gower, and on clear days up there the colours and textures to be seen across the peninsula are worth any detour — while the views further beyond are cosmic. It is possible to see much of the Glamorgan coast to the east, Somerset, Devon and Lundy Island round to the south-west, Caldey Island and Tenby more to the west and Carmarthen Bay and the Loughor Estuary closer to the north-west. Some of the Preseli Hills, Carmarthenshire Fans, Black Mountains and Brecon Beacons can also be picked out further away.

But to reach any of the beaches from Penmaen and onwards from the A4118 , whether on foot or by road, it will be necessary to drop down between some 200 to 300 feet — sharply sometimes at gradients of 20%, or 1 in 5. You can either continue along the A road and take the road to Oxwich noted on the page opposite, or try parking and taking either of the footpaths mentioned in the next two paragraphs.

The first option occurs at Penmaen Green down the lane to the left, along the route of the old road towards North Hills Farm. A right turn over a rise begins a descent towards Three Cliffs Bay, passing **Nott Hill** (NT), an outlier of Cefn Bryn and the only Gower cliffland that has acid soil and not limestone — indicated by rhododendron with the cover of gorse and bracken. The 5 acres of rocky hillside had been divided into building plots but they were steadily bought up by Miss E.R. Lee and presented to the National Trust in 1955. Now, with the Gower Commons Initiative, there is a project to re-establish the heathland plants that were native to the area in the 1920s. Then at the end of the narrow road a path cuts obliquely down the adjacent hillside to emerge at Pennard Pill, near the stepping-stones.

Three Cliffs Bay

The site of Penmaen Old Castle with Three Cliffs Bay beyond

A second footpath down from Penmaen begins at a car park further along the main road, on the left hand side. It leads to **Penmaen Burrows**, a low headland forming the western flank of Three Cliffs Bay and extending out to the Great Tor rock. Footpaths descend to the Three Cliffs and Pobbles Bay and also to Tor Bay and through Nicholaston Woods towards Oxwich. There are magnificent coastal views over many miles and also special features at Penmaen for those interested in prehistory to more recent times. **Pen-y crug** is one of six surviving chambered tombs on Gower and, at anything up to 5,500 years old, shares its design approach with Parc-le-Breos (above). But there is little to see at Penmaen Burrows, for many of the stones have collapsed around the entrance passage and the remaining side chamber and there are others that hardly show. The remains of **Penmaen Old Castle**, a ringwork also known as **Castle Tower**, is one of ten early earthwork castles (including Pennard, above) that were built as the Normans tightened their grip on Gower during the 12th century. It is on a promontory with a commanding view of Three Cliffs Bay and was constructed as a motte and bailey fort, guarded by a tall timber tower and reinforced with a limestone rubble bank and a deep ditch. After a relatively short time, it was abandoned before the mid-13th century and it is not known whether the Normans, who introduced rabbits to Britain, were responsible for the nearby 'pillow mound' artificial warren, or whether later medieval residents became concerned with the provision of meat and fur for their diet and clothing. There are legends here of *Staedworlango*, a settlement now said to be buried in the sand, but the only solid evidence lies in stone

4. Penrice Castle

Penrice's mock castle

The gateway, dating from 1793, serves as an entrance to the grounds of the modern 'castle' that was built for the Reverend Thomas Mansel Talbot, inheritor of the estate. His mansion was sited close to the former Penrice Castle, the seat of the powerful Mansel family, constructed in *c*.1240. The round keep survives along with the massive towers at the entrance and the tall curtain wall, rounded bastions and other features date from the closing quarter of that century — except for the stone pigeon house that was added in *c*.1500. The Mansels moved to a new fortified manor house at Oxwich Green in the early 16th century. The later Penrice Castle was built in the 1770s, and was extended in the Victorian era. The ancient castle is not in a safe state but it can be seen from a public footpath that strikes off to the left slightly further along the A4118.

walls in a depression that were part of the first Penmaen Church. This has long been succeeded by St. John the Baptist Church at Penmaen Green — well away from any risk of sand encroachment. Lastly, from relatively recent times, there is a double-fronted limekiln that is one of many to be seen on Gower and other limestone areas in south-west Wales being visited on these tours.

The A4118 continues from Penmaen past Nicholaston and the direction sign for Oxwich, Port Eynon and Rhossili, and then you take a secondary road to the left sharply down signposted to Oxwich Bay. It is not hard to miss, for facing you before the turn is the main Park Gateway of **Penrice Castle**.

Much of the property in and around **Oxwich**, including the beach and its car park, forms part of the Penrice Estate, although from 1983 most of the area of the National Nature Reserve had been purchased by the Nature Conservancy Council (now the Countryside Council for Wales). At the bottom of the steep hill, the road reaches a long and level section running between reeds and marshland that goes towards creating one of the richest varieties of coastal habitat in Great Britain — particularly for flowers, birds and insects. There is usually detailed information available near the car park on all aspects of the history, sea and shore, dunes, marshes, pools and woodlands.

Cottage in Oxwich

5. Oxwich Bay

The wide sweep of Oxwich Bay extends between the solid limestone cliffs of Pwll Du and the bold headland at Oxwich Point, while the soft shale eroded by the sea in between them has been built up by the tides as a shingle bank and covered with wind blown sand to form the dunes of Oxwich Burrows. These create the backdrop to the sandy beach that extends for two miles as far as Tor Bay at low tide. In the lee of the headland, it is good for bathing, boating, sand castles and walking and, served by the large car park, general stores, refreshments and public toilets, it is one of Gower's most popular attractions, being especially hectic during the summer school holidays and weekends.

Oxwich Bay and Point from Cefn Bryn

One of the quiet charms of Oxwich is the ancient St. Illtud's Church overlooking the bay on the wooded hillside. The minute chancel is thought to date from the 6th century, while the rest of the church probably comes from the 12th century. Beyond the chancel and close to the churchyard boundary there is the poignant, beautifully situated war grave and headstone of a sailor of the Great

St. Illtud's Church

War. Given up by the sea on 1 February 1916, his epitaph simply says: 'Known Unto God'.

The sea is said to have claimed an early rectory, while the most recent one formed part of the Oxwich Bay Hotel, on the way to the small village. At the crossroads, the road to the left leads steeply up a hill to reach **Oxwich Castle**, and continues towards Oxwich Green and the secluded beach at Slade.

From the car park there is a choice of two ways of reaching the A4118 — the first being to return along the road on which you arrived, driving between the marshes and back up the hill to the Penrice Park gateway. Alternatively, there is a left turn at the sign for Penrice and Horton, heading along the narrow road towards Oxwich Camping Park that continues through the village past numbers of attractive thatched and other cottages. This road ends with a T-junction facing the granary that dates to 1807 at Penmaen Old Farmhouse alongside the A4118. This is raised on 'straddle stones' as a safeguard against raids by rats and mice.

In each case you turn left onto the A road.

The granary at Penrice Old farmhouse

6. Oxwich Castle

Oxwich Castle gateway and heraldic arms

After acquiring Oxwich by marriage, the Mansel family moved from Penrice Castle and in 1487 the formidable Rice, or Rhys, Mansel was born at the castle overlooking Oxwich Bay. Between 1520 and 1538, by then already distinguished in royal service and knighted, he is generally thought to have upgraded the castle with the first phase of what, in those more settled times, was really a fortified mansion. Displaying his initials and the heraldic arms of the Mansels, quartered with those of the Scurlage and Penrice families, his rather ostentatious gateway was more decorative than defensive and the two-storey range on the south side of the courtyard chiefly comprised a great chamber, bedroom and domestic quarters. Later this part became a farmhouse and it now serves as the Visitor and Exhibition Centre. After Sir Rice died in 1559, Edward his son erected a taller and much more lavish east range of chambers, with three projecting towers. The main entrance was by a projecting stone porch and staircase that are now reduced to ground level, and the eastern portion of the main building and two of the towers have also collapsed. Still standing are the high walls facing the courtyard and the south-east tower up to its full six-storey height. After coming close to demolition, all the buildings are now being cared for by Cadw.

The first of the ruins to be met upon leaving the car park are of a stone dovecot, or pigeon house, that in Tudor times could well have been installed as a symbol of high social status. It contained some 300 nest-holes and ensured a regular supply of fresh meat. But one winter's day in 1557 the birds must have been caused extra flutters after a French ship grounded in the bay. A 'rescue' of cargo and prisoners by the Mansels led to a violent fight with followers of contesting claimants outside the nearby gateway and tragically Anne Mansel, sister-in-law of Sir Rice, was fatally struck on the head by a stone while attempting to calm everyone down.

7. Penrice

There is little indication at Penrice that until *c.*1700 it was actually the principal village of Gower. St. Andrew's Church faces the village green, and the base of the ancient village cross, and it dates from the early 12th century, and an all too common Victorian 'make-over'. The most striking feature from the outside is the huge size of the porch in relation to the rest of the building. To the left of it stands the 'Murder Stone' of a local widow where the inscription reads: 'To the Memory of Mary Wife of James Kavanagh of Penmaen who

St. Andrew's Church

was Murdered by (*here scratched out*) The 3rd of October 1829 Aged 75 years Prepare for Death Make No Delay She in a Moment was Snatched Away'.

Close by, the **Mountybank** is a large, overgrown earthwork that first appeared soon after the Norman Conquest, marking the first Penrice fortress prior to the raising of Penrice Castle in the mid-13th century. Northwards past Mill Wood the narrow road continues, with few passing places, to rise to Home Farm on the A4118.

Having turned left onto the A4118, before heading towards the next beaches it is worth considering a short detour that loops its way through the straggling hillside village of **Reynoldston**. It starts at the next right turn, to make towards the slopes of Cefn Bryn and first reaching Little Reynoldston. The road then continues to the Higher Green and King Arthur Hotel, close to what amounts to a meeting point between north and south Gower. Just about a mile northwards towards the B4271 and Llanrhidian there is a footpath leading towards a false crest of Cefn Bryn and **Arthur's Stone**, a burial chamber also known to the Welsh as **Maen Ceti** and the focus of different traditions, myths and legends. Although there has been some dispute about the true age, it is normally counted as one of Gower's six megalithic tombs and consists of two chambers beneath a huge capstone that is raised on stone uprights. There has been speculation about how the estimated 25 tons weight could have been raised on its supports, and wonderment that has produced the Welsh proverb: *Mal Gwaith Maen Cetti* — 'Like the labour of the stone of Cetti'. But more relaxed assumptions are that the ground beneath

Higher Green, Reynoldston

Arthur's Stone

what is actually a glacial 'erratic' of millstone grit could first have been excavated without great effort before being underpinned by the supports!

The road descends southwards from the hotel to rejoin the A4118, and a turning to the right towards Llanddewi and Scurlage and soon vehicles squeeze through the narrow main street of **Port Eynon** to reach its terminus at the public car park and beach.

8. Port Eynon

The marble statue of Billy Gibbs in the churchyard, and seen as you drive through Port Eynon

The sheltered sandy bay and rolling dunes that extend to the quieter village of Horton nearby attract streams of summer visitors to the camping, caravan and chalet parks that overlook the bay, or come for a day by the seaside. All are well catered for by gift and surf equipment shops, cafés, The Smugglers' Haven restaurant and the Ship Inn, with its distinctive port-hole windows. Anyone also interested in the history of Port Eynon might look towards the lee of the Point to the west, where much of the seafaring life of the village centred. Until 1916 this is where the self-righting RNLI lifeboat *Janet* was housed, but on New Year's Day disaster struck after the crew attempted to assist the *SS Dunvegan*, aground at Oxwich in rough seas. Twice the lifeboat capsized and Coxwain William Gibbs and two crew members were thrown out and lost. Afterwards it was decided to close the station and rely on the modern lifeboats at Mumbles and Tenby. Overlooking the A4118 at the corner of St. Cattwg's churchyard, the tragedy suffered by the villagers is commemorated by a life-sized marble statue of Billy Gibbs. Nearly 50 years later, the lifesaving tradition at Port Eynon Bay that had started with the launch of the first lifeboat, *A Daughters Offering*, in 1884 was revived by the inauguration along the shore at Horton of a seasonal Inshore Rescue Boat. The old Port Eynon Lifeboat House has meanwhile been adapted to become part of a Youth Hostel and just past it was Crowder's Quay, which figured in the 19th-century oyster fishing industry. In its heyday, up to 40 skiffs operated out of Port Eynon, fishing from the Bantrum beds beyond the Point and the Helwick Shoal (until recently marked by the lightship that is now berthed at the Swansea Maritime Quarter). The oyster catches were landed at Crowder's Quay and stored in 'perches pools' until they could be shipped to Swansea, Bristol and more distant ports, and expert eyes can still make out where they were. Outside the oyster season, the fishermen would work during the summer months in the limestone quarries, the bulk of which can be seen from the Memorial Stone to two founder members of the Gower Society that is visible from the shore on the headland, looking rather like a 'Day Marker'. The shallow waters of the bay are of high salinity, and on the shoreline at the rock pool end of the bay close to the Point there are the remains of an old salthouse, where seawater was partly evaporated then boiled to produce salt, mainly for curing fish and meat. It was demolished during the Great Storm of 1703 and two fishermen's cottages were afterwards built on the site. Their ruins now mark the site of *Ye Salte House*.

9. Coastal walk from Port Eynon

Except for Mewslade this is the last sandy beach along the south coastline for about six miles until Rhossili. From Port Eynon Point to the tip of Worm's Head there is instead the most thrilling walk in Gower. The limestone cliffs have formed into bent, tilted, contorted or broken rock formations, shattered into spectacular shapes or hollowed out as caverns and clefts while big seas and waves have frothed in whiteness and crashed along their feet. But the cliff path is not all easy going, can be dangerous in places and it is not really designed for smallish children or adults who are not reasonably fit or used to much walking. Best reached at low tide from down below within ¼ mile of the Point, there is the baffling **Culver Hole**, a rock cleft that has been closed for some 60 feet by a medieval wall pierced with round and rectangular window openings. Inevitably it has long been linked with zealous local smuggling, although the name could come from *culfre*, Old English for pigeon and therefore it could have been a dove house, or was it to do with the lost Port Eynon Castle once up above — and is there a secret passage leading to *Ye Salte House*, previously the domain of the somewhat lawless Lucas dynasty?

Nearly 2 miles further along there is a cave considered in archaeological circles to be unique in the British Isles. About 30 feet up above sea level, **Paviland Cave,** also known as **Goat's Hole,** was found in 1823 to contain not only the bones of prehistoric animals but also evidence of a ceremonial Old Stone Age burial, comprising parts of a headless skeleton, with ornaments and implements laid beside it. The bones were coloured red by iron oxide, and it was decided to call their owner The Red Lady of Paviland — until radio-carbon tests revealed that 'she' was actually a young man. Probably a strapping nomadic hunter who would have roamed some 25,000 years ago, when the cave and

cliffs were far inland and Britain was physically joined to the Continent across the present Bristol Channel, he and his kind would have had little problem in entering the cave. Now it is not easy to find and quickly isolated by rising tides. All attempts to reach it require tide-table and weather checks and some agility, and access presents dangers for the unskilled and ill-equipped.

Passing two Late Iron Age promontory forts high up on the cliffs on either side of **Deborah's Hole,** where other bones have been discovered (and now shown at Swansea Museum), the footpath heads inland behind Thurba Head, crowned at 200ft. with yet another fort. Then it drops to meet the rocky footpath coming down Mew Slade from Pitton and heading for Mewslade Bay (This is another 'slade' met since leaving Mumbles — a Gower term for a limestone valley opening out to the sea). Because of the ½ mile or so walk needed to reach it from the road

Three views of Mewslade Bay

Fall Bay

and the climb back up, **Mewslade Bay** rarely becomes crowded and when the tide is out, the sandy beach is excellent for swimming, ball games and sunbathing — as too is **Fall Bay** further along. Towering crags form a mighty backdrop that is popular with rock-climbers and, at one place, with some rather rare kittiwakes, but neither they nor the sands can be seen when the tide is in. Continuing on above, along what is virtually one long plant and bird nature reserve, the cliff path rises to round Tear's Point and come within sight of its climax at Worm's Head.

Climb back through Port Eynon, past the holiday park entrance then the road to Horton on the right, taking the first left turn onto the B4247 at Scurlage. The road heads for Rhossili past Pilton Green and until the early 20th century the road from Swansea would have come to an end at Pilton Cross. There was simply a narrow lane from there on and most travellers to and from Pitton, Middleton and Rhossili usually had to walk. Now the road continues past Pitton (and the signpost for the car park at Lower Pitton Farm which is down the narrow road to the left, serving the footpath dropping to Mewslade Bay), and Middleton. This is where, in School Lane, Petty Officer Edgar Evans, R.N. was born — who died with Captain Scott in 1912 during his expedition's attempt to return from the South Pole. There is a memorial to him in Rhossili Parish Church, which soon comes into sight on the right side of the narrow road that ends at the large car park above Rhossili Bay.

10. Rhossili and Worm's Head

Below the car park, the footpath to and from Worm's Head sets off at about 250 feet above beach level past the Worm's Head Hotel, the public toilets and the National Trust Visitor Centre in one of three former coastguard cottages. The well-used path leads towards the Old Coastguard Lookout, and as well as the sea views across Rhossili Bay there are on the landward side the remains of the Old Castle Iron Age Camp, former small limestone quarries and an area known as the Vile. This is divided into narrow strip-shaped fields, as a rare survival of a medieval open-field system. The old Coastguard Lookout now serves as an Information Point about the locality, not least tide times for explorers intending to continue on to Worm's Head, including those who have arrived along the cliff path from above Mewslade and Fall Bays.

Looked at from the Rhossili approach it is not hard to appreciate how some superstitious mariners, maybe in poor visibility, might have taken Worm's Head to be some form of marine monster, rising out of the sea. Certainly no worm, the mile-long promontory owes its name to the Danish invaders who called it the *Wurm* or *Orm*, meaning dragon or serpent (as at the Great Orme, Llandudno). The local people know it as The Worm, or *Penrhyn-Gwyr*, and the connecting rocky causeway over which the sea washes twice every 24 hours or so as the Shipway. The Worm becomes an island, and the causeway is only open for approximately 2½ hours either side of low water. Anyone remaining there outside this period is likely to be marooned for seven hours but strongly advised not to try crossing when the tide is

35

closing in, for many people have been drowned in such attempts. Public access is allowed to this National Nature Reserve and noteworthy sea-bird haven when tides allow and two islets connect by a barrier of rocks at the Low Neck to Devil's Bridge, a huge natural arch of limestone, and to the Outer Head. The high cliff at the end has an eerie-sounding blow-hole, another cave that had once contained the bones of prehistoric animals, and plunges for over 100 feet into the sea, where razorbills and guillemots often bob up and down in the swell and languid seals loaf on the rocks.

Rhossili Bay

Probably the finest view of the Worm, and the line upon line of breakers flooding in on the tide along 3 miles of Rhossili Bay, is from **The Beacon**, high on Rhossili Down. It is some 632 feet above the beach and the highest point in Gower, whereas the village of Rhossili is roughly half way up — so that to reach both, a stiff climb is unavoidable, but if you have the energy, un-missable. The sandy beach is a paradise for bathers, anglers, surfers and walkers — but not so for mariners, as is shown by the remains of wrecks, notably that of the barque *Helvetia*, which foundered in 1887. But not all disasters were caused by bad weather or poor seamanship alone, for during the 18th and 19th centuries ships were often lured onto the rocks of Worm's Head and other stretches of the coast with false lights held out by wreckers. Many local villagers were involved in the evil and sometimes murderous practice, and some of the clergy — although ever concerned for the safety of all sailors in their prayers — did not altogether condemn it. One preacher is said to have ended an entreaty with: 'But, if it be Thy will that they be cast away, send them ashore here Lord, and not among the wicked in the next parish.'

Directly above the beach is a long raised bench of glacial material formed by the process of 'solifluction', then covered by wind-blown sand and known as **The Warren**. Human bones were exposed there in 1949 and taken to be from an old burial ground, and in the wet winter of 1979/80, sections of drystone walling appeared, those of one domestic building measuring 55 feet long and 22 feet wide, close to the remains of another five houses. Further excavation exposed the near full-height walls of a 50 feet x 21 feet nave and 14 feet 7 inches square chancel of a church. It was thought to have been built in *c*.1150, just about half a century after the Normans conquered Gower, whereas the other buildings must have been part of the original, pre Norman, village of

Worm's Head

Rhossili. Village and church are said to have been engulfed completely by wind-blown sand early in the 4th century and the excavations having been backfilled, all that is left to see near there is the old white-painted rectory. This was built half way between the parishes of Rhossili and Llangynydd, which used to be the rector's responsibility. After rebuilding in the 1950s it was bought by the National Trust in 1995, modernised, and is now let to holidaymakers.

In today's village, **St. Mary the Virgin's Church** was founded during the 6th century and the present building dates from the 12th and 13th centuries and a 19th-century 'restoration'. Unique in Gower and rare in Wales, the doorway comes from the late Norman period, with outer dog-tooth moulding and an inner moulding of deeply cut chevrons that are typical of the second half of the 12th century. At the top of the left hand pillar is a 'scratch dial' that, with a stick in the hole, acted as a timepiece when the doorway was open to the sky — perhaps with the rest of the rare sculptural work, part of the old church on The Warren?

There are fine views of church and village from the steep path up to the **Beacon**, but there is little sign of any trees on the landscape because of the furious westerly winds. Seemingly just one solitary ash tree managed to survive for at least 100 years, but only by growing horizontally. There must be even better views for the hang-gliders and para-gliders who take off from just below the Beacon and soar above the cairns, round barrows, remains of a Second World War radar station and Sweyne's Howes, the two ancient burial mounds half way along the hill top of the Downs.

To head up the west side of the peninsula head back from Rhossili past Scurlage to rejoin the A4118 on which you turn left. Keep straight on at the sharp right-angled turn that the A road makes at Llanddewi and take to the minor road signposted through Burry as far as Burry Green, and then turn left towards Llangennith.

After evolving from a previous priory, **St. Cenydd's** at **Llangennith** (correctly Llangynydd) is the largest church in Gower and now dominated by a huge 13th-century tower with a typical Gower saddleback roof. It is on the lower side of a sloping green facing the Kings Arms inn, while 18th-century farm cottages, one of them now occupied as a Surf Shop, complete what forms a pleasant village group. The Atlantic Ocean swells that pour in between Burry Holms and Rhossili produce the rollers that earn Llangennith the title of The Surfing Capital of Gower.

To reach the Burrows and Burry Holms, take the left turn at the mini-roundabout at West Town and head for the Hillend camping site and car park. The coastline is dominated by the sand dunes of Hillend, Broughton and Llangennith Burrows (burrows is derived from *Old English* for mounds) and they were probably formed in the 15th century, when blown sand engulfed everything but the limestone cliffs and the Burry Holms tidal islet. (Another way to the Burrows leads from the mini-roundabout and the Broughton sign to the Broughton Farm static caravan park and through an area rich in wild flowers, including pyramidal orchids, sea holly and purple bloody cranesbill.)

11. Burry Holms, Broughton Bay and Whiteford Point

To commemorate St. Cenydd's Day, a visit is made each summer to the site of a wooden Celtic church oratory on Burry Holms, which can be reached at the north end of Rhossili Bay during a period of 2½ hours each side of low water. After Burry Holms the coastline veers north-east for the next five miles as far as Whiteford Point and the handsome Victorian lighthouse marking the south side of the channel to Llanelli until it was decommissioned in 1933. Unusually it was constructed of cast iron, with elegant balconies, and at high tide stands in 20 feet of water. From Spaniard Rocks the coast is rocky, with caves that include Gower's second Culver Hole, Three Chimneys — a natural arch, and a deep circular pool that gives its name to Bluepool Corner — a sandy cove when the tide is out. Then comes Broughton

Bay, which is regarded as dangerous for bathing, but also sorrowfully remembered as the scene of the worst ever maritime disaster on this coast. A fleet of 19 coastal sailing vessels of between 80 and 400 tons, outward bound from Llanelli, misjudged hostile changing sea and weather conditions on the night of 22 January 1868, and all but three of them were dashed against the rocks or had their bottoms knocked out by fierce thumping on the sand. Most of their crews were lost, as is described in an authentic account in *A History of West Gower (1877–94)*, an authoritative

Burry Holms seen across the burrows

work by the Reverend J.D. Davies. A renowned Gower historian and archaeologist, he was particularly well placed to report the tragic event, for between 1860 and 1911 he was also rector of the adjoining coastal parishes of Llanmadoc and Cheriton. And he was actually attending the weekly choir practice in Llanmadoc Church at about the time of the disaster.

From Llangennith the next leg of the tour first heads for the village of Llanmadoc and to St. Madoc's Church where over 30 of the dead sailors who were lost of the disaster of 1868 referred to in Box 11 are said to have been buried. Return up the road towards Burry Green and take an early left turn at Kennextone to pass a camping site then continue past the Britannia inn to **Llanmadoc**. In order to park, head for the 'honesty box' farm field car park down the lane to the right towards Cwm Ivy, just before the church. The present building looks north over the marshlands of the Burry estuary and dates

St. Madoc's Church, Llanmadoc

from the 13th century, although there is evidence, in the form of a lettered stone now set in the cill of the nave window, to indicate that the original foundation date is before AD 550. The highly versatile Reverend Davies was also a skilled wood-carver and he created the oak altar frontal and led the extensive church restoration of 1865 as well as the building of the Old Rectory across the road.

The villages of Llanmadoc and neighbouring Cheriton stand on ancient sea cliffs that are now well back from the sea, as can be appreciated from the churchyard by looking north beyond the old lighthouse — across the Loughor estuary towards 'the mainland' and south-west Wales. They form the gateway to Gower's north-west coast and, as it was from Llangennith and Broughton, to explore it is necessary to park the car, ease the legs into action — donning sensible footwear, allow for sudden changes in weather, keep an eye on the tides and stay on the footpaths.

12. Whiteford Sands and Burrows

At Cwm Ivy car park there is a sign indicating the way to the Whiteford Sands and Burrows, which are a botanist's paradise that leads to what has been described as 'the most bird-rich estuary lying wholly in Wales'. Some 45,000 waders have been counted there during the winter and as well as ducks such as wigeon, shelduck, teal and pintail, even a flock of eiders has remarkably been seen on the rocks off Whiteford Point — well away from their usual habitat much further north. For the keenest bird-watchers there is a 5 miles plod from Cwm Ivy, through the Corsican pines, along the saltings to a hide at Berges Island, perhaps to be followed by a return along the beach at the edge of the sea. Further to the east, Cwm Ivy Marsh leads towards Landimore Marsh, which merges into Llanrhidian Marsh. These are brackish places where only specialised salt-tolerating species survive, such as sea rush, sea purslane, sea lavender, sea meadow grass and glassworts. Plants like these cause the tidal waters to slow down, depositing some of their mud so that the land 'accretes', especially since the introduction of spartina or cord grass. These herbs are grazed by half-wild ponies and cattle that are owned by commoners — and it is to be expected that as a result their sheep produce meat that is at least as flavoursome as the much vaunted salt-marsh lamb from Le Mont St. Michel on the Normandy coast!

From the Cwm Ivy car park and Llanmadoc, turn left at the Britannia Inn and head to Cheriton, about ¾ mile to the east. Built probably in the 14th century, St. Cadoc's Church is on the left of the road and is known as the 'Cathedral of Gower', a distinguishing feature being its centrally placed tower. Restoration work in 1874 followed that at Llanmadoc and it included the rector's carvings of choir stalls, altar rails, altar and the embossed wooden ceiling. After serving the two parishes for 51 years, the talented and enterprising John David Davies died in 1911 and is buried in Cheriton churchyard.

The route continues towards Landimore, where a steeply descending lane branches off to the left to end at a car park at Landimore Marsh. Along a footpath to the west, **Whiteford National Nature Reserve** is rich in flowers, including several species of orchid, all flourishing because of the calcium-rich nature of the sand dunes. To the east, the mud flats and salt marshes of the Burry Inlet are among the most important places in Wales for duck, geese and waders that can roost and feed over the winter.

Until the silting process commenced in relatively recent times **Weobley Castle**, which now commands a cliff-top half way towards Llanrhidian would probably have been directly above the sea and not the present extensive salt-marshes. To reach it, return up the lane and turn left onto the road for Llanrhidian. The access drive appears on the left after about a mile.

13. Weobley Castle

In a commanding position at the top of a 150 feet sea cliff, but like Oxwich not a castle in any military sense, Weobley Castle is a fortified manor house offering a glimpse of domestic gentry life at the end of the Middle Ages. Most of the buildings that survive were built early in the 14th century and they are grouped round a small open courtyard with no curtain wall, except for a short section to the right of the simple gate. This is high enough for a mounted rider to pass through and at first floor level on his left was the solar, or private apartment for the lord and his family. A spacious Great Hall was arranged above the kitchen on the estuary side and from *c.*1500 this was reached from the courtyard through an imposing porch. The east range is thought to have been partly a guest chamber placed above a servants' hall and at the north-east corner there was a reredorter or latrine turret serving three levels in the adjacent wing. A two-storey structure on the south side probably included a chapel at the upper level, while the adjoining square south-west tower, which was originally freestanding and very sturdy, could be the oldest part of the entire building. To complete the circuit, the cistern turret to the right of the gateway

Weobley Castle

is so named because of a pit there that was used as a cistern to store rain water — seemingly the only source available for domestic needs.

Weobley escaped assault until the castle was attacked and damaged early in the 15th century during the Glyndwr revolt but it was quickly repaired and after passing to Sir Rhys ap Thomas of Dynevor, ardent supporter of Henry VII, it was extensively altered and rebuilt. But Sir Rhys's grandson and heir fell foul of Henry VIII, was executed for treason and the estate passed to the Crown and was sold to Sir William Herbert, earl of Pembroke. The castle was subsequently tenanted and used partly as a farmhouse, and after passing through the hands of the Mansels and Talbots it eventually became the responsibility of the Ministry of Works in 1911 and is now protected, conserved and opened up for public visits by Cadw.

After visiting the castle, return to the road and turn left for Llanrhidian, once a hub of thriving woollen and weaving activity. Its name derives from St. Rhidian who is thought to have founded a llan, or church, on the site of the present building in the 6th century. The present **Church of St. Rhidian and St. Illtyd** dates from the 13th century and the chancel and huge battlemented west tower (thought to have carried a beacon fire in threatening times) were added in the 14th century.

There are two ways to return to Swansea from Llanrhidian. One is to take the B4295, to the left of the petrol filling station, and pass beneath Cilifor Hill on the right. It is occupied by three massive ramparts that follow the contours to form the largest Iron Age fort in Gower, the defences then partly re-used in the Middle Ages and now leaving slight remains of a castle ringwork (on private land). At Crofty, at the edge of the marsh further along the road there is a link to the left that reaches a road that skirts miles of the coastal saltings. It is from here and neighbouring Pen-clawdd where people have gone out into the estuary for very many years to gather cockles for processing and then sale at Swansea Market and elsewhere. After passing beyond Pen-clawdd, the road runs beside the marsh all the way to Gowerton, where signs indicate alternative ways back to Swansea.

The second alternative route from Llanrhidian uses the B4271 to the right of the petrol filling station and shop and at Cilibion it meets the road from Reynoldston that has crossed Cefn Bryn Common, close to Arthur's Stone (above). A short distance up this road on the right is **Broad Pool**, an isolated Nature Reserve rich in plant, bird and insect life that is also a promising place to spot the semi-wild ponies that roam Cefn Bryn and other Gower commons. The B4271 continues beyond the junction through Pengwern and Fairwood Commons, Swansea Airport showing on the right, until it joins the A4118 that then runs through Killay and Sketty into Swansea.

Carmarthen

Seven miles inland from Carmarthen Bay at the highest tidal point of the Towy, the slope above the north river bank has been the scene of human occupation throughout recorded history, and probably ever since the Iron Age. First there were the Celtic Demetae tribe, then between 75 and 77 AD the Romans arrived and established an auxiliary fort as part of the task of subduing Wales. It stood at the south-west corner of a quadrilateral, connecting with straight roads running parallel with Cardigan Bay through *Bremia* (Llanio) and Trawscoed to *Canovium* (Caerhun**),** west to *Segontium* (Caernarvon and then extending eastwards to *Deva* (Chester) and down through the Marches via *Viroconium* (Wroxeter) and *Gobannium* (Abergavenny) to the legionary fortress of *Isca* (Caerleon).

A civic settlement developed immediately to the east of the fort and this came to qualify as a *vicus,* a self-governing local capital with an amphitheatre beyond for parades, contests and public events with seating for up to 5,000 people. There is a tradition that, after the Roman withdrawal in *c*.410 AD, a native community formed around a Celtic church dedicated to St. Teulyddog, possibly in the area of the later St. John's Priory.

This was the Age of Saints and also a time for legends, none more so here than that of the Celtic wizard and magician Myrddin Emrys, or Merlin, who mythically is supposed to have been born or discovered close by. The place name in Welsh duly became Caerfyrddin (Merlin's City), anglicised as Carmarthen. The legends tell of many places where Merlin is buried or imprisoned and the nearest can be found at the **Merlin's Hill Centre** at Alltyfyrddin near Abergwili, just to the east of Carmarthen. Close to the A40, there is a car park, picnic area and other wheelchair-friendly amenities at the heritage centre, while nature trails lead to the site of an Iron Age hill fort and stunning views of this part of Carmarthenshire.

Merlin pronounced several prophesies concerning Carmarthen, and the most oft-quoted to be somehow traditionally associated with his name was about an oak tree that stood until recent times at the end of Priory Street:

> *Pan gwympo'r dderwen Caerfyrddin a syddo*
> When Merlin's oak shall tumble down
> Tumble then shall Merlin's town

Eventually the tree stump had to be embedded in concrete and held together with iron bands, but then it became an obstruction to traffic. Not without some local trepidation the fragments were gingerly removed to be placed on display in a glass case and, as a conciliatory and so far effective gesture, a young oak was planted at the site of the Roman amphitheatre.

When Giraldus Cambrensis visited the town with the archbishop of Canterbury on their recruiting tour for the Third Crusade in 1188 he was still able to see brick wall remains of the Roman town. The Normans had arrived by 1094 and William fitz Baldwin is thought to have built their first castle a short way down the Towy at Rhyd-y-gors. By 1105 there was what was probably a motte and bailey defence on the present town

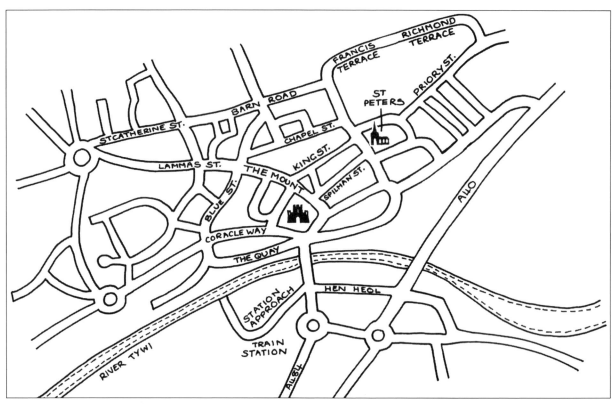

Carmarthen town plan

site overlooking the river, and an Anglo Norman civilian community that settled below had received a first royal charter of privileges from Henry I (1100–1135) by 1109. The established Welsh township to the east was allowed to remain, placed under the control of the prior of St. John Baptist from *c.*1127.

The Augustinian priory of St. John Baptist was one of a number of religious houses that were established by the Normans in recognition of the pope's support, part of a campaign to reorganise the Welsh Church while consolidating their hold on Wales. It functioned until the dissolution in the mid-16th century and is especially known as the place where the *Llyfr Du Caerfyrddin — The Black Book of Carmarthen*, was written. It is thought to be the work of one person in around 1250 and is so called because of the colour of its binding. It is one of the earliest surviving manuscripts written solely in the Welsh language and contains religious poems, many verses relating to figures of the Dark Ages, including Seithenyn and the drowning of *Cantre'r Gwaelod* (p.209), King Arthur, Myrddin and the town of Carmarthen. After passing through many hands it was purchased by Sir John Williams in 1904 and presented to the Welsh nation with numerous other priceless volumes and housed among the Special Collections at the National Library in Aberystwyth (pp.205-206).

Despite continual struggles between Welsh and English, including the capture and destruction of the castle by Llywelyn the Great in 1215 and sacking of the town by Owain Glyndwr in 1405, from being relatively small during the 12th and 13th centuries, Carmarthen came to flourish as one of the largest and most important towns in Wales. Receiving a Grant of Murage in 1223 it soon outgrew the small walled area around today's Guildhall Square, Quay Street and Bridge Street and in 1326 Carmarthen was declared to be one of 14 'Staple Ports' in the kingdom. It thus was licensed to deal in and export commodities such as wool, pelts, leather, lead and tin, and these export trades and entry of shiploads of wines from Bordeaux added to a role as the base for a lucrative fishing industry. All this activity brought increased prosperity and reinforced emergence of the town as the centre of commerce and royal government in south Wales that had followed disposal by the English in 1282 of the challenge posed by Llewelyn ap Gruffudd (p.246). The attacks by Owain Glyndwr in 1405 prompted rebuilding of the castle gatehouse, followed by an extension of the town walls to protect the eastern suburbs, and when the Act of Union came into effect after 1536, Carmarthen was well equipped to receive confirmation of its status, dating from 1284, as the capital of its eponymous county. With Brecon, Caernarvon and Denbigh, it also became a designated seat of the Great Sessions of Wales, a system of Courts that lasted until 1830. This formed part of a share of the wide functions vested in these capitals placed at the four corners of the country (subject until 1689, however, to the powers of the Council in the Marches based at Ludlow, Shropshire).

By 1600 the population of Carmarthen was approaching 2,000 and had recently been declared by William Camden to be 'the chief citie of the county' and an impression of how it then looked was produced in an *Atlas* in 1611–12 by historian and cartographer, John Speed. In vignettes, both to his map of Wales and the sheet *Caermarden, Both Shyre and Towne described*, the town is dominated by the 'castell' that guards a stone bridge across the 'Tovy', its 'Key' and shipping. The 15th-century town walls and gates were still there, as was the priory following its dissolution in 1559, while other features included St. Peter's Church and Street, Priory, Water, Spilman, Kings, High, St. Mary's and Key Streets, the market cross, St. Mary's Church and the mill. By that time, development had extended beyond the town walls, by the quay, along Priory Street past the eastern gates and Lammas Street in the direction of Haverfordwest, and beyond the subsequent Civil War earthworks known as The Bulwarks. These formed a part of the defences thrown up by Royalist forces and remain as rare survivors of the time when triumphant Parliamentarians slighted the castle, to render it finally useless as a fortification. The keep was later adapted as the county prison and then a new gaol was built between 1789–1792 to a design by John Nash (1752–1835). This was replaced from 1938, interrupted during the war, by the conspicuous chateau-style County Hall designed by Sir Percy Thomas Partnership, its steep angled slate roof covering today's Carmarthenshire County Council headquarters.

Carmarthen Castle

Regarded as 'a Town of Distinction', attracting celebrated residents such as Richard 'Beau' Nash (1674–1762), who later made his name at Bath, and Richard Steele (1671–1729), pioneer of the periodical press and editor of the *Spectator*, Carmarthen by 1770 was ahead of the population of most if not all other Welsh towns with at least 4,000 residents. But this supremacy was soon to come to an end with an explosive growth of large scale industrialisation in Wales. Llanelli, with its anthracite coalfield and belching factory chimneys, soon became by far the largest town in the county, as well as the 'Tinplate capital of the world'. The population of the small village of Cardiff in south Glamorgan in 1801 was minute but it soon soared as a result of a massive coal trade. In 1955 (after stiff competition from Caernarvon and Machynlleth), and by then a city, it assumed the title of Capital of Wales — once held convincingly by Carmarthen. Within two generations between 1780 and 1850, the population of Wales more than doubled from 530,000 to 1,180,000, largely through a process of rapid urbanisation, while the numbers of people working on the land fell even more dramatically. Inevitably the economy of agricultural centres such as Carmarthen suffered badly during the Victorian and Edwardian eras and some county and market towns stagnated or even shrank. The fortunes of Carmarthen benefited, however, from its prime location at the approaches to south-west Wales, combined with a long established role as principal administrative and social centre for a large surrounding region. After modest growth by the beginning of the 21st century the population was close to 20,000, while it stands at the meeting place of an exceptional number of trunk roads, not far beyond the end of the M4. But although recently provided with a

The Guildhall

new by-pass and road and pedestrian river bridges, at busy times it can still pay a price for the resulting commerce.

The communal and commercial life of the town used to be centred near the gateway to the castle and around the market cross, sited optimistically to ensure honest trading, but this has now been replaced by the statue of a gallant general, a son of the proprietor of the Ivy Bush Hotel in Spilman Street, who achieved fame in Afghan warfare of the early 19th-century. Nott Square is named after him, close to where most of what remains of the **castle** has been undergoing a worthwhile programme aimed at disentangling abutting building clutter and restoring and consolidating what is left. This mostly consists of the stone-revetted motte, the earliest surviving structure, part of a much rebuilt curtain wall and the 14th-century gatehouse with two battlemented towers supported by a corbel table.

Few other features of the town illustrated by Speed in the early 17th century now survive, for the town walls and gates, priory, St. Mary's Church, as well as the Franciscan friary have long disappeared and the 700-year-old Tywi stone bridge had been replaced. The main central street used for the medieval cattle market

Greyfriars Shopping Centre

is still in full use as it leads westwards from the castle through Nott Square and Darkgate into Lammas Street. The Neo-Classical **Guildhall** standing just off Nott Square dates from 1767 and once housed the Assize Court for three counties and various council offices, but most of the buildings along the main route are Victorian or later, as can be appreciated from upper storeys poised above the modern fascias and plate-glass shop-fronts. Just before the Tourist Information Centre on the left and the Royal Welch Fusiliers Crimea Monument, Mansel Street leads to the right off Lammas Street and its hotels towards the covered provision **market**. Rebuilt in 1981, this contains more than 100 units and has a widespread reputation for its

St. Peter's Church

impressive range of local produce, especially on Wednesdays and Saturdays when it is augmented by many outdoor stalls. In contrast, the modern although uncovered Greyfriars Shopping Centre comprises a set of 25 of the usual high street multiple stores to be found almost everywhere in towns of around this size. Lammas Street continues westwards to reach a further example of Carmarthen's past taste for military monuments, a 60ft.-high limestone obelisk to the memory of General Picton, who fell at Waterloo in 1815. On the left side of Lammas Street behind the buildings, Friars Park, formerly the site of the Franciscan priory of Grey Friars, was where Edmund Tudor, son of Owen Tudor and Queen Katherine of Valois, half-brother of King Henry VI and father of Henry VII, was first buried in 1456. (By command of Henry VIII his remains were moved at the dissolution to a tomb in the choir at St. Davids Cathedral, otherwise they might later have rested beneath an aisle of the Tesco supermarket that occupied the land by the late 20th century.)

From Nott Square in a north-easterly direction and running parallel with Spilman Street, King Street leads towards St. Peter's Church, on the highest ground in the older part of the town. Chiefly of the 14th century, it is not renowned for architectural merit but there is a Roman altar in the porch and some of the monuments are interesting. One of these incorporates a freestone effigy of Sir Rhys ap Thomas (d.1525) who, like Edmund Tudor, was transferred with his wife from the Grey Friars priory on its dissolution. His guarded, last minute support with a substantial force of well trained manpower was said to have been crucial towards the success of Henry Tudor after his landing at Mill Bay, Milford Haven in August 1485, and subsequent accession as King Henry VII in battle at Bosworth Field two weeks later (see p.120). Sir Rhys ap Thomas, knighted on the field, gained further preferment to become the most powerful Welshman in early Tudor Carmarthenshire.

Close to St. Peter's in Church Lane, the Victorian former Art School has since 1991 been converted to house the Oriel Myrddin Gallery of contemporary crafts and the regional art centre. Open all year, it mounts continually changing exhibitions and provides regular activities for people of all ages, as well as the opportunity to purchase from a range of artworks on offer.

Priory Street, beyond the church, is the only solid reminder of the Priory of St. John Baptist that once stood in that area east of the town and after passing the site of the **Amphitheatre** on the left, one of only seven left in Britain, the road crosses the River Gwili near its confluence with the River Tywi in the direction of Llandeilo to reach Abergwili.

Now almost a suburb of Carmarthen, medieval **Abergwili** was a small borough in its own right, boasting a weekly Friday market and at least one annual fair. In 1287 it was chosen by the bishop of St. Davids as the site for a collegiate church and this remained in being until 1541, when it was annexed to Christ College at Brecon (p.175). All signs of the buildings have now disappeared, but they stood between St. Davids Church and the later Bishop's Palace. This originated during the middle of the 16th century, but the present building followed it in 1903 after a fire and has become the County Museum of Carmarthenshire's eventful past, reaching back to exhibits of Roman times — all in delightful parkland surroundings. Merlin's Hill Centre at Alltyfyrddin Farm (see above) is slightly further along on the opposite side of the A40.

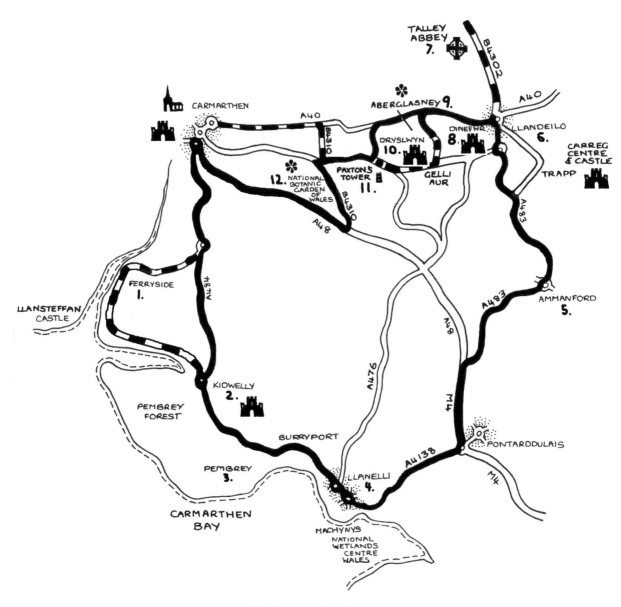

Outline map for Tour 2
The numbers 1 to 12 relate to the boxed information given within the tour

Tour 2 South-East Carmarthenshire

The tour chiefly uses A roads and includes a mix of pastoral landscapes, old historic sights such as Kidwelly, Dinefwr and Dryslwyn (and possibly Carreg Cennen) castles and Talley Abbey, remnants of the industrial past, Elizabethan and Tudor gardens at Aberglasney and the National Botanic Garden with its huge range of plants and habitats. Without detours the route amounts to about 50 miles.(OS Landranger 159).

The route starts from the Pen-sarn roundabout on the new by-pass, across the river from Carmarthen, and where the A48 heads off to meet the M4, and the A484 heads south to Kidwelly and then Llanelli. This latter is the road this tour takes.

The A484 passes close to the railway for a short distance before turning towards Cwmffrwyd and then heading south for Kidwelly. You can either carry on into Kidwelly, turning off to the right at the start of its by-pass to join a minor road leading into the older part of the town, towards the castle, or, to follow the estuary and pass through Ferryside, turn right in Llandefaelog. If taking this latter route, bear left at the fork soon reached, passing over a crossroads and then bearing right at the next junction. This will lead you into Ferryside. Follow the road along the coast and railway line and you'll come into Kidwelly. (For Welsh rugby enthusiasts, the hill-top village of **Llansaint**, perched above this route into Kidwelly, with its staggering views is the birthplace of London Welsh, Cardiff and Barbarians player, Gerald Davies, who has been described as a 'prime icon of a Golden Age of rugby' and 'arguably the finest winger of all times'. He gained 46 caps in matches for British Lions and Wales during 12 years, scoring 20 tries for Wales.)

---

1. Ferryside and the Towy Estuary

Ferryside is a quiet riverside village named from the service that once used to take pilgrim and other coastal traffic heading to the west across the mouth of the estuary to Llanstephan, under the protection of its castle in times of conflict. And when the tide was out exposing vast areas of sand, it was a hereditary custom for the tough women of nearby Llansaint, like those at Penclawdd in Gower, to go out each day in all weathers to collect cockles to eke out family budgets. The full sacks were loaded in panniers slung on donkeys and taken to the station for despatch by train to market (while some donkeys, so it was claimed, were smart enough to find their own way back across the sands without a driver!). But now the cockle beds and shiny sands are left to oystercatchers, redshanks and curlews amongst the many waders and other seabirds that feed in the estuary.

---

2. Kidwelly

The magnificent castle ruins at Kidwelly rank in south Wales with those at Pembroke (pp.99-101) and Caerphilly, but the first thing to appreciate is that it has the only place name in all Wales where the 'll' is pronounced as a single l. The Welsh form is Cydweli, and it seems that the 'll' must have crept

---

in at some stage during the process of anglicisation, in order to try and match Welsh names, not least that of neighbouring Llanelli with its daunting two 'll's! It was one of the oldest boroughs in Wales, although there is no evidence of any settlement at the mouth of the Gwendraeth Fach river before the Anglo Normans arrived in 1093. William de Londres built a first stronghold but it did not survive Welsh attacks and it was not until the reign of Henry I in *c*.1110 that the all-powerful Roger, bishop of Salisbury, established a castle and started to lay out a town on the north bank of the river. Attacks by Welsh partisans continued well into the 13th century and in the 1270s, early in the reign of Edward I, there was the first use of stone with a square curtain wall and cylindrical towers in the four corners, all tightly contained within the earlier enclosure. Extending into the scarp sloping down to the river close to the south-west tower, a distinctive semi-octagonal chapel was added, and early in the next century the outer timber defences were replaced by a further stone curtain wall and towers to produce a second enclosure. This made the castle concentric on three sides, and on the fourth side the south-west gatehouse, completed in 1422,

Kidwelly Castle

was flanked by semi-cylindrical towers with a wall bulging outwards to cover attacks from the river and up the scarp. Much of this impressive structure has survived, along with other parts of the castle, for it withstood an attack by forces of Owain Glyndwr in 1403 and did not suffer in the Civil War from the attentions of Cromwell's slighting gangs. But by the time the castle was taken into public guardianship in 1927 the ruins required extensive repair and conservation work and in 1984 this responsibility was inherited by Cadw. As for many of the historic monuments placed in its care, this body has published a booklet, *Kidwelly Castle* by John R. Kenyon, which sets out in detail, and lavishly illustrates, the history of the castle from the arrival of the Normans, provides a tour of The Gatehouse and Outer and Inner Wards and contributes several other supporting features.

Defended within a bank and ditch, the town and burgages established close to the castle by Bishop Roger amounted to no more than 8 acres in extent and it is evident that early suburban growth soon followed to the west — in the lower parts of present day Ferry Road and Water Street. Then called 'Scholand', the presence of the market cross shows that this became the commercial hub, but when in 1280 a murage grant by Edward I allowed revenues to be used for walling the settlement, only the southern part was so protected. While failing to take the castle in 1403, Glyndwr rebels entered and destroyed much of the old town and only some parts of the early 14th-century Gate and a short section of wall now remain. However to the south across the river another settlement was growing, close to where the bishop in *c*.1130 had founded a Benedictine priory. This was closed down upon the Dissolution of the monasteries but the fine priory church of St. Mary the Virgin survived and is now thought to be the best example of the Decorated Gothic style (*c*.1290–*c*.1350) in the St. Davids diocese. Cruciform in plan with a later 13th-century tower, and an unusually tall broach spire for Wales, it has a broad, aisle-less nave and spacious chancel. A 14th-century alabaster sculpture of the Virgin and Child has been brought back inside the church after being buried out of sight in the churchyard by a worried former vicar when it was over-venerated by members of his flock.

Growth during the 12th century was largely created by the cloth industry of Flemish settlers, who with the English and French made up the early town population as a way of consolidating Norman hold in the region. By early in the 13th century, Kidwelly had become a thriving trading port, having links with Ireland and further away in Gascony and Aquitaine, and its two townships became joined by a bridge in the 14th century. Yet by the time Henry VI granted the borough a new charter in 1444 the 'old town' was being described as 'waste and desolate', and seemingly was no better to John Leland almost a century later. Silting in the estuary was also creating a set back to navigation at the port, but in 1737 a factory was built alongside the Gwendraeth Fach river and the second earliest of all tinplate factories, it succeeded in making Kidwelly one of the largest tinplate manufacturing centres in Britain and functioned until 1941. Then, between 1766 and 1768, one of the first canals in Wales was cut to connect the anthracite pits of the Upper Gwendraeth valley at Carway to the coast at Kidwelly Quay and this was later succeeded by a railway extending to the harbour at Burry Port. The story of these great enterprises, and their effect on the economy of Kidwelly and district, can be found at the seasonal Kidwelly Industrial Museum. This is situated on the site of the old tinplate works and is signposted from the A484 town by-pass, where it serves as a heritage centre for many other aspects of Carmarthenshire's past.

Like many small trading ports, Kidwelly had its own ship-building yard and, being so close to Dylan Thomas territory, might well have been responsible for the *SS Kidwelly*, the boat of blind Captain Cat from *Under Milkwood*! Another Kidwelly claim to fame is that it is one of the very few places to feature in a favourite nursery rhyme. This one is known to generations of Welsh children as *Hen Fenyw Fach Cidweli — The Dear Old Lady of Kidwelly*, in which the singer always gets an extra sweet!

> The dear old Lady of Kidwelly
> A seller of sweets is she,
> Counts out ten for a halfpenny
> But always eleven for me.
> That was very good news for me, for me
> Counts at ten for a halfpenny
> But always eleven for me.

From the centre of Kidwelly take the B4308 to reach the A484 by-pass on which you turn right and head towards Llanelli, crossing over the route of Thomas Kymin's early canal as it heads for Kidwelly Quay, and then across the Gwendraeth Fawr river. The road closes in on the railway line on the right to cross flat marshy ground where there is soon a roadway leading right towards the **Welsh Motor Sports Centre**. This occupies the site of an RAF Second World War aerodrome and is now set out for Formula 3, autocross, go-carting, vintage car rallies and a range of other motor sports, all against a backdrop of Pembrey Forest stretching for 7 miles from **Pembrey Country Park** along Cefn Sidan Sands to Towyn Point.

3. Pembrey. Pioneering transatlantic flight and present seaside pleasures

Pembrey Sands

This is where, in June 1928, the celebrated aviator, Amelia Earhart (1897-1937), landed after a flight of 20 hours 40 minutes in the Fokker F7 seaplane, *Friendship*, from Trepasser Harbour, Newfoundland, to become the first woman to cross the Atlantic Ocean. Hailed worldwide, she and the two pioneering crew members afterwards received a ticker tape welcome in New York and attended a Presidential Reception in their honour at the White House. In 1932, Earhart succeeded Charles Lindebergh in becoming the second person to fly solo non-stop across the Atlantic, and after a spectacular flying career in 1937 she set out also to become the first woman to circumnavigate the world. But adopting the longest route of 29,000 miles around the equator, she and her navigator were lost in the Pacific Ocean, near the conclusion of their epic attempt.

Nowadays the nearest approach to aerial flight at Pembrey is probably parascending above the sands near the vast **Country Park**. Open all year, this hugely popular attraction now occupies the former site of a large ordnance factory and it has been landscaped to link with over 7 miles of famously safe, golden beaches, dune and woodland trails and picnic areas. There is a 130m dry-ski slope, a toboggan run and a miniature railway, while other activities can include horse riding, land yachting and orienteering. Golfers are accommodated at the **Machynys Peninsula Golf and Country Club** on the 7,100-yard links-style course created by Jack Nicklaus, built on old industrial land. The parish church, dedicated to St. Illtyd, dates from the late 13th century onwards and is noteworthy for its architecture, special memorials, and a rare example of a medieval circular stone pound for stray animals — a useful earner for church funds should they not be claimed.

The old village of Pembrey, or Pen-bre, has now merged with Burry Port, which grew chiefly from the export by sea of anthracite coal mined in the Gwendraeth Valley, and from its copper and tinplate activity. The A484 continues for another two miles towards the western outskirts of Llanelli, marked on the left-hand side by Stradey Park. This is the home ground of Llanelli Rugby Club, the 'Scarlets', who choose to adorn the tops of their goalposts with saucepans.

Upon entering Llanelli, today the largest town in Carmarthenshire, it is not easy to appreciate that, just like Kidwelly, it began as a small Anglo-Norman borough attached to a late 12th-century castle, or that St. Ellay's church, becoming visible ahead in Bridge Street by the River Lleidi, was founded even earlier. But although nothing now shows, the early settlement and castle are generally believed to have been situated to the west of the church around the present day leisure centre and playgrounds of People's Park, to the rear of the striking late-Victorian Town Hall. There are several visitors car parks close to the main road for anyone wishing to visit the town, otherwise carry on along the A484 through Llanelli.

4. Llanelli. One-time smoky furnaces, and the 'tinny', amid great scenic beauty

The small borough was not granted a royal charter until 1913, when the first mayor of Llanelli was elected, and little is known of the place throughout the Middle Ages. The antiquary, John Leland, in his *Itinerary* written in the 1530s mentioned 'a village where the inhabitants digge Coles', probably from surface seams of highly valued anthracite, a hard coal that burns with a non-luminous flame. Llanelli was hardly more than a small village until after the mid 18th-century, when by 1766 small vessels were being laden at the London Pier on the Lleidi estuary, known as The Flats, and small ironworks were entering production. In 1791 a blast furnace was built at Cwmddechau, close to the countryside about 1½ miles due north of the estuary, and soon this was acquired by the leading 18th-century iron-master, Alexander Raby, when the district became known as the **Furnace**, as it is now. It was not long afterwards that the furnaces of Llanelli were working day and night producing cannon and cannon balls for deployment in the Napoleonic Wars of the early 1800s, but economic factors encouraged diversification into copper smelting, coal mining, tin plating and steel making. Ruby built the famous **Dafren** tin-plate works in 1847, where thin iron sheets were coated with tin, mainly obtained by sea from Cornwall. By then tin-plate was already being used to can food and much later Llanelli produced Britain's first canned beer. Llanelli became the 'Tinplate capital of the world', was nicknamed 'Tinopolis', and at the height of its industrial expansion in the early 1890s, The Welsh Tinplate and Metal Stamping Company Ltd. were exporting kitchen equipment all over the world. The many products included 'Goat Brand' tin-ware supplied to branches of Woolworths everywhere and the enamelled saucepans with coloured rims soon resulted in the local nickname: Sosban.

It was something of a coincidence that there was a Welsh nonsense song *Sosban Fach*, and that Pembrey and Llanelli families holidaying at Llanwrtyd Wells should hear it sung at impromptu concerts there:

Mae bys Meri Ann wedi brifo	Mary Anne has hurt her finger
A Dafydd y gwas ddim yn iach;	And Davy the lad isn't well;
Mae'r baban yn y crud yn crio	The baby in the cradle is crying
A'r gath wedi sgramo Joni bach	And the cat's gone and scratched little Jon
Sosban fach yn berwi ar y tan	One small pan is boiling on the fire
Sosban fawr yn berwi ar y llawr	One large pan is boiling on the floor
Ar gath wedi sgramo Joni bach.	And the cat's gone and scratched little Jon.

But it was no surprise that before long, Llanelli adopted the song for its own, or that it should become the battle anthem of the Scarlets rugby team, or that extra verses should recall famous victories — such as those over the Australian Wallabies and New Zealand Maoris and All Blacks, or that the goalpost tops should be so splendidly adorned.

However, tinplating technique was to be revolutionised by mass production of metal in long strips at the massive new strip mills of Port Talbot and Llanwern. Llanelli's place as capital of the tinplating world was soon lost as many works in the town and surrounding villages were forced to shut down. Meanwhile as oil took the place of coal, exports through the port also declined and it closed, although tinplating continued in production at Trostre at the eastern, Loughor, end of the town.

The Tinplate Industry Museum has been established there and there are other displays at the **Parc Howard Museum** (below), along with examples of the output produced between 1840 and 1925 of the Llanelli Pottery Works. It will also be seen that Llanelli had a small place in transport history — as the terminus from 1839 of Wales' first railway, to Pontarddulais, to be built specifically for steam trains.

At the dawning of the Motor Car Age, it is where in Stepney Street the first inflated car spare tyre was devised on a spoke-less rim for fixing on a punctured wheel, to be known widely as the Stepney Wheel. Felinfoel beers were first brewed in the 19th century at the local inn, quickly gained favour at other pubs for their keeping qualities and flavour and such was the demand that in 1878 a brewery was built at the then village of **Felinfoel**, to the north of Llanelli. The founder was a brewer and tinplate manufacturer, and this connection has since played a part in the growth of the Felinfoel Brewery Company, especially in 1935 when 'Felinfoel' pioneered canned beer — initially to stimulate a faltering tinplate industry. Not very long afterwards, cans of 'Double Dragon' and other beers were being shipped to all Second World War theatres, and since then a high proportion of all kinds of drinks have been sold in cans, or 'tinnies'.

There has now been further industrial diversification in Llanelli, and into tourism which is playing an ever-increasing part in supporting the local economy. In this respect, there are very few industrial towns anywhere in Britain that lie as close to sea and countryside of such natural beauty and interest. In the town there are the popular covered market and pedestrianised shopping streets, close to parks, gardens and open spaces.The large Parc Howard has an ornamental park, playing fields and many other leisure facilities surrounding the former **Bryncaerau Castle**, seat of the prominent Buckley family. It enjoys sweeping views down to the sea and this castellated 19th-century mansion was the home of Sir Stafford Howard, who was in tin-plate and in 1913 became the charter mayor of Llanelli. He presented the house with a large area of parkland to the people of Llanelli on a 999-year lease, at five shillings per annum, and his mansion house has since become the town's museum and art gallery. Over to the west, between Stradey Park, and People's Park, **Sandy Water Park** caters for water sports on a large lake, while close to the A476 beyond Felinfoel to the north, on a National cycle network route, **Swiss Valley Country Park** provides a wide choice of outdoor activities and picnic sites in the scenic surroundings of the Cwm Lliedi reservoirs.

At the edge of the Burry Inlet on the eastern seaboard of Carmarthen Bay, and directly opposite Pen Clawdd in Gower at Penclacwydd (appropriately 'the hill of the gander'), a 500-acre reserve has been created to become the **National Wetlands Centre Wales** (admission charges). It is one of the nine visitor centres in Britain run by The Wildfowl and Wetlands Trust, founded at Slimbridge by Sir Peter Scott, and is open 7 days a week (except Christmas Eve and Christmas Day). There are large numbers of spectacular visiting or captive ducks, geese, swans and flamingos and particular pride is taken in the growing numbers of little egrets. From a local total of 13 in 1994, a Welsh record of 392 of the majestic 'snow white herons' roosted in the grounds and lagoon areas throughout September 2005. Up to 60,000 birds of different species often return to the estuary for the winter and the area is designated as a Site of Special Scientific Interest and a Special Protection Area. There are observation hides and family fun is available along landscaped walkways. On the Millennium Wetlands, children are able to explore Water Vole Valley and the Swan Maze and in June go on Duckling Day tours, while indoors there is an interactive 'Millennium Discovery Centre'.

National Wetlands Centre Wales

As mentioned above, carry on along the A484 through Llanelli and at a roundabout towards the east of Llanelli, take the A4138 Pontarddulais road (signposted for the M4) for some 4 miles to join the westernmost, final length of the M4 at Junction 48. Leave the M4/A48 at Junction 49 and the Pont Abraham Services to head on the A483 for Ammanford.

---

5. Ammanford and 'the Land of the Pyramids'

At the northern edge of the anthracite coalfield, close to the present boundary of the Brecon Beacons National Park, there was very little to see at the confluence of the rivers Amman and Loughor until the early 1880s apart from the Cross Inn on the square and a few nearby buildings. The place was actually named after the pub, and as it grew in size might have continued to be called Cross Inn, but to avoid confusion with another hamlet in the county it was renamed Ammanford, and Rhydaman in Welsh. Because of the location of the Amman Valley close to centres of the emerging tinplate industry there was a strong demand for coal to fuel the furnaces, so that the district came to be locally christened as 'The Land of the Pyramids' because of many resulting triangular spoil tips. Ammanford has since become one of the busiest places in Carmarthenshire, but despite having been an anthracite mining centre for over a century, it is far from being a typical industrial town.

Continue on the A483 towards Llandeilo. As the A483 and accompanying Heart of Wales railway line head northwards past Llandybie, the scenery becomes steadily more delightful as both close in on the western boundary of the Brecon Beacons National Park, to the right. (You can at this stage visit Carreg Cennen Castle by turning right from the A483 at Llandybie to take a minor road that turns right then left at Blaengweche before reaching Trapp and the magical sight of the castle, poised 300 feet up on the edge of a precipitous hilltop (see pp.194-195). There is a large car park at Castle Farm, and after the visit return to Trapp and turn right to continue along the minor road to rejoin the A483 in Ffairfach.)

If ignoring Carreg Cennen Castle, continue ahead into Llandeilo. The A483 enters the town over a steeply ramped causeway graced by a central stonework river bridge of 145 feet, built in 1848 and reckoned

Pastel shaded houses on Bridge Street in Llandeilo

to have the widest span of this type of construction anywhere in Wales. Curving elegantly to the right past pastel shaded Georgian houses, it climbs away from the Towy towards the top of the hill on which much of Llandeilo stands, cutting through the parish churchyard to enter the town's main Rhosmaen Street. Kerbside and off street parking can be reached by taking the first turning right into Crescent Road.

Having visited, or if you wish to pass through, then stay on the A483 (Rhosmaen Street) and you will meet the A40 at a roundabout on the far side of Llandeilo.

6. Llandeilo

St. Teilo's Church is traditionally associated with Teilo, an early 6th-century saint and it occupies a site that might well have been that of his *clas* or mother church, and this is where he is thought to have been buried. There are indications that a religious community continued there until the 9th or early 10th century, and that because of this Llandeilo had become a place of some consequence long before the appearance of the Normans and has been known as Llandeilo Fawr ('great') to distinguish it from other Welsh places with the same name. The early town originated near the river crossing and then stretched up the rise to embrace the church, occupying the areas of modern King Street, Church Street and Abbey Terrace. Devastation by the forces of Owain Glyndwr in 1403 required time for reconstruction, followed afterwards by gradual development of Carmarthen and Rhosmaen Streets until more determined growth during the 18th century served to consolidate the town's status and role in and around the Towy valley.

At this roundabout with the A40 you can either turn left towards Carmarthen to continue the main tour, or, to visit Talley Abbey, turn right onto the A40 in the direction of Llandovery, then almost immediately left on to the B4302, Talley being reached after about 7 miles. Talley is the anglicised name for Tal-y-Llechau meaning 'Head of the Lakes', both lying in a green and wooded valley among remote hills alongside the B4302. There is a visitor car park at the west end of the abbey and parish church.

7. Talley Abbey

Remains of the crossing tower and presbytery, Talley Abbey

The monastic community chiefly owed its presence at this idyllic location to the patronage of the Lord Rhys, who had not only effectively regained political, military and cultural control of his kingship from the Anglo Normans but, during the monastic revival era, also did much to revive its religious life. He had given support to the Welsh Cistercian abbey at Whitland (p.80) in the 1160s, is said to have secured the fortunes of Strata Florida Abbey (pp.238-240) and between 1184 and 1189 was solely responsible for founding Talley Abbey. When, after a lifetime of munificence towards the new monastic Orders, he died in 1187 he was buried at St. Davids Cathedral (p.136) — where his 14th-century tomb effigy is to be found.

Among the new Orders of the time were White Canons who lived according to the Rule of St. Augustine of Hippo (354–430) at the Abbey of St. John at Prémontré in north-east France. The mother house of the Premonstratensian Order, it established 37 abbeys across Britain — with just one in Wales. The white-cowled canons arrived at Talley with huge enthusiasm for raising a monastery at least as grand and as large as that at Strata Florida, but through lack of sufficient resources they were in the event forced to scale down their building plans. The church was to have been 240 feet long, but this had to be reduced by more than 70 feet and standards of sculptural ornament and decoration had to be reduced as part of a large catalogue of savings. Once installed, the community frequently endured hard times and were soon impoverished by jealous and other ungodly moves on the part of the abbot and their spiritual brethren of Whitland Abbey. These worries continued after the death of the Lord Rhys into the early 13th century and money problems were compounded by repercussions of the Welsh wars of Edward I later in the century and because of inadequacies there were times when rights at Talley had to be surrendered to English abbeys. Then came The Black Death, in 1403 a damaging visit from Glyndwr rebels and after a further chequered career, final Suppression came to the abbey in 1536 and abbot and canons were pensioned off. The canons' choir and presbytery of the abbey then continued to serve the needs of the parish until 1772, when a new parish church was built. Sited just to the north, close to the lower lake, this has since been rebuilt but the medieval abbey buildings were left to suffer from the elements and they collapsed or the materials were quarried for use in other buildings, possibly including the first new church.

Except for a 85ft.-high portion of the crossing tower, little now remains but stone outlines of the medieval church buildings and the grassed, once intended longer nave. A Cadw booklet: *Strata Florida Abbey. Talley Abbey* by David M. Robinson and Colin Platt sets out a full, illustrated account of the historical background of the abbey, the building processes, a tour of the remains and relationships between the fortunes of the two monasteries.

Cwmdu

On the way back to Llandeilo from Talley Abbey via the B4320, there is a further option on a quite different scale at **Cwmdu**, which can be reached by turning right at Halfway and driving down a minor road for just under a mile. It is a small hamlet where the National Trust acquired a terrace of empty and decaying 19th-century cottages, terminated by a Baptist chapel of 1839, and revived them in a carefully un-modernised state. The colour-washed row includes the General Stores, where it is said to be 'like going back in time to the first half of the last century', Cwmdu Inn and a holiday cottage that is 'furnished in a style in keeping with the Age'. Back at Halfway, the B4320 continues southwards to meet the A40 and the main tour route heading westwards.

Just over half a mile along the A40 towards Carmarthen a brown sign indicates the way to Dinefwr Castle off to the left. The side road leads to Carmarthen Street in Llandeilo and reaches the access drive to Penlan Park and the castle site close to the police station. There is a car park near the castle at Newton House.

8. Dinefwr Castle

For centuries the fortunes of Llandeilo were linked with those of Dinefwr Castle, perched high downstream on the long ridge overlooking the Towy and occupying the stronghold of Welsh princes of the Dark Ages. They once ruled over the kingdom of Deheubarth, which comprised most of south Wales west of Glamorgan, and after 1066 medieval Welsh lords followed them by commencing a stone castle. But the Norman advance into south Wales was swift and overwhelming, and for much of the 12th century Deheubarth and the neighbouring kingships were held under firm and almost continuous Norman

Dinefwr Castle

Newton House

control. But Welsh resistance did not cease, and in 1165 Rhys ap Gruffudd, the Lord Rhys (1132–1187), took the castle of Dinefwr and adjoining lands and retained them until his death. He was one of the greatest Welsh leaders of the 12th century and in holding his own against the Normans, he re-created his kingship and kept the peace with a strong hand, albeit under the over-lordship of the not too un-appreciative English king. He now rests in St. Davids Cathedral (p.136), while the Welsh-built Dinefwr Castle, the main seat of the kingship, is now regarded as 'historically one of the most important castles in Wales', as one modern patriot has put it.

Most of the stronghold is thought to have been the work of the descendents of Lord Rhys until 1280, when Wales was conquered by Edward I — and Dinefwr became an English royal castle. Building work was continued and in 1298 a small new borough was founded alongside the castle to the north of an existing Welsh town and known as Dinefwr Newtown (Y Drenewydd) and altogether English. With nearby Llandeilo, there were thus three small boroughs close to one another for a while, but by Tudor times the castle was abandoned along with its supporting boroughs and the Welsh were again gaining control of Dinefwr. In 1485, Rhys ap Thomas, a grandson of one of them, joined the cause of Henry Tudor at Bosworth and in return gained precedence throughout south Wales from Henry VII. His descendents lived on at Dinefwr into modern times.

A large new mansion was built on the site in the 15th century and, as **Newton House**, it was rebuilt in 1660, afterwards extended and re-fronted in a

Victorian Gothic style and in 2006 was being extensively refurbished. The parkland that surrounded both medieval castle ruins and mansion suited the tastes of the 'Picturesque' movement in its time (pp.257-258), and when in 1775 the celebrated landscape gardener, Lancelot 'Capability' Brown, visited there was little there that he could improve upon. The house and park with over 100 shy fallow deer and a small herd of rare white cattle are now owned by the National Trust, while the medieval castle ruins on its crag and much of the woodland belong to the Wildlife Trust West Wales. There is a nature trail that can be joined at **Penlan Park** in Llandeilo and followed through steep woods and across fields that are rich in wildlife to Castle Wood and up to the old stronghold.

The castle is in the care of Cadw and its illustrated *Guide: Dinefwr Castle. Dryslwyn Castle* sets out details of its history and provides a detailed descriptive tour.

From Dinefwr Castle return to the A40 and turn left. After about 3½ miles the road reaches Broad Oak where you can turn left onto a minor road to Llangathen and Aberglasney Gardens, 'one of the country's most exciting garden restoration projects'. The gardens are soon reached on the right.

9. Aberglasney. 'A Garden Lost in Time'

The origins of Aberglasney reach back over five centuries, perhaps before the 1470s, and there are continuous records of ownership of the estate since *c*.1603 when it was bought by Anthony Rudd (d.1614), the bishop of St. Davids. Each of his successors made a contribution in shaping the house and gardens until the 20th century, when misfortune left the house vacant and exposed. Then wartime requisitioning introduced unfavourable uses such as a major laundry and quarters for American forces, to be followed by vandalism, theft and outright neglect. The end of the century had almost arrived when, in 1995, what remained of the property was purchased by the Aberglasney Restoration Trust. An American benefactor donated the purchase price and contributions from other donors, trust funds, charitable foundations and a range of grants have combined to give Aberglasney a new lease of life after near terminal decline. One of the first tasks of the Trust was to retrieve the Victorian portico that had been illegally removed from the north façade of the listed mansion and advertised for sale in a

Aberglasney House and the retrieved portico

Palm and orchids in the Ninfarium

Cloister walkway

Christies catalogue. The resulting court case drew public attention to the critical state of Aberglasney and advanced the cause of its rescue and restoration. Soon, rampant weeds and many tons of earth and detritus fill were cleared, stonework was repaired or renewed and a programme of restoration came within sight. Opposite the house at the heart of the 10 acres of land, a garden had been considerably filled in to the top of a surrounding range of arches. This has now been restored to original levels and what has emerged is an Elizabethan/Jacobean cloister garden that is surrounded on three sides by a broad, arcaded walkway that offers views over the other gardens. It is probably the last remaining example of such Jacobean garden history to have survived in Britain, preceding the time when this formal approach was superceded by the more open parkland vistas favoured during the 18th-century Picturesque era.

The Cloister Garden parapet walkway continues along to the top of the formal Upper Walled Garden. This and the adjacent Lower Walled Garden provided the family and estate establishment with vegetables, fruit and flowers throughout the year (in the manner perhaps familiar to many who have already visited the restored lost gardens of Heligan in Cornwall), while the present Pool Garden could well have been preceded by a fish pond as another food source. Elsewhere there is what is thought to be a unique, centuries-old yew tunnel, while Bishop Rudd's Walk consists of a network of paths and bridges past rare and unusual plants and there is a wetland area and Pigeon House Wood to explore. Much of the rescue work was well under way when it was in a state to be afforded further prime-time TV coverage, while as the work of restoration continues, the latest scheme to be presented is called the Ninfarium named after Ninfa in Italy, a village abandoned in the 14th century where there is now a wild garden restoration initiative. At Aberglasney, the derelict inner courtyard of the house has been used to create a covered atrium, planted with sub-tropical species of plant that will help to generate all-year-round appeal at the Gardens, except on Christmas Day when it is closed. The admission tariff offers concessions for OAP and disabled garden enthusiasts, and children.

As a short detour the tour can continue by turning right on leaving the car park and driving for about 2 miles to join the B4300 beyond the Towy. The road ahead reaches the **Gelli Aur ('Golden Grove') Country Park** and its 60 acres of wooded parkland, where there is a further opportunity to sight fallow deer among wooded parkland. There is also an arboretum, an adventure playground, a visitor centre and a choice of nature trails. The florid Gothic style mansion with its crow-stepped gables, battlemented portico and tall polygonal chimney stacks at the centre dates from 1832 as the re-built seat of the Vaughans and earls of Carbery, a leading family of south-west Wales, and afterwards home to an agricultural college. To return to the main tour, turn left onto the B4300 to head for Llanarthne, 4 miles further on.

To continue with the main tour, return to the A40 and turn left towards Carmarthen. Dryslwyn Castle can be reached by turning left onto the B4297. This leads to a landscaped car park and picnic area below the castle and above the Towy.

The Towy snakes down the valley from Dryslwyn Castle

10. Dryslwyn Castle

Dryslwyn is third of the trio of Welsh castles (with Dinefwr and Carreg Cennen) that controlled the lush Towy valley during the Middle Ages. The castle ruins stand on an isolated steep-sided hill where it was possible to control one of the few crossing places before Carmarthen. Documentary evidence indicates that the castle existed in 1246, although it could well have been built some while before. By 1271

Dryslwyn Castle and the River Towy

it was in the hands of Rhys ap Maredudd (d.1292), a great-grandson of The Lord Rhys and last of the Welsh princes of Deheubarth, and by 1287 he had created one of the largest stonework castles ever to be raised by a native Welsh lord. In order to provide for victualling and other services it was usual for there to be an attendant township, and by 1281 the Welsh settlement lying close to the castle walls possessed a mill and was gaining strength and numbers from the right to hold an annual four-day fair after each St. Bartholomew's Day (24 August). A weekly market followed from 1324, but before then there was to be a radical change at Dryslwyn after a disaffected Rhys ap Maredudd mounted a revolt against Edward I. This provoked a determined siege that involved an army of *c*.11,000 men and the castle fell to the king. Recent archaeological excavations at the site have unearthed hugely damaging projectiles in the form of massive stone balls measuring more than 16 inches in diameter, and many of smaller calibre, that are likely to have been hurled at the castle walls by a siege engine known as a 'trébuchet'. In addition, the attackers undermined the castle walls to bring about their collapse and that of the Welsh garrison. On this occasion in 1287 some 150 of King Edward's workforce and some of his nobles were killed when the walls fell in over them.

Rhys ap Maredudd had previously escaped to Ireland, forfeiting his lands to Edward I, but he returned to Wales in 1292, was taken prisoner in battle soon afterwards, tried for treason and hanged — his body ignominiously trailed behind horses.

Little change was made to the castle after the English assumed control but the town was enlarged, partly to accommodate immigrant settlers from the Continent, and in 1324 was granted the right to hold an all important weekly market. But it was not long before decline set in, not least because of ravages of The Black Death (1347–51) and also when, in 1403 Owain Glyndwr took the castle. Although recaptured bythe English soon afterwards, the effectiveness of the fort was at an end and it was soon de-commissioned, with inevitable consequences for business in the town. The population started to move elsewhere and by the 17th century the site was all but abandoned. Today, all that is left showing on the surface are bumps and hollows of house platforms and roadways along the northern part of the hill, while the present road to the west side of the castle site is thought to correspond with Briggestrete, the ancient road which led from the town to the ford, some 100 yards upstream from the modern bridge, Pont y Dryslwyn.

The tour continues by turning right on leaving the car park to rejoin the B4297 as far as the B4800 crossroads. Turn right here and soon the road passes below a very strange looking edifice that is perched high up on the crest of the wooded height to the left. For nigh on two centuries this must have puzzled countless travellers along the Towy valley between Llandeilo and Carmarthen, during which time it has become known as Paxton's Tower.

11. Paxton's Tower

Erected by Sir William Paxton (1744–1824) to mark the victory and death of his friend, Horatio Nelson in 1805, it is difficult to fathom any of its neo Gothic features that connect it with the sea battle at Trafalgar or the famous admiral. The architect was Samuel Pepys Cockerell (a relative of the diarist) and in *c*.1808 he produced a weird triangular gatehouse affair with towers at each angle and three tall arches for the passage of carriages. There was a banqueting hall, boudoir and closet on the first floor and a central hexagonal turret above. But

Paxton's Tower across the fields

if a close sight of the Grade II* Listed Folly does not appeal, then the stunning panoramic views of the Towy valley from up there certainly should — reached by footpaths or a lane ending at a car park close to the viewpoint. Down below, the river can be seen to snake its way slowly down the unusually flat valley, past Dryslwyn Castle, prominent on its hill. Beyond and rising to 470 feet is **Grongar Hill**, which in 1726 became the title of a famous poem depicting the Towy valley scenery by John Dyer (1699–1758). He has been regarded by some of his admirers as a forerunner of Wordsworth and the Romantics, and another favourite poem of his, *The Country Walk*, was all about Aberglasney, where he was born when it was occupied by the Dyer family. Much later, Grongar again received a mention by Dylan Thomas, along with nearby Golden Grove (above), through the Morning Prayer of the Rev. Eli Jenkins in *Under Milkwood*.

Sir William's view to the south-west was towards his Middleton country seat and the tower can still be seen from the centre of the Estate, much of which has now become the National Botanic Garden of Wales. This is the final call along this tour and can be reached by turning left onto the B4310 beyond Llanarthne.

Alternatively there are two more direct ways back to Carmarthen, one by continuing westwards along the B4300, the other by rejoining the A40 at Nantgaredig after turning right onto the B4310, and then passing through Abergwili.

12. National Botanic Garden of Wales. 'A Noah's Ark for Plants'

The Great Glasshouse seen across a fountain

Built on the principle of plant conservation, the National Botanic Garden of Wales (NBGW) was the first botanic garden in the world of the new millennium and described by one enthusiast as 'A Noah's Ark for plants'. Noah limited his conservation effort by only embarking animals, seemingly not recognising that without plants they, including the human complement, could not survive for long. At the NBGW it is suggested that this omission has at long last been rectified, and it is not before time, for they reckon that without some action, 'by the end of this century we are going to lose between 30% and 70% of the world's plants'. The botanists and many other concerned people are convinced that 'plants are becoming extinct at a faster rate than ever'.

The history of **Middleton Hall** can be traced back to the early 1600s, and after the estate passed to William Paxton in 1789 he undertook extensive improvement works that continued until his death in 1824. But in 1931, the fine Neo Classical mansion that had been designed for him by Samuel Pepys Cockerell in 1793 was destroyed by fire, when the condition of the surrounding parkland and his much cherished lakes had also greatly deteriorated. It was all in this state when Carmarthen County Council bought the 586-acre estate and in 1978 the reincarnation of Regency Middleton, its crumbling walls and buildings and Paxton's famously designed landscape of watercourses, woodlands and meadows began to evolve. The County Council handed over the property and an estimate of £43.6 million was calculated as the likely cost of the project — half of the amount coming in 1996 as a Millennium Commission grant.

The Garden opened in May 2000 with entry through a circular Gatehouse, designed by Norman Foster and Partners, where admission tickets, Guides and other information are available throughout the year, except on Christmas Day when everything is closed. The spine of the Garden rises from there along the Lower and Upper Broadwalk to Millennium Square, the surviving buildings of Middleton Hall and the architectural climax of the **Great Glasshouse**, the Garden icon at its heart. Built to the design of Norman Foster and Partners, it is the world's largest single-span glasshouse, and is in the form of an elliptical torus 95m (311ft) long x 55m (180ft) wide, tilted seven degrees on its axis for maximum sunlight. The interior is maintained at 5°C above ambient temperature and kept from falling below 9°C. A fully controlled and natural airflow is regulated by 147 computer-controlled vents, while high-mounted fans blow blasts of air to simulate the windy conditions of Mediterranean regions that occur in various parts of the world. In early 2006 it was estimated that of nearly 3,000 plants in the Glasshouse, 160 species some from the Canary Isles, 90 from parts of Chile, 120 from southern California, 100 from the Mediterranean area, 230 from South Africa and 210 from Western Australia. An entire landscape of 3,500 sq. metres has been produced, recreating a natural ecosystem that is in parts hugely under threat. With a miniature ravine, rock terraces, a waterfall and lake there are representations of six different geographical areas and so it is possible to gain the impression of moving from country to country past an ever-increasing range of plant species. Here and everywhere else in the botanic garden, the plant collections are intended for scientific research and teaching and there are extensive facilities for seminars, workshops, lectures and conferences, as well as leisure courses. One prime object is to embrace the spirit of the World Environment Summit in Rio de Janeiro in aiming to document, understand and conserve the Earth's biological diversity and adopt sustainability as an essential theme.

But there is insistence that a visit to the Garden should also involve 'a day full of visual delights, heavenly scents,

Inside the Great Glasshouse

amazing stories, beautiful walks and unforgettable activities for all the family'. The importance of this showed during a worrying time in 2003, not long after the opening, when public support and visitor numbers were declining to crisis levels. The resulting national publicity brought an immediate response within Wales, and beyond. A new strapline: 'A Place for People. The Place for Plants' was devised to encourage visitors to meander past long, eye-catching herbaceous borders, garden lakes and the 'Rocks of Ages' — 700 million years of the geological past of Wales alongside an extremely rare and magical Double Walled Garden. In Millenium Square at the top of the rise, the Stable Block has a restaurant and houses a gift shop and gallery, an Exhibition pays tribute to the Physicians of Myddfai, legendary healers of the Middle Ages, and their modern successors (pp.184-185). Beyond there is an Energy Zone housing the Biomass Boiler that provides heat for the Glasshouse and other buildings, and the Living Machine waste treatment system, a range of interlacing lakeside paths, areas still under development — and much else. A 'Woodlands of the World' project is being planted on 40 acres to the south of the Great Glasshouse 'over about ten years or so' to represent other regions across the globe with similar climates to south-west Wales, such as southern Chile, south-west China, the Himalayas, north-west America, and Tasmania that enjoy similar mild, moist conditions. Grant aid of £700,000 is expected from the Millennium Commission for a tropical glasshouse to be sited within the double walled garden, inspired from the Victorian era and incorporating two 'lanterns' rising above the roof height to accommodate taller palm trees.

Finally this tour route leaves past the plant sales area and Garden entrance and left via the B4310 to join the A48 for the return drive to Carmarthen.

Tenby

In the Welsh tourism 'Oscars' of 2005, Tenby was voted the people's choice as 'My Special Place', their favourite in Wales, 'an iconic destination'. But this was not the first time for visitors to show their appreciation for this picturesque Pembrokeshire resort on the western side of Carmarthen Bay. Countless holidaymakers of many descriptions have been arriving there at least since Georgian times, while poets, writers and artists have been effusive in their choice of superlatives ever since a 9th-century Welsh bard wrote in praise of Dinbych in a poem: *Edmyg Dinbych* (Admiration of Tenby). He described the sea and coast around the fortress on the shore and this is thought to be the first documentary reference to the name of the place and to its small castle. John Leland visited in *c*.1540 and wrote of the charm of its setting, Richard Fenton referred to the beauty of Georgian Tenby, calling it 'Justly the boast of Pembrokeshire', while long after he was born there in 1878, the painter Augustus John (d.1961) wrote: 'You may travel the world over but you will find nothing more beautiful; it is so restful, so colourful and so unspoilt'.

Early in the 21st century it can still rightly claim to be one of the most picturesque traditional seaside resorts in Britain, most diverse and diverting. A great deal of its character and style comes from a unique cliff-top situation, above a small picture-book harbour, four safe golden sandy beaches — shelving gently into clear blue waters, and an adjoining bold and precipitous coastline that runs into the sea in a succession of headlands. It claims to enjoy a sunny and temperate climate, while the town possesses another distinct atmosphere that is created by tall surviving medieval town walls, battlements and towers, scant castle fragments and an elegant old parish church that all help to distinguish Tenby from other popular Welsh seaside towns and resorts, such as Llandudno and Aberystwyth (pp.201-206), that

Harbour Beach from below Castle Hill looking towards the town (left),
and from the town towards the castle

Tenby town walls (above left) and the Five Arches gateway (above right) and a section inside the walls (left)

were founded in more recent times. It was because of these and other attributes that in 1964 the Council for British Archaeology included Tenby in a select list of just 51 towns in Britain that were considered to be of national importance.

Wales abounds with cairns, hut circles and enclosures that date since the Bronze Age and from *c*.500 BC the Celtic peoples are known to have adopted exposed coastal promontories for their 'cliff castles'. Although no evidence has been discovered because of later disturbance, it is thought quite likely that the Castle Hill at Tenby was regarded as most suitable for the purpose and certainly by the middle of the 12th century, the site was favoured by the Anglo Normans. They built a modest castle there as part of a chain of strongholds and fortifications to try and consolidate their hold over the region. The Welsh were not, however, put off, and attacks by their forces culminated in 1260 when the town and castle were destroyed by Llewelyn ap Gruffudd. This led to a prompt decision to enclose the entire settlement of the time with a ring of walls, towers and gateways to reinforce the protection provided by the cliff-top castle. Work quickly began, to be supported by charters authorising the raising of levies to help with construction and maintenance costs. In 1457 further reinforcement, accompanied by an increase in the height of the walls, was directed by Jasper Tudor, earl of Pembroke (who after the Battle of Tewkesbury during the Wars of the Roses, would in 1471 be sheltered in the town as a fugitive Lancastrian with Henry Tudor, his nephew and the future King Henry VII, before they sailed from the harbour for the French coast into exile — to return in 1485 via Dale (p.120) for battle at Bosworth and the dawning of the Tudor dynasty). By 1540 John Leland was able to observe that: 'Tenby is a walled town hard on the Severn Sea in Pembrokeshire … The town is strongly walled and well gated, every gate having a portcullis made entirely of iron'. Notwithstanding this, feared threat from the Spanish Armada in 1588 caused further strengthening to be added to the south of the West Gate. It was not put to the test, and walls and three gates remained substantially complete until the second half of the 18th century when sections were cleared to make way for housing and, as often happened, stone was 'quarried' for other building projects. Despite this, there are still substantial tall lengths of town wall to be seen, pierced with the two tiers of arrow slits as specified by Jasper Tudor (d.1495). Five of the original 20 towers have also survived, with the much photographed **West Gate** and its 'D' shaped barbican with five arches — all part of Tenby's membership of the Walled Towns Friendship Circle, founded there in 1991 and now with some 150 members in almost 30 countries.

There are nearly 300 listed buildings of historical or architectural interest in the town. Most buildings within the walls date from Victorian times, although in some places with rather more of a Regency or Georgian dignity. They appear along tightly packed streets, alleyways and lanes dating from the Tudor period when, near the mouth of the Bristol Channel, Tenby was well placed as a port to conduct trade with the West Country, parts of Ireland and other regions of Wales and the rest of Europe. Thus in 1566 it is said that oranges imported through the harbour from Portugal were the first to be introduced in Wales (well in time to have relieved the Reverend Theophilus Evans of Llanwrtyd (pp.244-245) of his scurvy problem!). The main building to survive from that time is the unique

The Tudor Merchant's House

late 15th-century **Tudor Merchant's House** (NT) on Quay Hill, once fronting one of the main commercial thoroughfares between the walled town and the harbour. The present stone quay dates from 1328 and it was protected from a very early date by a long stone pier that for many years was the only one existing at a south Wales town. A principal function was to provide good shelter for the fishing boats that landed the catches

that formed the main economy of the town — the traditional industry from which it derived its centuries-old Welsh name of *Dinbych-y-pysgod* (Tenby of the fish), to distinguish it from inland *Dinbych* (Denbigh) in north Wales. The medieval pier was replaced in 1842 and further modified during the 19th century, and most of the fishermen's cottages and other buildings clustered around the harbour and small beach have been renovated and decorated in gentle pastel shades, along with the Georgian and Regency houses that climb gently towards the hill-top. Nowadays charter parties and other groups of keen deep sea anglers board fishing boats that steer past colourful leisure craft in the harbour and yachts entering regattas

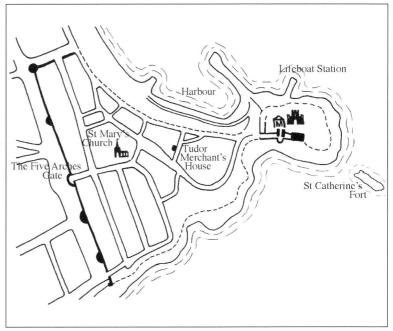

Map of Tenby

Laston House

and class championships hosted by Tenby Sailing Club — its clubhouse adapted from the former warehouse on the harbour-side. Also during the summer season, other boats ply frequently to and from the harbour, or from the castle beach at low tide, carrying day-trippers on the 20-minutes ride to Caldey Island, just half a mile south of Giltar Point, or they embark on extended cruises along the National Park Coastline.

The **harbour-master's office** is on the site of the old weighbridge house above the harbour at the approach to Castle Square. This is where in 1805 Sir William Paxton (d.1824) of Middleton Hall, Llanarthne in Carmarthenshire (now the site of the National Botanic Garden of Wales, see pp.61-62) leased council land on the small street, then called Laston, to build a stylish bath-house. There had for some time been a fad, supported by doctors, about the health-giving properties of sea water, and bathing machines for coy swimmers had been hauled onto the beaches since the late 18th century. Some people even drank the water, with added port or milk to taste! The first baths were lost in a fire within a few weeks of opening, but by 1810 separate pools for ladies and gentlemen had opened at today's **Laston House**. They were in use day and night, and in addition there were shower baths, sweating baths, vapour baths, fumigating baths and a cupping room with processes meant to stimulate blood flow to ease the common ailments of those who could afford it all. Above the entrance, and still to be seen, there was a quotation from Euripides (*c*.480-406 BC) that can be translated as 'All man's pollution does the sea cleanse'. So impressed was the council that the original Greek wording has long appeared as the Motto on the Arms of Tenby, while at the time Paxton was promptly admitted as a Freeman of the town. A wealthy London banker with great entrepreneurial skill and vision, he had built cottages to house the bath attendants and followed up with further schemes that included a new road and walkway close to the harbour and baths, an improved town water supply system and a new theatre in Upper Frog Street. For himself he converted the old Globe Theatre in Tudor Square into a fine town house, now called Tenby House, and lived there from 1805 until just before he died.

Until a few years before, Tenby had been suffering a miserable time of it. Started by the effects of the Civil War, this had been compounded by an outbreak of plague in 1650 that accounted for the deaths of almost half the population, and a huge decline in sea trade as a result. There was little recovery for the rest of the century and throughout the next. John Wesley visited in 1784 and wrote: 'There is not such a town in England — two thirds of the ancient town are either in ruins or vanished away'. However Tenby still had much to offer with its picturesque cliff-top location, clear sea water, sandy beaches and mild climate and Paxton's activity served as a catalyst to kick

Curtain walls of the castle with the museum showing just to the top right

start a trend among 'well to do' and fashionable visitors, long accustomed to the amenities of the inland spas, to turn to this spectacular, albeit rather remote, town as an alternative watering place. Furthermore, the Napoleonic Wars had put an end to the grand continental tours that had been so popular among the moneyed classes and they too looked elsewhere. In consequence from only 800 near the start of the century, by 1831 the population of Tenby had reached 2,100, rising to 3,500 by 1851. Wealthy visitors were thronging the town during the summer 'season' and were being catered for on the beaches and with several assembly halls, reading and card rooms and a choice of bowls, billiards, archery, fishing, horse riding and sailing. By 1828 paddle steamers from Bristol were calling twice weekly with large numbers of passengers and terraces of very presentable houses were built above the north beach and harbour, to be followed in around 1875 by the impressive buildings along the Esplanade overlooking the south beach and Caldey Island. At the start they were mainly private residences but were gradually converted into small hotels. **Castle Hill** received a great deal of attention and in 1865 was adopted as the site for the Welsh National Monument to Prince Albert, who had died two years before.

The statue of Prince Albert on Castle Hill, with an over-familiar visitor

One pathway built at that time leads past Laston House and a remnant of the curtain wall of the old **castle** and then above the **1905 lifeboat house** and slipway, most recently the Station of the R.N.L.B. *R.F.A. Sir Galahad*. This lifeboat was named in 1986 as a memorial to the dead and wounded suffered when the Royal Fleet Auxiliary ship was attacked whilst disembarking units of the Welsh Guards at San Carlos in 1982 during the Falklands operations. This Tyne Class self righting lifeboat was launched 364 times during its 20 years of service, saving 73 lives. But eventually the slipway could not be used because silting reduced the required depth of water at the point of entry and the lifeboat had to be moored offshore — to the detriment of vital reaction times. In March 2005, as the 11th lifeboat to serve the Station, and at one of 233 R.N.L.I. lifeboat stations in the UK and Republic of Ireland, the R.N.L.B. *Haydn Miller* took its place in a **new lifeboat house** a further short distance round the headland. Weighing 30 tonnes and constructed of fibre reinforced plastic, she has a crew of six, a range of 250 nautical miles and a top speed of 25 knots — starting with a launch speed down the slipway of 16 knots. For fair to moderate weather rescues in inshore waters, the R.N.L.I. also operates a fully inflatable boat.

The new lifeboat station

The new lifeboat station on the north side of Castle Hill was built, not without considerable difficulty, on the site of the 200ft-long Royal Victoria Pier. Itself built to celebrate Queen Victoria's Diamond Jubilee in 1897, this was opened in 1899 to accommodate excursion steamers bringing day-trippers from Swansea and Ilfracombe to the resort, for Tenby had become less exclusive by then. Numbers of more 'ordinary' visitors

St. Catherine's Fort

continued to arrive during the Edwardian era, swelling the considerable numbers of train passengers who had been arriving since 1866 along the new Whitland to Tenby line — and a new breed turning up in the cars and charabancs of the Motor Age. After just 50 years of use, maintenance of the ironwork pier was proving to be uneconomic and in 1953, much to the anguish of local anglers, it was added to the lengthening roll of other piers that had already sadly been lost to seaside resorts around the British coastline.

The footpath continues on to the far end of Castle Hill, passing the replica of the bandstand that had also been built at the time of the royal diamond jubilee. This is situated at a good point to view **St. Catherine's Fort**, sturdily built into the contours of the tiny island where once stood a chapel dedicated to the patron saint of spinners and weavers — Tenby trades until the 16th century. Completed with dressed granite blocks in 1870, the building was intended to form part of a chain protecting the new dockyard at Pembroke Dock from a feared overland invasion by the French through the harbour and beaches around Tenby. There was to be a garrison of 100 soldiers and officers, but as it turned out no cannon was ever fired except in annual practices and in 1907 the fort was disarmed and afterwards sold and fitted out by the new owner as a luxurious summer residence. But in 1940 it was sold again and sadly the island has since been unoccupied — apart from by a few seagull nests.

Further on along the south side of the hill the path reaches Tenby **Museum and Art Gallery**, the main indoor attraction of the town. Replacing the old National School, it was founded in 1878 and the collection and displays include archives of the ancient borough, which received its first charter in 1290 and the right to appoint its own mayor in 1402, while royal charters go back to the time of Richard III (d.1485). There are displays of the geology, archaeology, natural history of Pembrokeshire and the evolution of Tenby and many aspects of local history. The picture gallery concentrates on artists with close local associations and works by others which portray Tenby and its locality. They include Augustus John, who was born there, his highly regarded sister, Gwen, along with Nina Hamnett, Edward J. Head, David Jones, John Piper and others.

The museum building consists in part of what were probably residential quarters of the castle, close to the largely intact small gatehouse and protective barbican tower and the scrappy lengths of castle wall on that south side. The only other visible remain is the insignificant stone watchtower of just over 17 feet diameter, with an added square stair turret, that stands on the crest of the hill (and supports Tenby's sunshine meter). Beyond it is the old coastguard station, now privately occupied and still with highly enviable views

Hotels and houses on the Esplanade above South Beach

of Carmarthen Bay, across to Gower and Worm's Head and along the coastline and beaches on each side of Tenby. This peninsular site at the top of the hill presents a great variety of views. On one side the broad expanse of the **South Bay**, backed by sand dunes and extending for 1½ miles as far as Giltar Point has Caldey Island as an effective breakwater. **Castle Beach**, facing south, is in the lee of the Hill and St. Catherine Island and, with a mobile jetty, is the low tide embarkation point for the boats to Caldey Island. Around to the north side, the **Harbour Beach**, the smallest of the four, is where there is a great deal of activity worth watching, while the picturesque curve of **North Beach** extending to Monkstone Point, with its green trees, shrubs and

North Beach and Goscar Rock,
with the harbour and Castle Hill in the background

grey rock background and prominent sandstone **Goscar Rock** has been said to be often at its best in the mornings and early afternoons. All Tenby beaches regularly earn the European Blue Flag Award and those 'in the know' sometimes choose theirs for the day after checking the wind direction by the gilded copper weathercock on the octagonal 15th-century spire of **St. Mary's Church**. This is possible from many parts of the town, for faced in fine ashlar stone above a tall 14th- century battlemented tower to reach a height of 152 feet, the spire is a prominent landmark for miles around.

Apart from St. Davids Cathedral, St. Mary's is the largest church in Pembrokeshire and one of the largest medieval parish churches in Wales. There is mention of a church in 1100 and in 1210, Gerald de Barri (Giraldus Cambrensis, see p.91) is listed as rector of the parish — which would have had a much smaller church and, as was then often the practice, it is probable that he was not in residence, or even in Tenby. The church booklet, *A Short Account of the Building and History of St. Mary's*, describes and illustrates the development to the Perpendicular (*c.*1335–50 to *c.*1530) English Gothic rebuilding of the 13th-century church. Seen on entering through the west door, a striking feature is the high altar, set at the head of ten broad sanctuary steps. The church is crowned by an elaborate 'wagon' roof that dates from 1470 and has some 169 carved bosses, all but five dating from the 15th century. They include symbols of The Passion and of the Four Evangelists, foliage patterns, grotesque faces, mitred heads, mythical beasts, fishes and even a mermaid holding a mirror and comb. The late 15th-century 'wagon' roof of the nave is panelled like the chancel roof and has further bosses and figures, although most in the western half are plaster copies of some of those in the chancel.

Inside St. Mary's Church, the largest
parish church in Pembrokeshire

The many fine monuments date back to the early 14th century, a series of 15th-century effigies, monuments of the 17th century and a modern plaque to Robert Recorde (d.1558), a Tenby man of commanding genius and wide academic achievements, credited with being the founder of the English School of Mathematics and the first writer to use the symbols +, -, and =, and also to work out square roots (but being in no position to ensure that the image on the medallion is actually his — there are doubts). To the south-west of the church there are ruined remains of the 'College', although the church was never collegiate and it is thought that the stonework survives from a building for housing priests of the three chantries that lasted until 1547.

St. Mary's is one of the five churches of the rectorial benefice of Tenby and the other in the town is that of St. Julian, patron of ferrymen, innkeepers and others, which was rebuilt on the harbourside in 1878 as the 'fisherman's church'. It replaced the first chapel at the end of the medieval stone quay that had become a bath house in 1781, and then a blacksmith's shop, before it was demolished in 1842. Close to where it had stood, but now from the more modern quay, boats run every 20 minutes from Easter to October (but not on Sundays) taking visitors for three miles across Caldey Sound to Caldey Island — except at low water when a mobile landing stage on Castle Beach is used. Subject to weather and sea conditions, the crossing takes about 20 minutes.

Forming a natural breakwater for Tenby, **Caldey Island** is 1½ miles long and in places rather over half as broad and has had a monastery since the 6th century, probably during the Dark Ages and exposed to raids

by Norsemen during the 9th century, becoming Kald-ey (Cold Island). The Benedictines arrived as a cell of St. Dogmaels (pp.159-160) in 1136 and remained until the Dissolution when it entered private hands, at times becoming a haunt of pirates. In 1906 an Anglo Benedictine community arrived, built the abbey church in 1910, was received into the Church of Rome in 1913, dedicated the new abbey and church to St. Samson in 1919 and then ten years later moved to Prinknash Priory. The monastery was sold to the Reformed Cistercian Order from Chimay, Belgium, its present community of around 20 monks living according to the austere Rule of St. Benedict. Each day they attend seven services in the monastery church, starting at 3.15 am, but the Rule also expects them to set to manual as well as spiritual work and they maintain a prime beef herd, bake shortbread, produce hand-made chocolate and, rather differently from some of their religious brethren, they manufacture not liqueurs such as Chartreuse or Benedictine but a range of perfumes and toiletries derived from the wild flowers, gorse and herbs that grow

Caldey Island,
and one of the boats that takes visitors across

The 13th-century priory church dedicated to St. Illtud on Caldey Island (above) and one of the priory's farm buildings (left)

on the limestone at the north end of the island and on red sandstone at the south. Products are on sale in support of the community there and at the Caldey Shop on Quay Hill, Tenby. There is much else to see and do on foot by following the paths — the medieval parish church of St. Davids and the 13th-century priory church dedicated to St. Illtud, its stunted, battlemented tower surmounted by a far from upright spire but the centrepiece from the medieval Benedictine period thought to be of the most complete range of medieval monastic buildings in Wales. Paths leads to the lighthouse, the village tea gardens, post office and museum and to gain a closer view of the bird and seal sanctuary of the tiny high tide St. Margaret's Island, home to the largest cormorant colony in Wales — less than 1 mile from the mainland at Giltar Point and Penally. Then finally back to the fine sand and safe bathing of Priory Bay beach near the jetty before rejoining the Tenby boat.

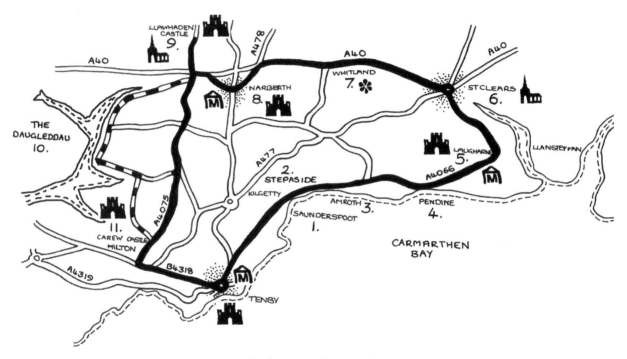

Outline map for Tour 3
The numbers 1 to 11 relate to the boxed information given within the tour

Tour 3   South-East Pembrokeshire

This tour uses a mixture of A, B and minor roads, visits the coastal settlements of Saundersfoot and nearby villages before reaching Pendine Sands that served for the early land speed records of Sir Malcolm Campbell, but was also the scene of a horrific ending for a popular competitor and the start by Amy Johnson and Jim Mollison of the very first east/west Trans-Atlantic flight. The route then heads to Laugharne with its castle, also the final home and resting place of the poet Dylan Thomas, then runs alongside the Taf estuary to reach St. Clears. It passes through Whitland and Narberth with a subsequent option to visit Llawhaden Castle. It then takes to mainly secondary roads for visits to Landshipping and Cresswell Quay on the Daugleddau. The last stop is Carew with its impressive castle ruins, Celtic cross, mill and church, and the route then returns to Tenby. The tour distance is about 45 miles without diversions (OS Landranger 158,159).

Leave Tenby on the A478 signposted to St. Clears, turning right onto the B4316 to travel into Saundersfoot.

---

1. Saundersfoot

During the late 18th century beginning of Tenby's gradual recovery from bad times, Saundersfoot hardly amounted to more than a small hamlet with a handful of houses. Yet from before Norman times it was known to be at the heart of a considerable coalfield. Starting in shallow bell pits, it was around here that coal mining began before any other part of south Wales, and with the Industrial Revolution came ever-increasing demands for the highly sought-after local anthracite. From the 18th century, shafts throughout the surrounding district were taken to depths of between 180 and 500 feet and thousands of tons

Saundersfoot harbour and beach

of the shiny black mineral were raised to the surface to be carted to the beaches of Coppet Hall and Wiseman's Bridge. Once there they were manually loaded onto brigs, which had been moored offshore, sometimes 30 at a time, after sailing from the east coast of England, the Guinness brewery in Dublin and much further. It is said that Queen Victoria was so taken with its high quality and low smoke emission

---

that she insisted that when she was on board the Royal Yacht, only Saundersfoot coal should be used to fire it.

Such was the demand that in 1829 the case had been made for a large new harbour, with connecting rail links to new collieries starting three and more miles away in the Begelly area and around Kilgetty and Stepaside. By 1833 the new facility had proved its value with the export of some 11,500 tons of anthracite and by the time the first main line railway service opened in 1866, annual loadings had more than trebled and the harbour afterwards served the industry for well nigh 70 years until the closure of Bonvilles Court Colliery to the west of the village.

Meanwhile the size and population of Saundersfoot had followed the expansion rate of the coal trade, helped from 1848 with the needs of iron production at Stepaside, but once the final shipments from the harbour had been made there might well have been severe local recession — as has widely been the case in so many Welsh coal-mining areas in the Glamorgan valleys.

Fortunately the collapse of the coal industry here was partly compensated for by the growing popularity of tourism and the attractions of holidays by the sea already found at Tenby, especially since 1866 once increasing numbers of visitors in their best Sunday suits, dresses and hats began to arrive by train. Just over half a century later, similarly dressed families started to follow in small black Fords, Morrises and Austins, motor cycle combinations and charabancs, the great influx receiving a further boost just before the Second World War with the passing of the Holidays with Pay Act. For all this, Saundersfoot offered great advantages of warm, clean and shallow sea and golden sandy beaches, straddling a fine large harbour that soon came to be appreciated as a picturesque and valuable leisure amenity and not just idle, redundant coal docks.

Like many such small seaside resorts it was a quiet and restful place for some time after the war, serving in part as an overspill or alternative to Tenby. Then came some all too familiar 1960s buildings along the seafront and cliff-tops, with modern housing developments among older parts of the village that combined to produce a marked change in local character to cater for modern holidaying tastes and needs. These now include a choice of pubs, cafés, restaurants, gift and novelty shops, amusement centres etc., while as a principal yachting centre of south Wales there are moorings for a large number of vessels in the harbour. The Saundersfoot Sailing Club has dinghy and cruise sailing and there are water-sports, sea fishing and boat trips to Tenby and further along the coastline for sightings of marine wildlife.

Saundersfoot lies on the Pembrokeshire Coast Path near its eastern limit at Amroth, and heading in that direction an unclassified road rises from the junction with the B4316 near the seafront and from opposite heads inland and then descends again to **Wiseman's Bridge**. In 1944 this is where, along the 10-mile stretch of beach extending eastwards to the mouth of the River Taf, Prime Minister Churchill and a gathering of 'Top Brass' assembled to witness full scale rehearsals for the 'D' Day landings. Known for its eponymous pub lying close to the beach, it is a small hamlet where at low tide it is possible to walk across the sands to Saundersfoot or, alternatively, follow the Coast Path in that direction through the tunnels that were made to take the former rail links between the local mines and the harbour.

2. Pleasant Valley to Stepaside
Pleasant Valley lives up to its name, passing inland for just over a mile to Stepaside. It is difficult to imagine now that, in the 19th century, this was a far from pleasant industrialised area of blast furnaces, foundries, brickworks, collieries, iron ore and limestone quarries. Instead, it has become a popular leisure venue, with a Craft Centre, Museum, Bird Park and other attractions of appeal to tourists.

3. Amroth

The pebbly beach below the pub at Wiseman's Bridge (above), unlike the sweeping sands, at low tide, at Amroth (below)

The south-east facing beach at Wiseman's Bridge is rather rocky in places as it continues towards Amroth, where at extreme spring low tides the stumps of trees may be seen offshore as vestiges of a 'drowned forest'. This dates from distant times when, as in St. Brides Bay, the Bristol Channel and Cardigan Bay, sea levels were much lower and there was a huge expanse of land and vegetation occupied by now long extinct animals. Some of their bones have been found in areas of blue clay out there, as well as flakes from primitive tools. A stream at the eastern end of the village marks the County boundary with Carmarthenshire and also one end of the 186 miles of Pembrokeshire Coast Path. The Carmarthen Bay Coastal Path offers further cliff scenery to the east as far as Pendine.

Amroth is also at one end of the Landsker (p.127), the invisible boundary crossing the county from Newgale towards the far west. **Amroth Castle** has known no warfare for it is a late 18th-century house, albeit built on the site of a now vanished Norman fortress. Close to the sea, it has now become a holiday centre, divided into apartments and with the grounds laid out with caravans, a swimming pool and children's play area. One mile inland along Knight's Way footpath, **Colby Woodland Garden** (NT) consists of 8 acres of secluded wooded valley planted with bulbs and a colourful range of rhododendrons and azaleas — at their best from early Spring until June. The Garden is open between April and October and it also has a walled garden full of horticultural treasures as well as more familiar plants that flourish in the mild enclosed environment. Beyond the walls there are enjoyable walks that pass through oak, ash, beech and sycamore woodland to fine viewpoints and to a National Trust shop and other amenities.

The way by road to Amroth first heads inland to **Summerhill**, where there is a right turn for this quiet little village stretching along a narrow sea front and storm beach of shingle thrown up above a long expanse of gently shelving sands, very popular during the summer once the tide goes out.

Now in Carmarthenshire, the road heads inland again, climbing high up through Marros before meeting the B4314 on which you turn right towards the coast, this time for the sharp drop down past the church through the straggling old part of **Pendine** village to sea level below the cliffs at the western end of the famous long stretch of sands. These are a great magnet for large numbers of summertime day-trippers and longer staying families, perhaps holidaying at one of the mass of caravan parks in the locality and making good use of the shops, cafés and other amenities on hand. There is a good path for walkers, climbing high above the sea from Dolwen Point, passing the banks of an Iron Age promontory fort and traces of the Bronze Age above Ragwen Point at the approach to Marros Sands. Looking ahead, there are views across the sea towards Tenby, while to the east there is the Carmarthenshire coast.

Near the start of the cliff walk, one of the functions of the Beach Hotel was to serve as headquarters for world-class motor racing events that took place here during the 1920s.

---

4. Pendine Sands. Exploits of Malcolm Campbell, J.C. Parry Thomas and Amy Johnson

Pendine Sands

Much of the dune and beach area was acquired for use as a firing and test range during the Second World War and is still owned by the Ministry of Defence, defined by warning notices, not least because of unexploded munitions.

The 7-mile long stretch of fine, hard sand extends at low tide from Gilman Point at Pendine towards the Taf estuary and during the 1920s became famous for the land speed record attempts held there. Between September 1924 and February 1927, Sir Malcolm Campbell (1885–1946), driving his 350 h.p. V12 Sunbeam, *Bluebird*, raised his average speed along the course from successive world records of 146.16 mph to 174.22 mph (before becoming the first driver to exceed 300 mph at Bonneville Salt Flats, Utah in 1935). But disaster struck at Pendine during another attempt in 1927 when the Welsh ace, J.C. Parry Thomas, was killed at a speed of 180 mph after losing control of his 27-litre car, *Babs*. As a mark of respect it was buried in the sand dunes, where it remained until 1969. Then it was exhumed and meticulously restored during the next 15 years for exhibition (between Easter and the end of each October) at the '**Museum of Speed**' in the village by the Beach Hotel.

Motor racing was evidently in the Campbell blood, for in 2002 Don Wales, grandson of Malcolm Campbell and nephew of Donald Campbell, set a UK Electrical land speed record at Pendine Sands in *Bluebird Electric 2* at a speed of 137 mph.

Situated well over to the west of Britain, the long expanse of flat, firm sand was also well placed as a runway for Amy Johnson (1903–41) and her husband Jim Mollison (1905–1959) when, in June 1933, they took off from Pendine in a de Havilland DH-84 Dragon 1 aircraft called *Seafarer* for the first non-stop, east-west trans-Atlantic attempt to reach New York. (Unfortunately they ran out of fuel and were slightly injured on crash landing at Bridgeport, Connecticut — and as a wartime transport pilot Johnson was to drown eight years later after being forced to parachute into the Thames estuary).

In Pendine turn right onto the A4066. On its way to Laugharne this skirts the base of the cliffs past Llanmiloe, now separated from the Pendine Sands and Burrows by a large expanse of marshland, with **Coygen Hill** soon rising on the right above the East Marsh. It was well known among early archaeologists for the lofty cave on its eastern face containing a rich deposit of bones of animals that have long been extinct in Britain, such as mammoth and woolly rhinoceros, now distributed among south Wales museums. There are remains of an earthwork fort at the top of the hill, and shell mounds said to contain relics dating back from the Dark Ages at least as far as the Bronze Age. Just to the north-east, closer to Laugharne, **Sir John's Hill** has become known to devotees of the work of Dylan Thomas through its association with one of his most ambitious poems, *Over Sir John's Hill*.

---

5. Laugharne, by a 'heron priested shore'

Pronounced 'Larn', the town also appears as Lacharn, Talacharn and was once Abercoran — 'mouth of the Coran'. This is the small river that enters from the north-west, passing alongside the castle before merging with the River Taf out in the estuary. The **castle** site was first chosen for a Norman fortification in the early 12th century but as a result of continual attacks by the Welsh, including both Llewelyns, the stone-built castle that has survived dates from the late 13th century and after, as it passed through several generations of the de Brian family — at a time when a new borough was chartered and **St. Martin's Church** was built somewhat

Laugharne Castle and the River Coran

apart to the north. The township of Laugharne was set out along what is now known as King Street, directly to the north of the castle, and seven centuries later burgage plots can still be recognised there. A similar pattern from the same period is displayed along Victoria Street, Market Lane and Wogan Street and there are indications that the Frogmore area across the Coran also has very early origins. The impressive, lofty castle ruins stand on a bluff overlooking the Strand and facing the estuary and green hills of the Llanstephan peninsula beyond. They were partly incorporated into a mansion during the reign of Henry VIII by Sir John Perrott (d.1592) who, as also at Carew (below), was enthusiastic about converting damaged castles into palatial residences (maybe stemming from his alleged condition as a natural son of the king!). There are remains of an early round keep and a late 13th- or 14th-century tower and gatehouse and the castle resumed a military role during the Civil War, being captured by the Royalists in 1644 and then retaken by besieging Roundheads and soon afterwards partially destroyed and allowed to become ruinous. In Georgian and Victorian times gracious gardens were laid out in the grounds and more recently these have been recreated as part of a consolidation and restoration programme that also provides for a discretely placed visitor centre. After much careful attention the castle is now open to the public during the summer months and is managed by Cadw, whose illustrated guidebook provides a history, detailed tour of the ruins and a series of associated features.

Close to the castle entrance, the tiny **Town Hall** dates largely from 1745 and one distinguishing feature on the south of its tower was a 10ft. square prison cell fitted with wooden chairs and pillows and known as the **Clink**. The township has moreover uniquely been governed by a Corporation since the reign of Edward I and at the annual election a portreeve, who still presides at council meetings, is invested with a chain of golden cockle shells and an enamel and gold coat-of-arms jewel. ('Port' comes from the Saxon word for a market town while 'reeve' was 'Gerefor' — an official. The shells represent long association with the local cockle industry). Once Laugharne was also a port in the maritime sense, but all traces of the harbour have now long been replaced by a sweeping expanse of salt marsh and creeks.

The largely Georgian main street leads towards St. Martin's Church, where beneath a simple white cross the overflow churchyard to the right is the final resting place of the Welsh lyric poet, author and broadcaster **Dylan Thomas** (1914-1953), and of **Caitlin**, his wife (d.1994). He was not the only writer or artist to be

Laugharne Town Hall and the Clink

drawn to Laugharne, for long before him in the early 1830s the landscape painter, J.W.M. Turner (1775–1851), was there to create a most dramatic and celebrated water-colour of the castle and seascape. The countryside poet, Edward Thomas (1878–1917), came and between the wars, the author Richard Hughes (1900–1976), best known for *A High Wind in Jamaica,* occupied Castle house, close to the ruins and wrote one of his novels in the gazebo on the south eastern curtain wall overlooking the estuary. But for most literary tourists, the main draw is the connection with the gifted Dylan Thomas — who also gained

The Boathouse where Dylan Thomas lived and worked for the last four years of his life and the cross that marks his grave in the churchyard

inspiration for a time in the gazebo when writing his short stories collected in *Portrait of the Artist as a Young Man*. Born in Swansea (pp.7-8), he afterwards moved around a great deal, first visiting Laugharne in 1934, living there in a fisherman's cottage from 1938, afterwards in New Quay for a time (p.218) before finally settling with his wife and family in 1949 for the last four years of his life in the now famous **Boathouse** beside the estuary, complete with a small 'Shack' workplace that looked out over the 'heron priested shore'.

Now the Boathouse has become a heritage centre, open each day and complete with a range of artefacts, cuttings, audio-visual presentations, a bookshop, tearooms and an outdoor terrace. Close by, it is possible to peer into 'The Shack', the old garage where Thomas wrote *Under Milk Wood* and much of his other work, while back in the town, but in no sense a shrine, **Brown's Hotel** is popular as the place where, as was his way until excess alcohol brought about his early death, he often drank.

In a story included in *Quite Early One Morning*, Thomas wrote that he just came to Laugharne 'one day, for the day, and never left; got off the bus, and forgot to get on again'. Whilst he remains there, this tour moves on up the valley — to shadow the River Taf upstream and head along the A4066 for **St. Clears**. As a bottleneck at the junction of main roads to parts of south-west Carmarthenshire, Pembrokeshire and holiday destinations in the west, until recently this place was a nightmare for motorists. But now there is a by-pass and living conditions have much improved in the town centre.

6. St. Clears/Sancler

Founded by a knight named St. Clare, St. Clears is thought to date from as early as 1153. A Norman motte and bailey **castle** was built in a strong position here on a peninsula at the junction of the rivers Taf and Cynin (rather in the manner of Newcastle Emlyn on the Teifi, see pp.230-231), and it was mentioned in 1188 during his recruiting drive in Wales for the Third Crusade by Giraldus Cambrensis. Subjected, as was commonplace, to several Welsh attacks, it is thought to have been abandoned during the 13th century but substantial remains of the mound have survived and are to be seen on the east side of Bridge Street, with the bailey leading towards the south. During the 12th century, a small Cluniac priory dependant on a church in Paris was introduced some way to the north, and upon its dissolution as an alien foundation in the mid-15th century, its **church of St. Mary Magdalene** became the parish church of St. Clears. It has a massive battlemented tower, like other churches in south-west Wales, but one rarity there is a fine Norman chancel arch with rich, robust carvings. It is likely that a civil settlement formed between castle and priory and there is a record of a charter dated 1393, a corporation and portreeve, and an inland port

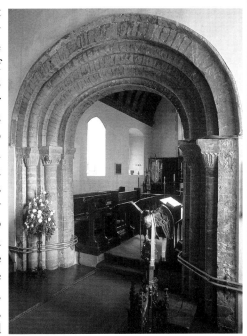

The chancel arch in St. Clears Church

and quay. Later, in the 1840s, the village and surrounding area became a centre of violence during the Rebecca Riots, contributing to reform of the toll-gate system of road maintenance charges. At the junction of several well surfaced, toll-free, main roads and relieved by its by-pass, St. Clears has now, however, become a peaceful base for holiday outings to many delightful parts of the region.

After leaving St. Clears, the route joins the A40 from Carmarthen and still not far from the River Taf, heads for **Whitland**, to visit which you must turn left onto the B4328.

---

7. Whitland/Hendy Gwyn and an early National Assembly

Rather Victorian in looks on the banks of a now tiny River Taf, the topography of Whitland has made it an important agriculture centre, never more so than when it served dairy farmers across a wide area with one of the largest milk factories in Wales.

Back in the 10th century, tradition has it that for around six weeks it was the venue for a very different form of activity. This was during the lifetime of Hywel Dda (916–950), king of Deheubarth, grandson of Rhodri Mawr the Great of Gwynedd (844–878) — and one of the greatest figures in Welsh history. He is said to have summoned a great assembly of some 1,000 lay and cleric representatives from all parts of Wales for the purpose of consolidating the diverse range of folk law and customs that had widely been in practice over previous centuries. The chosen men of substance and learning met at his hunting lodge — the Ty Gwyn ar Taf (the Old White House on the Taf) in the year 930, and after considering, amending or abrogating ancient law and drafting new provisions, produced a Code that formed the basis of Law in Wales for the next three centuries, and to an extent until the Act of Union in 1536. It was considered to be superior to the Law in England in many desirable ways and more advanced than in many parts of Europe, in subjects as diverse as land tenure, building regulations, fire precautions and equality for women. It has also left a revealing and rare picture of the public and domestic life and times of 10th-century Welsh people.

There is now no trace of Hywel the Good's meeting place, but instead there is the **Hywel Dda Interpretive Garden and Centre** on the site of the old market in St. Mary's Street. Said to be 'the only garden in Europe dedicated to the Law', it contains an apt exhibition and six small gardens, each representing (in Welsh) a separate division of the Law: Society and Statutes; Crime and Tort; Women; Contract; Court; and King and Property. These are illustrated on slate plaques, illuminated with enamels and decorated with various forms of artwork.

The Landsker (p.127) Borderland Trail passes close to the second site north of the town that guarantees Whitland its place in Welsh history. In the valley of the River Gronw there was the first Cistercian abbey in Wales, called *Alba Domus* or *Alba Landa*, and also *Blanchland* — anglicised as Whitland. It was founded in 1143 by the first Norman bishop of St. Davids, and although a daughter establishment of Citeaux (*Cistercium* in Latin) Abbey in France and ultimately subject to the authority of its abbot, the White Monks of Whitland were mostly Welsh, with Welsh sympathies. It became the mother abbey of seven other Cistercian abbeys in Wales, all of them under the patronage of Welsh noblemen, and two others in Ireland. But whereas there are still visible remains to be seen at Strata Florida (pp.238-240), Cwmhir and the other daughter abbeys, there is now hardly anything left above ground of **Whitland Abbey**.

The B4328 rejoins the A40 just to the west of the town where you continue towards Haverfordwest and after 4½ miles you reach the A478 and turn left to visit **Narberth**. There is some on street parking in the town, and a small car park to the left just beyond the Town Hall.

---

8. Narberth/Arberth and the Landsker Borderlands

On a rise just south of the main coach road, Narberth is centred in Arberth — 'yn Arberth', the surrounding agricultural district that produces its Welsh name and, by adding the 'N' from the phrase, also its English. Architecture in this compact market town suggests a prosperous time in Georgian, Regency and early

Narberth Town Hall (left) and castle remains (above)

Victorian periods, much of it coming from a successful market that served the local area. It was such that Tenby, suffering economically from the competition, in 1676 managed to have it shut down for 12 years. The picturesque, rather Disneyesque **Town Hall**, with the Royal Coat of Arms on the wall, was first built as a gaol and court on a central island site in *c*.1835 and was afterwards fitted with a turret and an additional storey. Among its occupants are the TIC and the **Landsker Visitor Centre**, Narberth sometimes being referred to as 'Capital' of the Landsker Borderlands. Its mid-13th-century **castle** lying south of, and downhill from, the Market Square was part of a chain that extended from Roch in the west to Amroth that served to separate Norman and Welsh Pembrokeshire, the 'Englishry' from the 'Welshry'. Now much ruined, it was rectangular in plan, with a Great Tower at the north-east corner next to the gatehouse (now gone) and with three drum towers at the angles and smaller towers mid-way along each of the east and west curtain walls, some parts of which may still be seen by the public, with disabled access, throughout the year. Much of the damage was caused by Llewelyn ap Gruffudd in 1257 and by 1609 it was reported to be 'decayed and wasted for 20 years and more' — although is thought to have been occupied for another 50 years or so. However the romantic tales and legends applying to Narberth appearing in the fabulous early Welsh stories of the *Mabinogion* and early Welsh chronicles, including those of Prince Pwyll's love for the beautiful Princess Rhiannon, are probably based around the nearby earth and timber **Sentence Castle** at Templeton, in the 'Englishry'. Dating from the end of the 11th century, this used to be called Narberth Castle but was burnt to the ground by Llewelyn the Great early in the 13th. Back in Narberth, **St. Andrew's Church** was founded soon afterwards, giving its name to Church Street, but except for the thin north tower and north nave wall, it is now the outcome of Victorian designs. Narberth's Victorian and Edwardian past is well represented in the small **Wilson Museum** towards the castle. There are many aspects of local history and culture, including costume and objects that used to be in daily use in the home (check opening time with the TIC). In the High Street, next to the car park, the **Queen's Hall** has been rebuilt to house an art gallery and café, while the auditorium caters for all types of concert and serves as a venue for exhibitions and antique fairs. In other parts of the town, as well as the castle ruins there are many buildings that add extra character, for example the De Rutzen Arms in Market Street, which began in 1832 with a covered market at the rear. More recently artists and craftspeople have been drawn to the now colour-washed houses and shops to make a distinct contribution to the 'atmosphere' and commercial well-being of Narberth.

Take the B4314 from Narberth (signposted to Haverfordwest) back to the A40 at Robeston Wathen, and on which you turn left. In a short while you will reach the A4075 to the left, which is the turning for Carew, but you may first wish to make a detour to see Llawhaden castle. If so, continue on along the A40 at this junction, and take the next right-hand turn and follow it for 1½ miles to **Llawhaden**. Apart from the castle, there is some good scenery, an ancient church with unusual features and part of a restored medieval hospice.

9. Llawhaden Castle and the bishops of St. Davids

Llawhaden Castle is one of the eight castles of the Landsker, but differs from the rest in being more of a strongly fortified bishops' residence than a military stronghold. A first earth and timber castle was built on a commanding position in 1115 by Bernard, first Norman bishop of St. Davids, only to be taken by the Lord Rhys and destroyed in 1193. It was recaptured by the English bishops early in the following century and never seems to have featured afterwards in armed hostilities — although garrisoned as a precaution during the Glyndwr uprising. Instead a succession of bishops of St. Davids made it one of their principal residences, each one adding further lavish refinements until the mid-16th century. Although now little more than a shell, there is still enough left of the deeply moated building, high and prominent on a steep-sided hill above the Eastern River Cleddau, to show that it was intended to appear more of an episcopal status symbol than an effective fortress. It still suggests grandeur and the taste for good living enjoyed by medieval bishops of St. Davids and their important guests. Medieval bishops spent much of their time on the move, attended by large entourages that needed to be housed and fed along their way. Dealing not only with spiritual matters within the diocese, they also called upon their numerous and often far flung estates in order to check that they were properly managed and partake of some of the produce. Of necessity all the travel created the need to house the bishop and his retinue and their horses and trappings, and soon after the Norman occupation Llawhaden became a principal residence. Occupation lasted until the mid-16th century, when the bishop of the time apparently stripped the lead from the roofs and started a process of 'redeployment' of stonework. What is left of the castle is now protected and maintained by Cadw, and includes parts of a twin-towered gatehouse, curtain wall and towers and lesser remnants of the hall block and associated private apartments, bakehouse and kitchen. Cadw have published a detailed and well illustrated guide: *Lamphey Bishops Palace. Llawhaden Castle*, with additional sections on *Carswell Medieval House* and *Carew Cross*, which are also in its care.

Llawhaden Castle

Down below the hill on the banks of the Eastern River Cleddau, **St. Aidan's Church** has a medieval nave and chancel,

south chancel aisle and west porch, and the distinction of having two towers, each one castellated. The diminutive outer one was the first to be built, and when in the 14th century it became necessary to move the building further away from the river, the new tower was placed against it.

Llawhaden had been growing into a large and significant borough from the late 13th century, along with the palace being built by Bishop Bek. In 1287, in Chapel Field at the west end of the medieval town, he founded a hospice for poor and needy wayfarers. It was the first to be provided anywhere in his vast diocese and a tall barrel-vaulted chamber has survived behind the modern village hall. A recess in the wall has been suggested as being for a ceremonial piscina. There are traces of a ditched enclosure surrounding the ruins.

Llawhaden Church with two joined towers

Return to the A40, turning left and then right onto the A4075 to rejoin the main route. On that short section of the A40 you cross Canaston Bridge, near where the eastern Cleddau approaches its highest tidal limit. (Locally received opinions are that in *c*.2100 BC, pillars of bluestone from the Preseli Hills were brought down here to be launched, taken down the Haven and up the Bristol Channel to build a phase of Stonehenge).

Having turned on to the A4075, you can either take the main road straight through to Carew, or take an additionally scenic route by taking the first right a few hundred yards along the A4075. If you take this route, you will first reach Blackpool Mill. Continue past the mill and after a further 1½ miles take what is in fact the next right. If you bear right at the next junction this will lead you to a dead end at the quiet and atmospheric Landshipping Quay. Returning to that junction and carrying on (or turning left in the first place!), then follow the signs to Cresswell Quay, another attractive settlement. Bear left once through the village and you will rejoin the A4075 on which you turn right to reach Carew.

10. The Daugleddau, estuary of the Two Swords

Blackpool Mill

In its woodland setting, the picturesque **Blackpool Mill** is in good condition for a building dating from 1813, uncommonly large and in effective use as a corn mill for nearly a century and a half. During the 1950s, like so many others, it might have been allowed to deteriorate or be converted to other uses, but it has been restored to working order since then and augmented by features such as a craft shop, model steam engines, a museum, mill caverns and a café — all serving to make it a popular attraction at this gateway to the Daugleddau. As well as this, it is conveniently situated alongside part of the westernmost stretch of the 50 miles Landsker Borderland Trail, where it connects with the Knights Way footpath that passes through Narberth to the end of the Pembrokeshire Coast Path, nine miles away at Amroth. It is also an ideal base for less energetic walks within the peaceful countryside surrounding this upper course of the Haven.

The main channel of the Daugleddau (*Dau* meaning 'two'and *cleddau* 'swords'), or what some have called The Secret Waterway is a good example of a drowned river valley, known as a ria, that extends from the coast towards the heart of Pembrokeshire. By the time it reaches the Cleddau toll bridge above Neyland the Daugleddau blends the waters of the Rivers Carew, Cresswell, the Western and the Eastern Cleddau and several smaller tributaries that have joined through secluded tidal inlets and creeks. The waterway winds past steep wooded banks that run down to the high tide mark, salt marsh vegetation and wide intertidal mudflats that between them provide a rich habitat for plants and animals and copious feeding grounds for waders and waterfowl.

Landshipping Quay is at the head of a short tidal creek (or pill), and like other estuarine settlements along the Daugleddau, such as Lawrenny, Cresswell Quay and Carew, until the 1860s the hamlet was a busy trading centre for its size, with berths for small sailing coasters that came in on the tides. They dealt in a wide range of commodities and also loaded the output of local small coal mines (for ever remembered at Landshipping after the major disaster where 40 men and boys as young as 11, possibly even younger, were drowned when the incoming tide broke through a roof of the Garden Pit on 14 February 1844).

Landshipping Quay

At the end of a creek to the east, one branch of the waterway reaches **Cresswell Quay**. Williamston Park to its west (NT) is now a nature reserve and a Site of Special Scientific Interest displaying a wealth of wild flowers near the salt marsh, disused quarries and a complex of man-made and now muddy creeks. As a wildlife 'hospital', the **Oiled Bird Rescue Centre** opened at West Williamston in 1980 and as well as treating birds contaminated by oil, it has been on extra alert during the regular migration period of young Manx shearwaters seeking to follow their parents from Skomer Island (p.122) to South America, normally between 20 August and 7 October. Many of the infant birds are blown off course and once grounded, often in brightly lit places, are not built to take off again. It is part of the role of the Centre to ensure that rescued

Cresswell Quay

birds are fit to proceed, and then at dusk to avoid voracious gulls, they send them on their way from a headland overlooking the open sea. (It is known from ringing records that thereafter the shearwaters will live above the oceans for several years before returning to their birthplace as adults — often to the same Skomer rabbit hole!)

Across the River Carew branch of the estuary, the gateway and two flanking towers of 13th-century **Upton Castle** have survived to form part of the present private residence and among the trees to the south-east, a Decorated period chapel contains a rare square-shaped Norman font and fine monuments incorporating figures of the Malefaunt family and others having a part in Upton's past. Outside there are relics of a medieval preaching cross. Signed for visits from Cosheston village two miles away (during seasonal opening days and hours), 35 acres of Castle Grounds are now said to contain over 250 different species of trees and shrubs and formal terraces as well as herbaceous borders, a rose garden and woodland walks running down to an isolated part of the Carew river, and to further picturesque views and wildlife sightings.

The A4075 continues on southwards and crosses the river at the head of the estuary by a narrow bridge to arrive at Carew, there being a car park across the bridge and near the castle on the right-hand side of the road.

11. Carew

For such a small village, Carew contains a great deal of interest and most visitors start with the magnificent **castle** ruins that they can see across the mill pond from the car park just before reaching the road bridge. The façade dates from Elizabethan times, but there have been much earlier appearances on the slightly raised limestone ridge. Recent archaeology carried out by the University of Wales, Lampeter, has indicated Iron Age occupation and there are indications of the raising of a heavily defended Welsh stronghold there during early Christian Deheubarth. In 1095 an earth and timber castle was built by the Anglo-Norman Gerald of Windsor, created Constable of Pembroke Castle by Henry I. He gained possession of the property at Carew by dowry through his marriage to the lively Nest, daughter of Rhys ap Tewdwr, prince of Deheubarth. Through many affairs and romantic experiences, such as a daring abduction from Cilgerran Castle (pp.228-229) by an infatuated Prince Owain ap Cadwgan, her irresistible charms earned her a place in history as the 'Helen of Wales', whilst becoming also a grandmother of Giraldus Cambrensis (p.91). Only the Old Tower now survives from this period and by the late 13th century the castle was held by the Carews, who carried out considerable work to the east side, and built the chapel and gatehouse and the western range, consisting of the Great Hall placed between two massive drum towers that were reinforced by spur buttresses that rose to first floor level.

In 1480 the castle passed from the Carew family and the next, most prominent occupant was Rhys ap Thomas (see also p.45). This was just

Carew Castle as seen from the north

Carew Castle as seen from the south-west

five years before the events opening at Mill Bay with the landing of Henry Tudor (p.120) were to change the whole course of history. To begin with, Rhys ap Thomas was not inclined to renounce his loyalty to King Richard III but after some hard bargaining at a meeting near Welshpool, he belatedly decided to throw in his lot with Henry, offering the services of a force that traditionally is said to have numbered between 1,800 and 2,000 men. They must have had a significant effect on the outcome of the battle at Bosworth and Rhys was rewarded with a knighthood, together with much of the pre-eminent role in south Wales that he had sought. It was during the years immediately following the battle that Sir Rhys rebuilt a substantial part of the castle as a sumptuous residence that matched his grandiose style. When he was admitted as a Knight of the Garter in 1507, he arranged a spectacular 5-day grand joisting tournament which brought 600 noblemen to Carew from all over Wales — probably the last such event ever to happen. But in 1531 his grandson was executed for treason and the castle reverted to the Crown until, in 1558, Queen Mary granted it to Sir John Perrot (her half-brother — if it is true that he was an illegitimate son of her father, King Henry VIII).

As was shown at Laugharne, he was a born castle 'makeover' enthusiast, and in the 1580s was responsible for the 7-bay long north range that displays two storeys of mullion-and-transome windows above a high basement as the focus of the many cameras pointed from the footpath across the mill pond to the north. There might have been more to photograph, but in 1591 he too was arrested for treason, condemned to death and forfeited his property and rights, but he died from ill-health in the Tower of London the following year and so avoided execution.

The south range was destroyed during the Civil War and was let later that century, soon to be robbed of much of its best masonry, while the outer ward buildings disappeared. Then in 1963 the National Park Authority acquired a long lease of the remains from the heirs to the Carews and joined with Cadw in an extensive programme of consolidation and conservation.

Carew Mill

The castle was sited alongside a tidal creek leading up to Carew and it would have had access to the sea on either side of high tide, until it was realised during the Middle Ages that the considerable fluctuations in water level could be harnessed to provide power for a grain **mill**. The creek was dammed, automatic gates were installed to admit the sea water to a 23-acre pond on the rising tide, then

Carew Cross

closed until the flow started to ebb. When the level had fallen enough, the water was automatically released again through a sluice to drive the two undershot mill wheels which worked the machinery operating the millstones and other equipment. The present four-storey building on the causeway follows a sequence of installations and dates from the mid-19th century, from when it continued in use until 1937. Restored later and linked by path with the castle, it is now the only functional tide mill in Wales and open to visitors throughout the summer — under the management of the National Parks Authority.

Close to the main road and within a fence just inside the castle grounds, the age of the **Carew Cross** can reliably be dated almost to the nearest year. A Latin epigraph relates to Maredudd, son of Edwin (and a descendant of Hywel Dda, see p.80) who had been a joint ruler of Deheubarth with his brother from 1033, prior to being killed in action in 1035. It is likely that the memorial was carved and erected close to that time, rising in two separate pieces to a height of 14 feet. The wheel-head was cut from carboniferous sandstone, and has flaked on the road side, and the shaft from a harder igneous rock that probably came from the Preseli Hills. It is all richly carved with intricate or interwoven patterns that are predominantly in the fashion of the Celtic Church, although also reflecting Irish, Saxon and Viking influences of that time.

St. Mary's Church, **Carew Cheriton** (near the junction of the A4075 and A477 south of Carew) dates from the late 14th century and is especially noted for its distinctive staged and battlemented west tower of *c*.1500 with a polygonal corner stair turret. Of particular interest inside are the tombs and effigies of the Carew family who held the castle for many centuries. In the churchyard, another unusual feature is a chapel over a vaulted charnel house that was once used for housing exhumed human bones.

From the car park by the castle, turn right onto the A4075 and then left at the junction with the A477, shortly thereafter taking the B4318 to the right to return to Tenby.

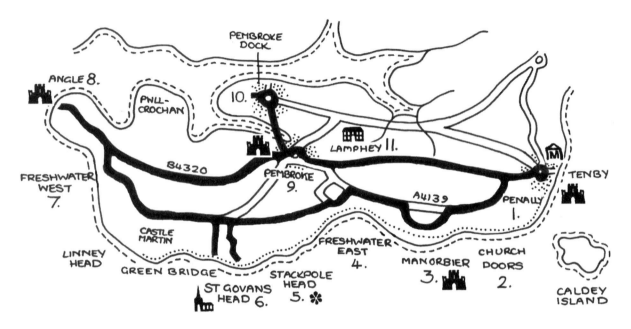

Outline map for Tour 4
The numbers 1 to 11 relate to the boxed information given within the tour

Tour 4   Westwards to Angle

On a mixture of A, B and minor roads, this route includes several bays and beaches (one, Barafundle Bay, which has no road access and where it is necessary to ease the legs into action in order to reach one of the coastline's most favoured, sheltered and secluded beaches), scenic views, Manorbier Castle, St. Govan's chapel, Angle, the town and castle of Pembroke and the various sights of Pembroke Dock and its fortifications and, finally, Lamphey Palace. The driving distance of about 40 miles includes some backtracking (OS Landranger 157, 158).

The tour leaves Tenby on the A4139 signposted towards Pembroke, shadowing the South Beach, and after 1½ miles reaches Penally.

---

1. Penally and Lydstep Haven

Penally is a small village on rising ground with good views of St. Margaret's and Caldey Islands, the surrounding sea and long stretches of coastline extending to Gower. The present parish church is built on the site of a *clas* or Celtic monastery on the village green and dates from the 13th and 14th centuries, and is dedicated to St. Nicholas, a 4th-century bishop of Myra in Asia Minor and saint of sailors, and of children (the original Father Christmas). Since 1995 the name of St. Teilo, said to have been born in Penally in the 6th century and later a friend of St. David, has been added as someone who, widely venerated during the Age of the Saints, functioned in the conversion of Britain to Christianity from his principal monastic foundation of Llandeilo Fawr in Carmarthenshire. Along with other stone relics from the early days of the 10th century, the 7ft-high **Penally Cross** is a wheel-head cross carved in a combination of Celtic and Northumbrian styles edged with cable mouldings and with three types of carving on the shaft. There are monuments in the church dating from *c*.1300 and one of the most poignant is the memorial to all who drowned when the Tenby Lifeboat capsized in 1834.

After Tenby and Giltar Point, the next beach is of sand and pebbles at **Lydstep Haven**, sheltered between the limestone cliffs of Proud Giltar and Lydstep Point. Served by a slipway and regularly earning the European Blue Flag Award, it is privately managed as part of the Lydstep Beach Holiday Resort (admission charges) and backed by ranks of caravans set out on land around the bay. It is reached along a private drive from the A4139 in Lydstep village that leads towards the resort car park and clubhouse at Lydstep Haven House.

On the headland beyond the caravan site and beach the National Trust has a car park and some 54 acres along coastline of 1¼ miles where paths lead to the pallid limestone rocks of Lydstep Head. At a great syncline or downfold, the strata were thrust into vertical positions at the time when continents collided some 290 million years ago. The cliff top abounds in typical limestone and salt tolerant flora and in the spring large numbers of seabirds, such as herring gulls and fulmars, nest in the cliffs and there are many other species in the scrub just inland. During 19th-century summers, quarrying was undertaken

---

down below, the limestone trucked on rails to the cliff edge to be lowered onto schooners lying at a sheltered anchorage, close underneath the cliffs, and thence taken to ports and kilns in west Wales or Devon.

Provided that tide tables are checked and understood, at low tide the Lydstep caverns are famously worth the effort of the steep descent to the shore and scramble over the rocks.

The route carries on along the A4139 through Lydstep and soon reaches the B4585 on which you turn left for Manorbier. Soon after a right-angled bend, there is a sign on the left for the Youth Hostel above the cliffs at Church Doors and Skrinkle Haven which you must take if you wish to visit these sights.

2. Church Doors and Skrinkle Haven

The Youth Hostel has been converted from a former army building and other relinquished military positions have become car parks, viewing points and picnic areas. A stairway leads far down the cliffs to a rocky cove, where Carboniferous Limestone to the east gives way to Old Red Sandstone. Two narrow bastions of limestone remain to project like walls out to sea, dividing the Haven into three, and being soluble they contain cave entrances that have locally produced the name of Church Doors for one. Down towards beach level there are dangers of rock falls and there is a real need to take care not to be cut off by the tide. Safe access is restricted at the time of writing and local advice should be sought before venturing too far.

Further along the B4585 there is another sharp turn, close to the castle entrance at Manorbier from where a minor road leads down to the left reaching the National Park Authority car park (charges) and then narrowly rising to a few smaller roadside parking spaces overlooking Manorbier Bay and Beach. If you wish to miss out Manorbier and continue on the main route, this follows the B4585.

3. Manorbier. 'Most assuredly without equal'

A path suitable for wheelchairs leads from the NPA car park to the top of the beach while other ways descend past a pebble bank to the Green Coast Award sandy beach below the high tide line and to well explored rock pools. It is generally safe for bathing and popular with surfers — but there is a warning about needing to show respect for a dangerous undertow. To the south, the rocky headland is called Priest's Nose and after about 300 yards from the beach the Coast Path passes **King's Quoit,** a Neolithic burial chamber that has been there for some 5,000 years. It comprises a long capstone slab facing towards the Bay that appears to have fallen from the adjacent, near vertical outcrop of coarse Old Red Sandstone and been propped with smaller slabs, probably left without a covering mound. Near the headland, close to the path there are several deep, scary but spectacular chasms where it would appear that bands of soft shale have been eroded by the sea from between beds of the harder sandstone.

Manorbier Beach

Manorbier Castle

High on a coomb running up from the Bay, a fairy-tale medieval castle stands on a low spur, while the even older church of St. James faces it from an equally strong bank that lies opposite. All these features at Manorbier (pronounced manor-beer) make it one of the most appealing places throughout the National Park. One well-travelled writer declared that this part of south-west Wales was at once the most beautiful and productive, Pembrokeshire the most attractive and Manorbier most assuredly without equal, 'the most pleasant place by far'. But this was not hyberbole by a modern travel 'hack' but part of a long tribute written in Latin and it came from a medieval scholar, high churchman and, not to be surprised at, a local boy with a lasting affection for his birthplace.

Born in the castle in *c.*1147 this was **Gerald de Barri**, and until his teens he would have worshipped at that church and often relished an idyllic coastal scene that was not essentially different from all that is still enjoyed today. His family name came from Barry Island, off the Glamorgan coast, and William, Gerald's father, was a Norman knight who had married well to Angharad, a daughter of the Norman governor of Pembroke, Gerald of Windsor, and of Nest — who was a grand-daughter of the all powerful Rhys ap Tewdwr. Gerald was sent to the Benedictine Abbey at Gloucester when he was old enough, and afterwards spent a period in Paris before returning to Wales to hold several livings, including Tenby, Angle and Mathry in Pembrokeshire as well as becoming a prebendary of Hereford, a canon of St. Davids and, from 1175 when he was still only 28 years of age, archdeacon of Brecknock (see pp.168-169). Although he must often have been absent from his residence at Llanddew and the diocese on other affairs, he retained the title until he resigned in 1203, until then, while turning down offers at Bangor, Llandaff and two Irish sees, constantly hoping that one day he might become bishop of St. Davids — and archbishop of a Wales that would be independent from Canterbury. Then in his mid-50s, he devoted himself largely to writing a total of 17 books, some of them becoming invaluable source material of 12th-century history. He died in obscurity in 1223 and is thought to have been buried at St. Davids Cathedral.

The outer walls and battlements of the de Barri family home are still remarkably intact and in a good state of preservation after all this time, thanks to the durability of the local limestone and mortar used in their construction, and also because Manorbier was not involved in any serious conflict. It was much more a stately mansion than a military fortress until it degenerated into a farm during the 16th century.

Manorbier Castle main gateway

Today's main entrance way follows a path that crosses what is left of the outer ward, passing a 16th-century barn to arrive at the inner ward through the gatehouse. The former guard room has now become a shop where it is possible to obtain an authoritative guidebook. The booklet provides a history covering details of the de Barri baronial estate, of the buildings and defences as they evolved from the 12th century until reaching their prime in the late 13th and changes that then took place from the 14th through to the 20th century. Just past the shop, part of the 16th-century barn was converted in the 1880s into a modern house, now a holiday home, and flowering herbaceous borders and seats were placed around the walls of the inner court. Rooms in the adjacent Round Tower have been used as bedrooms for guests, including RAF servicemen of two World Wars. Before then, during the 19th century, many cellars are said to have been adopted by smugglers, while now Manorbier Castle provides a romantic setting for films and theatre — with an inevitable reputation as a haunt of ghosts.

If you walk for 1½ miles from Manorbier along the Coast Path towards Freshwater East (i.e. with the sea on your left!), you suddenly come upon **Swanlake Beach**. Formed from sand, shingle and rock, it is in one of the most secluded coves in Pembrokeshire and is recommended as a good place 'to get away from it all ... with plenty of peace and quiet'. Certainly rather a magical place, it is set among high red sandstone cliffs, facing south and benefiting from afternoon sun. The rock pools are absorbing, bathing is safe and you are unlikely to be sharing with many other people, for the beach lacks a car park.

From Manorbier continue along the B4585 and after about ¾ mile turn left onto the A4139 and follow the signs for Freshwater East. The A4139 runs through Jameston and Hodgeston as far as the outskirts of Lamphey, where you turn left on the B4584 for Freshwater East, where a good road descends steeply to reach two car parks, one on the left for the disabled with a wheel chair path to a viewpoint above the beach, and the main one on the right.

4. Freshwater East

The contrast here with Swanlake Beach (see 3 above) could hardly be greater, for Freshwater East has been accessible and very popular ever since before the Second World War. This is clear from the sprawling range of buildings that must have been put up on the hillside above the beach before better management was introduced under the post-war Town and Country Planning Acts and, from 1952, by National Park measures. Then in the 1970s, Trewent Park holiday park was set out in the valley to the west of the bay, complete with self-catering holiday homes, chalets, a touring caravan site and shop. The sand and shingle beach faces east in an arc and is sheltered from prevailing winds by Trewent Point, regarded as safe for swimming and good for sailing, canoeing, water skiing, surfing and fishing. Also there are good walks, but in the Burrows behind the beach everyone is especially urged to keep to the marked footpaths. These dunes have been created over time from on shore winds that have driven sand grains inland to build up around the obstacles and slopes here, and are particularly notable also at Tenby, Freshwater West, Whitesand, Newport and Poppit. The habitat is fragile and colonisation by dune plants such as sand sedge, spurges, sea holly,

Freshwater East

sea bindweed, chickweed and lichens that lead to a thickening turf is compromised by trampling feet. Roots of selected plants, notably marram grass, penetrate for many feet, helping to stabilise the dunes as the grass allows the build up of further sand — provided they too are not disturbed.

Moving on, the Stackpole Road begins just beyond the car parks and climbs past East Trewent, running nearly parallel with the undulating Coast Path that passes the rocky headland of Greenala Point and the Iron Age promontory fort at its summit. Take the next left turn to descend to **Stackpole Quay** (or carry straight on if you wish to by-pass this spot and head straight into **Stackpole**). To reach the village from Stackpole Quay, backtrack past the strongly built estate lime-kiln on the left and take the first left turn to rejoin the road that leads to Stackpole.

5. Stackpole

In 1976, the National Trust acquired 2,000 acres of the Stackpole Estate between Stackpole and Bosherton, for the previous 300 years the heart of the Cawdor family estate in south-west Wales. Long before that, Stackpole was a Norman holding and through the centuries was extended to become a highly desirable county estate of productive farms, woodlands, sandy beaches, dunes and miles of spectacular sea cliffs. Built towards the end of the 18th century a short walk from today's spacious car park (charges except for NT members), **Stackpole Quay** enabled coal and other goods to be landed for use at Stackpole Court and on the estate, and limestone from the quarry to be loaded for burning in kilns along the coasts. It also acted as an anchorage for the Cawdor family yacht, the *Speedwich* and, still thought to be Britain's

smallest harbour, is now in use by local fishermen, small boat-owners and for outdoor pursuits based at the Stackpole Centre. This is at Home Farm, part of a range of historic farm buildings that survived the demolition of the Hall. There are six self-catering cottages, three group houses, a hydro-therapy suite, leisure suite and other recreational facilities, while outdoor activity includes canoeing, rock-climbing, abseiling, cycling, horse-riding, music and drama. Close by, Stackpole for Outdoor Learning is a National Trust residential 'environmental centre' that operates throughout the year and is open to applicants of all ages. Close to the main car park, the Trust has converted other old estate buildings into well designed holiday cottages and, just above the quay, the equally favoured Boathouse Tearoom. Nearby, another initiative has seen the old quarry adapted for rock climbing, abseiling and other physical activity, along with picnic and barbecue sites and viewpoints of the stunning coastline. At closer range, careful study of the rocks in the area reveals interesting geological features and a bounty of fossils.

Stackpole Quay

Barafundle Bay

Barafundle Bay is not served by a road or car park, and the only way to reach the beach involves an initial climb joining the Coast Path from sea level up to the headland and then a steep descent down steps to what in 2004 was voted 'the Best Beach in the UK'. Small wonder that the Cawdors kept it strictly to themselves, that they chose to bequeath the family name of Lort to a cave on one side of the bay and Griffith Lort's Hole on the other, and that the wall straddling the arched gateway at the top of the steps was felt necessary to keep out the park deer. East facing, the beach is sheltered from prevailing winds, and the golden sand, high bathing water quality and general good management consistently earn it the annual Green Coast Award. The Coast Path continues onward from the far side of the beach to circle Stackpole Head, one of the most spectacular promontories in Pembrokeshire, amidst a wealth of wildflowers spread above awesome limestone cliffs, with sea caves, blow holes and sheer–sided coves and in the company of colonies of breeding guillemots, razorbills and kittiwakes, even occasional islander puffins.

The National Trust boundary embraces **Stackpole Warren**, the name indicative of Norman times when rabbits were introduced for food and fur. But this limestone plateau with its blown sand cover forms a landscape that dates at least as far back as the Bronze Age (*c*.2,500–800 BC), perhaps even to the Mesolithic period (*c*.10,000–5,000 BC). Archaeologists have found remains of hut circles and field systems of the more recent Iron Age (*c*.800 BC–AD 43) and are sure that there is still much else waiting to be discovered. In addition to all the overlying sand and bracken, there is a turf of lime-loving grasses and many other plants that are grazed by cattle, sheep and ponies, and maybe even descendents of the original rabbits. This special habitat supports butterflies and many other invertebrates, while for the botanists the important plant communities include the really rare lichens that contributed towards making the Warren part of the designated 500-acre National Nature Reserve lying within the Trust's 2,000-acre Stackpole Estate.

Also included are the triple waters of the **Bosherston Pools** that formed part of the development of the Cawdor seat at Stackpole Court. Rebuilding of the earlier mansion began in 1734, to be followed by further remodelling, alterations and embellishments. Ancillary works such as construction of the stable block followed during the rest of the century, while the grounds overlooking the adjacent valley were artistically laid out with gardens, greenhouses, walks and other features. Then after half a century the scenery was transformed by the damming and flooding of the valley that crossed the estate near the mansion to form a long, narrow freshwater lake. It produced a magnificent vista that ran down past the mansion towards the sea at Broad Haven, while crossed at its north end by a stylish one-arch bridge carrying the main entrance drive and, part way down, by an elegant eight-arch bridge. Controlling dams were discretely positioned, and by the mid-19th century two further sheltered valleys had been dammed, to merge at a central lake just to the rear of the beach and creating what is still the largest expanse of open water in the National Park. After Stackpole Court was demolished, the lakes, adjoining areas of marsh and woodland of the large Estate acquired by the National Trust in 1976, duly became part of the Nature Reserve jointly managed with the Countryside Council for Wales.

The famous **Lily Pools** are within the western arm of the lake and are at their best when the white flowers (the native *Nymphaea alba*) are in bloom in early summer, while the highly fertile water that is fed from springs percolating through the limestone supports large populations of indigenous aquatic plants, pond-dwelling invertebrates, countless fish, shy furry animals, including otters, and rarely seen birds. From among more than 18 miles of footpaths linking the lakes, woods, cliffs and beaches, walks alongside the lakes can be joined from Stackpole Quay, the Warren, Broad Haven beach, the Coast Path — and from the National Park car park at Bosherston.

To the south of the village a lane leads off left to **Broad Haven South** beach and the car park (NT) above the dunes at the head of steep steps down to the sands. Broad Haven South is the estate's second sheltered sandy beach and is regarded as safe for swimming, good for fishing and well situated for a wide choice of walks for those not wishing to spend all their time lazing on the beach. The stream running down the north side of the bay drains from the Bosherston Lakes, while the isolated limestone stack just offshore is mysteriously known as Church Rock.

Continue below Belvidere Hill to join the B4319 to the south of St. Petrox on which you turn left, and then left again along the road to Bosherston. Beyond Bosherston, the road continues south towards St. Govan's Head, which shelters the former small harbour of New Quay just to the east, at the foot of a deep valley in the rocks. There is a good car park where the road ends at Trevallen, and blocking a steep and narrow ravine in the cliffs is the tiny medieval Chapel of St. Govan.

6. St. Govan's Chapel

St. Govan's chapel is surrounded by many wild stories and legends, down even to the precise number of narrow steps leading to and from it and its actual date of origin. But sober thoughts suggest that the present single vaulted nave and bellcote were a reconstruction of the 13th century to benefit pilgrims visiting the healing well of Govan, a 6th-century holy man.

St. Govan's Chapel and the nearby coastline to St. Govan's Head

The Castlemartin Firing Range — and Wildlife Conservation

This is divided into 'Range East' as far as the **Elegyg Stacks** and the **Green Bridge Natural Arch**, and 'Range West' onwards past Linney Head to Furzenip and Gupton Burrows. Both sections may be out of bounds during the week for training operations that can involve live shells, mortar bombs and grenades, but general public access as far as the Green Bridge is usually permitted at weekends and over bank holidays. Beyond that point access is generally forbidden, but throughout the year the National Park Authority organises guided tours by bus or on 3, 6 and 10 mile rambles that explore the archaeology, history, geology, biodiversity and scenery on the Range. Numbers are limited and no-one under 11, or dogs, can go, warm clothing and sturdy footwear are advised, booking is essential (at 01239 820912) and everyone going meets at Pembroke TIC at The Commons (see below). There is limited optional transport from Pembroke/Pembroke Dock. Information Centres in the area are also helpful about Range access arrangements.

Those who participate can assess the ecological outcome of robust military activity in this large 'no-go' area. Tank and other vehicle movements and targeting obviously cause damage, but movement has been restricted to constructed tracks and firing is directed to specific areas and is not all over the place. A high proportion of the total acreage is thus undisturbed and, unlike modern intensive farming practice, it is not drenched with herbicides, insecticides or artificial fertilizers, or have its hedges and trees widely grubbed up. From 1948, such 'unimproved' land across the one-time Stackpole Estates livestock and arable farmland within the Ranges has encouraged many native wild flowers and plants to flourish, aided by winter grazing livestock brought down from the Preseli Hills. These sheep and cattle both provide natural fertilizer and also keep down invasive, smothering scrub, gorse and long grasses. All this process supports many species of insects, butterflies, birds and mammals whose habitats are so threatened elsewhere and it leads to the designation of many parts of the Range as Sites of Special Scientific Interest.

The Green Bridge of Wales

Retrace your route back to the B4319 on which your turn left towards Castlemartin.

When access is allowed, you may wish to take the lane to the left just beyond the Camp and the village of Merrion which leads to a car park above the much-photographed Elegyg Stacks and the Green Bridge Natural Arch, 'bird rich' like the entire coastline with razorbills, guillemots (*elegug* is Viking for guillemot), fulmars, kittiwakes, shags and others — even perhaps rare choughs and peregrines.

Then, either return to the B road and turn left, or if you have chosen, or been forced to carry on in any event, continue along the B road through Castlemartin to descend nearer to sea level at the approach to the long and impressive sweep of rocks, golden sand and pebbles that is breezy Freshwater West.

7. Freshwater West

Freshwater West

Overlooking the beach from the south, just above the firing range limit at Little Furzenip and the beach, a last remaining thatched seaweed storage hut has been rebuilt by the National Park Authority and volunteers as a reminder of days when edible brownish-purple seaweed (*porphyra umbilicalis*) was farmed from intertidal rocks around here. After drying on the draughty hut floors, the seaweed was sent off to Swansea to be boiled into laver bread, or *bara lawr*, combined with oatmeal and fried with bacon. It was a staple, inexpensive part of the diet of Welsh miners in the Valleys and is still available at Swansea Market, Llanelli and elsewhere, some of it even in tins. Now regarded as something of a delicacy, at least by those who can bring themselves to face the dark, glutinous appearance, the texture and the taste, it is sometimes called 'Welsh Caviare'.

The beach faces due west, receiving Atlantic rollers with the full force of the western wind behind them — highly popular therefore with surfers and the venue for Welsh, English and European Amateur Championships. This time any red flags are meant to indicate danger for bathers from an undertow on the ebb tide, strong currents and quicksands. Many ships have come to grief on the shore, forced in by strong westerly gales. One of the most tragic of all disasters occurred in 1943 when two unwieldy army landing craft, unable to shelter at Fishguard or Milford Haven, foundered in heavy seas just off the beach. Very many young Royal Marines and crew were drowned, leaving just three survivors despite brave rescue attempts from a Royal Navy sloop, six of whose sailors were also lost.

There is safety these days in all the rock pools at the south end, and when most of the sand disappears at high tide, the National Trust sand dunes provide a good alternative as long as everyone keeps to the marked paths — for they are classed as a Site of Special Scientific Interest. Another example of botanic, as well as historic interest lies just offshore, where the stumps of forest trees, drowned some 5,000 years ago, may with luck still be seen at the lowest tides — just as at other coastal stretches met on these tours. Not far inland, there is also another example of a Neolithic burial chamber, not unlike that at Manorbier (above) in the form of a sandstone capstone supported at one end by three uprights. Named the **Devil's Quoit**, it is visible at Brownhill Burrows, close to the B4320 from Pembroke and just to the right of the junction where we turn left for Angle.

Continue along the B4319, turning left where it meets the B4320. The road terminates after a right turn in the village of Angle that leads towards Angle Bay and a limited amount of parking at the end.

8. Angle. Oil and Whisky Galore

At the entrance to the waterway at the remote tip of the long peninsula on the southern side of Milford Haven, Angle was little more than a remote fishermen's hamlet not so long ago, and a reminder has existed in St. Mary's churchyard since 1447, when the small Fishermen's **Chapel of St. Anthony** was built. Another memory of those times is the building that lies just to the north, sometimes known locally as **The Old Rectory**, but originally designed to serve as a defence against pirates who lurked in the Haven. A Grade I Listed Building, this is a tower house, or pele tower, three storeys high — its original entrance reached only by ladder to a first-floor doorway. Far more widespread concern existed during the 16th century because of the thought that the Haven might be invaded by the Spanish, and in 1580 an **East Block House** was built on the headland to operate as a defence in association with a **West Block House** on the opposite Dale peninsula. Apprehension about the vulnerability of the Waterway continued into the 18th century, by which time the French were the main worry. More elaborate lines of defence were devised, but only partly implemented because of cost. Horatio Nelson observed early in the 19th century that he regarded Milford Haven as one of the finest natural harbours in the world, but it took more than another half-century before further defensive steps were taken. These involved the construction of an expensive series of massive forts, armed with the latest guns — but by then they were too late, the French threat had passed and never a shot was fired in anger from any of them. One fort was at **Chapel Bay**, to the west of the modern Lifeboat Station and in 1863 another, planned to be closer to the naval dockyard, at Popton Point just to the east of Angle Bay. Although regarded as one of 'Palmerston's Follies' because of all the wasted effort and costs, approximately 100 years later it was to acquire a very useful, although altogether different function.

By the 1950s the demands of **oil** and petroleum production required the use of ever increasing sizes of tankers and many more refineries, but places with the necessary depths of water, suitable land and a sufficient labour force were rare. However Milford Haven satisfied all requirements and long jetties started to appear from 1959 — linked by pipe-work to adjacent or distant refineries. Of the five oil companies arriving up to the early 1970s, BP opened its ocean terminal at Popton Point in 1961 and soon some 9 million tons of oil were being pumped for refining over 60 miles away at Llandarcy, east of Swansea, facilitated by high-tech uses of the company's 19th-century fort. But it was not long before changing economic and other factors caused the installation to close and be cleared. The jetties were leased to Texaco, which covered 550 acres further upstream at Rhoscrowther and linked by underwater pipe-work with the Gulf refinery on the north shore. Downstream, opposite Angle Bay and Point, Esso had also departed, but after 13 years, operations at South Hook and Herbrandston were under way to refurbish the long jetty to bring two berths back into use. They are intended for gargantuan tankers that are to bring shipments of liquefied natural gas (LNG) from Qatar in the Gulf, and the aim from 2007 is to provide the UK with 20% of its entire gas consumption needs by a 196km National Grid pipeline from here through Tirley in Gloucestershire. The costs include an amount for protecting a 1,000 year old coral bed, for linking the tankers to re-gasification plant on land and the conveyance of rubble and redundant material by sea to reduce inland lorry movements — the Gulf state and the petro-gas giant Exxon Mobil sharing the total bill.

Directly opposite, sheltered away from the main waterway, **Angle Bay** (or East Angle Bay as locals sometimes call it) is a good anchorage for leisure craft and the shallow water and mud is popular with waders and ducks but is not good for bathing, rock pooling or building sandcastles. For this, the sheltered sand and rock beach at **West Angle Bay** at the other end of the single, long village street is much better, about a mile to the west. It has a large car park and a café near what remains of the former brickworks and there are good views of the shipping passing up and down the fjord-like waterway, and across to **St. Ann's Head**.

West Angle Bay and Thorn Island Fort

Nothing shows above the surface to indicate the reefs in the narrow entrance channel, or close to the coasts, but the grounding off St. Ann's Head of the tanker *Sea Empress* in 1996 and pollution of many miles of coastline and much of the sea with 77,000 gallons of oil is a lasting reminder of the hazards that exist out there. The cliffs to the east of the bay lead round to the ruins of the Elizabethan tower and the 19th-century East Block House, referred to above, and also the disused wartime RAF radar station site near the Rat Island spur, and then southwards towards Sheep Island, Parsonsquarry Bay, Guttle Hole and Freshwater West. To the right of the car park, tracks lead up around the point towards Chapel Bay fort, and above that on **Thorn Island**. This was built from 1852, later 'made over' into a hotel, and in 1894 was the scene of another disastrous grounding, when the *Loch Shiel*, bound for Adelaide, foundered with 7,500 cases of high proof whisky, a great deal of beer — and dynamite. Those who have read the book

Whisky Galore, or seen the film, will guess what ensued between the villagers and customs men as the cargo started to float ashore. Over to the north-west, close to South Hook Point and the deep water jetty for Exxon Mobil's huge LNG tankers is the fort at **Stack Rock**, another of 'Palmerston's Follies' that was not needed to fend off the French.

Angle, like many place names in these parts, is thought to have Norse origins and to indicate the corner or turning point at the entrance to the Haven. It is also the end of the road and where this route turns to begin the journey back towards Tenby. Retrace your steps to the junction of the B4319 and B4230, this time keeping left on the B4320, passing above the Haven and the Texaco refinery. Major explosions at the plant in 1992 and 1994 caused very worried villagers of Rhoscrowther to sell up their homes to the company for demolition and move away, along with the post office and pub and closure of the medieval St. Decuman's Church. Further east at Pwllcrochan, the oil-burning Pembroke Power Station, built between 1963 and 1972 as one of the largest of its kind in Europe, was demolished at the end of the century because of crippling fuel costs.

After Hundleton the road passes Monkton and the Priory Church just before reaching the A4139 at Pembroke, where a right turn leads to convenient car parks and the TIC at the area known as **The Commons**. This is where the gasworks, slaughterhouse, tanneries, an iron foundry and other noxious trades used to be, while still remaining to the south is Orange Gardens, the neatly set out 19th-century suburb built to house Pembroke Dockyard workers.

9. Pembroke. Birthplace of a Royal Dynasty

Originally marshland, The Commons was near the eastern end of one of two prongs of the tidal Pembroke River that lay some three miles upstream from the Haven waterway. This was navigable as far as Monkton Bridge and between the two creeks there was a long, high ridge of carboniferous limestone. It formed a commanding and eminently defendable prominence in a region of fertile soils, equable climate with ready access by water to the sea, and inevitably attracted human settlement. This seems to have started up to 12,000 years ago during the last Ice Age when a large cavern in the rock, now known as **The Wogan**, was occupied. Artefacts indicate that cave dwellers followed periodically throughout later periods of the Stone Age, into the Bronze Age and up to the end of the Roman occupation. Up on the surface, there is a strong likelihood that the promontory was adopted as the site of an Iron Age Fort, and that it later became a building plot for a local nobleman. There is no doubt that it appealed as a base and stronghold for the invading Normans, and at the western end in 1093 they built a fortification 'from wooden stakes and turf', as Giraldus Cambrensis was to put it almost a century later. However this was strong enough to hold out against early attacks by the Welsh, and following creation of the first Earldom of Pembroke the county was granted palatine status of full independence for the next four centuries until the reign of Henry VIII, Pembroke having

Pembroke Castle showing the massive round keep built by William Marshal to the left of centre

*The castle and quay from Mill Bridge
across the Pembroke River*

already received its first royal charter from Henry I. Endowed with these privileges and related administrative and commercial advantages, Pembroke flourished and was immune from the debilitating 13th-century Welsh wars being suffered elsewhere, but unease led to reinforcement of the defences. Work on the present **castle**, including its massive cylindrical keep, and on the solid stone walls that surrounded the town were initiated by William Marshal (the third earl from 1189) and continued for many years afterwards by his successors. Governed by the narrowness of the limestone ridge, these established the shape of the town along a single, long main street lined with houses on some 227 burgage plots sloping down to the town walls and towards the creeks. There were North, East and West main gates, a small pedestrian postern gate for late-comers after dark and six wall towers. Of these, Barnard's Tower at the north-east corner of the settlement was the most important, covering as it did the only side of the town that was not protected by water. The Normans brought in immigrant settlers as the sole occupants and these were expected to provision and service the castle garrison and take up arms to defend the territory if required. The native Welsh population was kept outside.

Ownership of the castle passed through several hands with many vicissitudes of fortune and effects that generally involved dilapidation and neglect, until it became the turn of Jasper Tudor. Unlike many of his absentee predecessors, he took up residence at Pembroke Castle and for the first time for more than 150 years became closely interested and involved in its upkeep. His 'hands on' approach produced much essential renovation work, as well as new features that could well have included the detached 'mansion house' in the Outer Ward. He also attended to the needs of other parts of his lordship, like those of Tenby in the late 1450s (above).

Jasper Tudor had received the earldom of Pembroke in 1452 from his half-brother, the Lancastrian King Henry VI (d.1471), son of Queen Katherine of Valois, widow of Henry V (d.1422). His older brother, Edmund, was made earl of Richmond but died at Carmarthen in 1456 (p.45) and afterwards his 14-year-old widow, Margaret Beaufort, was received under Jasper's protection at Pembroke Castle. Quite believably within the Henry VII Tower, she bore their only child, immediately the new earl of Richmond, on 24 January 1457. But the Wars of the Roses were looming, and led by Jasper Tudor in 1461, the Lancastrians were decisively defeated at Mortimer's Cross in Herefordshire by forces under Edward, duke of York, who later that year became King Edward IV. Taken captive, Owen Tudor, the second husband of Queen Katherine and father of Edmund and Jasper, was beheaded at Hereford, and deprived of his earldom, for the next ten years Jasper became a fugitive before setting sail from Tenby for exile in France with his 14-year-old nephew, Henry Tudor. A further 24 years would pass before they returned to Wales with an army via Milford Haven, near Dale, to confront Richard III in battle at Bosworth (p.120), and for Jasper to regain his title and castle.

Without an heir, Jasper's firm influence died with him in 1495 and afterwards the Act of Union brought the old County of Pembroke under Crown control, from 1536 leaving the castle with no obvious future role. However in 1642, unique among Welsh towns, Pembroke declared for Parliament at the start of the

Civil War and the castle was strengthened to serve as a base for the local force commander, Colonel Laugharne. But in 1648 the town changed sides in support of the imprisoned king and was then subjected to a daunting two-month siege under the personal direction of Oliver Cromwell. After the garrison finally surrendered, one of the three rebellious leaders held in the Tower of London, mayor John Poyer, drew the short straw in a grim lottery ordered between them and was accordingly executed by firing squad. Cromwell also ordered that the castle be slighted 'so that it may not be possest by the enemy', leaving the Great Gatehouse and adjoining towers along the south frontage severely damaged — along with much of the town and its walls. As was then common

The barbican entrance to Pembroke Castle

practice, further destruction was caused by the 'quarrying' of stone by townspeople for new building projects and this only ended when the Victorian antiquarian, J.R. Cobb, began a process of restoration. He was followed energetically by Major General Sir Ivor Phillips from 1928 with a comprehensive and costly programme that was completed at the castle just before the Second World War, just in time for troops of the Royal Fusiliers to be quartered in the Outer Ward.

Now owned and managed by the Pembroke Castle Trust, it is the largest and most important castle in Wales not in State care and exceeded in size in the south only at Caerphilly. The Trust has helpfully published a very readable, well illustrated guidebook by Neil Ludlow, *Pembroke Castle. Birthplace of the Tudor Dynasty*, and it is available at the Castle Shop near the entrance.

However, before exploring the inside, visitors would first do well to take in views of the stunning exterior of the castle, and starting from the TIC and car parks at The Commons, the best way to do this is to head westwards on foot for Monkton Bridge. There was formerly a quay here, with warehouses, a boatyard and busy commercial area, ships arriving from the Pembroke River and sea where there is now a barrage. This controls the tidal flow, retains water levels in the Castle Pond, prevents flooding of the Commons area in the winter and admits small craft into the pond through a water gate at high tides. Some of the best views can be gained by following the edge of the pond and crossing this barrage to face the building from the north. Then retrace your steps to reach the path immediately below the castle.

As another rewarding diversion, on a hilltop above and to the right just off the B4320 road from Angle, the **Priory Church of St. Nicholas and St. John** is on the site of an early Celtic Christian church. It was founded in *c*.1098 when Arnulf de Montgomery, who had received the castle from his father Roger, the Marcher earl of Shrewsbury, established a Benedictine priory at Monkton. After the Dissolution the 13th-century nave was another to be retained as the parish church and then renovated towards the end of the 19th century. Standing in the churchyard to face east, it is not difficult to appreciate why Oliver Cromwell should have chosen to mount his heavy guns there to pound the castle and town during the siege of 1648. Nearby, **Monkton Old Hall** contains remnants dating from the 14th century, was possibly the priory guesthouse and has now been restored for use by the Landmark Trust, while **Priory Farmhouse** is in the form of a 14th- or 15th-century fortified tower house, complete with a medieval dove-cote close by.

Westgate Hill, leading into the walled town from Monkton Bridge, begins at the site of the old West Gate close to where there is a group of medieval cottages, the oldest dwellings in Pembroke. This is the shortest way to the castle entrance, whereas a longer but very rewarding way takes to the footpath below the base of the castle, along the southern edge of the Castle Pond. It is where the return walk from the barrage (above) reached, and soon the route approaches the huge cavern in the rock called the **Wogan**, where puzzlement over the origins of the name have led to suggestions that it stems from 'ogof', which is Welsh for cave (and likewise pronounced locally with a short 'o'). The Normans built a large Watergate across the mouth of the cavern and used it for storage and probably as a boathouse — whence a spiral stair leads up into the Great Hall block of the castle. The path continues on to the South Quay, and starting point of an informative *Pembroke Town Trail* prepared by the Pembroke Civic Trust Society. It is possible here to reflect on how very busy this spot once was, crowded with sailing ships from France, Spain, Ireland and further abroad as they joined the British coastal traders. Daniel Defoe recorded a good idea of the scene in *c*.1724 in his account of *A Tour Through the Whole Island of Great Britain,* when he found Pembroke to be 'the largest and richest, and at this time, the most flourishing town of all S. Wales. Here are a great many English merchants, and some of them men of good business; and, they told us, there were near 200 sail of ships belonged to the town, small and great …'. There was sea trade at the quay until as late as 1961, and when the *Town Trail* was compiled, the last vessel, the *Kathleen and Mary* was still to be seen as St. Katherine's Dock in London. The quay ends at the **Mill Bridge** at the bottom of Dark Lane and the site of the North Gate — demolished in 1820 because of the heavy volume of traffic! The Mill Bridge carries the A4139 towards Pembroke Dock, but it is also a tidal barrage dating from the Middle Ages. Until 1956, when the mill was burnt out, it operated in an admirably 'green' and sustainable fashion by admitting water at high tide and then releasing it through the mill wheel with the ebb. This arrangement can still be seen in operation during the summer months at Carew (pp.86-87).

Dark Lane leads off to the right to join the appropriately named Main Street, and another short step leads to the castle entrance. Now called the Mill Pond Walk, the path continues onwards past a frequent population of water birds as far as the Pembroke and Tenby Railway embankment, built to cross the river in 1864. A tunnel connection through it leads to the Upper Mill Pond where many more bird and mammal species can be found at the nature reserve. The path turns with the old town wall line when they reach Barnard's Tower, where Blackhorse Walk leads southwards towards the East End and the site of the town's East Gate. This spanned Main Street and from there the wall line continues southwards by Gooses Lane until it turns towards the west to reach what is left of a rectangular tower, superimposed by a 19th-century summerhouse or gazebo. Then there is the site of another of the six wall towers and a limekiln built into the wall. Little of the southern section of wall shown on John Speed's Town Plan of 1610 has survived between there and the West Gate.

From East Gate Square, Main Street leads towards the town centre and castle, first reaching a number of fine Georgian and Victorian houses. Notable among these, especially for the high quality of its interior features, is No.111 Main Street. Built early in the 18th century and re-fronted in *c*.1840, it is one of some 90 Listed Buildings in the town and just one of the reasons why in 1977 the central area was designated as a Conservation Area of Outstanding Merit, having before that in 1964 been included on a select national list prepared by the Council for British Archaeology. **St. Michael's**, close by, is one of the two town centre medieval churches, their parish boundaries meeting at Elm Tree Square, the former site of the town gallows and stocks. Here Melbourne House and Hamilton House date from *c*.1810, sharing a pediment at the end of Hamilton Terrace and found at the start of where the Main Street shops and other commercial premises begin to appear. The York Tavern is one of the oldest pubs in town, close to New Way which drops steeply down to where it made the first planned break in the wall since it was built, but actually 'new' almost 300 years ago. Pembroke, by its nature, had many taverns and pubs in the past and some still exist along Main Street, notably the 18th-century King's Arms and the Lion Hotel former coaching inns. The shop fronts and signs are all too typically modern, but as in other historic towns there are many early 19th-century façades to be seen above fascia levels. They are contemporary with the **Town Hall**, set slightly back from the road, while opposite, the unmissable **Clock House** dates from nearer the middle of the century and afterwards, when it was extended and the tower rebuilt. Alongside to the north and, except for its massive tower, almost hidden away behind buildings is **St. Mary's parish church** at the corner with Dark Lane. Probably the older of the two in the town centre, it

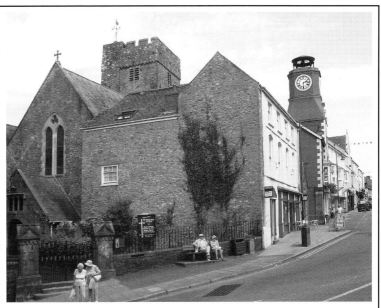

St. Mary's Church, Clock House and Main Street, Pembroke

dates from the late 12th and early 13th centuries but has some earlier traces that suggest that it might have been the church of the early Norman town.

Main Street meets Westgate Hill at a dropping off point at the main castle entrance, ticket office and shop. It was to complicate matters for an attacker that the Great Gatehouse was unusually defended here by a barbican. This is a fortified outwork and first line of defence. The Castle Trust *Guidebook* starts with the Outer Ward defences and then describes the Inner or Horseshoe Gate, leading to the Inner Ward, Chapel, Great Tower, wall turrets, Wogan Watergate and other structures. It also contains a background history that reaches back before the arrival of the Normans and also special features that include the Welsh ancestry of the Tudors, an explanation of the purpose of the castle and how it functioned, the way of life there and details of its architecture. From the end of May to the end of August, although not on Saturdays, the Trust conducts a number of guided daily tours, while the castle and exhibition rooms are open seven days a week throughout the year, except at Christmas time and on New Year's Day.

One way back to the TIC and car parks is down Westgate Hill to Monkton Bridge and then left for The Commons.

The rocky peninsula on which the town was built long ago determined a confined layout that still offers no real scope for any improvement in 21st-century through traffic measures. For the next leg of the journey it is therefore necessary to drive up Westgate Hill on the A4139, past the castle and briefly enter the town centre, before turning left into Dark Lane to cross Mill Bridge to head over the hill towards Pembroke Dock, about 2 miles to the north. Once through the narrow railway tunnel, you turn left at the T-junction and then go straight over the roundabout and traffic lights beyond to enter Pembroke Dock. Signs along lead to the ferry within what remains of the former dockyard and seaplane base.

10. Pembroke Dock. Warships, Royal Yachts and Flying-boats

The Story of Pembroke Dock could hardly differ more from that of Pembroke, for until 200 years ago there was little else but flat fields at the then small hamlet of Paterchurch, alongside the Milford Haven waterway. The nearest busy activity was 4 miles downstream at the Royal Naval Dockyard on the opposite shore where vessels had been built and launched since the closing years of the 18th century. They included the *Nautilus, Lavinia, Milford* and, in April 1814, the 74-gun *Rochefort*. Then that year the Admiralty decided to transfer the dockyard inland and upstream to Paterchurch, where the government already owned areas alongside deep inshore stretches of the waterway. Early in 1816 the sister 28-gun frigates *Valorous* and *Ariadne* slipped into the water there to launch a 106-year history of major shipbuilding at Pembroke Dock. Some of the finest ships of the Royal Navy were built from then until 1922, in a total of 260 military and civil vessels that included frigates, corvettes, submarines, wooden-wall battleships, a sequence of five royal yachts and many swift light cruisers for deployment in the First World War. Of all these, in 1834 the *Tartar* was a paddle boat and the first steam man-of-war, twelve years later the sloop *Conflict* was the first warship to be fitted with a screw propeller, the 80-gun *Lion* became the largest vessel in the RN of 1847, the *Duke of Wellington* the largest wooden-wall ship ever to be built, the *Windsor Castle* with 116 guns, the *Prince Consort*, the navy's second only ironclad of 1860, and finally the Admiralty oiler, *Oleander*, launched in 1922.

The dockyard provided specialist as well as unskilled work for more than 2,000 men during its heyday, first for building wooden-wall vessels and from the 1860s the ironclads. It eventually covered 90 acres and had 13 building slips beneath whale-back roofed ship sheds, while alongside the burgeoning activity at the yard, Paterchurch was absorbed in Pembroke Dock, to become the largest township in Pembrokeshire and one of the earliest 'new towns'.

The first houses at Front Street were built close to the river immediately to the east of the dockyard wall and they were followed by many others in a grid pattern of military precision, set well apart to facilitate the delivery by road of cumbersome raw materials. The opening of the GWR rail link and terminus in 1864 helped further in this, while permanent buildings went up on Llanion Hill by the end of the century to replace the defensible barracks and huts of the large military defensive force. But by then there were the first indications that the shipyard facilities were not up to the changing needs of the Royal Navy, which included numbers of very large Dreadnaught type battleships. Redundancies followed from 1906 and then early in the difficult post-war period further disaster struck when, on 22 June 1922, a serious fire precipitated closure of the dockyard, which followed four years later. There was no alternative work for the many skilled tradesmen or labourers and many were forced to move away, and in a town ravaged by unemployment the depleted spending power led to many bankruptcies throughout the area. Then in 1930 the yard was transferred

Sunderland flying-boat WL824 flew from Pembroke Dock during the war. Now a rarity at the RAF Museum, Hendon

to the Air Ministry and soon two Supermarine Southampton reconnaissance flying-boats entered service with No. 210 Squadron of the RAF, to be joined by Short Singapore III bi-plane flying-boats during the mid 1930s. These were immediate predecessors of the mono-plane Short Sunderlands — with a range of 2,980 miles these were to see the longest period of service in first line duties in its original designed role of all aircraft of the RAF. It entered squadron service at Pembroke Dock in 1938 and soon after the outbreak of war in September 1939 became quickly involved in the rescue of crews from torpedoed ships and the scourge of German U-boats during their attacks on merchant ships and convoys in the Battle of the Atlantic. With defensive as well as aggressive armament, the Sunderland earned the nickname of the 'Flying Porcupine' from German fighter pilots. During the mid-war years 'PD', as it was fondly known, became the largest operational flying-boat base in the world and at one count there were almost 100 flying-boats present in the water or in service areas, mainly Sunderlands but probably also the formidable Consolidated Catalina long range (4,000 miles) amphibious aircraft. (During the war F/O J.A. Cruikshank of No 210 Squadron was awarded the VC for his courageous attack on a submarine by a Sunderland, while on 7 May 1945 the 196th and final U-boat sunk by Coastal Command went to a Catalina of the same squadron).

But inevitably the air base, naval oil storage tanks, barracks and other installations at Pembroke Dock attracted the attention of the Luftwaffe as prime targets and the first bombing attack took place in July 1940. From then on the dock area and town suffered terrible damage from a succession of raids, the most dramatic when many of the 17 oil tanks at Llanreath received direct hits. Augmented by brigades from several parts of south Wales, a large number of firemen were killed while fighting the fierce flames and the skies were blackened for many days, choking the town and surrounding areas. Other raids followed and in May 1941 many lives were lost and nearly 2,000 homes damaged, along with the ordnance factory, while the gas works and the Three Crowns and Prince Albert pubs received direct hits. The last big raid was mainly with incendiary bombs in June 1941, involving further loss of life, but several years would pass before rebuilding work could start. One outcome of the raids was that small fighter stations were quickly sited around much of Pembrokeshire, the disused runways still recognisable on the Ordnance Survey sheets from Carew to St. Davids and Templeton to Fishguard.

The Sunderland base at Pembroke Dock closed in 1957, causing further depletion of the local economy that was resulting from the departure of the military forces, closure of the naval refuelling service and of small ship repair yards. But there were first signs of a new use for the waterway and in 1960 Esso opened the first oil terminal and refinery, to be followed by four other oil companies. The Milford Haven Port Authority was also encouraging leisure and tourism enterprises and in 1979 a Ro-Ro

One of the plaques on the eastern dock boundary along Commercial Road commemorating aspects of Pembroke Dock's history

ferry terminal was opened at the former dockyard. By the end of the century it had been adapted and enlarged to enable Irish Ferries to operate twice-daily freight and passenger services, taking 3 hrs 45 mins sea-crossing time to and from Rosslare.

Along the eastern dock boundary a 12ft-high wall borders Commercial Road as it heads towards Front Street (above), and has been used to mount a special series of plaques illustrating Pembroke Dock's past history, including the horrific blitzes and the happily remembered Sunderland era. Until the 1930s, ships landed cargo at the nearby quay alongside Front Street while now a raised walkway extends beyond the high tide line to the north-east **Martello Tower**. This was constructed in 1851 with an artillery piece on the roof as a small island fort of grey limestone ashlar, to defend the exterior of the dockyard wall in conjunction with the smaller south-west gun tower at the end of Fort Road. Since 1758 there had been another gun platform between the two at Pater Point but this was demolished in 1903, preceded by the disarming of the north-east tower in 1882. This was restored in 1994 and opened as a museum displaying features to illustrate its role during the 19th century aimed, as it turned out unnecessarily, at defending the shipyard against attack by the French.

The Martello Tower off Front Street

The Cleddau Bridge as seen from Hobbs Point

Hobbs Point is another place of interest that fronts the waterway a short distance upstream, just west of Llanion Hill. The pier and slipway there were built from 1830 to form the landing stage for the Irish packet boats plying to and from Waterford, and until the mid century it was the terminus of the Irish mail coaches from London. They came by today's A477 London Road and Pier Road and visitors can also now see where the river ferry from Neyland used to berth before the Cleddau Bridge opened in 1975, and where ships that had been launched down the dockyard slipways were often fitted out before commissioning.

Still used by pleasure boats, this is a good vantage point for marvelling at the slim and elegant proportions of the fine box-section form of the **Cleddau Bridge**, raised on six slender piers half a mile upstream above the waters of the Daugleddau — but remembering also the four workmen who were killed in 1970 when a section collapsed as it was under construction.

Looking across the Milford Haven waterway from Pembroke Dock

Both the A477 and A4139 can be followed to leave Pembroke Dock. At the roundabout on the edge of the town, head straight across on the A477 and then almost immediately right onto the A4139 back into Pembroke. Cross the Mill Bridge, then swing left along Main Street through the town centre. At the roundabout at the far end, go straight across onto the A4139 Tenby road. After about 2 miles you will reach Lamphey.

Brown signs here indicate **Lamphey Bishops Palace**, just off the main road past the tall embattled medieval tower of St. Faith and St. Tyfel Church and at the end of a short, shady avenue of trees.

11. Lamphey Palace. A Break for the Bishop

The medieval bishops of St. Davids were powerful prelates who exercised not just great religious power and influence in the diocese but also joined in important affairs of State in London and elsewhere. There were doubtless times however when they needed to escape as it all became too much, but whereas in the 21st century a self-catering fortnight in a holiday cottage might serve to recharge episcopal batteries, it would certainly not have been sufficient for a bishop of 700 years or so ago. The earliest reference to somewhere for the bishop to take his ease as a wealthy country gentleman dates from 1259 and the

The inner gatehouse beyond the archway (left) and the late Perpendicular chapel block east window of c.1522 (right)

days of Bishop Richard de Carew, but most of what can be seen today is thought likely to be the work of the very creative and artistic Henry de Gower, bishop from 1328 until 1347. He has been credited with the more than 27-yard long great hall at the eastern end of the site, distinguished by an arcaded parapet felt to be of the same order as those at St. Davids Bishops Palace (pp.133-134) and Swansea Castle ruins (p.11), although lacking their refinement. Below the ruins there is still a vaulted undercroft running for the full length of the ground floor, probably provided as a cool room. The courtyard was remodelled within a battlemented wall at this time and beyond it there were fishponds, fruit orchards, vegetable gardens and a great expanse of parkland providing for a thriving agricultural economy. Later work in the early 16th century included the chapel, with a finely proportioned Perpendicular window, attached to the northern wall of the old hall, but before long the palace was dismantled and passed to the Devereux family. Robert Devereux, earl of Essex and favourite of Elizabeth I, spent his early days there, but from the time of his execution for treason in 1601, Lamphey started to deteriorate and in the 18th century parts of the ruins were converted to farm buildings and in the 19th the site was turned into a walled garden. Now it is in the care of Cadw and the *Guidebook* by Rick Turner provides an illustrated history and tour of the buildings and grounds, along with other relevant features.

Decorated arcading similar to that at St. Davids Palace and at Swansea Castle

A drive leading from the car park near the palace entrance reaches the fine Lamphey Court, which is now converted to a country hotel, while to return to Tenby, backtrack towards the main road, and at the junction at the end of the driveway to the palace, turn left onto the minor road that runs along the ridgeway, turning left at the junction as you descend near Penally towards Tenby, and left again onto the A4139 into the resort.

Haverfordwest

Somewhat confusingly there are two Cleddau rivers in Pembrokeshire, an easterly one springing from the Preseli hills to approach the sea past Llawhaden and beneath Canaston Bridge, and the other over to the west with its source high above Fishguard. They join at Landshipping to merge as the Daugleddau (which means two rivers of the Cleddau), then to be joined by the Carew and Cresswell rivers and lesser streams to enter the Milford Haven waterway, (Aberdaugleddyf), that flows past the towns of Neyland, Pembroke Dock and Milford Haven to reach the sea at St. Ann's Head.

They have been crossed at places by tracks and roadways where the water levels and banks have allowed, and at the lowest practicable point before the Western Cleddau widens out from a steep-sided valley into mud flats and becomes tidal, the river bed of solid rock came into use as Haefer's Ford. This was from *haefer*, Norse for a goat, but the crossing was also well placed to profit from human passage, especially as there was the great commercial advantage of navigable sea access, albeit some 20 miles away at St. Ann's Head. There can be little doubt about the existence of an early settlement on the high rocky outcrop above the ford, and none whatever about the strategic significance of the site seized by the Normans when they reached the area soon after the Conquest. Probably built of timber, their first castle was founded in *c.*1110 by Gilbert de Clare, first earl of Pembroke, while Henry I sent groups of immigrants from Flanders to colonise the area and oust the native Welsh population. The small town that developed above Haefer's Ford became known as Haverford, in Welsh Hwlffordd, something of a corruption, but it was not until early in the 15th century that the word 'west' was added to Haverford to end any confusion with Hereford (army ford) in England. William Shakespeare later called it 'Har'fordwest' and this is how it is often still pronounced locally. Castleton, the early settlement, was small and confined to the area west of the castle close to St. Martin's Church, and not until the turn of the century did the town really begin to grow and be protected by walls, after a borough charter was granted by William Marshal, the then earl of Pembroke, creating burgesses and a merchant guild.

By 1188, when Giraldus Cambrensis, Gerald of Wales, visited with the archbishop of Canterbury on their recruiting drive for the Third Crusade, the castle had also been rebuilt in stone, while in *c.*1210 a **priory** was founded and endowed beside the river. Dedicated to St. Mary and St. Thomas the Martyr, this was a foundation of Austin Canons, known as the Black Canons as were those at Carmarthen (p.42) and Llanthony because of their habit

Haverfordwest Castle

The remains of the priory lie beyond the new County Hall and across the river, and include these raised gardens

and who also observed the rule of St. Augustine. Major excavations since 1983 have exposed extensive foundations of the priory and monastic buildings, the church measuring some 160 feet in length and 90 feet across the transepts of the cruciform building. The slight remains of the transepts, west end of the nave, and the footings, together with a reconstruction of the unexpected discovery of raised monastic gardens, now planted with species of the medieval period, can be reached from Quay Street.

In 1220 the town was attacked and badly damaged by Llywelyn ab Iorweth (the Great) but by the end of the century had recovered to become a sizeable and thriving borough. The castle, too, had been greatly built up by Eleanor of Castile, wife of Edward I and royal holder of the lordship of Haverford — in between raising their 16 children!

By 1324 Haverford contained 360 burgage plots, indicating a town of significant size for those days, comparing favourably with 421 in Cardiff, 281 in Carmarthen and only 70 in Caernarvon and 112 in Conwy in north Wales. A further sign of its importance was the presence of four churches, in addition to the priory and a Dominican friary founded in the mid 13th century in today's Bridge Street, between the two lanes called the Friars and the Hole in the Wall. Much success arose from the advantages of sea-borne trade through Ireland and along the coastline with outgoing cargoes of wool, hides, corn, malt and coal carried by barges and sea-going vessels of up to 250 tons burden. By the time the 10-year-old Richard II had ascended the throne in 1377 the town had further expanded to contain 422 burgages. But then external events took a turn after confidence in the king had waned because of his misrule, for when he landed at Haverford in 1399 he was seized by Bolingbroke's men, taken to Flint Castle, forced to abdicate and soon afterwards died 'in suspicious circumstances' at Pontefract Castle. Returning from exile, Henry Bolingbroke, earl of Derby, assumed the throne as usurper to become King Henry IV and in the consequent turmoil and widespread social crisis, the Glyndwr rising erupted in the following year. In 1405 the town was captured by a French force allied to the Welsh cause, although the castle was besieged but not taken. The Cleddau enabled vital supplies to reach the inhabitants of the borough, as when it was besieged in 1220.

Incorporation as the 'County and town of Haverfordwest' by royal charter in 1479 introduced autonomy and the offices of mayor, sheriff and other dignitaries. Henry VIII confirmed county status for the town in 1545 and under the Tudors and early Stuarts the continuing coastal trade led to a prosperous era. But the Civil War brought deep recession and left the town 'destitute and depleted', a state compounded by the return from the 1470s of a further devastating bout of the Black Death that this time accounted for a fifth of the total population, estimated by the mayor in 1651–2 to be of 'some 2,000 souls'. Cromwell, meanwhile, had ordered the **castle** to be slighted to prevent any further military use, and, as was then usually the case, the townspeople used much of what was left as a limestone and sandstone 'quarry' for their other building projects. Thus, although the castle still looks impressive from down below, a climb up the hill reveals that it is now hardly more than a shell of curtain walls and towers, much of it attributable to the efforts of Queen Eleanor. During the 19th century the outer ward was used for a prison, now the County Record Office, while the Haverfordwest Museum is in the former prison governor's house. Apart also from the hilly medieval street system and churches within the former walled area, the centre of the town is primarily a creation from the 18th century, when some of Pembrokeshire's top people kept town houses in Haverfordwest. **Foley House** in Gaol Street, designed by locally born John Nash, is often referred to — sometimes because of the shocking roughcast applied to its original stucco exterior in the 1950s. Another past celebrity, born in 1758 in a town house in Hill Street, was General Sir Thomas Picton, whose military career was ended by a musket ball to the head at Waterloo in 1815.

However the 19th-century personality who left the most enduring impression across much of the face of Haverfordwest was William Owen, the county surveyor from 1832. As Haverfordwest Civic Society's *Welcome to the Visitor* records, he radically remodelled much of the worst parts of the town and was responsible for the **Shire Hall** in 1837, only one of a number of his fine public buildings. 'He transformed the eastern approach to the town by creating new streets (Victoria Place and Picton Place), built the New Bridge (which he financed himself) so forming an extension of the High Street'. As well as all this, he was mayor of Haverfordwest four times and, as the Civic Society concludes, 'Haverfordians still walk, literally, in his shadow'. (But at the heart and capital of a scenic county such as this it is a pity that they also have to walk in the shadows of far less worthy contributions to the townscape from post war architects, developers and planning committees of the 20th century).

The South Wales Railway from Newport reached the town in 1853 and not only provided greater mobility for Haverfordians, it also created an effective link between industrial Wales and the agrarian south-west. This helped greatly to reduce transport costs for farmers, especially for supplies of lime needed to 'sweeten' their acid soil, for other effective fertilizers such as guano and basic slag, and for conveying produce to feed hungry mouths through new markets in the smoky new communities. The consequent rise in countryside productivity during the second half of the century was reflected in what was being spent on building works or house extensions in the towns, extensive restoration works at the churches and by 1900 ten Nonconformist chapels had risen in Haverfordwest. In 1888 the borough was merged with Pembrokeshire and became the county town.

The rail service was, however, to have an immediate impact on the river trade, while competition from Milford Haven, much closer to the sea, intensified as it expanded as a town and port. Soon the quay alongside the Western Cleddau, so much used and extended from medieval times, fell quiet as the port went into steep decline and the river silted up, while the mayor retained in name only his ancient function and title of 'Admiral of the Port of Haverfordwest'.

Part of the riverside is now again commercially active as the **Riverside Quay Shopping Centre**, across the river from a large **indoor market** on stilts where some produce is still brought in from the local area. A

The indoor market opposite the Riverside Quay Shopping Centre

fortnightly outdoor Farmers' Market is also reminiscent of early medieval times when produce and articles were brought to be sold each week at the Sunday market in St. Mary's churchyard. Nowadays, however, all goods arrive by road and nothing comes up the Cleddau.

With a population of *c.*12,000 inhabitants by the early 21st century, Haverfordwest is at the hub of Pembrokeshire as a major shopping, professional service, educational and administrative centre with major roads radiating to everywhere else in west Wales.

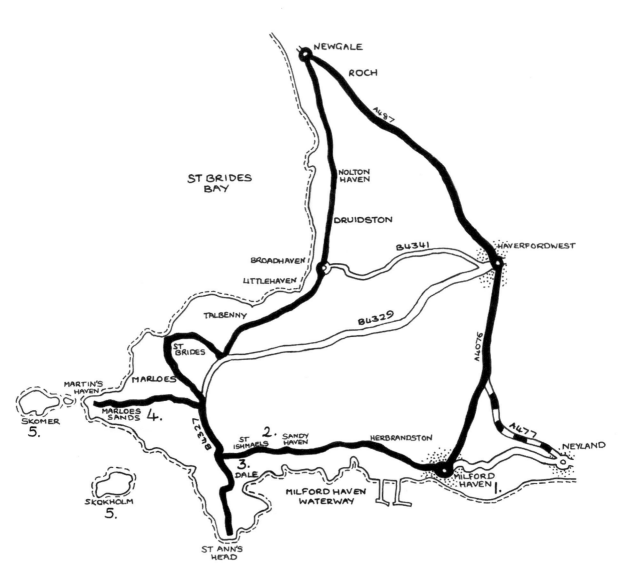

Outline map for Tour 5
The numbers 1 to 5 relate to the boxed information given within the tour

Tour 5   Milford Haven and St. Brides Bay

This tour is largely on B and minor roads and explores, as its title suggests, the coastline around Milford Haven and St. Brides Bay. It can include visits to Dale, the St. Ann's Head peninsula, Marloes and Musselwick Sands, Martins Haven and a departure point for boat trips to Skomer and other off-shore islands, Little Haven, Broad Haven, Druidston Haven, Nolton Haven and Newgale Sands. Without any detours the distance is about 35 miles (OS Landranger 157).

Starting from Haverfordwest, the route follows the A4076 south-westwards towards Milford Haven, past the A477 junction for Neyland just beyond the straggling village of Johnston. The approach to Milford Haven at Steynton is marked by the hilltop medieval **church of Sts. Cewydd and Peter**. It was altered and restored during the 18th and 19th centuries, and in the nave there is a 6th-century stone cross with letters carved in Latin and Ogham scripts. The road continues towards the waterfront at The Rath, and a raised look-out view of a panorama of the Daugleddau Waterway and its range of interesting features and activities. To park and take in the view, when you reach the church on the left just above the waterway, turn left (in effect you continue straight ahead), and then right at the T-junction and park along this road.

---

1. Milford Haven and Neyland

Standing high above the waterway it is possible to reflect over much of what has happened to the town of Milford Haven, or Milford as it is also called, during 200 years of faltering development and periods of boom and debilitating bust. Until the late 18th century, except for small settlements at Hakin and Castle Pill, there was little but acres of farmyard and an ancient sailors' chapel, but they became parts of a large Pembrokeshire estate that passed in 1782 to Sir William Hamilton upon the death of his first wife, Catherine Barlow — of the well-to-do Slebech family. He recognised the potential of his well situated inheritance but, based overseas as a career diplomat, he was unable to be on hand to plan and implement any projects. But in order to create what he envisaged as a new riverside town, he made a start in 1790 by securing Parliamentary powers to 'make and provide quays, docks, piers &c. and to establish a market with roads and avenues …'. Some time later he was also able to appoint a forceful, enterprising agent to act on site on his behalf, his nephew Charles Greville. By the end of the 18th century, three long streets were laid out in parallel on a gridiron pattern as Hamilton Terrace, Charles Street and Robert Street, and Greville also built a riverside quay, a Customs House and a hotel.

Ideas had formed about promoting Milford as a trans-Atlantic port in competition with Liverpool, of establishing ship-building yards, and also pursuing a novel way of meeting a lucrative demand for lamp oil, mainly for street lighting. This was at around the time of the American War of Independence, when Quaker whalers of Nantucket Island, Massachusetts, were out of favour and meeting difficulties for remaining supporters of the king. Greville, with government support, offered inducements for some of them to resettle at Milford in order to set up a whaling industry that would produce sperm oil. In doing

Commemorative statue of a fisherman above the Haven opposite the jetties for the Texaco refinery

this, they also, quite surprisingly for them, built a brewery. It was also a time when the Royal Navy needed to build up the Fleet for combat against the French, and the Admiralty was encouraged to place orders for warships to be built on the riverside.

In 1802, at the height of his fame in combating Napoleon, Admiral Nelson was invited to visit the embryo town and the Haven, along with Sir William Hamilton and his second wife, the gorgeous former Emma or Emily Lyon — and by then Horatio's mistress. He found no difficulty in praising Milford Haven waterway in a speech, bracketing it with Trincomalee in Ceylon to be the finest of all natural harbours that he knew, and he also supported Greville's naval dockyard initiative. Two men-of-war had already been built and launched in 1801, and following upon Nelson's words of encouragement, the total of vessels provided for the Navy increased to seven by 1814. But after a property dispute and other troubles, the dockyard was transferred that year to Paterchurch (Pembroke Dock, pp.104-106).

The resulting economic setback for Milford was compounded by the collapse of the whaling operations, partly due to the introduction of coal gas for lighting and therefore a huge fall in demand for sperm oil. By 1820 the venture was largely over and the whalers and families had mostly returned home. Riverside activity in building merchant vessels did, however, continue for much of the remaining century at small shipyards at Hakin, Hubberston Pill, Scotch Bay and Castle Pill. In addition, corn and other local produce was being shipped to Bristol and in 1845 alone, 66,100 tons of coal left Milford by boat. But the vital task of building Milford Docks was not completed until 1888 — far too late to attract any trans-Atlantic commerce. Milford had also lost out significantly when Neyland was chosen as the terminus of the broad gauge railway line from Paddington in 1856, for the town had to wait another seven years before the track entering the town was laid alongside Hubberston Pill.

With the completion of the main work at the docks and the introduction of a rapid rail service of fish trains to the markets, Milford was able to begin recovery from yet another period in the doldrums. It was fitting in September 1888 that the first vessel to tie up at the docks was a steam trawler, *Sybil*, and during the years until the 1950s, it would be followed at Milford by a regular fleet averaging some 100 fishing vessels and an industry often employing 4,000 people, either afloat or on shore. Catches reached a peak in 1946, when some 60,000 tons were landed immediately following the wartime reduction in trawling in the western and Irish fishing grounds. Milford had rapidly become the fourth ranking fishing port in Britain, first in Wales, and memories survive in the town of the time when the boast was that 'each week day was a pay day', and when, as well as good wages, members of the crew also received a share of the catch.

But during the 1950s decline set in, some of it put down to the polluting effects upon inshore waters of Milford's second oil industry. This time it was not whale oil but crude from the Middle East, and in 1960 at South Hook Point by Stack Rock, Esso officially became the first company to commence deliveries of oil at a new deepwater jetty and berths in the Haven and through pipelines to a huge oil refinery inshore at Herbrandston. This followed closure of the Suez Canal in 1967, when the longer voyage around the Cape in waters unrestricted by a canal meant a change to much larger crude oil tankers. Other companies were also attracted to Milford Haven by the depth of water and berthing opportunities, close to suitable land and a sufficient labour force. BP soon followed in 1961 with an Ocean Terminal near Popton Point and Fort Popton on the opposite shore, linked by long pipeline to the Llandarcy refinery beyond Swansea (now closed). Then in 1964 came Regent, now Texaco, to the east at Rhoscrowther. On the north bank, jetties for Gulf Oil were built in 1968 on the shore between Milford and Neyland near Wear Point and an inland refinery for Amoco (now Elf/Murco) was served by pipes laid from a jetty at Gelliswick, near the derelict Victorian Fort Hubberston. In 1969 the *Esso Scotia* berthed to become the first 250,000 ton Very Large Crude Carrier, or VLCC, to enter a British port, and by 1974 Milford Haven, in terms of tonnage, had become the largest port in the UK. But before the end of the century, higher costs of crude oil, North Sea output, changing economic factors and a surplus of refining capacity had caused all but two of the five oil installations to close, leaving one at Robeston West and that of Texaco across Man of War Roads to the south at Rhoscrowther, although with a new use also in mind for the initial Esso jetty.

Neyland

Four miles further upstream from Milford, opposite Pembroke Dock, Neyland had also been involved in shipbuilding for the Royal Navy, launching during the late 18th century the 74-gun *Prince of Wales* and the frigate *Milford*, and despite losing government contracts continued to build small merchant vessels until the end of the 19th century. Then early in the second half of the century, the Railway Age was gathering momentum in Wales and by 1854 the broad gauge line had reached Haverfordwest and I.K. Brunel (1806–1859) was seeking to establish a rail and sea link from Paddington to the south of Ireland. The best chance available at the time was by an extension of the South Wales Railway through Johnston to a terminus and port on the Milford Haven Waterway at Neyland. By August 1856 sufficient had been achieved to open a twice-weekly packet boat service to Waterford and an extensive rail and port infrastructure was set up during the remainder of the decade on land alongside Westfield Pill, at what came to be called for a time, New Milford. This venture was soon augmented by a ferry service to Hobbs Point to convey passengers and freight across the river to and from Pembroke Dock and beyond, but Brunel's real ambition for a speedy ferry service to Ireland, and also the chance of securing transatlantic passenger business, had been to base a rail terminus and port on the Irish Sea coast of west Wales. An opportunity finally arose half a century later, at Fishguard (pp.147-148), and in 1906 the first ferry sailed from there for Rosslare, and the packet boat service ceased at Neyland. Unlike the disappointing experience of the Haven ports, from 1909 transatlantic passenger liners also began to call — but only during the short few years leading up to the First World War.

There was intense activity throughout the Haven during both World Wars. The Admiralty requisitioned many trawlers for mine sweeping, patrols and other naval duties, although despite the dangers some fishermen did go out to sea, joined early in the First World War by 24 refugee trawler crews who had brought their boats and families from Belgium. A wide variety of warships anchored off the naval dockyard, while hundreds of merchant ships assembled in the Waterway to make up convoys for perilous ocean crossings and huge numbers and variety of vessels appeared prior to the Normandy invasion. Sometimes there was also the unfamiliar sight of scores of flying-boats, based at RAF Pembroke Dock for anti-submarine and surface ship attack duties and convoy protection over the Atlantic. These were fuelled with aviation fuel through underwater pipes from large Air Ministry underground tanks, and at Newton Noyes, near Milford, there was a major Royal Naval Armament and Mine Depot.

Near Brunel Quay at Neyland a large reinforced concrete slipway was built to enable the Sunderland and Catalina flying boats to be hauled to parking areas on shore and for access by landing craft — and this feature is now much appreciated by anglers and small boat owners.

Ambitious hopes of Neyland becoming the southern terminus of a Manchester to Milford Railway project were realised in very small part (p.240), but finally the station was closed in 1964 and the track bed to Rosemarket and Johnston converted to a country walk and 'off road cycle route'. There is instead also a 380-berth marina and waterfront and a statue of Brunel, the great engineer to whom Neyland owes its foundation. Between 1908 and 1914 there had been a busy fish market at the quayside, but new facilities at Milford then led to its transfer there.

In 1926 there were more local repercussions following closure of the Pembroke Naval Dockyard and one later blow came in 1975 with the opening of the Cleddau Bridge (p.106) and consequent redundancy for the Hobbs Point Ferry.

Milford Haven Port Authority and a future for the 21st century

A submerged river valley, or ria, running inland for 10 miles and beyond, between ½ mile and 1¼ miles wide and with depths in places of at least 6 fathoms, the Milford Haven Waterway has been well known to seafarers at least as long ago as the days of the Vikings, who are responsible for its name. Valued in their turn by Normans and Flemings, in 1588 the locally born historian George Owen rather extravagantly described it as 'the most famous port of Christendom', while William Shakespeare wrote '… how far it is to the same blessed Milford; and by the way, tell me how Wales was made so happy as t'inherit such a haven' (Cymbeline). As a traveller, social and economic historian, as well as author of *Robinson Crusoe* and *Moll Flanders* and some 500 other books, about a century later Daniel Defoe added his eulogy in *A Tour Through the Whole Island of Britain*. He described it as 'the fairest and best road for shipping that is in the whole of Britain … for about twenty miles within land', although was rather in doubt about earlier claims that 'a thousand sail of ships may ride in it, and not the topmast of one be seen from another', which he thought 'merits confirmation'. Admiral Lord Nelson found much in its favour at the start of the next century, and it is all the more surprising that the 1802 embryo town of Milford he was then visiting has still barely reached a population of 14,000 — two hundred years later.

But in 1986, as successor to the Conservancy Board, the Milford Haven Port Authority was created with jurisdiction 'bounded by the high water mark on the shores of Milford Haven and its approaches … as far as the tide flows'. Soon afterwards it bought the Milford Docks Company and, aided by EEC funding, rapidly completed a £10 million regeneration scheme, opening the new **Milford Marina** in time to host the start of the International Tall Ships Race in the summer of 1991. Responsible for 200 square miles of waterway containing the fourth largest freight port in the UK and the biggest port in Wales, supporting two major oil refineries and an oil storage terminal, set in Britain's only coastal National Park, the Authority provides port, harbour and associated services.

Looking over Milford Marina, an area being redeveloped with offices and shops around the marina

These include wharfage, stevedoring, fishing industry support, ship repairs, marine and leisure facilities and functions at the Pembroke Dock Ferry Terminal that opened in 1979.

In 2006, looking ahead into the early 21st century and an expected expansion following the arrival from Qatar of Liquefied Natural Gas, or LNG, towards the end of 2007, the Authority was preparing to commission and consider ambitious outline expansion plans for a Milford Haven Outer Marine Facility that would provide commercial berths, an outer marina, a cruise liner berth and 'associated landward infrastructure and development'.

From the statue of a fisherman on the waterfront, the route soon reaches a junction with Hamilton Terrace on which you turn left to pass the roadway to the **Museum**, housed in the old 1797 Custom House, the docks, marina and train station, to continue through Hubberston. Milford Haven Golf Course is just beyond to the west and to the right there is then a close view of the Elf/Murco oil refinery complex, extending northwards towards Robeston West. Soon afterwards the road enters the National Park and reaches Herbrandston. Here you can turn left down a narrow road (also the course of the Coast Path) leading towards Sandy Haven beach, and a small car park if you wish to stop. The route otherwise continues westwards towards St. Ishmaels and Dale.

2. Sandy Haven and St. Ishmaels

With a sandy beach and outcrops of rock, Sandy Haven lies sheltered by cliffs immediately to the west of South Hook Point and the eastbound route of the Coast Path passes between the shoreline and the former Esso refinery boundary before turning in the direction of Milford. For anyone with an appetite for the past, it runs close to the site of an Iron Age promontory fort, matched by another one across the bay on Great Castle Head. At the Point, South Hook Fort dates from 1863 and its field of fire relates to that of the Stack Rock Fort, lying just off-shore. Each was garrisoned by more than 150 men and they bristled with guns at the time when there were fears that the Haven might be attacked by the French.

Consistently earning Green Coast and Seaside Awards, the beach reaches up Sandy Haven Pill for 1½ miles to Rickeston Bridge, and the Milford to Dale road, drying out at low water. While the water quality is graded as 'Good', because of unpredictable estuary currents it is not recommended for swimming in, although popular for sea angling, sailing and canoeing. Close to the car park, Ferry Cottage was once associated with a boat crossing to the west side of the creek, but except for the two hours each side of low water, the alternative today involves a journey by road of about 4 miles between the two crossing points. But for the four hours or so while the tide is out there are stepping stones leading towards the west shore and, only then, to the small Sleeping Bay. The westbound Coast Path rises above it to head along the cliffs over Butts Bay and Longoar Bay, and the path to the right towards St. Ishmaels. This starts at the small hamlet of Sandy Haven, where a narrow road leads past a well-preserved limekiln, together unusually still with its weighbridge, and the ruins of the lime-burner's hut. At St. Ishmaels, a path from the cricket ground heads south towards the cliff top to meet the Coast Path, whence there are steep steps descending to the small Lindsway Bay, sheltering between Great Castle Head and Watch House Point, the site of a coastal artillery position in the First World War. The restored medieval church of St. Ishmael stands in a lonely, idyllic valley that drops down to Monk Haven, just to the west. This is thought to have been used in Neolithic times and during the Age of the Saints, and inlet and track were favoured during the frequent medieval pilgrimages to St. Davids as a safer alternative to sailing the often hazardous, storm-bound coastal course.

The route then continues to Dale past Herbrandston and the head of Sandy Haven Pill to reach St. Ishmaels and then approaches the B4327, on which you turn left for **Dale**, where there is a car park (charges).

After passing the car park, the road enters a clockwise one-way system, running along the sea front past a chandlery, boatyard, café, the Griffin pub and Dale Yacht Club, before coming to a side road ending at **Dale Point**.

A second side road from the one-way circuit climbs **St. Ann's Peninsula** and reaches the National Trust car park at Kete, some 200 feet above the adjoining sea level.

---

3. Dale, St. Ann's Peninsula and the return of Henry Tudor

On an isthmus site at the entrance to an important waterway and sheltered from prevailing Atlantic storms it is hardly surprising that Dale should have attracted settlement over the years. It is bounded by evidence of occupation reaching back to the Bronze and Iron Ages, and of defensive works from the time of Thomas Cromwell in *c.*1540 and his fears of a Spanish invasion culminating in the building of West and East Blockhouses in the 1580s, of the Napoleonic Wars period and of installations for the Royal Navy, Army and Royal Air Force during the Second World War. Its name derived from the Norse word for 'valley', Dale became one of Pembrokeshire's leading sea trading ports during the 16th and 17th centuries and as well as its fishing, boat building and other traditional activities, surprisingly engaged in brewing to produce and export the popular Runwae family ale. But by the 18th century output had ceased, along with most other village work, apart from some fishing and boat building, and the place was almost deserted. Across the road from the car park there is a long curved sand, pebble and rock beach that is claimed to be the sunniest spot in Wales and is a consistent winner of Blue Flag and Seaside Awards. There is a wide slipway for trailed boats and the landing stage is usable for long periods at either side of high water. The outlook is towards the east, across the sheltered Dale Roads towards Stack Rock, the oil tanker jetties and as far as Milford and Pembroke Dock. Dale has now become a hugely popular sailing, boating, windsurfing and water-sports centre.

A side road from the clockwise one-way system leads to **Dale Fort** at Dale Point. Close to evidence of Bronze and Iron Age occupation it was built in 1856 as part of a first line of defence of the waterway that also included **Thorn Island** and **Stack Rock** forts, and soon afterwards a second **West Blockhouse** fort. It mounted seven 68lb and two 32lb guns and there was barrack accommodation for 70 men, but it was as well that no attack came, for the smooth bore cannon would have been no match for breech-loaded, rifled guns that soon armed the evolving steam-propelled warships. As it is, a **Field Studies Centre** was established at Dale Fort in 1947, and further along the Coast Path, beyond Castlebeach Bay and Watwick Bay, West Blockhouse Fort was restored in 1986 by the Landmark Trust for use as holiday flats in one of the best surviving features of the Victorian military defences of the Haven.

A second side road from the one-way circuit leads to St. Ann's Peninsula. During the Second World War an area of land at Kete became *HMS Harrier*, an extensive land-based Royal Navy Air Direction School that accommodated up to 800 staff and

The landing stage and slipway at Dale Roads

trainees in 100 classrooms, offices and living quarters. Training involved the use of electronic simulators by which radar technicians were taught how to detect enemy aircraft before they could attack friendly ships — and direct fighter planes on to them. No aircraft could be spared for training in the early days and the Navy had to improvise with 'Stop-me-and-Buy-One' tricycles requisitioned from Walls Ice Cream Co. Each 'enemy' trike was fitted with a radio-telephone, compass and metronome for beating time, and the job of the operator was to detect it and direct 'friendly' trikes to the attack! Later on, aircraft from local air stations would fight sea battles between Kete and the Smalls Rocks (p.131). The base was closed in 1960, the site cleared and afterwards all was acquired by the National Trust.

Separated from Kete by **Great Castle Head**, a Late Iron Age fort of *c*.100 BC above it and Westdale Bay, *RAF Dale* was engaged in anti-U-boat patrols in the Bay of Biscay and protecting convoys in the Western Approaches, but in September 1943 the Royal Navy took over as *HMS Goldcrest,* a shore-based Fleet Air Arm station for twin-engined and night fighter training and front line operations. It officially closed in December 1947, but unlike Kete, left numbers of RAF and Admiralty buildings behind.

From the car park at Kete a service road provides a walking route with good views of the Haven towards St. Ann's Head. It makes for a pleasant although sometimes boisterous walk for half a mile in following the coastline south of Little Castle Point and another hillfort, Frenchman's Bay and a small creek called 'The Vomit'. After rejoining the Coast Path, the roadway passes the former coastguard station to reach **Cobblers Hole** where, alongside a helicopter pad, there is a fenced section from which it is possible to see at close quarters a superb example of acute folding and faulting of the eroded rock face. The Coast Path passes through a gate from the service road at the lighthouse and makes for Mill Bay and the east coast of the peninsula before turning towards Dale.

A very visual example of folding and faulting that has occurred in the earth's surface at Cobblers Hole

St. Ann's Head serves as a bastion to shelter Milford Haven against the worst effects of the most tempestuous and frequent gales known at any headland in Wales, although passage to or from the waterway is not altogether free from hazard in almost any conditions. To the south east, Crow Rock and Toes off Linney Head have claimed many victims, while memories are still fresh from the ecological disaster caused by the *Sea Empress* oil tanker that grounded off the St. Ann's headland in 1996. But dangers do not end there, for although the Haven approach appears wide, just below the surface almost in mid-channel there are two groups of

St. Ann's Head lighthouse and foghorn

dangerous reefs, with only two usable channels through which shipping must pass. Before the days of lighthouses and radar, beacons were lit on the headland at night near the Haven entrance, and close to St. Ann's Chapel where sailors could offer thanks, or pray, for a safe voyage. In 1714, two coal-fired lighthouses were built by the owner of Dale Castle to mark the Haven entrance, under a lease by which he was able, not always amicably, to collect dues. These were replaced by Trinity House in 1800 by low and high towers, and the former was later adapted to serve as a coastguard station, until the service was moved to Milford. The other was rebuilt in 1841, near the site of the old chapel, to a height of over 40 feet and 150 feet above mean sea level, converted to mains electricity with standby generators in 1958, joined by a service helicopter pad, and automated in 1998.

Of all movements through the Haven entrance below St. Ann's Head over the centuries, few can have been as epoch making as that on 7 August 1485, when a flotilla of ships brought Henry Tudor, fugitive Lancastrian claimant to the English throne, back to Wales almost to within sight of his birthplace at Pembroke Castle. Fourteen years before, at the battle of Tewkesbury, the House of Lancaster had suffered a decisive reverse of power, causing Jasper Tudor to seek exile for himself and his then teenage nephew, away from the clutches of the Yorkist King Edward IV. Granted asylum in France, he hired a barque at Tenby in September 1471, but blown off course in bad weather, made landfall in west Brittany. The mischance resulted in many complications that could have resulted in the Tudors being forcibly returned to England, especially from 1483 following Richard III's usurpation of the throne after the death of Edward IV.

But in 1484, and secretly slipping out of Brittany, he managed to enter France where the king and government were more in support of his political and dynastic aims, much to the alarm in England of Richard III. It was in these new circumstances that Henry drew up his invasion plan, successfully persuading the French king, Charles III, to provide practical aid.

Equipped with funds, ships and about 4,000 men, half of them French, with some 1,000 Scots and 400 English exiles among them, Henry was able to set sail from Honfleur and the River Seine on 1 August 1485 and, meeting no opposition in the Channel, landed after six days at Mill Bay, just inside the Sound and out of sight of Dale village. The force disembarked, their weapons and artillery were unloaded and the night was spent around Dale before an early departure was made towards a warm welcome at Haverfordwest. Then came a long march through Cardigan, Aberystwyth, Welshpool, Shrewsbury and Stafford, reinforcements joining them along the way, all culminating on 22 August in victory over Richard III and the Yorkists near the village of Bosworth.

The acclamation of Henry on the battlefield as King Henry VII ushered in a royal Tudor dynasty that would lead to prosperity in the kingdom for nearly 120 years, until the death of Queen Elizabeth I, and also mark the ending of the Middle Ages. Within six months, Henry had married Elizabeth of York, daughter of Edward IV and niece of Richard III, thus uniting the houses of York and Lancaster in the Tudor Rose. They also produced eight children, among them the future King Henry VIII.

From the car park at Kete, perhaps following close to Henry Tudor's trail from Mill Bay of 1485, return to the one-way road at Dale which heads left towards the north side of the valley, to pass footpath and narrow lane approaches to the small sand and shingle beach at **West Dale Bay**, the entrance to **Dale Castle** — a relatively modern castellated house built into scant remnants of the medieval castle of the knightly family of Vale, and St. James the Great parish church. Then it heads north, back to the B4327, past the new car park and a sighting to the left of a large stone-built windmill tower at Windmill Farm, dating from the early 19th century and now rather a rarity in Pembrokeshire

You can take either of the next two road junctions on the left to Marloes where signs point towards **Marloes Sands** and the large NT car park. (At Runwayskiln there is a Youth Hostel in a cluster of farm buildings.) These are near Marloes Mere, where villagers once gathered leeches as a profitable side line to equip grateful doctors for their blood-letting treatments. The Mere has been drained since then and has become a plant-rich wetland habitat, specially appreciated by wintering wildfowl and other birds. The beach is reached along a ½ mile footpath and this may be a reason why it are not likely to be crowded, despite a reputation as one of the most scenic of any to be found along the Welsh, or any, coast.

---

4. Marloes Sands, 'The Three Chimneys' and Gateholm Island

The curved mile-long beach is made up of sand and shingle, lying over extensive jagged rock that projects above the surface seawards for some distance. This pattern arose because of colossal earth movements of some 400 million years ago, also when the colourful cliffs at the rear of the beach were formed from horizontal layers of a wide series of Silurian sedimentary sandstones, mudstones, conglomerates and other rocks that were up-ended in steeply dipping, in places near vertical, courses. The footpath from the car park reaches the beach close to rocks that are rich in the fossils of brachiopods, trilobites, corals and other marine creatures. Across to the south-east of the sands, the near vertical '**Three Chimneys**' were relatively soft mudstone and harder sandstone before they were up-ended and then eroded at different rates to produce the striking feature that projects from the cliff face. To the west of the footpath entrance, **Gateholm Island**, like Skokholm lying in good view out to sea, has outlived other formations because it is comprised of Old Red Sandstone, its distinctive colouring caused by iron oxide staining.

Gateholm can be reached on foot at low tide. Meaning 'goat island' it helps to shelter Marloes Sands, but at such an exposed and inhospitable spot it is surprising that it should also have been adopted for considerable human settlement. Yet there are signs of occupation that archaeologists have dated from the Late Iron Age onwards and although much of the evidence has been smothered with plant material, more than 100 stone hut foundations have been identified on the plateau, sufficient to cater, it is thought, for up to 250 people, with only rain to supply their fresh water. The generally received conclusion is that the first occupants, although not Roman might have arrived during the Roman era, and that the Iron Age village was converted into a Celtic Christian monastery in or around the 6th century, during the Age of Saints.

Just to the west, **Albian Sands** was named after a paddle steamer that foundered there on her maiden voyage in *c*.1840, and now marking the eastern limit of the **Skomer Marine Nature Reserve** (below).

Martin's Haven

Returning to Marloes church, turn left back onto the 'main' road for the final run towards the end of the Marloes peninsula, at the NT car park (charges) for **Martin's Haven**. The roadway descends to the sheltered stony cove and a boat landing stage past a Wildlife Trust and South West Wales (WTSWW) sales and information centre, a covered exhibition about the Skomer Marine Nature Reserve, public toilets, and runs alongside a stone early 19th-century Deer Park wall. Let into an alcove there is a small *c*.1,000-year-old inscribed Celtic ring cross that was unearthed by NT employees. Rising to almost 200 feet, the Deer Park that may or may not have seen any deer at such a spot, is near the westernmost tip of the peninsula and contains one further promontory Iron Age fort to be seen along these coastlines. It provides fine views out to the volcanic rock Midland Isle (NT), even there with traces of ancient human settlement, and beyond it to Skomer. A regular boat service operates from Martin's Haven and the village of Dale to Skomer, Skokholm, Grassholm and other special excursions are also made.

---

5. Skomer, Skokholm and Grassholm Bird Islands

Skomer

Accessible by boat from 1 April to 31 October, the Skomer crossing takes about 15 minutes, and as well as the Boat Fee payable on board, there is a Landing Fee that contributes towards wildlife conservation costs on the island. Named by the Norse *Scalmey*, meaning the Cloven Island, it is an exposed 800 acres of volcanic rock, home to one of the most spectacular and accessible seabird colonies in Europe. Like the other two islands, it is part of the Pembrokeshire National Park, a National Nature Reserve and a Site of Special Scientific Interest and managed by the WTSWW under a lease from the Countryside Council for Wales (CCW). But it also bears signs of human occupation at least as far back as the Iron Age, as a promontory fort shows, and there are signs of later settlements, pastureland systems, stone-walled houses, folds and enclosures as well as a good harbour at North Haven. Indeed, it was farmed until 1958.

Puffins nowadays occupy burrows on the cliff-tops until mid-summer, and there are razorbills, guillemots, kittiwakes, herring gulls, great and lesser black-backed gulls and many other species to be seen in abundance. Feeding far out at sea during daytime with the storm petrels, the internationally important population of Manx Shearwaters cannot be seen until the evening, when they often appear in huge rafts offshore. Only towards midnight do they return with eerie, raucous calls to their underground nests in rabbit burrows, hoping to elude the predatory gulls. Many grey seals can be seen on the rocks throughout the year, especially near the Garland Stone, and from late August until October the females land to produce their pups and to mate. It is thought that rabbits were first introduced from Spain to this country by the Normans — and the island is inhabited by thousands of them. The combined effect of their grazing and contributions adding to all the sea-bird droppings enables a great variety of wild flowers to flourish, despite the salt spray and high winds. In spring, the most striking are the carpets of rabbit-resistant bluebells, while as on many coastal cliff-tops in Pembrokeshire, there are widespread red campion, thrift and sea campion among the displays. Amongst the birds, insects and small mammals moving among the vegetation it may just be possible to spot an elusive, and unique, Skomer vole.

In addition, the sea surrounding Skomer and the Marloes peninsula forms part of a statutory **Marine Nature Reserve**, one of only three in the UK, partly because it is at the northern limit for many warm water species found more commonly in the Mediterranean, as well as being a habitat for subjects from far northern latitudes. Managed by the CCW, the Reserve covers over 16 miles of coastline and its role is explained and illustrated at the Martin's Haven exhibition. It deals with the shape of the shores and the animals and plants living there, life on the steep and extremely exposed cliffs and on the wave-swept rock slopes, rock platforms and sheltered beaches. Different habitats teem with all kinds of life, not just familiar species such as seals, fishes, crabs and lobsters, and on the sea bed there are, for example, more than a third of all seaweed species, 75 different sponges and 40 species of anemone and soft coral. It is the stated purpose of the Marine Nature Reserve to conserve this wealth of habitats and wildlife and protect it from damage and disturbance.

Skokholm

Across Broad Sound, 2½ miles south of Skomer and surrounded by fierce tide-races, Skokholm also obtained its earlier name from Norse sources. It was 'The Islet in the Sound', from *Stokkr*, meaning a sound or seaway, and *holm*, meaning islet. Much smaller than Skomer and of Old Red Sandstone, it amounts to just 260 acres, 1 mile long and ½ mile across the widest point. The earliest written reference appears in an early 13th-century charter to the de Vale family. After centuries of change, it was again owned by the occupant of Dale Castle (above) for 300 years and in 1927 was leased to the distinguished naturalist, author and subsequent Founder of the West Wales Naturalists' Trust, R.M. Lockley. With his wife and daughter, and 10,000 rabbits and 80,000 birds as neighbours, he lived there until forced out by the onset of war in 1939. (For a while it was thought that the War Office would fortify the island because of its commanding position on the seaward approaches to Milford Haven, but nothing happened). Lockley had leased the island for £26 a year, with an option to purchase within two years, but could only just about afford the rent — even though the capital cost could have been nothing like the £650,000 raised in 2006 by the WTSWW, with aid from public donations and various grants, so that its future as a wildlife haven could be secure!

The Lockleys used up much of their resources in re-roofing and restoring the tumble-down island buildings, but in 1930 their budget received a magnificent boost when, for the £5 agreed with underwriters, they were able to acquire many hundreds of pounds worth of timber, tons of house fuel, fittings, gear and various other valuable items, salvaged from a topsail schooner, the *Alice Williams*, that had been wrecked on the island. Otherwise managing to be largely self-sufficient, the family sold rabbits, eggs, crabs and lobsters on the mainland to pay for anything else they needed. And throughout his time on the island, Lockley researched and documented many of the species there, producing studies of the life histories and migratory patterns of shearwaters, storm petrels, puffins and other sea birds. With *The Island*, a classic study of Skokholm's ecology, his numerous other published works have included *Shearwaters*, *Puffins*, *Grey Seal*, *Common Seal*, *Man Against Nature*, *Ocean Wanderers*, and *The Private Life of the Rabbit*.

By 1946 the island had been re-occupied as a bird observatory, the lighthouse restored to service, although now unmanned and powered by solar panels, while the old cottage near the centre has since been 'Listed' Grade II and other buildings converted for occupation by staff and up to 15 residential visitors or volunteers. A Site of Special Scientific Interest, it is part of the Skomer and Skokholm Special Protection Area and of the Pembrokeshire Special Area of Conservation.

But of all the birds to be seen there, or on Skomer, there are no resident gannets. In order to see any of these, it is necessary to sail 9 miles west-north-west to the tiny island of Grassholm, the Norsemen's 'Green Islet'.

Grassholm

Since 1947, owned and managed by the Royal Society for the Protection of Birds as the first reserve it ever bought, Grassholm is the only gannetry in Wales and numbers of birds at the breeding colony there have since grown steadily. At the time of Ronald Lockley's departure from Skokholm in 1939, when the total was cleverly thought to be precisely 11,992, by 1952 there were 17,000, and in 2005 increased to 32,409 pairs, meaning 32,409 nests of seaweed and various bits and pieces, packed onto the small 21-acre igneous rock islet — now the third largest colony in the world. Numbers are such that when the birds are present until the autumn migration, large areas of Grassholm show up as white from viewpoints on the distant Pembrokeshire mainland. The island is otherwise uninhabited, which is hardly surprising in view of the deafening cacophony of jostling, fighting and squabbling among the closely packed birds. Because of the risk of disturbance no landing is allowed, but there is much to see from visiting boats as the gannets plunge headlong all around into the sea after fish. There are accounts of the birds dropping for 50 feet, and even as much as 75 feet, depending on the depth of the hunted shoals, wings half closed until they are pressed tightly to the body just as it is about to strike the water. The huge forces are such that neck and wings of the birds are specially developed to act as cushions upon impact, while the bill has no nostrils that could allow water to be harmfully forced into the head.

After returning to the Martin's Haven car park, turn right to the road back to Marloes to follow a route running northwards along the **St. Brides Bay** coastline. There are several sandy beaches and picturesque coves, some of them busy and well serviced during holiday seasons, while there are others that are quiet and peaceful. First among these is **Musselwick Sands** on the opposite side of the Marloes Peninsula neck to Marloes Sands and rather closer to the village. The only public access is just before the built-up area on the left, where a footpath descends for just over half a mile to the beach, being steep in places and with rocks to cross. There are warnings about instability of the cliffs, but the sands are splendid when the tide is out, as are the views across the Bay.

Anyone with a taste for prehistory should follow the adjacent Coast Path for a mile and a half northwards to an Iron Age promontory fort at Tower Point, and to the **Nab Head**, where traces of Mesolithic, or Middle Stone Age (10,000–5000 BC) Man have been found. The place name comes from knap, a term for stone chipping, and shaped flints, pierced beads and a variety of stone tools and weapons has been uncovered at the chipping floor.

After taking the left-hand exit road from Marloes, the route briefly rejoins the B4327 on which you turn left before taking the first left turn towards **St. Brides Haven**, a small cove within Old Red Sandstone cliffs where there is car park down a lane to the left and a sheltered north-west facing beach of shingle, pebbles and, at low tide, sand. Allowing always for adverse currents it is good for swimming and sub aqua diving and regularly earns Green Coast and Seaside Awards. The church is dedicated to St. Bridget — Brigid of Kildare (c.450–c.523), abbess and saint, who was revered only slightly less than St. Patrick himself. Although remaining in Ireland, her cult came to Wales with 17 dedications as St. Bride or Ffraid Santes, and also extended far elsewhere during Irish movements of the 5th and 6th centuries. There is an early Christian cemetery between church and beach and stone-lined graves have been exposed in the cliffs near the lime kiln at the head of the cove.

From the car park, the route leaves along the road to the left at St. Brides Cross and meets the B4327 again at a crossroads, where you turn left onto another minor road that passes the overgrown disused airfield of *RAF Talbenny*. This entered service in 1942 in association with RAF Dale, under 19 Group Coastal Command, and engaged in anti-ship and anti-submarine sweeps in the Bay of Biscay and on enemy harbour installations. It also received a Ferry Training Unit and aircraft of Transport Command and was used as an emergency and weather diversionary airfield, closing finally in December 1946.

Broad Haven West

Unbelievably, **Little Haven** was once a mining centre but has now been readily transformed into one of the popular holiday villages along this coast. Instead of the coal schooners sailing from the sheltered beach there are now pleasure boats, canoes, water-skiers and

Broad Haven West

wind-surfers. The beach faces north-west, away from prevailing south-westerly winds, and the slipway is shared with the on-shore lifeboat. The village is well provided with shops, pubs and 'eateries'.

Keeping an eye on the tide, it is possible to walk along the sands while it is out, to the next beach to the north at The Settlands and further on to **Broad Haven West**. Otherwise there is a narrow coast road or, better, the road through Walton West that leads to Broad Haven and the first of its public car parks (charges).

Broad Haven (West), so named to distinguish it from Broad Haven (South) on the south coast, regularly merits a Blue Flag as well as a Seaside Award and has been a popular resort since the early 1800s. With a large sandy beach along the length of the village and an open west-facing bay it is good for swimming, sub aqua sport, canoeing, surfing, sailing and wind surfing. There are three slipways, a choice of car parks, various forms of accommodation, including a youth hostel and a National Park information point. To the north of the beach, the coastline has long interested geologists for its stacks, arches, folds, and the huge rock shown on the map as the Sleek Stone.

This being Wales, **Druidston** might immediately be thought to have a connection with druids, but locally pronounced 'Drewson' was actually named after a 12th-century Norman knight who settled there, Alfred Drue. **Druidston Haven** is a long sandy west-facing beach backed by steep cliffs on three sides and it lies just off the narrow coast road to the north of Broad Haven, reached along two footpaths down a stream valley. Because of strong currents it is not suitable for bathing, nor is it a good place for the physically disabled, but just half a mile back towards Broad Haven and suitable for wheelchair access, complete with a car park, there is a superb look-out position above **Haroldston Chins**. This is where the Neolithic or Bronze Age track, The Welsh Way, linking Whitesands, St. Davids and Monks Haven, St. Ishmaels reached St. Brides Bay and the Irish Sea, so avoiding the hazards of the sea voyage round the exposed headlands.

The coast road climbs out of the valley at Druidston, only to drop down again at **Nolton Haven**, another coalmining centre until the early 20th century. It has a small south-west-facing cove of sand, shingle and rock pools with cliffs on either side and a car park over the road. Another Green Coast and Seaside Award winning beach, it is suited for swimming, sub aqua diving and water sports provided that unpredictable currents, especially at low tides, are respected. No sign remains of the quay built in 1769 for the export of anthracite and culm, but a flat grassy terrace above the beach used to serve as a coal storage area where loads were brought along rails by trolley. **Trefrane Cliff Colliery**, overlooking the sea to the north, worked from *c.*1850 until 1905, its shafts 300 feet deep and sloping under the sea. When it closed there were still estimated to be 230 million tons of un-worked reserves beneath St. Brides Bay between Nolton and Newgale. Now all that is left above ground at Trefrane are a solitary ruined chimney-stack, sparse foundations and some spoil heaps.

The road climbs again, alongside Rickets Head, and after passing the disused colliery site it reaches the southern end of **Newgale Sands** and the first of three car parks, near the last of which it joins the A487 at its approach to Newgale (pp.128-129).

Turn right here to climb this main road towards Roch, Simpson Cross and the **Motor Museum** there, and finally back to Haverfordwest.

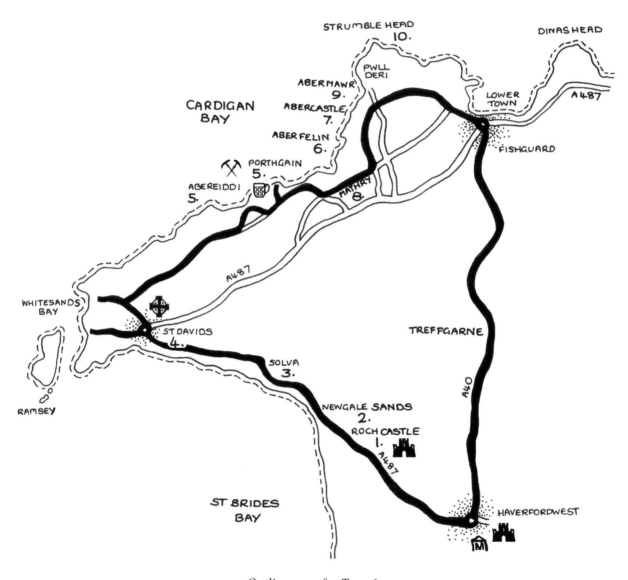

Outline map for Tour 6
The numbers 1 to 10 relate to the boxed information given within the tour

Tour 6   St. Davids & West Pembrokeshire

The tour makes use of the A487 and A40 as a framework for visiting one of the most scenic areas of south-west Wales, turning to minor country roads to reach spectacular stretches of rugged coastline around the St. Davids and Strumble Head peninsulas and some interesting inland features. It also includes the city of St. Davids with its very individual cathedral and remains of the bishop's palace. At Fishguard there is an opportunity to take a 'short cut' southwards back to Haverfordwest. The main triangular route is about 45 miles long, and an idea of distances involved in any side trips to the coast or inland may be judged from OS Landranger Map 157- *St Davids & Haverfordwest/Ty Ddewi a Hwlffordd,* strongly recommended.

From Haverfordwest take the A487 west towards St. Davids. Although Haverfordwest is far into south Wales, there is a distinct 'Englishness' about the town that many visitors do not expect, no more than how it came to be called 'Capital of Little England Beyond Wales'. But this has nothing to do with some legendary or imaginary territory, as there are two tangible features along the A487 on the way to St. Davids. First there is Roch Castle, some 6 miles to the north-west, and secondly Brandy Brook, which flows beneath the road near the Duke of Edinburgh inn towards its outfall in St. Brides Bay at the village of **Newgale**. This marks the western end of the boundary separating the 'Englishry' from the 'Welshry', since the 12th century known as the Landsker (a Norse word for 'frontier' or 'divide').

The Landsker Line

In the year 1600 a Pembrokeshire historian, George Owen (1552–1613) wrote that 'The shire is taken to be divided into two parts, that is the Englishry and the Welshry … The upper part of the shire is occupied by Welshmen'. To the south, the incoming 'Normans, Flemings and Englishmen … utterly expelled the inhabitants thereof and peopled the county themselves'.

This divide, or landsker, had already been established by invading Norsemen and during the 11th and 12th centuries powers on either side of the imaginary line built more than 50 castles to consolidate their positions. For the Anglo Normans, Roch Castle, 2 miles inland from St. Brides Bay, is the north-west marker of a rank of castles along the Landsker that continued with Haverfordwest, Picton, Wiston, Llawhaden, Carew, Narberth to Amroth Castle in the south-east, with Laugharne in Carmarthenshire at the very edge.

North of the line, many of the inhabitants are likely to be bi-lingual or Welsh-speaking, and Welsh place names predominate, while long ago to the south the language and traditions produced 'Little England Beyond Wales'. The differences remain marked by the languages, accents and place names, and noticeably also by the church architecture. Ever conscious that they were not welcome and open to attack, the unloved Anglo Normans and Flemings built sturdy churches, with tall, fortified towers, whereas the Welsh north of the line had more modest buildings, most likely just with a small belfry tower, or chapels, and situated in remote country places to serve the scattered pastoral communities.

---

1. Roch Castle

Built by the de la Roche family in the 13th century at the north-west limit of the Norman invasion of west Wales, the D-shaped multi-storey tower of Roch Castle is perched on a volcanic outcrop that has coined its name, and which is seen for miles around as it looks down towards Newgale Beach and across a wide expanse of St. Brides Bay. It had an uneventful time up to the 17th century, when in 1601 it was purchased by William Walter of Trefran, but in 1644 the castle was garrisoned for King Charles and featured in heavy action as it changed hands. After the Civil War had ended, Walter left for London to

Roch Castle

seek compensation for all the damage caused, taking with him Lucy, his daughter. For a time she became a well-documented 'lady of pleasure' of King Charles II — and in 1649 bore him a son. As the eldest of his illegitimate children, the boy James was acknowledged by the king and made duke of Monmouth, and among many honours, invested with the Order of the Garter. Lucy meanwhile vanished from the history books.

By 1900 the castle ruins were in a really poor state but were rescued and considerably 'made over' by the 1st Viscount St. Davids and by the 21st century were being let for self-catering holidays. The prominent main tower has five bedrooms and guests may climb up to the battlements to take in the stunning views. The west wing below has three bedrooms, and all the accommodation is bookable between March and the end of November, and over Christmas and the New Year.

After passing a further 2 miles beyond Roch, the A487 drops towards the coast, turning at the junction with the minor road from Norton Haven to run a little above mean high water level alongside the great pebble beach that for more than 2 miles backs the sweeping expanse of Newgale Sands.

2. Newgale Sands

The high bank is thought to date from the Ice Age, when multi-coloured stone from the cliffs to the north of St. Brides Bay was deposited by rising sea levels to be continually pounded and shaped as pebbles by violent wave action. The prevailing westerlies have often driven the sea over the bar. After the colourful 12th-century churchman, Giraldus Cambrensis (p.91) had crossed Newgale Sands in 1188, he wrote of the winter of 1171–72 'when the

Newgale, as seen on the approach from Haverfordwest

wind blew with such unprecedented violence that the shores of south Wales were completely denuded of sand'. Tree trunks and subsoil that had long been buried were once more revealed and 'the sea shore took on the appearance of a forest grove …'. Now, more than 800 years later, stumps of a drowned forest can still at times be seen at low tide off the north end of the beach. Very much longer ago, anthracite coal measures were formed between Newgale and Little Haven — as will be realised from the ruins of **Trefrane Cliff Colliery**, just beyond the southern end of the sands. The biggest in the coalfield, it was 300ft deep, slanting under the sea, and worked from 1850 to 1905. The coal was initially shipped from Haverfordwest Quay and then Norton Haven but extraction of coal here dates back to *c*.1439 and, according to one assessment, there are still some 230 million tons of un-worked reserves between Newgale and Norton, and under the sea.

Facing west and exposed to winds from the Atlantic, **Newgale** is now popular for surf-boarding, kite-surfing, kayaking, sea angling and other water sports, while sunbathers, sandcastle builders and swimmers, ever mindful of the powerful undertow, are comforted by the regular 'Blue Flag' award that recognises the high water quality.

After crossing Brandy Brook, the A487 climbs steeply out of Newgale towards Brawdy and the disused RAF Station near Pen-y-Cwm which is now a Business Park. (Once renowned for its air displays and regarded as one of the finest UK military airfields, it was operational from early 1944, in part engaged in meteorological duties in the Atlantic and Bay of Biscay in connection with the D Day operations. Transferred to the Royal Navy in 1946 as *HMS Goldcrest II* (Dale was *I*), it was a base for Fleet Air Arm operations, often in conjunction with the carrier force, before being taken over by the Army (as the third of the Services to be there). After turning west, the northern sweep of St. Brides Bay ends abruptly here with a sharp move towards spectacular cliffs and coves, headlands and small harbours — firstly the fjord-like inlet at **Solva**.

Brandy Brook at the western end of Newgale Sands

3. Solva
Described in guidebooks as 'a sophisticated sailing village', 'a classically picturesque haven for yachtsmen, artists and retired people' and 'one of the most charming and attractive coastal villages in Britain … with a charming selection of shops, pubs and restaurants (not to mention the lobster and crab dishes)', even with an enterprising 'Nectarium' for breeding rare tropical butterflies and moths, it is inevitable that newcomers now outnumber original Solvaites. Below the Gribin, a rock-crested ridge crowned by a hillfort, the harbour lies in a valley that was gouged out by meltwater flowing southwards at the end of the last Ice Age. When sea levels subsequently rose, it was submerged and, just as the much larger instance at Milford Haven and at Porth Clais (below) it is known technically as a ria. Almost secretive, it was largely hidden from the roving eyes of pirates and other hostile seafarers and the creek has been in undisturbed use by fishing boats from at least as far back as the 14th century. In 1776, six trading ships operated out of Solva, by 1820 the number had increased to some 30, varying between 20 and 250 tons burden, and

by 1848 berths were being advertised for passage to New York for £3, half price for under 14s and nothing for infants, inclusive of water, fuel and bed places (for the voyage of between 7 and 17 weeks). The 1851 Census showed a population of 1,252 and there was a need for nine warehouses, but two years later the railway arrived at Haverfordwest and from then on everything changed. By 1856 there was just a single trading ship and by the 1901 Decennial Census the population had dropped to 730, and rose by only another 100 during the next 50 years. As the largest of the Dewisland harbours, Solva in its heyday was greatly involved in the export of corn and butter, largely to the hungry, growing population of Bristol, while the chief imports were of coal and limestone.

Limekilns and uses of lime. Solva had one of the greatest concentrations of limekilns in the region, their purpose being to produce lime to improve its acid soils and increase crop yields. The limestone (calcium carbonate) came principally from West Williamston, near Carew and the coal from Hook on the Western Cleddau and Nolton (above). The original ten Solva kilns, and another by the Gwadn Beach near the coast, were loaded from the top with small pieces of the stone while the lower part was filled with small coal or culm and ignited by firewood. The resulting quicklime (calcium oxide) was then carted away to be spread on the soil and 'slaked' by the elements, when it dissolved to form the alkali that neutralised the acid soil and increased the fertility of the ground. Lime was also used with sand and water to produce mortar and in limewashes on

Solva harbour at high and low tides

Limekilns at Solva

walls, including those of St. Davids Cathedral and many other churches in the land where the Puritans chose to cover over religious medieval wall paintings. Most kilns were sited as close as possible to the sea and generally removed from settlements, but this was not so at Solva. In Victorian times (long before the Clean Air Act), the smoke, fumes and carbon dioxide from up to ten kilns belched out over the village — it was certainly not 'a favourite holiday village' then! Neither had it been all plain sailing for ships passing along the rocky coastline or out in the bay.

Horror on The Smalls. One vicious hazard lying 21 miles off the coast here is The Smalls, a group of partly submerged rocks, appearing no more than 3.5 metres above the highest tides. Prior to the late 18th century they accounted for many shipping losses, until in 1775 the owner resolved to instal a beacon. But instead of briefing a specialist engineer he chose a musical instrument maker for the task. His materials were mainly wood and after he had assembled the parts on Gwadn Beach, near the coastline at Solva, he erected them on the outermost rocks in the form of an open octagonal structure, perched on nine legs of timber and cast iron. His idea was that the wild seas would pass through the supports with minimum effect on the lantern — and it worked for more than 50 years, before necessary repairs after a great storm extended its life for many further years.

Soon after it was completed the first two keepers were on station to tend the oil lamps above the tempestuous Atlantic waves — for up to four months at a time. But in 1801 there was a gruesome incident that produced a major sea-change in Trinity House manning policy. One of the two keepers fell ill, and then died, and his colleague, facing the predicament that he could be accused of the man's murder, lashed the dead man to the outer gallery of the lantern. Because of bad weather, relief was a long time coming and weeks later his mind had gone and he was in a really bad way. Since that time, until all lighthouses were converted to automatic working, Trinity House always stationed three keepers at every one. Standing 41 metres high, the present masonry lighthouse is similar in design to that at Eddystone and was built in 1861. It was surmounted above the lantern by a helicopter deck in 1978 and converted to automatic working in 1987. The safety of shipping no longer relies on the light from oil lamps, for the Smalls Lighthouse off Solva is now powered by wind and solar energy and the equivalent of a 35-watt lamp is visible in clear night conditions for up to 20 miles.

The Haverfordwest road was originally one of three principal approaches to St. Davids and passes near the city's former RAF Coastal Command airfield. Part of a chain of coastal bases, it was operational from 1943 in anti-ship and anti-submarine duties but there is now little left to see. However in 2002 it briefly came to life again as the site for the National Eisteddfod of Wales, hosted by St. Davids.

The National Park Visitor Centre
at the approach to St. Davids

There is a landscaped 'Pay and Display' car park and distinctive fairly new **National Park Visitor Centre** at the entrance to the city. Another highway arrives from the north-east after passing Fishguard, while a third, extending for just a mile, begins in the south-west at the small harbour of Porth Clais. This was the main gateway to the outside world at the time when visitors to this extreme far west part of Wales came not overland but along sea-lanes to reach what amounted to a marine crossroads connecting the Irish Sea, south-west England, Cornwall and Brittany.

4. St. Davids — miniature City, and Dewisland

In what has been termed 'The Age of Saints' following the departure of the Roman legions, devout travellers arrived with a strong Christian faith and deep attachment to monastic ideals, and in the mid-6th century Dewi Sant (as the Welsh call St. David) founded a monastic settlement here as its first abbot/bishop. There is a firm tradition that David had been born to St. Non at a spot close to the cliffs still marked by the ruins of St. Non's Chapel, and that he was baptized where the River Alun joins the sea at Porth Clais. He placed his monastery a mile upstream on a sheltered platform at a bend of the

St. Davids Cathedral

steep-sided river valley. Continuing as the seat of a bishop after his death in *c*.589, it was known by the Welsh name of *Mynyw*, and the Latin *Menevia*, and gained from its pivotal position on the busy western seaways off the 'Land's End' of Wales. But this also had drawbacks, for between 645 and 1097 it was plundered and ravaged on 13 known occasions, among the most violent in 999 when Vikings killed Bishop Morgenau and in 1080, Bishop Abraham. In 1081 William the Conqueror arrived as a pilgrim, while also viewing the potential of the coastline as a suitable departure point for expeditions to Ireland, and for a policy meeting with Rhys ap Tewdwr prince of the royal house of Deheubarth.

When the Welsh line of bishops ended in 1115, Henry I imposed the first Norman bishop on the monks. Bernard, a stranger to Wales and Celtic traditions, undertook a thorough reorganisation of the community as a non-monastic foundation, with a chapter of canons, and extended its territorial boundaries. Supported by the Pope, in 1120 he secured a 'privilege' that amounted to canonisation of David as a saint and the making of St. Davids as a centre for pilgrimage that lasted throughout the Middle Ages. Indeed, there was soon a declaration that two pilgrimages to St. Davids were equivalent to one to Rome, expressed in the Latin rhyme *Roma semel quantum: bis dat Menevia tantum*, a distinction only ever shared with Santiago de Compostela in northern Spain. Confirmed as bishop of the church of St. Andrew and St. David, Bernard embarked on a modest rebuilding of the cathedral and consecrated it in 1131. Pilgrims came in increasing numbers, prominent among them King Henry II, arriving through Porth Stinan in the autumn of 1171 (soon after the martyrdom of Thomas Becket at Canterbury Cathedral) and again on return from his expedition to Ireland the following Easter. His lavish gifts to the chapter were but a small part of all the offerings that were collected 'by the dish-full' from pilgrims, and after 50 years ambitious plans began to be drawn up for a much more magnificent cathedral. The new work started soon after the appointment in 1178 of Peter de Leia as the third of the Norman bishops and continued for more than three centuries as the basis for the splendour of the present church.

Although it is thought to be at least the fourth ecclesiastical building to occupy the site since the 6th century, nothing seems to be known about any civilian settlement before the appointment of Bernard as bishop. However Henry I had granted a charter of civic privileges in 1115 and shortly afterwards the profile of the cathedral became raised to an international level through the papal decree of 1120. A need developed for feeding and accommodating the increased number of pilgrims and a local surge in commercial activity was helped further from 1281 by a charter granting a twice-weekly market and two

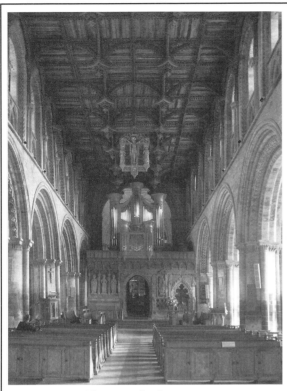

The nave looking east

yearly fairs, and there was even some sea trade through Porth Clais. Under the patronage of successive bishops the small town grew steadily as the economic centre of the district and by 1320 contained a community of 130 burgesses, most of them Englishmen.

Prominent amongst the bishops appointed to the diocese of Menevia was Henry de Gower (*c.*1278/1328-47) who was probably born on the Gower peninsula near Swansea (where he later founded a hospital for clergy of his diocese and seemed to have had a hand in the rebuilding of the castle, see p.11). He is regarded as a great builder-bishop and directed building work at the cathedral and various episcopal residences and manors, including St Davids itself, Lamphey (pp.107-108) and Llanddewi in Gower.

Within the cathedral the abiding, most prominent feature of his episcopate is the finely carved stone choir screen, or *pulpitum*, that closes off the choir from the nave. Designed in the Decorated style, like much of the masonry of the cathedral it is constructed of the tough, subtly coloured sandstone quarried from the nearby sea cliffs at Caerfai and Caerbwdy. Un-symmetrically occupying part of the front bay of the Norman nave, and forward of an earlier stone screen that stood under the west arch of the tower, it probably dates from the 1340s and incorporates de Gower's tomb at the southern end. Until 1571 it was surmounted by a rood loft that was afterwards replaced by perpendicular coving, other work during the 19th century and the 20th-century organ loft. Also in de Gower's time the nave, presbytery and eastern chapels were remodelled, windows enlarged to admit more light and a middle, subsequently central stage was added to the tower.

De Gower also undertook the complete rebuilding of the **palace** to the south-west of the cathedral. Enough of this *Palatium* among the other buildings has lasted to illustrate the great difference between the affluence and power of the medieval bishops of St. Davids and the asceticism of their saintly founder. He and his community lived their ordered life of prayer and hard work on the bare necessities of life, dressed in animal skins and with no possessions to call their own. As abbot, David was even stricter with himself, becoming known as 'David the Waterman' (*Dewi Ddydwr*) for his way of only

The bishop's palace by the cathedral

133

drinking water, and perhaps for standing for long periods in cold water 'to subdue the flesh'. De Gower's palace was intended to display the power and affluence of the Church and was designed with two sets of spacious rooms along the sides of an imposing quadrangle. Each one had is own great hall, living chambers and a chapel — that on the east side providing private accommodation for the bishop. The south range was the grander, with a ceremonial Great Hall measuring some 88 feet long and largely lit by a superb Bath Stone wheel window, set within a moulded frame of purple Caerbwdy stone — still all complete. The palace was built in the Decorated style of Gothic architecture and with distinctive arcaded parapets decorated with chequered stonework and just under 200 individual sculptures, a mixture of human heads, animals and mythical creatures mainly acting as carved corbels.

The wheel-shaped window in the Great Hall of the bishop's palace

The west range is the earliest surviving part of the palace, probably built in the 13th century and later modified and now mostly in ruins.

The palace and walls of the close are in the care of Cadw, and details of their history, from the beginning up to the Reformation and subsequent decline, a tour of the three ranges, the undercrofts, the exterior and the cathedral close, as well as separate features and information about St. Non's Chapel, are contained in a well-illustrated guidebook: *St Davids Bishop's Palace* written by J. Wyn Evans and Rick Turner.

After de Gower died in 1347, any further work at the cathedral was compromised by the onset of the Black Death and only in 1365 is there any record of further building, when space between the nave and river was used to found a college of vicars choral. Houses, a common hall and the Chapel of St. Mary were provided by 1382 for the priests who, separate from the cathedral foundation, performed the duty of ensuring that divine offices were properly sung. By the end of the following century the state of the nave roof and a pronounced outward lean by the southern arcading headed a catalogue of further remedial works that appear to have been completed during the years leading up to the Reformation. As it was not a monastic body, the chapter did not become involved in the dissolution of the monasteries — and in fact gained by being entrusted with the tomb containing the remains of Edmund Tudor, grandfather of King Henry VIII, upon its removal from the dissolved Grey Friars' house at Carmarthen (p.45). Nevertheless dissolution of the College of St. Mary, the vicars choral and the chantries in the cathedral chapels, combined with the ending of pilgrim income quickly led to neglect and ruin at both cathedral and bishops' palace.

William Barlow (1536–48), the first Protestant bishop of St. Davids, would have much preferred his cathedral to be more centrally placed in the huge diocese at Carmarthen, but consent was not forthcoming. The abandonment of St. Davids would probably have resulted in the total ruin of the cathedral. As it was, by 1610, John Speed's map showed a mere 51 houses and most of the former burgages abandoned, causing the contemporary historian William Camden to declare in *Brittania* that it was only 'a very small and poor Citie and hath nothing at all to make shew of'. However the original street pattern, formed largely by Catherine Street, Goat Street, Nun Street and the High Street, can still be made out in the 21st century, as can the market cross in the centre of the (triangular-shaped) Market Square, and the burgage pattern has substantially survived. But early in the 21st century, St. Davids is still hardly more than a village in extent, its resident population about 2,000, relying on the cathedral for its courtesy title of city (and the 1920s naming of its City Hall in High Street) until 1995. That year, Queen Elizabeth II by Charter granted St. Davids (*Ty Ddewi* in Welsh) the full status of City, the smallest in Britain.

Its economy relies heavily on seasonal tourism, for which it is well equipped with a range of accommodation, shops and catering facilities. Everyone is inevitably drawn from Market Square down The Pebbles towards the **Tower Gateway (*Porth y Twr*)**, the sole survivor of four gates that gave access to the cathedral precinct from the bishops' borough outside the Close Wall. It is built against the 13th-century octagonal tower where the eight cathedral bells are hung.

The relative ground levels are such that this is still well above the main body of the cathedral, down in the dip, and it is necessary to descend a flight of 39 steps, known as the Thirty Nine Articles, before reaching a further downward slope at the approach to the south door and porch. Alternatively it is possible to proceed a longer distance down Tower Hill without encountering steps. At the opposite side of the nave there is a well-stocked bookshop (one with an even wider range stands outside the cathedral across the river immediately to the west) where it is worth investing in the dean's illustrated Guide: *St. Davids Cathedral. The Cathedral Church of St. Andrew and St. David.*

Looking east there, it is possible to appreciate with awe all that the Dean describes as 'the unique blend of Peter de Leia's grand arcades, the splendour of Gower's rood screen, the magnificence of the early 16th-century ceiling and the 20th-century organ case'. It is also possible to note the upward slope of about 3 feet in the nave floor and the outward lean of the southern arcading, sources of great past concern. Opening with some words about Dewi Sant, the effects of Vikings and Normans and the part played by Giraldus Cambrensis (p.91), the booklet covers the medieval construction phases, including the building of the nave roof and ceiling, rebuilding by John Nash of the west front, its further rebuilding as part of a wholesale restoration between 1862 and 1877 by Sir George Gilbert Scott, and subsequent restoration by his son, Oldrid, of roofless aisles and chapels that had long been open to the skies. Beyond the 14th-century choir screen, the present stalls date from the late 15th or early 16th centuries and the bishop unusually occupies the position on the south side that in other cathedrals is normally the dean's stall (that side of the choir hence known as *decani*). Another unique situation is that, since the Middle Ages, the Sovereign has been a member of the Chapter of St. Davids. The only monarch to occupy the First Cursal royal stall in the choir is Queen Elizabeth II, when she visited the city in 1955 and again for the Distribution of the Royal Maundy in 1982. The far from religious carvings of the 16th century beneath the tip-up misericord seats are worth examining closely for what has been described as their 'wit, irony, invention and keen observation'. But awkwardly sited beyond, in the centre of the presbytery, is the tomb of Edmund Tudor, earl of Richmond and father of King Henry VII. It is close to St. David's shrine, while to the east, on the outside of the former 12th-century external wall, lies Holy Trinity Chapel and the original pilgrims' recess and, contained in an oak casket, bones that some believe

The tomb of Edmund Tudor

are those of David and a local saint, Justinian. The tomb of Rhys ap Gruffudd, greatest of south Wales princes (pp.54, 56) is in the south choir aisle, being just another example of the great wealth of interest that is to be found in this noble and historic place as it continues to observe a daily round of ordered worship, first introduced by its founder, David, patron saint of Wales, in the middle of the 6th century.

The Dewisland peninsula and seaboard to the south and west of St. Davids and surrounding area have evidence of occupation from long before David's time, when prehistoric man dwelt on the coastal fringe. The earliest signs are flint scatters at Clegyr Boia, just west of St. Davids that suggest the presence of a Middle Stone Age community of some 6,000 years ago. Excavations there in 1943 revealed house structures of the first Welsh farmers, the later Neolithic people who are more often recognised from their burial mounds or cromlechs such as the huge Coetan Arthur (Arthur's Quoit) at St. Davids Head and Carreg Samson (Samson's Stone) further to the north at Abercastle. A Bronze Age track leading from lands to the east and across the Preseli hills ended at Whitesands as a port for Ireland — and the copper and gold of the Wicklow Hills, the standing stones or menhirs in the region dating from their era of around 1500 BC. There are many Iron Age hilltop forts on coastal promontories, such as that on the Gribin at Solva, and what has been described as 'a remarkable Iron Age treasure house' at St. Davids Head. Best seen before the bracken grows in June, this is Clawdd y Milwyr (the warrior's dyke), the earth and collapsed drystone wall and stone hut-circles adjoin traces of the irregular field system between the headland and Carn Llidi where the Iron Age, and perhaps earlier, people farmed. Unique in Britain, it is regarded as representing at least 2,000 years of agriculture.

There is no conclusive evidence that the Romans set foot to any extent in the south-west beyond Carmarthen (p.49), although a tradition persists that there was a

The pilgrims' recess with its casket of reputedly saintly bones

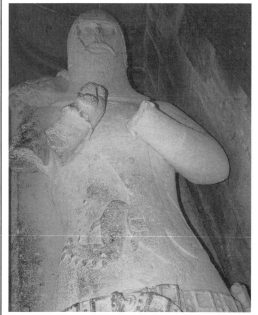

The effigy of the Lord Rhys ap Gruffudd

Coetan Arthur near St. Davids Head

fortification at Whitesands called *Menapia*. Also shown on some maps is *Occipitarvm Prom* at St. Davids Head, named by Ptolomy, the Roman geographer of the 1st century AD, as the oldest recorded feature on the coasts of Wales and thought to mean 'the Promontory of the Eight Perils', quite possibly referring to the rocks of the Bishop and Clerks that stretch westwards from Ramsey Island.

After the legions departed from Britain in 410, much of the country lapsed into the Dark Ages, but in the Atlantic zones to the west there was instead the 400-year-long 'Age of the Saints' that brought Sts. David, Justinian and Elvis to the peninsula and left the many other saints' names of places, churches and chapels on the wider map. That of the coast also indicates the presence of the Norsemen during the concluding centuries of the first millennium. Thus from *Holmen*, meaning 'a small island' came Skokholm, Grassholm and Gateholm; Ramsey, Caldy (Caldey) and Skalmer (Skomer) came from the word meaning 'a larger island', and *Vik* produced Goodwick as 'a bay with a safe anchorage'.

These were also times of myth, legend and folklore, the shading of fact and fiction, history and fantasy. The traditional story in the *Mabinogion* of Culhwch and Olwen relates to the landing of Twrch Trwyth, transformed from a king into a monstrous boar with seven young pigs, at the harbour of Porth Clais (below) when heading for Nevern and the Preseli Hills pursued by King Arthur and his men. Not far away the profoundly ascetic hermit, Justinian, reputed friend of David, after being executed by disaffected Ramsey Island disciples, is said to have walked carrying his head across the treacherous Sound, first to be buried on the mainland and later at the cathedral. Legend also has it that where David was born during a great gale, a healing spring gushed forth at what is now known as St. Non's Well. Another altogether different story goes that Black Bart, creator of the Jolly Roger, used to sally forth on his piracy raids from the now respectable Solva harbour.

Much use has been made of the striking purple-red sandstone quarried from the sea cliffs of Caerbwdy and Caerfai. They are among some of the oldest and most colourful rocks in Britain and elsewhere along the coastline they can range from grey, blue, red, purple, buff, green and pink sandstones to various shades of volcanic rock. Across this, the most westerly peninsula of Wales, they have imaginatively been thought to compete with the carpets of spring flowers and riotous colours of the early summer blooms that flourish in the mild 'Atlantic' climate that is influenced by the warm waters of the Gulf Stream that keep the coastline almost frost free. Golden gorse blazes throughout the year and even on New Year's Day at least 50 plants may be found in flower. But although spring comes early, autumn is late to leave and the annual sunshine record is the highest in Wales, it is the wind that governs the climate of the peninsula, as is shown by the shortage of trees and distorted shapes of the bushes. It is said that over 30 Force 8 or greater gales are expected every year, a high proportion between October and February when frontal squalls may blow at 90mph or more, gathering so much sea spray that plants on the exposed coast have to be adapted not only to buffeting in the wind but repeated drenching in salt water. The closest landfall beyond the prevailing north-westerlies that sweep in from the Atlantic Ocean is in South America, and the pounding seas have created a rugged coastline of cliffs and coves, headlands and harbours, bays and beaches of breathtaking beauty.

Nearby beaches. The nearest bathing beach to St. Davids is just over half a mile away at **Caerfai**. The quite sheltered south-facing beach, its rock pools and caves are reached down a steep but fairly short path from a small car park but offers only rocks and boulders until the ebbing of the tide exposes the firm sand. It regularly receives Green Coast and Seaside Awards and is in an impressive setting of tall but unstable sandstone cliffs. Some of the best and most colourful of these have been quarried from medieval times for the building and maintenance of the cathedral fabric, and so have those at **Caerbwdy**, immediately to the east beyond the Penpleidau headland and its large once heavily defended Iron Age fort. Caerbwdy is also a south-facing bay, with some sand beyond the rock and pebble beach at low tide. It can be reached both from the Coast Path and a footpath leading for just over a ½ mile from the A497

Top right: The ruins of the chapel traditionally associated with St. Non
Above: The 1930s' medieval looking Chapel of Our Lady and St. Non
Right: St. Nons Bay

at Pont Clegyr. This passes an unusually large square lime-kiln dating from 1815 and owned by the bishop, sited just above a ruined mill.

The Coast Path has come from Solva and after reaching Caerfai it heads onwards to **St. Nons Bay**, close to the reputed birthplace of St. David. The way there by road is via Goat Street in the city centre, turning left at the sign for the Warpool Court Hotel and passing its entrance drive to reach the coast down a narrow lane that ends at a small car park. There is what remains of a Bronze Age stone circle in a field just to the west, while closer down below are the scant ruins of a **chapel** that has traditionally been associated with St. Non, the mother of St. David. The present remains probably date from the 13th century. Propped up within the enclosure is a stone with an incised cross that is considered to be from between the 7th and 9th centuries. **St. Non's Well**, close by, is beneath a low barrel-vaulted well house built in the early 1800s, and with the shrine and enclosure restored in 1951. Up above, the **Chapel of Our Lady and St. Non** was built in 1934 in a medieval Pembrokeshire style and using stone from the ruins of the now vanished Whitewell Priory not far away. It began as chapel to the large stone house that enviably overlooks the bay, until in 1939 this was converted to a retreat house and centre for spiritual refreshment.

Erosion by the sea of heavily faulted sedimentary rocks down below has resulted in a hugely varied range of gullies, caves, arches and stacks, while up above them the flowers alongside the Coast Path are especially abundant along the next leg towards Porth Clais.

A signed road takes a similar route from the centre of St. Davids to **Porth Clais** as the River Alun that passes the west front of the cathedral, while a short distance to the north-west of the little harbour is Ffynon Dewi (David's Well) where David is said to have been baptised by Elvis, bishop of Munster. Ireland's mountains could be seen across the sea on clear days, and whereas passage might have been relatively easy to St. Davids, according to Giraldus Cambrensis 'covered in one short day', travel by land to much of west Pembrokeshire must have meant heading over rough ground for a windswept 'back

The harbour at Porth Clais

of beyond'. The Dewisland peninsula was, however, close to the meeting place of Celtic sea lanes that extended not just to Ireland but also the coasts of west Wales, south-west England, Brittany and to the rest of the world. The long and narrow inlet at Porth Clais at the mouth of the River Alun, where the bishop probably landed, provided the closest sea access for the monastic community that, years later, David was to found a mile upstream. It was to feature in *The Mabinogion* and serve early Christian missionaries, pilgrims, soldiers, traders, Vikings, pirates and the bishops' special palace guests — and more recently, coal merchants, lime dealers and pleasure boat owners. The inlet is half closed across the mouth by a stone breakwater that could date from Norman times, then rebuilt in 1722, while at the head of the creek there are two former trading quays, two stone quarries and four limekilns. The NT car park occupies the site of the former town gas works that had functioned until the 1950s, fed from steam coasters with coal which was also carted to St. Davids or used in the form of culm to fire the limekilns. Records refer to two 8-ton trading ships operating from the port in 1566. Nowadays there are anchorages for a few small boats, while the near vertical rock strata facing the sea are popular with climbers and abseilers.

From here the coastline to Port Lyski and round the headland towards Porth Stinian is famously bold and beautiful, offering the first glimpses of Ramsey Island and the shattered satellite islets and rocks to its south. The coast path passes traces of the 19th-century Treginnis copper mine, once almost at the cliff edge, before reaching the most westerly point of mainland Wales at Penmaen Melyn. This is directly opposite the fearsome line of rocks known as The Bitches. These reach out far across the Ramsey Sound where the spring tides roar through them at up to 7 knots to create a striking white water spectacle, sometimes attracting 'adrenalin junkies' and occasional world championship kayaking events. At Castell Heinif the Coast Path comes to another promontory Iron Age fort before reaching Porth Stinian, the end of the narrow road from St. Davids and a small car park.

The ruins of the early 16th-century **St. Justinian's Chapel** at Porth Stinian are on the site of the former Celtic oratory where the saint was first buried, before his remains were taken to the cathedral. Like the chapel dedicated to St. Patrick, further north at Whitesands, St. Non's and others on the coasts, it could have been placed there for sailors or pilgrims wishing to offer prayers for a safe voyage before setting off, or of thanks after a safe landing. King Henry II landed here in 1171 and the year after, and in recent times in 1912 the lifeboat station and slip was built and, in these hazardous waters, has been much called upon ever since. The slipway is also in use by boats making sight-seeing trips to and around Ramsey Island, North Bishop Island for the puffins and shearwaters, and longer cruises to see countless gannets, minke whales, porpoises, dolphins or to catch mackerel, pollack and trophy fish.

Ramsey Island/Ynys Dewi, an island nearly 2 miles long and up to 1 mile wide with magnificent cliffs and 400ft-high twin hills of igneous rock, Carnllundain and Carnysgybor, is owned by The Royal Society for the Protection of Birds and has a small reception area with limited facilities for a restricted number of visitors between Easter or 1 April, whichever is sooner, and the end of October. During the spring and early summer it teems with thousands of breeding kittiwakes, guillemots, razorbills and other seabirds that, after eradication of a great rat invasion, now again include underground-burrowing Manx Shearwaters. It is also a good place for choughs, the rare red-legged, curved beaked members of the crow family, and peregrines, as well as many other species to be seen inland. The island is rich with flora, early bluebells followed in spring by carpets of thrift or sea pinks and acres of purple heather. With Skomer and the mainland the island also supports the largest numbers of Atlantic grey seals in southern Britain, when during the autumn breeding season more than 400 white-furred pups can be born on the shingle beaches below the cliffs. Autumn is also the time to

Atlantic grey seals

witness the passage of migrating birds, some to over-winter here and others heading south for warmer climes.

An easy stretch of the Coast Path from Porth Stinian heads for the tip of the peninsula at Point St. John, where there are fine views along the northern end of Ramsey Island and westwards towards the Bishops and Clerks reefs, then a change of direction towards the small sandy beach at the north-west-facing Porthselau. Other ways there involve a walk of about ½ mile along a rough track linking with the St. Davids/Porth Stinian road, or by parking at Whitesands and walking along the Coast Path, or at low tide perhaps the beach. There is a *c.*570 million years' old curiosity for geologists along the Coast Path between the beach and Ogof Golchfa, known as the Cambrian basal conglomerate. Conglomerate is rock comprising pebbles or cobbles set in a matrix of finer material, but here the stones are purples, reds and whites made of quartzite, jasper and ash from the underlying Precambrian rocks and it is worth looking for outcrops close to the path.

Whitesands (*Porth Mawr*) is one of the most popular beaches in Pembrokeshire and so it can get very crowded at the height of the holiday season, while the B4583 access road signposted from the A487 north of St. Davids may suffer traffic jams. There is a large car park (charges) and sometimes this can also be overwhelmed, but usually it provides ready access to the beach and slipway, and also to a café, shop and other amenities. The beach earns its regular European Blue Flag and UK Seaside Awards for high water quality and there is the added magic of its superb setting, glorious sunsets seen from the west-facing outlook and a number of contrasting walks starting and finishing at handy parking places. The way from Whitesands past Porth

Whitesands Bay and Carn Llidi

Lleong to Porthmelgan must be among the most heavily used stretches of the entire 181 miles of the Pembrokeshire Coast Path, partly because of the stunning views all around and, with luck, the chance of sighting unfamiliar wildlife.

The sandy beach at **Porthmelgan** faces south-west towards Ramsey Island and the Bishops and Clerks reefs and requires a walk of nearly a mile from the Whitesands car park, making it relatively secluded. In addition to the sand there are intriguing rock pools and caves at low tide but swimmers need to be wary of the big waves. Beyond the cove the Coast Path continues onwards to Warrior's Dyke, an Iron Age fort not far from the tip of the peninsula at St. Davids Head (*Penmaen Dewi*) and then turns to pass close to Coetan Arthur, a rather basic Neolithic burial chamber dating from *c*.3500 BC.

From St. Davids take the A487 towards Fishguard but only just past the edge of St. Davids, turn left on the B4583 towards Whitesands (for which see the end of Box 4 above). There is no other car access to the coast before Abereiddi and it is best shadowed by taking to the St. Davids to Llanrhian minor road, turning left at the direction sign for Abereiddi and dropping steeply to the car park above the beach.

5. Abereiddi, Porthgain and their Industrial Revolution

The black sand creates a rather drab effect but does not deter summer visitors (any more than at Lanzarote in the Canaries), nor does it extend to the clarity of the sea water, which consistently earns Green Coast and Seaside Awards for Abereiddi. The scene early in the 19th century was, however, very different while the narrow road bringing tourists down to the beach was instead, as at neighbouring Porthgain, an integral part of heavy quarrying activity. This started in *c*.1830 at the slate-blue cliffs of Trwyncastell on the headland to the right of the north-facing beach, and added to deliveries of culm and limestone for the limekilns, small sloops were loading with slate during the summer months. They had to be run ashore at high tide, loaded with up to 30 tons of stone and floated off on the next tide, for it was not practicable to build a harbour and berths for larger, more profitable vessels. However about 2 miles away there was the relatively sheltered haven at Porthgain and by mid-century a tramway had been built along the intervening valley and work was in hand to develop the harbour. Although the life expectancy of Abereiddi slate was, at *c*.40 years, only about a quarter of that quarried in Caernarvonshire it had the edge at that time because of this close access to carriage by sea and production continued for the remainder of the century. By 1890 a quarry of five well constructed galleries, amounting to a depth of 150 feet, was capable of producing more than 80,000 slates per month. But by 1904 competition from, by then, rail-borne consignments of superior North Wales slate forced closure and during the 1920s a narrow passage was blasted from the sea to flood the quarry and provide shelter for small boats. Because of the predominant colour effects of the slabs this has become widely known as 'The Blue Lagoon' — and north of the beach there is a wheelchair-friendly path that passes ruined quarry buildings and quarrymen's cottages to approach it.

Part way along, the Coast Path bears off to the right, passing further ruins and the mysterious Abereiddi

The Blue Lagoon and the Abereiddi Tower on the headland

Tower on the Trwyncastell headland, its origins guessed to be anything from a navigational day-marker, an 18th-century Pharos tower, to a social meeting-place. After half a mile along the margins of Barry Island, the path arrives high above **Traeth Llyfn**, a west-facing golden sandy beach down in a setting of impressive but unstable cliffs. There is an alternative way there through Barry Island Farm to a private car park near the Coast Path, but either way access to sands and rock pools is down some steep metal steps — which should be kept within reach to avoid being cut off by a rising tide. Further along at **Penclegyr** two levels of a disused quarry show how the stone, andesite (for practical purposes called granite) used for a variety of purposes (see below), was raised up one incline by cable, along a railway through a cutting from the other, to be conveyed in wagons along the then named 'Jerusalem Road' to huge processing machinery further east at Porthgain. The path follows the same route as far as a steep flight of steps that descend to the harbour, which may also be reached by driving down the road from Llanrhian.

There have been arguments for all relics of the short-lived slate, granite and brick industry at this scenic part of the National Park to be cleared way, filled in, tidied up and 'landscaped', while there are those who are not bothered by the disturbed appearance. But there is a strong case for preserving a reminder of the great effort that came through often difficult times from here towards the end of the Victorian era in providing roofing and other essential building material (even gravestones) for the rapidly expanding towns of England and Wales. And of how, afterwards, the demands of the new 20th-century Motor Age were first met by supplying setts for street paving, and then stone chippings that were said to be 'second only in hardness to the granite of Aberdeen', for countless road miles of 'macadamised' base-courses and top surfacing.

Porthgain

The Sloop Inn has been at Porthgain since 1743, and for many years from a century later the liquid lubrication dispensed there must have been greatly appreciated by quarrymen, brick-workers and seamen in the dust-laden and smoky atmosphere. Now, early in the 21st century, it has changed from being a workers' to a walkers' pub, offering Real Ales, bar and evening meals and special Sunday lunches while also acting as a museum of relics and old photographs of Porthgain, and a source of further local information and literature as found in *Porthgain & Abereiddi. A Century of Industry* by Peter B.S. Davies, and *The Railways of Porthgain and Abereiddi* by J.C. Jermy.

The 'village green' and car park areas almost opposite the pub are close to the sites of the brick kiln and drying sheds and the newly re-roofed Machine House beyond — where bricks were formed by uniquely processing slate and slab waste, then to be passed to a large Hoffman Kiln beneath a 100ft-high chimney to emerge at a rate of some 50,000 per week. Next to the slate mills opposite were the enormous storage bins and crushed stone chutes that still dominate the west side of the enlarged harbour, and beyond them the tunnel entrance to the Porthgain Slate Quarry. Above are the remains of the stone crusher and screening buildings, other roofless and derelict operational sheds and buildings and evidence of many tramway track-beds, including the route to the Penclegyr Roadstone Quarry.

Passing 'The Street' of renovated, and now 'Listed', workmen's cottages that have ironically been re-roofed with Caernarvonshire slate salvaged from a wreck, the route then rises to Llanrhian before turning left to descend to sea level at Aberfelin, or Aber Draw, below the village of Trefin.

---

6. Aberfelin and *Melin Trefin*

Not really ideal for bathing, the beach is of sand, shingle and rock pools within a small west-facing cove hemmed in by unstable cliffs — calling for caution if approached. Roadside parking spaces above the path down to the beach are very limited in number. Beside the bridge, the old ruined corn mill that gave the cove its name (*melin* or *felin* meaning mill) inspired locally born Crwys (1975–1968), Archdruid of the Gorsedd of Bards between 1939 and 1947, to make it the subject of his highly regarded poem in Wales, *Melin Trefin*. The Coast Path passes through and meets with superb views and features of interest on the way to Abercastle, such as signs of the Trwyn Llwyd Quarries that were in production through most of the Victorian era, and the double-banked Iron Age promontory fort at Pen Castell Coch, where it is also worth taking in the stunning coastal views to the south west and chance sightings of fulmars.

The road climbs again through **Trefin**, the largest of the coastal villages between St. Davids and Goodwick, where there was an episcopal palace in the 14th century, but leaving few traces either of the building or any road access. There is then a further descent to the coast at Abercastle, providing a further example of a drowned valley or ria.

---

7. Abercastle. *Cwm Badan* (Valley of Boats)

Facing north-west and sheltered from the south-westerly gales, the harbour has provided safe anchorage for cargo boats at least as long ago as a first recorded mention in 1566. Sloops were based there in 1811 for trading with Bristol and Liverpool and among the wide range of cargoes have been consignments of slate, grain, dairy produce, salted herring and pilchards, while imports have included anthracite, culm and limestone for the four local limekilns, including the well-preserved survivor west of the harbour. One very special landing took place in 1876 when a small open fishing dory arrived with a solo crew on board. Alfred Johnson was the first person ever to sail across the Atlantic single-handed from west to east and the plaque of Welsh slate on the quay wall by the slipway records that he left Gloucester, Massachusetts, that year on 15 June and arrived safely at Abercastle on 10 August.

Just inland, west of the beach of muddy sand and shingle close to a public footpath, is one of the most imposing surviving megalithic tombs in south-west Wales. The huge conglomerate capstone of **Carreg Samson** is over 16 feet long and almost 10 feet wide, resting on three of the six uprights and is thought to have been used for over 100 different burials some 4,500 years ago. What is visible is just the central chamber, and although no-one really knows for sure, it is thought that the entire tomb would have been encased with boulders and covered with a mound of earth.

The road from Abercastle rises towards the conspicuous hill-top village of Mathry and is one of several ancient approaches that reveal its importance as a market centre during the Middle Ages, while the Farmers Arms pub in the centre of the village also acts as a reminder.

8. Mathry

There were strong Church property interests in the rich agricultural area, out of which Mathry became regarded as 'The Golden Prebend' because of heavy grain crops and rewarding clergy income. At the topmost part of the village the squat Holy Martyrs Church stands in a circular churchyard that suggests prehistoric origin, although the building was 'restored' in the spirit of the late 1860s. It occupies a superb vantage point for a wealth of views extending towards the Preseli hills, round to long lengths of the stunning northern coastline.

Mathry Church

A road heading east descends from the village to join the A467 St. Davids to Fishguard road at the junction with the B4331 to Castle Morris. At a crossroads about 1¼ miles along the main road there is a sign that indicates the **Llangloffan Farmhouse Cheese Centre**, a short distance along to the right. Based in Manchester, Leon Downey was co-principal viola with the Hallé Orchestra in 1977 but that year decided 'to get away from the clamour of cities and motorways', moved to Pembrokeshire and discovered the Abermawr Valley. He also started making and selling cheese at Llangloffan, and since then at certain times of the day it has been possible to watch parts of the production process and at most others visit the tea-room, sample and buy the products in the shop — or just wander about and examine his cows.

A sign pointing left announces the **Melin Tregwynt woollen mill**, first established in 1912 but following in a centuries-long tradition of the woollen industry based there. It has a special reputation for pure new wool blankets and throws and again it is possible, from Mondays to Fridays, to follow the processes, and all week to examine and buy the goods in the shop and take refreshment in the café.

9. Abermawr and Aberbach

The beach at Abermawr is made up of sand, pebbles and rock and skirted by cliffs that extend westwards towards the Penmorfa peninsula and another Iron Age promontory fort, and northwards towards Aberbach beach. The water is classed as of 'excellent' quality and good for bathing and surfing, always subject to the currents, and with Aberbach offers good sport for sea anglers. This is another part of the coast where stumps of a submerged prehistoric forest can be exposed offshore at very low tides after major winter storms. In more recent times Abermawr is said to have appealed in 1851 to Isambard Kingdom Brunel (1806–59), engineer to the GWR, as a suitable location for the terminus of his railway from London, and as a port for the competitive Irish and international shipping trade. There are still traces of some preliminary measures, but in the event he chose Neyland (pp.115-116) for the rail terminus instead and from 1856 this connected for the next 50 years with a prosperous ferry service to Ireland. At Abermawr the only link established across the Irish Sea followed in 1873, when an underwater cable was laid from the Submarine Telegraph Cable Hut that, now converted to another use, is still to be seen from the small car park and narrow road that leads towards the Strumble Head peninsula.

The road runs alongside the marshland that is trapped behind the Aberbach storm beach and then turns left to head with the coastline for Pen-Caer (the Strumble Head peninsula). Walkers on the Coast Path follow a generally easy stretch past Pwllcrochan and turn north-eastwards at the Penbwchdy headland for over a mile of what is regarded as one of the great cliff walks of Wales. They can reach a point at more than

450 feet above the sea level of Pwll Deri as they stride towards a Youth Hostel that can hardly be bettered for either setting or spectacular views. It occupies the former village school, has a family bunk room and during the spring-time sea-bird breeding season can be popular with 'twitchers', and in September and October spotters of Atlantic seals and their new pups. At Dinas Mawr, alongside the group of offshore islands and stacks to the south of the bay there is a further Iron Age promontory fort, while high above, at almost 700 feet above sea level, there is the hill-top fort on Garn Fawr. These are just some of the many prehistoric sites that are a reminder of the early origins of mankind in south-west Wales, and the Strumble Head peninsula has much evidence of human occupation ranging back to the Neolithic, or New Stone Age, period and the early introduction of agriculture. There is little known evidence in south-west Wales of any active Neolithic settlements however, the nearer of only two being at Clegyr Boia at St. Davids (p.136) and the other at Coygen Hill near Laugharne (p.77). It is thought that Clegyr Boia may afterwards have been adapted and fortified during the Iron Age, not far from the group of dwellings, ancillary buildings and field system of that period at St. Davids Head (p.136).

The narrow country road from Aberbach and Tregwynt rises towards Trefasser, continuing on to Pwll Deri and the Youth Hostel, while a right turn and then a left leads to the eastern foot of Garn Fawr, and there is an opportunity here to park and ease the legs into action to follow a track to the craggy summit at 699 feet above sea level and soak in some of the greatest views in south Wales. Then on to Strumble Head/Pen Caer, the nearest point to the Irish coast, to see the Trinity House light house on Ynys Meicl (St. Michael's Island). Built in 1908 beyond a very narrow gap crossed by a footbridge, its light ranging out for 26 sea miles, it was meant for the safety of ships passing between Ireland and the new Fishguard harbour at Goodwick. It is within sight of the South Bishop light marking the northern entrance to St. Brides Bay, 18 miles to the south west, and now unmanned was converted to automatic operation in 1980 and monitored from a control centre at Harwich on the North Sea coast.

---

10. Strumble Head Peninsula, and a short French Invasion

In 1789, Revolution had broken out in France, which became a Republic from 1792, and the following year Louis XVI and Marie-Antoinette had been made to take the path of many aristocrats to the guillotine. There was a new Revolutionary Government by 1795, and in February 1797 a very strangely constructed expeditionary force set sail for Britain with the aim of fomenting revolt against the 'ancien régime' here and to introduce 'liberty, equality and fraternity' to the down-trodden citizenry. One approach was to be through Bristol, but this was thwarted by adverse high winds and the ships headed further north, to be sighted off St. Davids Head, where false British Colours were recognised from the alien French rigging and an attempt to land at Fishguard Bay therefore anticipated and driven off by cannon fire. General Tate, their ageing Irish American commander, thereupon tacked round Strumble Head to disembark his force and stores above the inlet of Aber Felin at Careg Gwastad Point. In late February, at one of the wildest parts of the coast and lacking present-day cliff-scaling tackle, he faced his first great challenge — as today's winter users of the Coast

Strumble Head lighthouse and Irish Sea ferry

Path can appreciate by looking down the cliff face from the **stone memorial pillar** that was erected 100 years later. The frigates had rapidly up-anchored and were sailing back to France, and upwards of 1,200 assorted soldiers, former jail birds and felons had to make it to the top of the cliffs, where they began looting, drinking heavily and generally upsetting the neighbourhood. But meanwhile, after mobilising the local Yeomanry and some reinforcements, Lord Cawdor of Stackpole had moved swiftly and effectively into action and in a very short while the motley collection of French aggressors was surrendering arms on Goodwick Sands and being packed off as prisoners to Haverfordwest and elsewhere.

Thus ended the last invasion of Britain! Over the past 300 years the incident has bred many legends and yarns. Were the invaders really duped by the sight of Welsh women wearing their red skirts and tall hats to make them look like red-coated military reinforcements, and did a sturdy cobbler woman from Llanwnda really round up 12 Frenchmen by herself, equipped only with a pitchfork? Certainly there is a memorial to a Jemima Nicholas to this effect in Fishguard churchyard, and at the **Royal Oak Inn** in the town they treasure the table that was used when the surrender documents were signed.

The road leaving the car park at Strumble Head meets a T-junction, where a left turn leads down towards Stop-and-Call, with an opportunity to divert left to Llanwnda. Although restored during the 1880s, St. Gwyndaf's Church was founded much longer ago, even before Giraldus Cambrensis (p.91) was appointed as rector. Four centuries before his time, Asser, friend and biographer of King Alfred, spent his early days locally. The whole parish is particularly rich in prehistoric monuments, added to which the scenery looking down towards the north and out towards the sea is truly breathtaking.

Finally the road descends through Goodwick to reach the end of the A487 from St. Davids and Haverfordwest.

In making its return to Haverfordwest as an alternative to the now much longer A487, this tour follows the A40 (to pass Goodwick and Fishguard to head towards **Wolf's Castle**, where road and railway cross over and join with the Western Cleddau river to pass down the Treffgarne Gorge. The name of the village comes from the little known motte and bailey castle built at the junction of the Cleddau and Anghof rivers by a Fleming called Wolf at the time of the Norman Conquest, at the fringe of the Landsker. The River Anghof springs from the Preseli hills and, about 1¼ miles upstream, flows past Sealyham where the terrier breed originated in the 1860s.

The manor of Treffgarne was owned in the 14th century by the family of Owain Glyndwr's mother and from this it is widely believed that in *c*.1359 he was born here.

Just over 2 miles from the county town, the A40 reaches **Haverfordwest Airport**, its history harking back to 1942 when it was built for service by the RAF. After a disturbed and not altogether spectacular war, it closed in early 1946 and in 1952 was acquired by Pembrokeshire County Council. Many changes and enhancements later, including a new hangar, terminal building and control tower, there is now regular light aircraft use by charter and pleasure flights and for fixed wing and helicopter flying training, while since 1989 Withybush Airfield, as it is often called, has also hosted International Air Rallies, 'Fly-ins', competitions and various other events.

The County Showground and Withybush General Hospital follow as the A40 continues past Prendergast to skirt part of Haverfordwest town centre, before heading towards Carmarthen.

Fishguard

Well before Fishguard was founded by the Normans, late in the 11th century, its connection with the sea and fishing had long been recognised by the Vikings in giving it the Old Scandinavian name of *Fiskrgauthr,* meaning a fish yard. Little is known about these early days, not even the actual position of the settlement, apart from what can be surmised about the siting from the 13th century of St. Mary's Church. Unlike St. Davids 16 miles down the coast, the setting of a cathedral, birthplace of the nation's patron saint and seat of the diocesan bishop, it has not featured in history to any extent until the late 19th century apart, that is, from a bizarre episode that was played out in February 1797. In scenes resembling something of a French Farce, the Royal Oak Hotel in the Market Square figured in the signing of the surrender documents after the collapse of William Tate's chaotic invasion attempt (pp.145-146), while at Goodwick Sands his inglorious assault forces handed over their weapons before being marched off to the local jails. A print of the town at the time shows the buildings set out across the rising ground above the bay, at just about the time when the bountiful herring fishery, shared with the other ports along the Irish Sea coast, had failed after the shoals had abruptly left. This caused widespread job losses, but with the advantage of a deep water harbour, sheltered from the worst storms by the Strumble Head peninsula, Fishguard was nevertheless able to challenge Haverfordwest in the variety and volume of its sea-borne trade, and with added scope for setting up a competitive ship-building industry.

By the mid-19th century, the Railway Age was arriving in Wales and in 1852 the line reached Carmarthen and there were thoughts about continuing on to Fishguard, as the nearest port to Ireland for entering the profitable ferry trade. This would provide competition for the LNWR route through north Wales to Holyhead, but the South Wales Railway opted instead for the shorter land route to Neyland in Milford Haven and the service to Waterford opened in 1856, becoming a part of the GWR network in 1863. But the Great Western would nevertheless have preferred Fishguard as the terminus as it would reduce the crucial distance to Ireland by 35 sea miles. But not only that, there was another ambition — to capture some of the transatlantic passenger traffic from Liverpool, the primary entry port to Britain, and Fishguard was 115 miles closer to New York.

The opportunity came in 1899 when the GWR took over the Fishguard and Rosslare Railways and Harbour Company and work began on the huge task of quarrying a platform out of the Goodwick Cliffs and using the stone towards the construction of a near ½-mile long north breakwater out into the bay. The large covered railway station had four platforms, operational installations included a four road Churchward design locomotive depot, there were covered cattle pens for the valuable cattle import trade and the grand Great Western Hotel, now the Fishguard Bay Hotel, was built for the comfort of travellers. An inaugural transatlantic service to New York started on 30 August 1909, and in *Our Home Railways* the following year, W.J. Jordan wrote 'Soon after it was ready, some of the South American liners began to use it as a port of call on the homeward journey and so well adapted did the arrangements prove for quick despatch that the great Cunarders followed and now it is known as being 4½ hours from London on the quickest

American route'. Great ships such as *RMS Mauretania*, Booth Line and Blue Funnel liners sometimes called during the remaining few years before the start of the Great War, but did not return afterwards. The coastal waters of the Irish Channel became part of the war zone in 1914 and quickly faced the menace of German submarines. Numbers of merchant ships and fishing vessels were attacked to the south of Ireland by torpedoes or gunfire, culminating in the sinking by *U20* of *RMS Lusitania* in May 1915 with the loss of 1,198 passengers and crew. The U-boats were known to lurk in the shelter of the rugged Irish shoreline and Fishguard harbour was therefore regarded as an ideal site for a Royal Naval Air Service seaplane base as one of the counter measures. Six aircraft of No.245 Squadron were usually moored just outside the north breakwater and they made several sightings on patrol, although no confirmed 'kills', but at least provided a deterrent.

Fortunately for the GWR — and certainly the local economy and job prospects at Fishguard and Goodwick — the Irish ferries remained. Towards the end of the centenary year of the Fishguard-Rosslare shipping route, Stena Line, the operating company reported that in 2005 it carried 600,000 passengers, 52,000 freight vehicles, 147,000 cars and over 2,500 coaches across the Irish Sea, making for a significant trade and tourist link between the two countries. The 54-mile crossing on board the *Stena Europe* 'Superferry'

took 3½ hours, while between April and September it was possible to speed across on the *Stena Express* catamaran in just 2 hours.

Much port activity can be seen from the sand and shingle foreshore at The Parrog, where in 1797 the defeated French surrendered their weapons, and despite being quite close to the Ferry Landing Stage and installations is regularly credited with a Seaside Award and good water quality. Other attractions include the Ocean Lab building and TIC and the sail training centre where boats can be launched for three hours either side of high tide.

The old harbour, now called **Lower Fishguard** or Lower Town, is over to the east at the mouth of the River Gwaun, hence Fishguard's long established Welsh name of Abergwaun. At the end of Quay Street near the junction with the A487 Newport Road there is a sculpture called *Scadan Abergwaun – Fishguard Herrings* to reflect the historic herring industry of Lower Town. A plaque close by adds a reminder that here was the scene of the filming of Dylan Thomas' *Under Milkwood* in 1971 (p.8), when the harbour-side village was transformed into *Llareggub*. The long curving quay

Two views of Lower Fishguard, the old port

on the east side of the river was rebuilt at Cwm Abergwaun in the 1780s after a long history of modest shipbuilding and coastal trading that extended to Ireland and Chester and is lined with picturesque houses and cottages, ending with a high wall and slipway. Visible from there, high up to the right on Castle Point are some of the ancient cannons of **Fishguard Fort**. It overlooks Fishguard Harbour and was first built in 1779 following a raid by the privateer called *The Black Prince*, when a demand of £1,000 for the return of a captured local ship, and as a ransom for the town, was refused. St. Mary's Church and some houses were damaged in the ensuing bombardment and after that, Fishguard was grudgingly allotted eight 9-pounder guns in 1781, to be manned by three invalid gunners from Woolwich. Some time after becoming the HQ of the Fishguard Fencibles it sprang into action in 1797, firing, it is said, three shots and some blanks when one of General Tate's ships were seen entering the harbour, causing it to beat a hasty retreat round the Point. (No one seems to be quite certain as to whether the gunfire was intended to deter the French — or signal the townspeople to head for the hills!)

Looking across Fishguard Fort, briefly used in the action against the French Invasion of 1797, to the new harbour and one of the Irish Sea ferries

At the top of the Newport road beyond the harbour there is a car park on the left. At the end of the footpath leading to the fort, its guns and remaining buildings, there is another splendid view of Fishguard Harbour, and to the north east the complex run of cliffs leading towards Dinas Island.

Scadan Abergwaun — Fishguard Herrings

Fishguard Bay and the Strumble Head peninsula from Pwllgwaelod (see Tour 7)

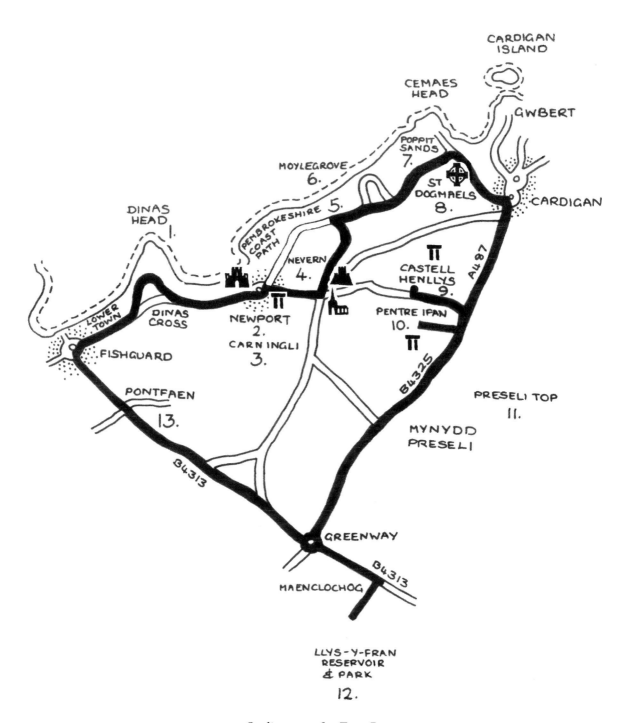

Outline map for Tour 7
The numbers 1 to 13 relate to the boxed information given within the tour

Tour 7   North Pembrokeshire & the Preselis

The route follows A and B roads in the main, but takes to minor country lanes in order to reach parts of the coast. It is essentially a scenic tour of both coastline and the Preselis, but includes the settlements of Newport and Nevern, the remains of the medieval St. Dogmaels abbey and the prehistoric sites of Castell Henllys and the Pentre Ifan burial chamber. The total distance excluding detours is about 40 miles (OS Landranger 145, 157).

The limekiln at Pwllgwaelod

Take the A487 out of Fishguard towards Cardigan through Lower Fishguard. Following the coastline up to ¾ mile inland, the A487 arrives at the scattered village of Dinas. Here you can carry on along the A487 or turn left onto a narrow winding road passing through Bryn-henllan and dropping down to a car park (charges) and well-preserved limekiln behind the award winning beach at Pwllgwaelod. Facing west across Fishguard Bay the small sandy bay is good for bathing, fishing, sub aqua diving, canoeing and sailing — and it is a popular place for meals at The Old Sailors pub and licenced restaurant.

---

1. Dinas Island / Head

There is a choice of at least two good walks, the first along the flat, push-chair friendly path leading for about ½ mile through bird-rich woodland and open freshwater boggy ground to **Cwm-yr-Eglwys** at the eastern end of Dinas Island. (Not really an island, it is rather a promontory that has been partly separated from the mainland during the Ice Age as a result of melt-water action along the line of the modern footpath).

One of the English meanings of Dinas is 'a fort' and as there are so many signs of Iron Age promontory fortresses along the Pembrokeshire coastline, it is surprising that no evidence of anything of the kind has so far been seen on Dinas Island. It used to be called Ynys Fach Llyfan Gawr, meaning the little island of Llyfan the Giant and has always served to shelter Fishguard Bay from the easterly winds and Newport Bay from the westerlies. During the Second World War, the Island Farm was rescued from dereliction by a renowned lover of islands, the naturalist Ronald Lockley (1903-2000) (see also p.123) who described the experiences in two of his 50 and more books, *The Island Farmers* and *The Golden Year*, and who first surveyed the route of the Pembrokeshire Coast Path before its adoption.

The National Trust came to own the farm and Dinas Island more recently and aims to 'integrate productive farming with environmental enhancement'. Currently this has involved the tenant in the introduction of a flock of 1,800 pedigree Lleyn ewes, natives of another projection into the Irish Sea further north in Gwynedd. Renowned for their 'hardiness, prolificacy, easy lambing, strong mothering instincts, good milking and easy handling' they are being added to a small stud flock of Sussex sheep and a Hereford cross steer beef enterprise.

Any achieved environmental enhancement can be judged along the 3-mile section of the Coast Path that rises 465 feet to Dinas Head on the second walk from Pwllgwaelod beach past wildflowers and butterflies and towards fine coastal views and the sight inland of the Preseli hills. Walkers continuing along the east side reach Needle Rock and, in season, nesting razorbills, chocolate-jacketed guillemots and raucous herring gulls, before returning to the mainland at Cwm-yr-Eglwys. The 'eglwys' is St. Brynach's, a 12th-century Celtic type church where the belfry and part of the west wall are all that remain after storms in 1827, and most spectacularly following the great *Royal Charter* hurricane of October 1859 (p.217) when this gold-laden ship and 113 other vessels were wrecked along the coasts of Wales. At the entrance to the churchyard there is a small model of *The Cwm Trader*, a coastal trading brig typical of the many lost ships that plied the waters off Pembrokeshire and Cardiganshire at the time. It had a largely flat bottom, with a relatively shallow draft, and would have sailed into the bays at high water to be unloaded at low tide by horse and cart. Another storm in March 1979 caused further severe damage to the churchyard, but since then a sturdy wall has been built and the small, award winning cove down below shares the benefit of its shelter and the cliffs on either side and is popular at holiday times for the sand and shingle north-east-facing aspect across Newport Bay.

Cwm-yr-Eglwys

Retrace your steps to the A487 and turn left towards Cardigan once more (or if you've carried straight on) the next port of call is **Newport**, *Trefdraeth* in Welsh — meaning 'the town by the shore', not too easily confused out here with its much larger namesake in Monmouthshire. The land around much of this tour bears evidence of extensive human occupation during prehistoric times, and half way to Newport and clearly visible on the left-hand side of the road at **Cerrig y Gof** there is a circle of five cromlechau, or chambered tombs. It is thought to be unique and possibly associated with the landscape of Bronze Age cairns, hut circles and enclosures, indicated close to the south on the OS map, rather than with monuments of the earlier Neolithic epoch.

The A487 enters Newport as West Street, meeting Parrog Road from the estuary on the left. It has the nearer and more sheltered of the town's beaches, but because of unpredictable currents it is not favoured for swimming. There are a slipway, moorings for pleasure craft and the Boat Club lodged in an adapted early

19th-century quayside warehouse. There is limited parking in Newport itself, but if visiting the second of the town's beaches, it is best to follow the A487 to the bridge across the Afon Nyfer, River Nevern, and continue on to a signposted left turn to pass the golf club and reach the large car park (charges) above the large open expanse of Newport Sands. (If just choosing to pass through, continue along the A487.)

---

2. Newport. Town by the Shore

Facing north-west, **Newport Sands** can become windy, an attraction for wind-surfers if not always sunbathers, who might choose to find shelter at the rear of the sand dunes. These have been formed from on-shore winds blowing sand inland to create a fragile habitat, calling for consolidation by the planting of marram grass. To be effective in preventing erosion and the loss of rare dune species, this needs to be free from disturbance by trampling feet. This is another coastal area along these shores where evidence of a 'drowned forest' sometimes shows close to the low tide line. It could have been associated with the wooded area around the Afon Nyfer Valley from times up to 10,000 years ago, before sea levels rose to their present levels — the timbers afterwards preserved through immersion in salt water and burial in the sand.

Newport was 'new' near the end of the 12th century when, as the surviving street pattern regularity suggests, it became a planted borough, close to the **castle** built by the Norman William fitzMartin (*c*.1155–1209) as *caput*, or chief base, of the barony of Cemaes. His former seat had been at the large motte and bailey castle of Nevern (below), but in 1191 he was driven out by the Welsh led by Rhys ap Gruffudd, the Lord Rhys (his own father-in-law!). His attempts to establish a new ring-work castle and the 'new port' nearer the estuary met with further Welsh resistance, first by Llywelyn Fawr in 1215 and then by grandson Llywelyn the Last in 1257 and the present structure, on a spur of Carn Ingli above the southern end of the town, was rebuilt in stone from *c*.1280. This castle was attacked by the Welsh in its turn in 1408 by Owain Glyndwr, and by the mid-1700s was in ruins, and so it remained for some 200 years.

Meanwhile the borough, new capital of the Marcher Lordship of Cemaes, had been granted a Charter of Incorporation with the right to hold a weekly market and an annual fair every 16 June. From then on it flourished steadily during the years leading up to the time of the Glyndwr rebellion, the population approaching 1,000 — more than half way towards that of the present day, more than six centuries later.

Much success would have come from its position on the coast, with an advantage as a busy trading port. This continued, and by the mid-16th century, ships at the Parrog quay on the estuary are known to have been trading with Bristol and a little shipbuilding was starting. Newport became an important wool centre and this resulted in a lively export trade, matched by the herring fishery that despatched cured products to Ireland, France and Spain and, later on, slates quarried from local cliffs. All this occurred before the days of land passage by coaches, lorries and vans along metalled roads, and the seas provided not only for many forms of personal travel but also the carriage of a wide range of goods and materials. Shiploads of limestone and coal arrived at the Parrog to supply the limekilns by the quay, whilst small vessels, such as the brig *The Cwm Trader* that is modelled at Cwm-yr-

Part of the remains of Newport Castle with the later mansion

153

Eglwys (above), engaged in port to port general trading. They would call in at the Parrog to set out produce and other wares for sale, perhaps like the practice at modern 'Farmers' Markets' — except that captains would probably also load up with locally produced goods for sale at other ports of call along the coasts, such as Solva, Angle and Tenby, and up the Daugleddau waterway to Haverfordwest.

If you walk back up into town you want to head into Market Street, one of parts of the surviving Norman street plan, which leads up towards the castle remains. In 1859 the twin-turreted north gatehouse of the castle was built into a modern dwelling for Sir Thomas Lloyd of Bronwydd in Cardiganshire and the attractively merged medieval and Victorian result continues in private occupation, and is out of bounds.

Close by to the east, **St. Mary's Church** was founded by William fitzMartin near the same time as his castle. It was enlarged in 1834 and afterwards, and is noted for its large cruciform plan and that of the Norman 13th-century west tower. Gravestones in the churchyard attest to the seafaring activity of many 19th-century parishioners.

The economy of Newport now relies heavily on tourism, catered for by a full range of shops, pubs, hotels, a Youth Hostel in Lower St. Mary's Street and the National Park Information Centre in Long Street — also along the line of the medieval street system.

The Cnapan Restaurant at Ivy House on the East Street part of the A487 serves as a reminder of the lively game that was once played on this stretch of the coast, for hours and even sometimes days. It originated during the 14th century and in his *Description of Penbrockeshire in Generall*, George Owen (1552–1613) provided a vivid account of a contest that makes present-day rugby football seem rather a tame and gentle affair. After the wooden ball was boiled in oil to make it slippery, the object was to prevent the opposing side, or parish, from taking it into their own territory. 'At some of these matches', Owen wrote, 'there have often times been esteemed two thousand foote beside horsemen … a great thing to see a thousand naked men thus grippd together and beating one another over the head as hard as they are able'.

The road to the left beyond Lower St. Mary's Street leads north eastwards down Penybont past Cromlech House, so named because behind it is **Carreg Coetan Arthur** (or **Arthur's Quoit**) burial chamber. Through radiocarbon analysis of the burnt wood from cremations it appears to date from around 3500 BC, the sides of the well preserved chamber formed by four upright stones, two of which support the large wedge-shaped capstone. It is sited unusually close to the estuary and sea level, seen as a possible indication that the first prehistoric farming settlers landed here with seed corn and domestic animals, to make their way up the Nyfer Valley to begin cultivating the northern slopes of the Preseli hills.

Coetan Arthur

154

3. Carn Ingli. The Place of Angels above Newport

Its other name Carn Engyl Lle, the Place of Angels, the rough open hill of scattered rocks is said to have been chosen until his solitary death in *c*.570 by St. Brynach (below) for a hermitage, so that angels could minister there to his spiritual needs. The vast igneous outcrop at the top had been taken in to an Iron Age hillfort, covering some 9 acres, and there are still remains of many of the huts that were protected within the defences, while drystone round house footings can be seen outside them to the north-east and south-west.

Overlooking Newport from near Carn Ingli

If you've stopped in Newport, or headed down past the golf course and stopped at Newport sands you'll need to find your way back to the main A487 coast road in Newport, and continue in the direction which you entered Newport and head towards Cardigan. The next stop is Nevern with its St. Brynach's Church in the Afon Nyfer Valley. For this, in only about 2 miles out of Newport, turn left on the B4582 which is soon reached. The road passes the Trewern Arms in the ancient hamlet to arrive at the entrance to St. Brynach's churchyard, close to a mounting block, one of two left in the county and a relic of the times when parishioners rode to church. You want to park somewhere near here. Dark ancient yews, including a tree that can exude drops of red resin, resembling blood according to gory old legends, border the drive from the gateway to the church porch.

4. The Church of St. Brynach and Nevern Castle

Brynach was a devout Irish Gael who founded seven local churches during the 6th century, of which this has become one of the most interesting in Wales. Yet it is just one of a remarkable number of antiquities in the vicinity. The squat Norman tower extends the full width of the church and dates from the 12th century, while the rest of the building is late Perpendicular (from between 1425 and 1525), was restored in 1864 and, together with the tower, subject to further attention in 1952. Although cruciform in plan, it is just noticeable that, for some reason, the chancel is set slightly out of line with the nave. Beneath a stone vaulted roof, unique in Pembrokeshire, the Trewern-Henllys Chapel occupies the south transept where on the east wall a brass tablet commemorates George Owen of Henllys, Lord Marcher of the Barony of Cemaes, Elizabethan historian and geologist — author of *Description of Penbrockeshire in Generall* (above). Two stone slabs, dating from maybe the 5th century, are embedded in the window sills, one inscribed, in Latin: *Maglocvni* (miscut *Maglocvvi*) *fili clvtor*, and Ogham: *Maglicunas maqi Clutar [i]* (read left to right). The meaning of both is '*(the monument) of Maglocunus (Maelgwyn) son of Clutorius*'.

Ogham is an ancient 4th-century alphabet of 20 characters, here in the Irish branch of the Celtic language called Goidelic which is found

St. Brynach's Church

widely in south-west Wales. It is formed with notches for vowels and parallel lines on either side of, or across, the edge of a stone for consonants. Repeated at St. Brynach's in Latin, and sometimes elsewhere in the native language, these monuments help to provide the key to the Ogham alphabet (see also St. Dogmaels parish church, below). The second stone slab, 62 inches long by 12 inches wide, bears a cross of cords or ribbons in slight relief, formed at least in one instance in what has been seen as a stylised, crucified body. Discovered in 1906 in the wall of the passage to the priests' chamber over the chapel, the two stones are thought to be contemporary with the time of St. Brynach.

St. Brynach's Cross

With a faintly lettered double inscription, another stone has been removed from the farm of Cwm-gloyn, farther up the Nevern valley, and placed outside the church, close to the east side of the porch. It is a memorial to Vitalianus and said to be one of the oldest examples of this type of monument, possibly dating from the 5th century. Nevern's famous **St. Brynach's Cross** stands at a full height of 13 feet alongside the path, further to the east just outside the south transept. Below the 24½-inch diameter cross, each of 21 carved panels has a pattern of Irish type interlacing ribbon with no beginning and no end, a symbol of eternity, while two compartments on the east side each contain a swastika form of cross and, with the west side, abbreviated descriptions in the peculiar alphabet found in the earliest British writings — such as *dns* standing for *dominus*, 'Lord'. There is no certainty about age, but comparison with the workmanship and precise dating of the Carew Cross (p.87) points to the 10th or 11th centuries when it was probably carved as a memorial to some respected local chieftain. The high cross of Nevern became a scheduled ancient monument in 1950, and it is also a long-standing part of local fantasy and legend. St. Brynach, like St. Francis, had a particular affection for birds and animals — in his case especially cuckoos, who were equally devoted to him. Long after his death, the first cuckoo of the year was always said to have perched on the stone every 7 April, on his feast day, and Mass in honour of the saint would not begin until the call was heard. But according to the above mentioned George Owen, on one occasion the bird was late and 'being scarce able once to sound the note, presently fell dead'. But, he added, 'This vulgar tale, although it concerns in some sort church matters, you may either believe or not, without peril of damnation.'

The ancient yews of the churchyard have tended to encourage growth of moss and lichen to obscure a little of the stone pattern in places, while the informative church guidebook offers a reminder 'of the use the Welsh made of these sinewy trees in the days of archery, and of how the English learnt from them the use of the long bow, used with such effect at Crecy and Agincourt.'

The elevated ground to the west of the church was occupied as a stronghold during the Iron Age, and later by local Welsh chieftains such as Meirig (Meyrick) of the Arthurian tales, and Cuhelyn. Not long after 1066 they were ousted by Robert fitzMartin who, whilst leading an expedition from Devon, found the location suitable for establishing a Marcher lordship to centre on the Welsh commote of Cemaes. The Normans proceeded to improve and strengthen the earthwork stronghold with a massive bank and ditch and they raised a tall motte, surmounted by a round tower. Further features were added during the course of the 12th century in creating one of the most elaborate and extensive motte and bailey castles in west

Wales. But in 1191 it was lost to the Lord Rhys and William, grandson of Robert fitzMartin, moved the Norman headquarters by two miles to Newport. But by the early 13th century, **Castell Nanhyfer**, as it is shown on the OS map, seems to have been abandoned and by George Owen's time it was 'utterly defaced', although, he added 'yet doth the seat thereof show at what strength it was in times past, being seated on a high hill … and strengthened by a mighty dyke hewn out of the main rock.' With the demise of the castle, the medieval importance of Nevern, as shown by the size of the church, also went into decline.

From the river side of the church in Nevern you want to take the minor road up past the remains of the castle. The road then rises to Gethsemane and on to a T-junction below Foel Goch. Turn right here to run parallel with the coastline and continue along the road to **Moylegrove**. (After less than a mile, the first turning to the right leads towards the first of another two burial chambers in the 'Newport Group' — at **Trellyffant**, its capstone pocked with puzzling cup marks. It is on private land and permission to visit the tomb should be obtained at the farm. The next turning to the right heads for Penlan Farm, where permission is also needed to visit the **Llech-y-Tribedd** ('the stone on the tripod') tomb, also known as the Altar Stone, Llech-y-Dribedd and Samson's Quoit. Again the capstone focuses on Mynydd Carningli as the view from the monument takes in a wide sweep of the north Preseli hills. In their alignment it is evident that these monuments ignore the nearby presence of the sea.)

(For those who are feeling energetic and wish to see more of the seascape — and are moderately fit and with a bit of stamina — with due regard for the weather there is the Coast Path between Newport and Cemaes Head, that then heads onwards towards the start of the National Trail near the landing stage at the northern end of St. Dogmaels. They should wear a pair of strong walking boots and take proper wet weather clothing and plenty to eat and drink, as well as camera and binoculars, for in order to appreciate the wild and beautiful cliff scenery it is advisable to allow a full day, perhaps at least 8 hours if not 100% in training. There are some taxing stretches in places, not least towards the end, and it is of course best to arrange for return transport before starting.)

5. Pembrokeshire Coast Path. Newport Sands to St. Dogmaels, past Ceibwr Beach
The Coast Path opened as a National Trail in 1970 between Amroth on the south-east coast of Pembrokeshire and St. Dogmaels in the north-west of the county facing Cardigan across the Teifi estuary. On plan it covers a distance of 186 miles, but it is not so easy to measure the extent of the undulations to be faced along the way, although a grand total climb of 30,000 feet has been indicated. Of these, more than 3,000 feet occur along the tough 16-mile walk between Newport and St. Dogmaels — although there are also long lengths of fairly level going at up to 500 feet above the sea between the rises and falls. The initial 6 miles stretch to Ceibwr at once involves a stiff climb beyond Newport Bay to reach the top of the cliffs below Morfa Head and, within a short distance reaches a height of 492 feet where the flanks of Foel Goch run down to the sea.

From here as far as Ceibwr, and recently also at Dinas Island and on Strumble Head, the cliffs are being adopted as nesting places by fulmars, graceful gull-like petrels who lay their egg on the inaccessible ledges. Easily distinguished from noisy herring-type gulls, they have silver-grey upper parts, a white head and under parts, no black wing-tips, but most of all they have an amazing aptitude for using air currents close to the cliffs by the effortless use of their long, glider-style wings. They originate from Iceland and are relatively new to these coasts and a century ago there was only one colony in all Britain. Since then, fulmar eggs were first laid in 1949, on Skomer Island (p.122), and the species has gradually become more established, probably nourished in part by sharing waste offal from commercial fishing in the Irish Sea — and maybe also fish wastefully dumped because of European quota restrictions.

The savagery of winter storms is shown everywhere along this shattered coast, by the huge landslips along Traeth Cell-Howel and slumps of rock by inaccessible bays backed by monumental cliffs, leading towards the promontory Iron Age fort of Castelltreryffydd, now difficult to make out because of land slippages. The path descends steeply to Traeth Bach, a small rocky bay, and Pwll y Wrach, the Witches Cauldron, a massive collapsed cave — the consequence of devastating marine erosion. The path climbs steeply again to cross another headland to arrive at **Ceibwr Bay** and its pebble beach, somewhat under half way towards the end of the walk.

Ceibwr Bay

Just over ½ mile up the Awen stream valley, formed as a glacial overflow channel, the village of **Moylegrove** provides opportunities for a break, even perhaps a much quicker way back to the start, by road. Alternatively it could be a setting off point for the westward walk along the Coast Path or for the second leg of the walk to Poppit Sands and St. Dogmaels. This is certainly a good place for enjoying some of the most scenic parts along the Trail, with every chance of seeing Atlantic grey seals in late August and September, but it is not recommended for swimming.

Close to the shore there is a memorial to Wynford Vaughan-Thomas (1908–1987), war correspondent, versatile broadcaster, author, traveller and champion of Wales (also pp. 3, 8), who used to own Patchyn Glas, a wild headland on the south side of Ceibwr Bay, then conveyed it into the care of the National Trust in 1984 as a contribution to Enterprise Neptune (now Neptune Coastline Campaign), and who, incidentally, as President of The Council for the Protection of Rural Wales, officially opened the Pembrokeshire Coast Path on 16 May 1970.

On the Newport side of the bay there is a rare example of a 'raised beach', a flat platform thought to have been formed when the land surface eroded some 125,000 years ago when sea levels were higher, while dropping into the sea on the opposite side and dominated by a steep anticline or up-fold, there are faulted bends of rock which result from compression in the earth's crust many millions of years before that.

The Coast Path climbs again steeply from the beach, passing Pen-castell Iron Age fort and flanking Foel Hendre at the approach to the complex layering and folding of the cliffs culminating at Pen yr Afr. But first the Path zig-zags steeply back down to sea level to cross the valley stream at Pwllygranant, before gaining height again to reach the top of the cliffs above Traeth y Rhedyn. More climbing follows with the turn north-eastwards to master the highest point of the entire National Trail, which is above Traeth Godir-coch at over 575 feet above the sea. From then on it is mostly downhill and towards Cemaes Head, but before losing too much height it is hugely worth soaking in the expansive coastal views back past Dinas Head and Fishguard Bay towards Strumble Head and St. Davids Head, and onwards above the Teifi estuary to Cardigan Island, the low cliff line of Ceredigion beyond and, with luck on a clear day, a sighting of the distant mountains of Snowdonia and the Lleyn peninsula.

The track down to Allt-y-goed advances to a lane running past the Poppit Sands Youth Hostel that then leads to the car park and lifeboat station at Poppit Sands. From there the B4546 takes over to carry the final stretch of the National Trail to its northern terminus at the St. Dogmaels slipway.

6. Moylegrove, and a bride's dowry

The English name originated in Norman times as the Grove of Matilda, the land forming part of the dowry upon her marriage to Robert fitzNorman of Nevern (above). The small stream and a narrow lane run for ¾ mile down to the rocky inlet at Ceibwr that, in past times, must have created some temptation for a little smuggling and was certainly well used by fishermen and customers of the coastal traders who landed at the bay. Small ships delivered anthracite culm and limestone to load the now disused limekiln so that local farmers could sweeten their acidic soil with the quicklime produced. There is scarcely more spare room by the beach nowadays, and very little car parking space, so it is best to park in Moylegrove before any visit.

The road climbs sharply away from Moylegrove to head for **St. Dogmaels**, a fishing village on a bend of the River Teifi before it widens out into the estuary. It has a small north-facing beach but the more popular sands lie nearer to the river mouth and sea along to the end of the B4546, served by a large car park (charges) and other facilities.

7. Poppit Sands

The last, or first, of the many beaches found along the Pembrokeshire Coast Path, Poppit Sands are well patronised during holiday seasons, being close to Cardigan and on the tourist trail. Facing north-east across the wide Teifi estuary, the large sandy beach is spared prevailing south-westerly winds and offers scope for sports that include canoeing, surfing, wind-surfing and water-skiing where annual Blue Flag and Seaside Beach Awards are regularly gained. But there are warnings for swimmers and others about unpredictable tidal and estuary currents that can create dangers, which is recognised by the posting of lifeguards and an inshore rescue boat at busy times.

Features of greatest interest at St. Dogmaels are the remains of the medieval abbey, and that of its setting on or near ground that has been associated with Christianity ever since the 6th century.

8. St. Dogmaels. Abbey of St. Mary

Dogmael is known to have lived early in the Age of Saints in Wales that, for the next four or five centuries, followed the collapse of the Roman Empire. Little is known about him, except that he was locally, as well as in Anglesey and Brittany, recognised as a saint because of his Christian devotion, piety and integrity and this led to the establishment of a religious settlement at Llandudoch under his leadership. A reputed cousin of St. David, he must have shared some of his austere and testing ways for, according to one account, as head of the community he urged the monks to participate in a daily dip in the River Teifi, whatever the season! Thought to have been in the form of an early monastery or *clas* church, his was one of a number to appear by the 6th century in Wales. In 988 it became the turn of Llandudoch to suffer the attentions of Viking raiders, like St. Davids and other churches along the Welsh coast as far north as Llanbadarn (p.207). Partly as a result, there is now little evidence above ground of the ancient monastery and the remains to be seen today formed part of the monastery founded early in the 12th century by Robert fitzMartin, the Anglo Norman lord of Cemaes (above). During the early years following the Conquest, the Normans had observed an obligation from Rome to replace the poor buildings and strange customs of the *clasau* of the Welsh Church, where monks could marry, own property and hold rights to be passed on by heredity. After assuming his lordship, one of the first acts for Robert was to set about founding a new stonework monastery, to be served by personnel from one of the French religious orders. However monks would not simply present themselves at Llandudoch, as aspiring novices might have done for St. Dogmael some six centuries before, and it became necessary for him to head across the Channel to recruit the nucleus of a community. He chose the Reformed Benedictine abbey of Tiron in northern

The ruins of St. Dogmaels Abbey

France, where the monks were among orders who strictly interpreted the Rule of St. Benedict in their daily lives. Returning with a prior and 13 monks he founded a priory and five years later this was upgraded to an abbey after he had repeated the process with further monks. It was established with ceremony in 1120 as the only Tironian abbey that was to appear in Wales or England, at about the same time as a Benedictine friary of Anglo Norman monks were settled at Cardigan across the Teifi, and immediately seeded a small new priory on Caldey Island (pp.70-71).

These were turbulent times throughout the area, with continued conflict between the Welsh princes and the Normans, not deterring further visits also from marauding Scandinavian pirates. Nevertheless building work at the abbey continued during most of the 12th century and in 1188 the community was able adequately to accommodate the archbishop of Canterbury and Gerald of Wales, archdeacon of Brecknock, during their recruitment drive for the Third Crusade. Incidentally not long after that, Gerald and the abbot of St. Dogmaels were in competition for the bishopric of St. Davids: there was much ungodly argument and dispute extending as far as Rome, and eventually neither of them was appointed.

The 13th century started well, but much damage to the fabric of the abbey was suffered during the Edwardian wars and the 14th century brought further financial worries, compounded by the devastation of the Black Death of 1349. By 1402 only the abbot and three monks remained at the abbey and the original solemn monastic vows of poverty, chastity and abstinence were seemingly observed only by their avoidance. This and other shortcomings called for admonition by the bishop of St. Davids, and by the time of a further episcopal visitation a century later there were three more monks, the buildings were in much better shape again and monastic life had been revitalised, the majority of the monks 'of good and honest conversation and obedient to the abbot'. But not for long, for in 1536 St. Dogmaels was one of hundreds of monasteries and other houses that were closed as a result of the dissolution ordered by Henry VIII. Most of the abbey and its possessions were leased, and then sold, to a John Bradshaw of Presteigne in Radnorshire and he built a mansion somewhere within the abbey precincts. There is no sign of it now, and eventually in 1834 the abbey remains passed over to the State and are now 'protected, conserved and promoted' by Cadw. It has published a customarily well-presented booklet: *Cilgerran Castle. St. Dogmaels Abbey. Pentre Ifan Burial Chamber and Carreg Coetan Burial Chamber.*

For St. Dogmaels it details a history of the abbey, the monastic life, the development of the abbey buildings and a tour of the old walls remaining above ground. This last feature begins at the west end of the abbey church, progresses along the nave towards the presbytery and the crypt and the substantial remains of the north transept that was rebuilt in the early 16th century. The trail continues from the south transept around the cloister, taking in the outer parlour, the west range and remains of the chapter house and other principal monastic buildings, ending with the separate late 13th-century infirmary block.

The abbey church was adapted for parochial use after the dissolution, but early in the 18th century a new church was erected alongside it. In 1847 this was replaced at the north side of the abbey by the

present parish church of St. Thomas as the latest religious institution to appear on or near the site of the Celtic church of Llandudoch. Within there are some inscribed stone slabs thought to originate from the 8th or 9th centuries as boundary markers for the sanctuary area of the ancient Christian monastery, while at the west end there is a 7ft-tall memorial pillar that dates from the 5th or 6th century. It would have marked the grave of 'Sagranus, son of Cunotamus', who perhaps was a local chieftain, and it is carved both in Latin, and also Ogham with an alphabet of notches and strokes along a straight line that bears comparison with the principles of the modern Morse Code. Here was an opportunity to find the key for deciphering the hitherto baffling markings, between the Latin: *Sagrani Fili Cunetami* and Ogham: *Sagragni Maqui Cunatami* (Maqui relating to the Gaelic 'Mac', and the Welsh being '(M)ab' or 'ap' = 'son of').

Known as 'The Sagranus Stone', it has been seen as an early example of the skill of Welsh stone-carvers that culminated in the superb artistry and craftsmanship of the surviving stone crosses to be seen during these tours at Nevern, Penally and Carew.

The B4546 through St. Dogmaels shadows the River Teifi upstream to a roundabout, at which you turn right onto the A487 in the direction of Newport and the Preseli Hills.

The road rises quickly to pass the B4582 junction at Crossway, reaching **Eglwyserw** and the picturesque Serjeants Arms inn, said to date from the 17th century. St. Christiolus Church is Victorian in build, but stands within a circular churchyard that signifies pre-Christian origins. At the far end of the village there are vestiges of a Norman **castle** in field boundaries and woodland on the right and ¾ mile further on, the **Dyfed Shires and Leisure Farm** at Carnhuan offers a wide seasonal variety of covered and outdoor activities that include ploughing and harrowing demonstrations on this 'real working farm'. Nearby there is an ancient standing stone, just one of a huge number of prehistoric relics such as stones, cairns, burial chambers, hillforts and ancient roadways in which the rolling moorland ahead is so rich. They register human occupation hereabouts for at least 5,000 years, largely through burial structures for their dead. Most of the dwelling places would not have been sufficiently robust to survive the passing of the ages, and this can be appreciated (daily from April until the end of October) from what can be seen a short distance away at **Castell Henllys**. It will entail a short diversion from the main route by continuing on the A487 Newport road and following the brown signs which lead off to the right (otherwise turn left onto the B4329 to follow the main route).

9. Castell Henllys Iron Age Fort. Stepping into the Past

Recreated Iron Age houses at Castell Henllys

Here is the site of a defended Iron Age fort dating from between 600 BC and the 1st century AD where, as well as a number of roundhouses there were animal pens, a smithy, a grain store and other facilities. Archaeologists were able to uncover sufficient of the foundations to find important information about the site and in the 1980s work started to recreate four thatched roundhouses and some other buildings in their original places. The largest and final building, the Chieftain's House, was completed in 2000, and the results of the whole enterprise have appeared in the BBC *Surviving the Iron Age* series. Included around the area there is an exhibition centre, a self-guidance trail with a series of informative interpretation panels, as well as a scheme of twice-daily guided tours that provide an insight into past and present life in the fort and out in the surrounding land.

From Castell Henllys turn left back along the A487, and then right onto the B4329. If you wish to visit Pentre Ifan burial chamber, then turn right in Brynberian, the over the crossroads of minor roads, otherwise continue on the B4329. After a mile and a half from the hamlet approaches the road approaches the impressive burial chamber.

10. Pentre Ifan

Of the six surviving Neolithic monuments within the Newport Group that are focused on the rocky outcrops of Mynydd Carningli, Pentre Ifan Burial Chamber is a scheduled ancient monument with a 16ft-long capstone supported at a height of 7 to 8 feet above the ground on the points of three uprights — one of the finest tombs of its class in Britain.

Pentre Ifan

Continuing along the B4329 steeply upwards, it reaches the watershed at Bwlch (meaning 'pass') -gwynt ('wind'). The car park here is 1,300 feet above sea level and well placed for easing the legs into action to broaden the experience and thrill of being high up in the hills.

11. Preseli Top, and Bluestone pillars for Stonehenge

The Preselis are best explored on foot, in good walking boots, with adequate wet weather clothing (the annual rainfall is said to be *c*.60 inches and the rivers springing here supply much of Pembrokeshire's needs), something to eat and drink — and a good walking map, especially as mists can occur very suddenly and the open exposed moorland is a very different environment to that of lowland Pembrokeshire. Also, although there are public rights of way and permitted access paths it is important to remember that the land is privately owned, and this thought should also extend to the many ancient monuments that are not to be damaged or disturbed in any way.

Bwlch-gwynt is a good starting point for heading around the slopes of Foel Eryr — Hill of the Eagles — towards the upper Gwaun Valley, or eastwards along part of the Golden Road Path in the direction of the mountain village of Crymych, passing a turning for the highest point of the Preselis.

From the Bronze Age cairns at the summit of the 1,760 feet Foel Cwmcerwyn there are immense views when the weather is right, reaching north to south from Caernarvonshire to Devon, east to the Brecon Beacons and west even to Ireland's Wicklow Hills. First it is necessary to skirt a forestry plantation for about a mile along the path before turning right for Preseli Top. After that it follows the summits across territory that shows signs that it has been of major significance from the Bronze Age, when it lay on a trade route to and from Ireland, and through the Iron Age into the Roman period. One puzzling example close to the path is Beddarthur, or Arthur's Grave, made up from a dozen standing stones set out in an oval circle probably more than 2,500 years ago — and not likely to have anything to do with King Arthur, alive or dead. Across the valley, Carn Menyn, is an outcrop of frost-shattered rocks and a source of bluestone pillars for the inner ring of Stonehenge in far away Wiltshire. There has been much argument about how, some 3,500 years ago, blocks of the spotted dolerite, rhyolite and volcanic ash quarried here, weighing up to 4 tons each, came to be transported in large numbers to Salisbury Plain nearly 200 land and sea miles away. The generally received explanation is that they must have been sledged on rollers as far as the tidal Eastern Cleddau river, maybe near Blackpool Mill (p.53), then rafted down Milford Haven and out to sea, before being finally dragged inland to Stonehenge by a huge gang of men.

On the opposite slope, Carn Alw was an Iron Age hillfort on the side of a natural outcrop, and outlines of associated round huts still show in the area. Far more rare (cf. Pen-y-Gaer above Llanbedr-y-cennin in the Conwy Valley), is the pattern of sharp upright stones below the west side known as chevaux de frise, a defensive feature, rather like a raised modern minefield or tank trap, meant to break up attacks on foot or horseback.

After another 1½ miles the path reaches the east end of the range, and looking down on Crymych from almost 1,200 feet above sea level is the 'Hill of Three Cairns', or Foeldrygarn. Regarded as one of the finest surviving hillforts in Wales, its life-span could well have been around 1,000 years, starting with the Late Bronze Age and continuing as a large Iron Age fortified settlement into the Roman period. The Three Bronze Age cairns are at the top level and within the lower enclosures are large numbers of depressions which seem likely to be the bases of scores of Iron Age huts, similar to those recreated at Castell Henllys (above).

From Bwlch-gwynt, continue along the B4329 to the junction with the B4313 where the main tour turns right to follow the Gwaun Valley to Fishguard.

There is a temporary diversion at the crossroads here by first turning left onto the B4313 and driving for 2 miles to Maenclochog. Beyond the church at the far end of the village the minor road ahead is signposted to Llys-y-fran Reservoir and Country Park.

12. Llys-y-fran Reservoir and Country Park

The man-made reservoir covers 212 acres and not only provides much of Pembrokeshire's needs for water but also many opportunities for out-door sport and recreation. There is a footpath all round the lake, in woodland and along nature-trails, water-sports are catered for where people bring their own craft, while there is a hire service for cyclists and anglers. The park claims to be the 'largest game fishing venue in west Wales' and towards this is equipped with a boathouse where 36 loch-type, petrol-engine fishing boats are available for hire — and there are specially designed boats for disabled anglers, including those in wheelchairs. Thousands of trout are released from rearing cages each year to join the indigenous population of wily 'brownies'. In 2005 the biggest fish caught weighed 9lb 12oz.

There are also a children's Adventure Playground, a Visitor Centre, licensed restaurant and several other amenities.

If the diversion has been followed, it will afterwards be necessary to backtrack to the B4313/B4329 crossroads at Greenway and the New Inn.

The main tour continues down the B4313 as it shadows the Pontfaen Brook downstream towards its confluence with the River Gwaun.

13. The Gwaun Valley and River

The River Gwaun has descended from its source high on the slopes of Foel Eryr and, for most of the year flows gently down the valley past prehistoric remains, areas of ancient woodland that are supporting their rich habitat, and farmland. Little has changed there over the centuries since some 10,000 years ago, when far greater volumes of water, running beneath melting ice masses, carved out the deep valley towards the end of the last glaciation. The tremendous forces left Cwm Gwaun, the Gwaun Valley, with deep-sided gorges as one of the prime examples of its kind in Britain. As it is all best explored on foot, the National Park Authority has helped by creating the Golden Road Path, from down by the harbour at Lower Fishguard via Bwlch-gwynt (above) to Crymych, along a route that must date back more than 3,000 years. The main centres in this quiet unfrequented valley are at Pontfaen and Llanychaer, whose people have become known for holding on to some of their old ways. This has shown since 1752, when the Julian calendar followed in Britain until then was replaced by the Gregorian version — but not in Cwm Gwaun, and *Hen Galan*, the Old New Year, continues to be celebrated by local families on 13 January (not that they are ever likely to miss out on anything happening around 1 January as well!)

Two narrow roads turn off the B4313 to the right for Pontfaen, on the far side of Picton Mill Bridge, for the Dyffryn Arms pub and small, restored St. Brynachs Church. Much older are the cross-carved memorial stones standing in the churchyard — they date back at least as far as the 9th century. The Baptist Church, a short distance upstream from the pub, is perhaps the most impressive building in the hamlet. Cilrhedyn Bridge is the next river crossing over to the right, and it is good that, in conserving such a magical valley landscape, the National Park Authority has established a Woodland Centre that aims to promote good woodland management there. On the near side of the three-arched bridge over the Gwaun, Llanychaer follows next and has become known for nearby **Parc y Meirw** (Field of the Dead), at *c*.130 feet in length the longest megalithic alignment of stone pillars known in Wales.

Finally the B4313 continues to shadow the Afon Gwaun until it reaches the A40 junction in the centre of Fishguard, and when the river at last enters the sea through the small harbour at Lower Town.

Brecon

The earliest known settlements close to the upper reaches of the River Usk are the Iron Age (*c*.800 BC – AD 43) hillforts that were placed at strategic points above its course. **Pen y Crug** was sited on a moorland hilltop at some 1,088 feet above sea level to the north west of modern Brecon, and built by tribesmen who were the direct ancestors of the modern Welsh people. These were small dark people known as Brythons and they spoke a language called British, the precursor of Welsh. The smaller **Twyn y Gaer Fort** was established at 1,203 feet a short distance upstream on a flat topped hill on the opposite side of the valley at the highest point of Mynydd Illtud, within walking distance from the National Park Mountain Centre (see p.181). These forts served the Celts as defended look-out points, settlements and places of refuge during times of tribal warfare or attack from predatory animals or cattle raiders. At other times the people farmed and lived on less exposed lower ground. During medieval and Tudor times the poor quality land within or close to the ramparts of such ancient hillforts came to be used for the building of Pillow Mounds. Shown on the OS maps as at Mynydd Illtud, these were a few feet high and meant for the systematic management of rabbits in organised warrens, tunnels often lined with stone to encourage breeding. The animals were introduced by the Normans, possibly from Spain, during the end of the 12th century. Interestingly a rabbit and a dog appear on the corbel of the south wall of Kilpeck Church in Herefordshire. These date from *c*.1150/60 and were carved by sculptors inspired, in part, by work seen on the pilgrimage route to Santiago in Spain. The rabbits provided people of that time with a regular supply of fresh meat (rather as did pigeons kept in dovecotes), with their added advantage of having soft coney fur for clothing. Only later on, when the animals escaped from their confines, did they start to become a costly pest.

Roughly half way between the two hillforts and much nearer river level, the Romans arrived at Aberyscir soon after AD 61 to quell challenges from the recalcitrant Celts and their blocking of the mineral-rich lands to the west. The first fort, of turf and timber, was constructed in a magnificent setting at what was a focal position at the southern hub in a network of Roman roads. This linked the gold, copper, lead and other mines along with other resources which they wished to exploit. It was named **Y Gaer** and is thought to have been known to the Romans as *Cicvitvm*, a key site among a number along the River Usk beyond the legionary fortress of Caerleon (*Isca*) which included Usk (*Burrivm*), Abergavenny (*Gobbanivm*) and Pen y

Remains of the Roman fort at Y Gaer

Gaer. The 3.25-hectare site was probably first occupied by an auxiliary Spanish cavalry force of 500 men, known as Ala Hispanorum Vettonum, who were intended for operations against the Silures but there is no longer any sign of their clay and wood fortress. This was covered by a stone fort in *c*.AD 140 and the ruins of walls, angle towers, gateways and the guardhouse are to be seen at Y Gaer farm, immediately to the south of the farm buildings. The site is visible from the A40 Brecon-Sennybridge road and to reach it on foot there is a marked footpath just over 2 miles long leading from Fennifach Road, west of the town. The fort is a Scheduled Ancient Monument and privately owned, with a right of public access. Y Gaer and its environs were excavated in 1924–5 by Sir Mortimer Wheeler and later by others and their finds are to be seen in the Brecknock Museum in the centre of Brecon and at the National Museum of Wales in Cardiff. There is evidence of more than one rebuilding, and even a period of abandonment at the end of the 2nd century, and it is thought that a final programme of refortification and other work may have taken place during the 4th century, although there are indications that the fort was abandoned not long afterwards. The area within the ramparts has in recent times been ploughed out. From the west gate of the fort there are traces of a way to the ford over the River Yscir and a lane to the west of the church in the direction of Trecastle, and from there largely taking the route much later followed by the turnpike road to Llandovery (*Alabvm*). At up to some 1,300 feet above sea level this passes the former marching camps at Y Pigwn, and the subsequent fortlet, running well above the present A40 from Brecon, down in the Gwydderig valley to the north.

Not unusually, little is known about Dark Age occupation of the area, except that it is possible that in the early part of the 5th century Brocan or Brychan, a semi-legendary leader of half Irish descent, is thought to have ruled over this part of Wales. (Different stories tell that he had three wives and up to 50 offspring who included 24 especially devout daughters). The 'land of Brychan' came to be known as 'Brycheiniog' and Brecknock was adopted as an Anglicised form. In Welsh, the County of Brecknock is referred to as Sir Frycheiniog, although Brecon is known to the Welsh as Aberhonddu because it straddles the River Usk at its junction with the River Honddu.

The Normans were quick to appreciate the strategic advantage of the ridge on which the town now stands and it soon gained a **castle**, together with a **priory** served by Benedictine monks from Battle Abbey in Sussex and with the grant of 'the church of St. John the Evangelist without the walls'. (The hamlet of Battle just to the north west of Brecon may testify to the link once existing with the Sussex town and site of the Battle of Hastings). Thus the castle, priory and church developed west of the River Honddu soon after 1093 when Bernard de Neufmarché from Neufmarché (Newmarket) in Normandy overcame Rhys ap Tewdwr, the local ruler, and by 1110 he had control over the entire Welsh princedom of Brycheiniog.

Builth and Hay appeared as settlements at this time and at Brecon the earth and timber motte and bailey castle which he established on the site was later replaced by stonework, quite probably partially 'quarried' from the deserted Roman fort of Y Gaer. During the Later Middle Ages it had grown to become a principal royal castle of the Welsh Marches, ranking with Chirk, Montgomery, Ludlow, Wigmore and Monmouth. But now all that remains to overlook the river and bridge is a section of the great hall of 1280 extending alongside the Castle

The hall of the castle (centre) with the Castle Hotel to the left

Hotel and a nearby fragment of the original 12th-century '**Ely Tower**'. This was named after John Morton, bishop of Ely, who was imprisoned there in the 15th century, while today it comprises part of the present diocesan bishop's address.

Brecon Cathedral

Brecon Cathedral

The Benedictine priory church continued in existence until the dissolution of the monasteries in 1537 and then St. John's became the parish church. In 1923, following upon the separation in 1920 of the Church in Wales from the Church of England as a separate province of the Anglican Communion, it was fittingly chosen as the cathedral of the newly created Diocese of Swansea and Brecon. To appreciate the commanding hill-top position of the cathedral, high above the River Honddu and the town, the best approach is along The Struet, turning left over the Priory Bridge. Priory Hill rises steeply from the bridge, following round the ancient wall of the priory grounds on the right and comes to a pedestrian gateway leading to an entrance to the cathedral close at the south west corner. Also here is the tastefully restored monastic Tithe Barn, opened in 1995 as the imaginative **Heritage Centre**, a café, as well as the Canonry, Almonry and Deanery buildings.

It is known that the Norman church replaced an earlier place of worship on the site but there is now no trace of it, or much of what Bernard de Neufmarché built in the late 11th century. The formidable building of old red sandstone seen today was started in the 13th century, firstly by the patron and Lord of Brycheiniog, the notorious William de Braose II, known as 'The Ogre of Abergavenny' for his murderous treachery there. He was succeeded by Humphrey de Bohun and the chancel, transepts and tower were probably added in his time and in the 14th century were followed by the rebuilt nave. The sturdy appearance of the building, which is emphasised by the embattled parapets and strong tower, made it seem 'half church and half castle' in its turbulent early days.

The nave is entered by the north-west porch and it is considered to be a fine example of the Decorated period (*c*.1290–*c*.1350), but even more highly regarded is the chancel, 'one of the choicest examples of the first phase of Early English [*c*.13th century] style in the country'. The nave is far less ornate by comparison, its massive plain octagonal pillars rising high before breaking into arches — although during the Middle Ages its plastered walls would have been colourfully painted. The intricately carved font near the west end (bearing comparison with those at Eardisley and Canon Frome

Looking east along the nave in Brecon Cathedral

in Herefordshire) is just about the only relic of the Norman parish church which extends back to the time in *c*.1172 when Giraldus Cambrensis was archdeacon of Brecon (see below). Near it is a rare 12th-century Cresset Stone, hollowed out with 30 holes for fat or grease and floating wicks to serve as monastic night-lights. It would not always have been possible to take in the present long and impressive vista from where it and the font are now placed, for a great Rood Screen long separated the chancel or choir from the nave, the monks' part from the people's part. This bore a gigantic rood, a representation of The Crucifixion. It was the famed *Crog Aberhonddu* (Brecon Cross) of miraculous powers and celebrated in the poems of 18th-century Welsh bards.

At the east end of the north aisle, half way up the nave to the left, is St. Keyne's Chapel, formerly the Guild Chapel of the Corvizors (shoemakers) which they dedicated to their patron saints Sts. Crispin and Crispinianus on whose feast day the Battle of Agincourt was fought in 1415 — as anyone who knows Shakespeare's *King Henry V* will doubtless be aware. The north transept, or Battle Chapel, where the main feature is the triple lancet set high in the wall, is entered by the chancel under the tower. Beyond is the Havard Chapel, rebuilt in the 14th century by the Havards of Pontwilym, who were of Norman descent. Once the Lady chapel of the church, it has been dedicated since 1922 as the Regimental Chapel of the locally based South Wales Borderers — the Old 24th — now the Royal Regiment of Wales. Its beauty and dignity provide a fine setting for the two Rolls of Honour commemorating fallen officers and men of the South Wales Borderers and the Monmouthshire Regiment, and enhanced by the stained glass windows, paintings and many Regimental Colours. There is a special place for the Queen's Colour of the 1st Battalion, 24th Regiment of Foot, carrying the unique Silver Wreath of Immortelles at the top of the pike. This was ordained by command of Queen Victoria to commemorate the valour of Lieutenants T. Melville and N.J.A. Coghill in their attempt to save her Colour from the blood soaked battlefield of Isandhlwana, and also the heroic defence of Rorke's Drift during the Anglo Zulu War of 1879 (see below). To the east of the south transept, the St. Lawrence Chapel was rebuilt upon ancient foundations by W.D. Carõe, the St. Davids diocesan architect. After 1923 he was also responsible for other work following the adoption of St. John's as the cathedral, not least the high altar reredos. His sensitive work in restoring the small chapel as part of the ancient building has earned him the rare distinction of being regarded as 'a self-effacing architect'. Remembered here is Wilfrid Seymour de Winton (1856–1926), a considerable benefactor among many of his family, whose actions included the return of the Priory House and its grounds upon his death.

Further details about the cathedral fabric, its fittings, of two periods of restoration work by Sir George Gilbert Scott between 1861 and 1872 and much else are in publications available at the Cathedral Heritage Centre. Its frontage to the B4520 is worth seeing on the way back down to the Priory Bridge as it displays fine restored gargoyles and 17th-century mullioned windows. From there The Struet leads off to the right towards the town centre.

Gerald the Welshman

A left turn at the junction leads towards **Llanddew**, about 1½ miles away, where the **palace** was the residence and administrative centre of Giraldus Cambrensis (1145–1223) when, from 1175 to 1203, he was archdeacon of Brecknock. Born at Manorbier Castle near Tenby (p.91) he was known also as Gerald de Barri and was in fact one part Welshman, a son of the grand-daughter of Rhys ap Tewdwr, last prince of Deheubarth (southern Wales), and three parts Norman, being the son of a Norman noble. As a dynamic and colourful cleric and writer his influence extended far beyond the then diocese of St. Davids. For political reasons he was twice thwarted in an obsessive ambition to become its bishop, and also in making the Welsh Church independent of Canterbury. Nowadays he is best known in connection with his journey through Wales in 1188 with Baldwin, archbishop of Canterbury, on a recruiting and fundraising journey for the Third Crusade. Of some 17 books, all written in Latin, his *The Journey through Wales* (*Itinerarium Cambri*) and *The Description of Wales* (*Descriptio Cambriae*) are regarded as being among the few authentic accounts of the geography and social and economic conditions of the Principality during the early Middle Ages. He died in obscurity in 1223 and is believed to have been buried in the precincts of St. Davids Cathedral.

First mentioned in AD 500, the **church at Llanddew** is the oldest in the former county of Brecknock and formerly a 'clas' church, a mother church with monastic buildings. The present huge church of St. David comes from the 13th century and has been described as 'unsurpassed for the combination of perfect plainness with perfect excellence'. The vicarage was built in 1869 on the site of the archdeacon's castellated palace opposite, where all that remain are a 14th-century doorway, part of a wall and the roadside **Bishop Gower's Well** of reputed pure water, once to be shared by all with those living within the wall.

Llanddew Church (top) and remains of the bishop's palace

East of the Honddu

Its present population numbered at around 7,500, Brecon developed as a strongly defended Marches town during the late 12th, early 13th and 14th centuries. The Struet is the main approach from the north and in the centre it joins with High Street Superior, Ship Street and Bridge Street to form the top bar of a T-shaped junction. The Watton, from the south-east, continues to the junction as The Bulwark and High Street Inferior and forms the stem. Happily there has been no attempt to 'modernise' these original street names, as city fathers at other towns have done. They follow the original street pattern — although there is a local feeling that Ship Street has been corrupted from Sheep Street. These roads once passed through the 13th-century oval-shaped circuit of sturdy masonry walls at the Struet Gate, at the junction with High Street Superior, The Watton or East Gate, near the Shirehall and the Bridge or West Gate at Bridge Street. The other major gate, the Watergate, faced the north bank of the River Honddu close by. These gates were demolished in the interests of better traffic flow in 1775 and most of the walls and ten equally spaced towers had gone by the end of the 19th century, leaving small surviving portions along Captains' Walk and near Free Street.

Bethel Square lies between the main car park and the centre of town and is dominated by the striking former Calvinist Bethel Chapel of 1852 which has been sensitively converted into a branch of Boots the Chemists. An archway leads to a crossing with Lion Street and, dating from 1770, the **Guildhall** occupies the site on the right along Tredegar Street and up to High Street Inferior. It was Victorianised in 1888 when the open ground-floor corn market was walled in and the site had previously been occupied by a two-storey timbered town hall built in 1623 by John Abel (1577–1674), 'The King's Carpenter', of Herefordshire. (He was also responsible for the Leominster Town Hall, still to be seen at the Grange Park there, and

Looking across Brecon's rooftops to the Brecon Beacons

Bethel Square

The Brecknock Museum

work at Abbey Dore and Kington in Herefordshire). It had in turn replaced an earlier town hall that could well have been connected with the large medieval market place extending north-westwards from the church. This triangular site had been built upon by the time John Speed published his map of 1610. Fronted by a fine arched entrance, the present **Market Hall** is on the opposite side of the road along High Street Superior.

Opposite the Guildhall there are 16th- and 17th-century houses, including the former **Shoulder of Mutton Inn** where Sarah Siddons (1755–1831) was born and which is now named after the famous actress. They are among a large number of listed buildings of Special Architectural or Historic Interest in the central Conservation Area of Brecon, which in 1967 was placed on a special Council for British Archaeology list of 35 Welsh towns with historic centres meriting preservation.

Further down High Street Inferior is the largely 14th-century **St. Mary's Church**, from 1923 the parish church of the town of Brecon when St. John the Evangelist Church was chosen as the diocesan cathedral. Its prominent 90ft Buckingham Tower is named after Edward Stafford, duke of Buckingham, Lord of Brecknock — born in Brecon in 1477. Stafford built it in 1521 essentially for military purposes and not actually as part of the church (but on the orders of Henry VIII he was executed that year as the last Marcher Lord to revolt against the Crown). As the victim of brutal 'restoration' the church is no architectural gem, either from outside or within, but a recent east window of 1989 designed by John Petts of Abergavenny is worthy of approval. Just outside it, in the centre of the Bulwark where it meets High Street Inferior, there is the Wellington monument, clearly a popular rendezvous, then continuing down to the former Watton or East Gate at Watton Mount there is evidence of the former residential character of the area. This still shows at the mid-18th-century town house which is now the Conservative Club, the Georgian Wellington Hotel and the *Brecon and Radnor Express* buildings.

The **Brecknock Museum** displays quite a different image at the junction with Glamorgan Street and Captains' Walk. Originally built in 1839–43 to designs by architects Thomas Wyatt and David Brandon as a classic Shire Hall, of Bath Stone and with massive Doric Pillars and portico, it was meant to impress as an awesome venue for the Courts of Assize and Quarter Sessions and as the chief meeting place of the County Council. The courts continued there until 1971 and after local government re-organisation Breconshire County Council ceased to exist. The Brecknock Museum, which had been established in 1928, had until then been in cramped quarters at the Independent Chapel in Glamorgan Street but in 1974 it was transferred to the vacated building. There it became what is regarded as one of the finest and liveliest small museums in Britain, retaining the Assize courtroom as a reminder of legal dramas once played out there. A vivid tableau, complete with model figures of judge, jury, accused, witnesses, lawyers and other participants, has with some adaptation very cleverly been set up with a computerised lighting system and a sound recording of the proceedings. The museum provides a good introduction to the many great attributes of the old county of Brecknockshire. One special exhibit is the log boat found in 1925 on the bed of nearby **Llangorse Lake**, radio-carbon dated from between AD 760–1020. This is thought to have been used by occupiers of the crannog, or artificial island settlement, on the lake during the 9th and 10th centuries (see box p.178). In addition the building contains fine Welsh works of art, not least those displayed in the restored Grand Jury Room.

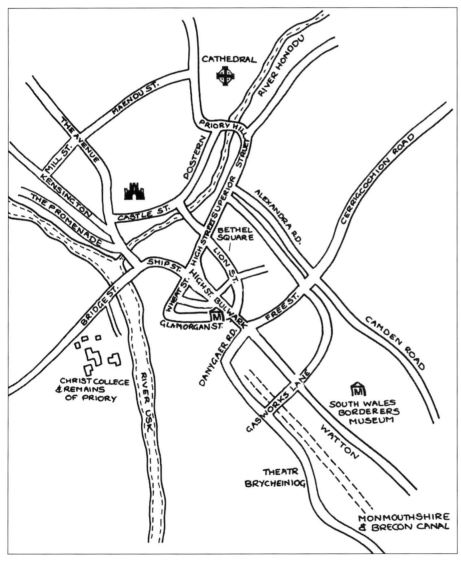

Plan of Brecon

Brecon Barracks, South Wales Borderers Museum and Dering Lines

A quarter of a mile along the left side of The Watton (B4601), which is planted with 24 lime trees in honour of the South Wales Borderers (as once having been named the 24th Foot), is a complete Victorian barracks complex. Built in 1842, it provided for infantry as well as cavalry and included officers' houses and a military hospital. A forbidding-looking keep was added in 1877 and Brecon became a military centre for Brecknock, Radnorshire, Montgomeryshire and Monmouthshire. The Depot of the South Wales Borderers was established in 1873 and the barracks has become the Headquarters of 160 (Wales) Brigade, formed as part of the 53rd Welsh Division in 1915 and commanding all the army units located in Wales. It also houses 53 Signals Squadron (Volunteers) 900 Troop of the Territorial Army. In 1969, the South Wales Borderers and The Welch Regiment were amalgamated to become The Royal Regiment of Wales. Treasures and details of the exploits of all these forces are to be seen in the Regimental Museum, installed in the barracks in 1934. This was moved in 1961 to its present site in the old militia armoury, built in red brick in classical style in 1805 for the Brecon Militia during the Napoleonic Wars. The Medal Room contains over 3,000 medals, including 16 Victoria Crosses. There is a display of weapons and pictures and paintings, dioramas and drums, assegais and ammunition, uniforms, buttons and badges contributing to a unique and memorable collection.

A special Anglo-Zulu War display records the heroism and utter tragedy of actions in which the 24th Regiment was involved on 22 January 1879, at a rocky outcrop known as Isandhlwana in what is now Kwazulu Natal Province, Republic of South Africa. Incompetence by the Force Commander, which included woefully underestimating his enemy and misreading vital signs, resulted in the slaughter of over 1,300 well-equipped British troops armed with Martini-Henry rifles and Gatling guns together with other forces, facing the mere assegais, battle clubs and shields being wielded by the Zulu 'impis' of King Cetshwayo, unwillingly goaded into action by the British.

Almost nobody lived to tell the tale and the account in the Museum relates that just *six* men of the Regiment escaped the slaughter. Under orders to try and rescue the Queen's Colour of the 1st Battalion, the adjutant, Lieutenant T. Melville, joined by a wounded Lieutenant N.J.A. Coghill, did manage to reach and cross the Buffalo River (the Natal/ Zululand Border) safely but they were then caught and killed. The Colour was retrieved from the swollen waters ten days later and, had they survived, these officers would each have been recommended for a Victoria Cross. Twenty-eight years later, on 15 January 1907, King Edward VII approved their award of posthumous, backdated VCs.

Later, on 22 January 1879 nearly 3,000 Zulus, fired up by their success at Isandhlwana, reached a small garrison manned at the border crossing by some 130 men of B Company of the 2nd Battalion in a redoubt some ten miles away at Rorke's Drift. They faced fierce and determined attacks until, despite the odds, the Zulus were beaten off by the early hours of the next morning. This action formed the basis of the iconic film, *Zulu*, starring Michael Caine and Stanley Baker in the roles of Lieutenants Bromhead and Chard, each of whom was awarded the VC among the total of 11 for that day (belatedly followed 12 months later by another fully deserved by Commissary T.J. Dalton). This count was far more than for any single engagement in British history — just one was awarded on D-day, 1944. There was clearly great heroism at Rorke's Drift that day, but it has often been put that the treatment of this much smaller event was a huge example of Victorian 'spin' — designed to draw national attention away from the humiliating, botched Battle of Isandhlwana a few hours earlier.

Next to the barracks there are the Headquarters offices of the **Brecon Beacons National Park** and the Breconshire County Court and less than a mile further on at the eastern edge of the town is **Dering Lines**. Named after Sir Edward Dering who raised the 24th Regiment in 1689, it was built as No 21 Infantry Training Centre in 1930 and countless soldiers have trained there since, including more than 27,000 during the Second World War. The camp became the Wales Brigade Training Centre in 1946, the

Parachute Regiment Battle School was set up in 1960 and it became the Infantry Training Centre Wales in 1995, running a wide variety of some 41 courses for the Regular and Territorial Army. The permanent military and civilian staff includes three platoons of a Gurkha Company (Mandalay) demonstration training support unit of 120 soldiers, whose families arrived from Nepal to join them at Brecon in 1997. They were soon accepted by the local community in jobs and at schools in the area and so became another example of the long-standing social and economic effect of the military presence in and around Brecon, not least as a major source of employment.

Across the A40 it is possible to detect the tranquil waterway which is known affectionately to many as the '**Mon & Brec**'.

Brecon and Abergavenny Canal — and *Jazz Aberhonddu*

The Brecon and Abergavenny Canal is a section of the Monmouthshire and Brecon Canal and starts from its new terminus at the **Theatre Basin**. This can be reached by joining Rich Way at its junction with The Watton closer to the town centre. It was constructed between 1796 and 1812 to the design of Thomas Dadford Junior by navigators, who were the original 'navvies', for the most part using only picks, shovels and wheelbarrows. Lying almost totally within the National Park or along its borders, it has 18 aqueducts, a 375-yard long tunnel and only six locks, with five in one place, along 33 miles of waterway which winds its way along the mountainside contours of the Usk Valley. It ends at Pontymoile, near Pontypool, joining the Monmouthshire Canal and the original connection to Newport and the sea. Most of its water enters over a weir on the River Usk half a mile upstream of the town, passing through a pipe to a culvert in the end wall of the basin. The original Act of 1793 authorised a system of connecting horse-operated tram-roads over distances of up to 8 miles from the canal and there were at one time around 200 miles of track. These were used to convey a wide range of materials such as farm produce, manure, fertilizers, lime, coal, and — importantly — the products of the Clydach Valley ironworks. The wooden canal barges, generally about 63 feet long and 9 feet wide and drawing 3 feet when fully loaded, could carry up to 24 tons. Trade rose rapidly to a heyday during the 1820s, but as everywhere else, the birth of the steam railway led to a steady decline in canal business so that a hundred years later there was little left. The final toll was collected in 1933, leaving the canal merely a carrier from the River Usk weir to meet downstream needs for water. The entire waterway inevitably deteriorated until, in 1963, it was taken over by British Waterways. After much restoration it had reopened by 1970, so surviving the local railway

The canal basin and Brynich aqueduct

system which caused its commercial downfall. Shortened now by 200 yards at the Brecon terminus it was greatly improved by a regeneration scheme in 1997. Two new basins were built and the towpath to Brynich lock and the impressive four-arched aqueduct across the Usk was widened and resurfaced for walkers, cyclists and the disabled. This corresponds with a 2-mile long section of the Taff Trail rich in wildlife and along part of what must be one of the loveliest waterways in Britain. For those 'just messing about in boats', at no faster than 4 miles per hour and usually less, their narrowboats, dayboats and canoes

Theatr Brycheiniog

are provided with mooring bollards, winding points, water, sanitary and rubbish disposal facilities and a picnic area. For the less adventurous the 'Dragonfly' trip boat operates from Easter until November from the Theatre Basin in front of the new **Theatr Brycheiniog**. Opened in April 1997, this has an auditorium with 436 seats for the enjoyment of drama, dance, music, opera and children's events and there is also a waterfront bar and bistro and a gallery where exhibitions regularly change. Great emphasis has been placed on affording full access for all, such as providing for wheelchairs in the stalls and balcony, tactile signage for patrons with sight problems, an infra-red system for the hard of hearing, adapted toilets and reserved car parking.

Each third weekend in August it is also a key venue for the Brecon Jazz Festival. For the 21st annual event in 2004 the small town played host in its superb setting to what were thought to be as many as 70,000 revellers, up to 950 at a time taking the places of stalls in the Market Hall, with its distinctively earthy atmosphere, and at several other venues under cover and in the open. Since the launch in 1984 a very lively carnival atmosphere has developed with the aid of street and shop decorations, marching bands, street music and up to 100 concerts of world class jazz. These are given by the greatest of international names and they enable the die-hard fans as well as a more mainstream audience to move between different gigs and styles of music.

The River Usk and Christ College

Canal Road has been built beyond the basin over a short infill section of the canal and it then continues past the end of Danygaer Street to join Captains' Walk. This has been called after a Captain Phillips of Glamorgan Street, who laid it out as a promenade during the 18th century, although another story is that during the Napoleonic wars it was a favourite path of interned French officers. It runs alongside the line of the Town Wall towards the Brecknock Museum and Glamorgan Street, where the Magistrates Court now occupies the inelegant 1960s headquarters building of the former Breconshire County Council. Further along on the left is Buckingham Place, a large stone building from the early 16th century, and then come the Georgian buildings of Wheat Street and a left turn into Sheep Street. Here is Brecon's sole half-timber fronted building and then the Public Library, opened by Prince Charles in 1969. With the Magistrates' Court (above), and the Police Station in Lion Street, this stands out as the third major architectural eyesore to react against its context and to blight Brecon's distinctive Georgian and Victorian central townscape.

The Usk Bridge is further down the road, past the Watergate. This leads off to the right across the Honddu and past the former town mill beneath the castle. Originating from 1563, the seven-arched bridge across the River Usk was highly placed in the Council for British Archaeology listing of 1967 but soon afterwards its fabric and appearance were to suffer badly as a result of design and reconstruction works which were totally out of character with its ancient stonework. Upstream on the right there is a **Promenade and riverside walk** leading to boating, play areas with a large car park and these all share with the bridge the striking and ever changing views of the foothills and Beacons away to the south.

The 16th-century Usk Bridge with its ugly 1970s walkway

In the foreground on the down-stream side of the bridge is **Christ College**. It is on a site that has been occupied for over 750 years, starting from *c.*1250 when Dominican or teaching friars established their friary there. The chapel of the College dates from that time and although much restored it must be the only building of a medieval friary in Britain still used for regular worship. Two halls with fine 15th-century timber roofs have also survived but no other monastic buildings remain. After the dissolution of the monasteries the prebendal college of Abergwili, near Carmarthen, took over, its school endowed with an annual income of £53 on lands and in the buildings of the old friary. In 1544 Henry VIII chartered 'the College of Christ of Brecknock' as a grammar school so that 'the Welsh rudeness might soon be framed to English civility'. The prebendal body was abolished in 1853,

View of the Brecon Beacons from across the Usk

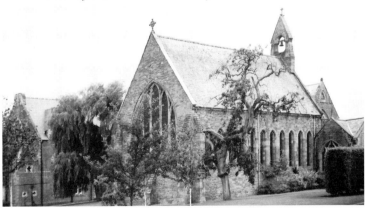

Christ College chapel

the school was re-founded in 1855 and new buildings in Venetian Gothic style were built by Pritchard and Seddon, diocesan architects. Christ College, one of only two acknowledged public schools in Wales, has since expanded as a co-educational boarding school for 11 to 18 year-olds and by 2004 took some 110 girls and 215 boys.

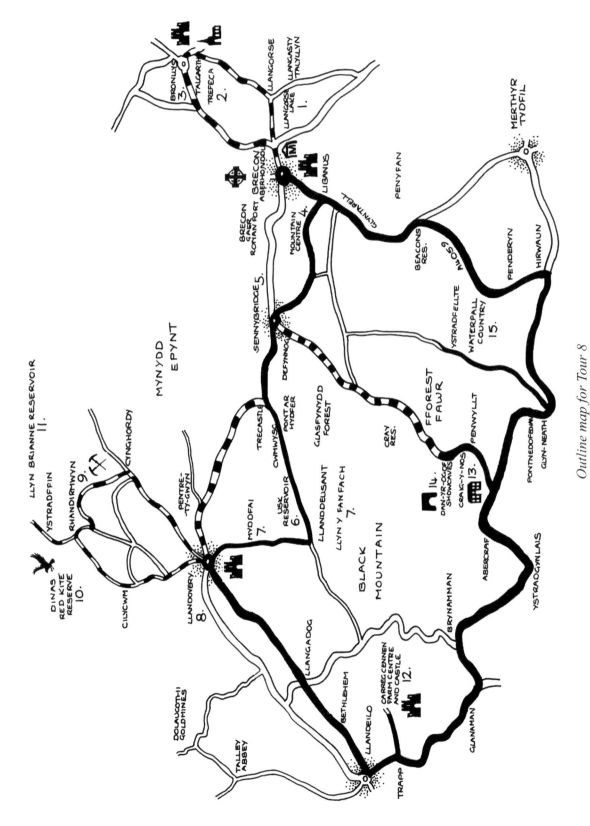

Outline map for Tour 8

The numbers 1 to 15 relate to the boxed information given within the tour

Tour 8   Western areas of the Brecon Beacons

A small tour to Llangorse lake and area (which can be busy in the height of summer) is followed by the main tour which heads through the Beacons on a mixture of A roads and fairly straight minor roads to Llandovery with its castle. A side trip on minor roads leads to Brianne reservoir. The western side of the Beacons is then shadowed, again on a mixture of A and minor roads, and likewise the south of the mountains, taking in Carreg Cennen Castle in its amazing hill-top location and with its underground cavern, caves at Dan-yr-Ogof and waterfalls and further scenery on the return journey. The distance of the initial Llangorse loop is 20 miles, and of the main tour 100 miles. (OS Landranger maps 146, 159, and 160).

The Brecon Beacons National Park

This park covers some 520 acres of mostly private land, including the mountain range from which it takes its name and the Black Mountains, where its eastern boundary is also that with England. Some 40 miles to the west it includes part of Carmarthenshire, while to the south it comes close to the once heavily industrialised South Wales Coalfield. The upper reaches of the Usk lie in the park, the river flowing eastwards through Brecon, the largest town in the park and its administrative centre, before turning south-eastwards, passing between the Black Mountains and Brecon Beacons towards Crickhowell to enter Monmouthshire. The enclosed farmland of the lowland Usk provides a strong contrast with much of the park, which is comprised of mountain ranges, secluded lakes, 19 reservoirs within or close to its boundaries, fast flowing streams, deep cwms and wide expanses of wind-blown moorland. There are some 1,250 miles of public paths — and almost one million sheep! Much of the soil of the park is derived from Old Red Sandstone which also protrudes as rock outcrops in many places. The highest point in the park, and in southern Britain, is 2,907 feet above sea level on Pen y Fan, a claim closely challenged by the adjacent Corn Du at 2,863 feet. Both summits are capped by a protective layer of hard sandstone and conglomerate when other ranges of softer stone have been worn away through erosion by wind, rain and ice. As the land falls towards the coalfield valleys to the south there is a change of foundation to Carboniferous Limestone and Millstone Grit. Along the courses of the Rivers Mellte, Hepste and Nedd Fechan in the country around Ystradfellte, and at the head of the Neath Valley, water erosion has produced falls as tall as 90 feet and labyrinthine cave systems which have so far been discovered to extend to at least 35 miles. There are signs of human settlement extending back to Neolithic days shown by the remains of chambered long barrows, Bronze Age cairns, standing stones and stone circles, Iron Age hillforts, Roman military camps, Norman castles, a remarkable heritage of religious and secular buildings and reminders of the industrial revolution from its earliest days.

Llangorse Lake was the site of a small man-made island of brushwood and stones just off the northern shore, on which was built a crannog, a name derived from the Irish *crann*, meaning tree, quite possibly as a protection against armed attack. Although no longer occupied, the island is still there and Llangorse Lake has become the most visited attraction of the entire park.

If you want to undertake just the main tour go to page 181.

The short tour starts at the roundabout on the western end of the Brecon by-pass and takes the A40 towards Abergavenny, but not for long. Turn left at the next junction signposted for Llanfrynach and Llangorse. There is then an option to turn right in the Llanfrynach direction via the B4558 to visit the canal lock and obtain a fine view of the canal aqueduct from the Lock Bridge across the River Usk, or walk to it along the towpath from the small car park and canalside picnic area. Otherwise stay on the minor road signposted for Llangorse, turn sharp right and then continue to follow the signs as the road first climbs and then descends to reach the village sign for Llanfihangel Tal-y- Llyn. The second part translates as the 'lake head' and the road continues on towards the village of Llangorse where there is a sign pointing towards the car park at the head of the lake.

1. Llangorse Lake

A rebuilt crannog, or lake dwelling, on Llangorse Lake

Llangorse Lake lies north of the Usk Valley and at the foot of the western face of the Black Mountains in a lowland basin left after the last Ice Age. The retreating glacier deposited a mixture of debris in the form of mounds or moraines at its side and front, as others had done to produce Llyn y Fan Fawr and Llyn y Fan Fach to the west of the Park. Unlike them, Llangorse Lake, or Llyn Syfaddan, is quite shallow and with a natural wealth of dissolved nutrients it sustains a great range of plant life, especially reed beds. This bounty in turn attracts a rich variety of birds and other wildlife, all accounting for early designation as a Site of Special Scientific Interest in 1954. Measuring over 1 mile long, with a circumference of 5 miles and a total area of 327 acres, as a naturally formed freshwater lake it is second in size in Wales only to Lake Bala in Gwynedd, also in a glacier-formed hollow.

It would have been an obvious attraction from early days for its abundant food supply of fish and fowl and in 1868 signs of Iron Age occupation were unearthed. Positive evidence has also arisen that an offshore **crannog**, or lake dwelling, was built in stages between AD 889 and 893 and that for a time it served as a royal residence for the local Welsh King of Brycheiniog. Less clear are aspects of the story set out in *The Anglo Saxon Chronicle* for the year AD 916 describing a Mercian attack directed by Aethelfleda, Lady of The Marches, daughter of King Alfred the Great and sister of Edward the Elder, King of Wessex and England. It does not explain why the wife of the British king and 34 men were taken away captive to Mercia, but as to the attack there is scientific evidence of a significant fire during the 10th century at the place then referred to as Brycenamere and Brecknock Mere. Some 270 years later the chronicler Gerald of Wales (see p.168-169) described the location when referring to the attack in his *The Journey through Wales*. As a local resident of Llanddew he was well able to relay local folk legends of a drowned city, covered with buildings, rich pasture-lands, gardens and orchards, and so may also have had close knowledge of the plentiful pike, perch, trout, tench and large eels then certain to have been available. These would certainly have been familiar to the owner of the dugout canoe which was discovered in 1925 in a well-preserved state beneath the water to the east of the island and radio-carbon dated to between AD 760 and 1020, and now in Brecknock Museum.

Dugout canoes would have caused no great harm at the lake, but nowadays there are concerns about the effects of power-boats, water-skiing, wind-surfing and even yachting in causing changes to the range of underwater and other plant life, even the loss of some rare species and sensitive invertebrates. In particular, depletion of the important reed sites by wash can cause detriment to breeding warblers and buntings and also reduce the amount of refuge for water rails, coots, wild ducks, great crested grebes and sometimes even more exotic visitors. The worries of conservationists, and others who are equally concerned about the ecology of the lake, are somewhat eased by the concentration of the caravan site, sailing club, cafeteria, P.G.L. Adventure camp, jetties, motorists, car parks and visitors on part of its north side only, and by measures aimed at restricting numbers and speed of boats on the water.

Instead of returning by the same route, an alternative way back to Brecon involves a right turn from the access road from the lake and then a left turn in the village to join the B4560 in the direction of Talgarth, Bronllys and the westbound A470. The hamlet of Trefeca is reached after 3 miles where a sign on the right indicates 'Coleg Trefeca. Cartref Howell Harris — The Home of Howell Harris 1714–1773'.

2. The Methodist Revival and the growth of nonconformity

The immediate beginning of the Revival is usually traced back to the conversion of Howell Harris at a sermon at Talgarth church in 1735. It was to become one of the most significant religious and social movements in the history of Wales. Harris worked in collaboration with Daniel Rowland (1713–90) and William Williams Pantycelyn (1717–1791), who it was once said 'provided the spiritual sound track with his unique hymn-writing ability'. At his

Trefeca College

enlarged home at **Trefeca**, Harris housed a community of over 100 people, known as 'y Teulu' (the Family), so that they could be taught from among 70 rural trades and crafts, such as weaving, carpentry, farming methods and spinning, for many of these people had been evicted from their farms or sacked because of their support for him. Then in 1768 a theological college for the training of young Methodist preachers was funded at the nearby College Farm by Selina, Countess of Huntingdon, a close supporter of Harris and of much Christian evangelistic work. The Presbyterian Church or Calvinistic Methodist Church of Wales was established in 1823 which now uses the college for lay training conferences, courses and retreats.

Harris was an itinerant preacher for 39 years after his conversion and died in 1773, still a lay Member of the Church of England. Nearly 20,000 mourners are reported to have attended his funeral, when he was buried under the same stone as his late wife, Anne, in front of the altar rails at **Talgarth Church**. There is a plaque commemorating his life and work on the south wall of the Lady chapel as another place of pilgrimage for those who honour his connection with the Methodist Revival. By the middle of the 19th century this movement had influenced the Baptist and Congregationalist Churches to the extent that Wales had become predominantly a nonconformist country. Many chapels, even villages, met on these tours have names originating in the Holy Land from those early days, such as

Libanus, Bethlehem, Salem and Bethesda. A century later there were some 164 nonconformist chapels in Breconshire alone, 131 of them built since 1811. Some are still well attended, but others have been adapted to varied uses, or stand empty and forlorn.

There used to be a castle tower twinned with that at Bronllys, a further ½ mile up the B4560. Bronllys Castle is signposted to the right and served by a convenient layby opposite the pathway entrance.

3. Talgarth and Bronllys

Saint Gwendoline's Church is unusually dedicated to one of the many pious daughters of Brychan (see p.166). It is thought possible that the present parish church and churchyard occupy the enclosure which once contained the earliest inhabitants of Talgarth in the age of the Celtic saints: these enclosures are called 'Llanau' in place names, such as neighbouring Llangors, Llanfilo and Llaneigon. The situation of the present 15th-century building can thus be said to go back to the time when Wales became both Welsh and Christian — but much of the interior has since suffered from the hands of Victorian 'restorers'. Much of the village below the church also dates from the 19th century and at one time it had a full quota of chapels, as well as pubs and some 65 shops. The South Wales Sanatorium, which opened with 304 beds in 1920 as the largest in Wales, used to provide employment for much of the population and the local economy also enjoyed the advantages of a tramroad route, then a rail service as well as the important road between the Wye and Usk valleys. But now Talgarth is much quieter, although it still operates a market, serves as an important centre for the local farming community and acts as a tourist base at the north-western end of the Black Mountains. There is a Tourist Information Centre at the 13th-century, tall pele tower and former look-out post at the Ennig bridge.

    Bronllys Castle is on high ground above the junction of the Llynfi with its tributaries Ennig and Dulas and consists of a 16m high 13th-century round tower with a vaulted basement and a high level entrance. It is thought to be on the site of a late 12th-century motte, established by Richard fitz Pons of Clifford, Herefordshire, and was often modified until 1521, when it became 'beyond repair'. St. Mary's Church is unusual for Wales in that it has a detached tower of medieval origin. There are seven in neighbouring Herefordshire and like many during times of border assaults it served as a refuge for women, children and even animals. In 1887 the 12th-/13th-century nave and chancel suffered from 'restoration' but there are still interesting old features in the church. They include the ancient font and a 16th-century Tudor screen, typically between nave and chancel, depicting a green man with his foliate head sprouting leaves from the mouth.

The B4560 joins the A438 in the centre of Bronllys (though this will soon change with the opening of the by-pass). Turn left and follow the signs for Brecon. Go straight over the first roundabout onto the Brecon by-pass, and turn left at the second in the direction of Merthyr Tydfil and Cardiff. You will now be on the A470 and have joined the start of the main tour (see opposite page).

The main tour starts here.

From the roundabout on the eastern end of the Brecon by-pass, take the A470 to head for Merthyr Tydfil and Cardiff, close to the River Tarell, for the 3 miles as far as Libanus. Turn right at the brown sign for the **Brecon Beacons Visitor Centre** at the far end of the village and follow the other direction signs up the winding minor road for the next 1½ miles before crossing a cattle grid and turning right at a further brown sign and then another right to enter the car park (pay and display).

---

4. National Park Visitor Centre

On a moorland ridge at 1085 feet above sea level the Centre commands superb views of the highest mountains in South Wales and is open daily, except on Christmas Day. It provides all the information needed about the Park, reinforced by a shop offering local books, maps and souvenirs. There are exhibitions, a 60-seat lecture and conference room, award winning tea rooms/restaurant and a comfortable lounge. Parking for disabled visitors is placed close to the building, where all parts are accessible by wheelchair. The Centre makes an ideal gateway for exploration of the Park, whether by a gentle stroll on the adjacent common or for a more ambitious walk in the mountains. As seen from the common, these form a chain running from east to west, falling naturally into four sections or ranges. In the centre is the Brecon Beacons range and the highest point about 3¾ miles away on Pen y Fan at 2,907 feet above sea level, just

The National Park Visitor Centre and views from nearby of Pen y Fan and Corn Ddu

to the west is the Fforest Fawr range, once part of a medieval hunting ground, while over to the east are the Black Mountains. Confusingly these are at the opposite end to the quite different Black Mountain, away to the far west.

After leaving the Centre, turn right at the sign for Brecon and Merthyr, and another indicating unsuitability for HGVs and coaches, and after a left turn pass over a cattle grid to cross the common, intersecting the line of the 1st-century Roman road (or *sarn* — causeway) between Y Gaer (pp.165-166) and Neath (*Nidvm*), 30 miles to the south-west. This is one of many Roman roads in Wales also labelled as Sarn Helen and thought to have been named after Princess Elen of *Segontium*, wife of the Emperor Maximus in the 4th century. Across to the right, with no public access, is Castle Mound which once carried a defensive round tower some 50 feet high and possibly built in the 13th century by Prince Llywelyn ap Gruffudd. After more cattle grids there is a descent between hedges to join the A4215. Turn right here, observing the sign to Dyfynnog and once past the hamlet turn left at the sign for Brecon and Llandovery, passing the blue village sign for Sennybridge to meet the A40 at the Usk Railway Inn. Turn left here towards Llandovery.

---

5. Sennybridge, Mynydd Epynt and training the Modern Army

At the confluence of the Rivers Usk and Senni, Sennybridge is at the beginning of the Vale of Usk which runs eastwards between Mynydd Illtud and the southern extension of Epynt. On the west bank of the Senni, **Castell Du** is the ruin of the 14th-century keep of the Constable of Fforest Fawr, once used as a prison for robbers and offenders against forest laws. Much later, the coming of the Neath and Brecon Railway in 1872 transformed the local rural economy and then in 1939 the army appeared. The **Sennybridge Camp and Training Area** was requisitioned and built up and some 60 years later the present Army camp is providing for tough experience in realistic conditions for regular, reserve and cadet units across some 30,000 acres of the main training and field firing area on Mynydd Epynt. This is mostly a broad and wild plateau of fairly uniform height lying at about 1,250–1,500 feet and outside the Park, covered by blanket bog and grass where live firing can take place during around 260 days a year, with artillery firing on 40 days and also some live firing from ground–attack aircraft. Some 200,000 service personnel were said to have trained on these rugged hills of Breconshire during 1999 and because of the obvious dangers, red flags fly continuously along the range boundaries. Unescorted access is not allowed other than along appropriately signed roads and it is always best to discuss plans either at the National Park Information Centre in Brecon or at the Sennybridge Camp. There will always be unexploded live ordnance lying about the range, dating from the Second World War onwards, and nobody should venture off approved routes. The surrounding area is thinly populated and, despite all the military and air activity, there is great scope for conservation of fauna and flora that might already have been lost in less restricted parts of the country.

After leaving Sennybridge, continue along the A40 as far as **Trecastle**, which was an ancient royal seat of Brycheiniog and has remains of a tree-clad but well-preserved motte and bailey **castle** on the right

*The warning column
by the side of the A40*

as you enter the village which is thought to have been first built in *c*.1095 by Bernard de Neufmarché. Trecastle is on the route of the Roman road from Y Gaer which runs for 3 to 4 miles along the ridge of Mynydd Bach past Y Pigwn to *Alabvm* near Llandovery. Ten miles west of Brecon, the village was a regular stage for a change of horses on the Gloucester to Llandovery mail and stagecoach route and its welcoming inns have long made it a suitable starting point for the exploration of western areas of the Park and of Epynt.

For the next stage of the tour, therefore, there is a choice available between the old stagecoach route via the A40 down the Gwydderig river valley to Llandovery (see the paragraph below), or a totally contrasting way there, heading high up to the Usk Reservoir, then below the long escarpment of the Carmarthenshire Black Mountain, one of the finest pieces of mountain scenery in South Wales, towards a remote fairyland, rich in folklore (see two paragraphs below).

In taking the direct A40 to Llandovery it would be as well not to emulate Edward Jenkins, the driver of a mail coach which passed this way just before Christmas, 1835. After over-indulging in pre-seasonal spirit at one or more of Trecastle's hospitable inns, he loaded up and set off behind four freshly-changed horses and was soon thundering down the wooded river valley and through the hamlets of Llywel and Halfway, totally out of control. Upon facing a cart laden with farm produce coming the other way, his evasive action resulted in the horses, crew, passengers, mail and baggage hurtling down a steep bank for over 120 feet, the coach finishing up in several pieces against a tree beside the River Gwydderig. Miraculously no one was badly injured and the horses were soon in harness again, but afterwards a roadside pillar was erected near the spot as a warning to everyone against the perils of early 19th-century drink driving. Over a century and a half later the warning column remains by the side of the A40 — still a reminder for inebriated drivers of the motorcar age. Apart from a much improved road surface and other refinements the route has not changed very much. (A short detour avails itself if you wish: a little further down the hill, a sign points right to Pentre Ty Gwyn, then another in blue leads to Cartref (home of) William Williams Pantycelyn who was the most prolific and famous of Welsh 18th-century hymn writers.) Once in Llandovery, make a left turn to follow the sign to the main car park on the former market site below the castle ruins.

The hugely rewarding detour from Trecastle recommended here is indicated by the brown sign for the Usk Reservoir, pointing left from the A40 just before the Castle Coaching Inn. The minor road soon crosses the River Usk at Pont Newydd and climbs in roller coaster fashion past a sign for Cwmwysg, Llanddeusant and Abercraf and through Pont ar Hydfer, where the River Hydfer joins the Usk. The gradual climb approaches moorland and fine views of the broad escarpment of the Carmarthen Fans to the left, its appearance continually changing with variations in light and shade. All around there are glorious views over dozens of miles of lonely, unfrequented country, with hardly a building in sight — just sheep. But soon the area becomes increasingly covered by regimented blocks of man-made coniferous forestry, here a clue to the proximity of the Usk Reservoir. If you want to stop and visit the reservoir, then follow the brown sign pointing in the direction of Cronfa Ddwr Wysg one mile away to the right beyond the dense pine plantations, otherwise carry on ahead.

---

6. The Usk Reservoir

Completed in 1955 at Cwm Wysg and the most recently built reservoir in the National Park, it is 1,050 feet above sea level and covers 280 acres of the upland reaches of the Usk. Cars can park at the approach to the dam and everyone can walk across the top to the other end, or drive there by continuing on and down alongside the spillway to reach the opposite shore. There are picnic tables close to the water and the lucky children of Trecastle Primary School have their own 'Environment Area'. The road eventually runs out but there are public footpaths and cycling routes around the reservoir and as well as many plant species, a range of wildfowl, woodland birds and other fauna is to be seen. Or caught — for this has a reputation as one of the finest trout fisheries in Wales, where natural brown trout are regularly supplemented by restocking with 'brownies' and rainbow trout. Tickets are available between March and October from a dispenser and fly fishing (although it can be rather windy), spinning and worming are currently permitted. There are also opportunities for boating and canoeing.

The road now leads through the Glasfynydd Forestry Commission wood to reach a cattle grid and car park at Pont ar Wysg. As this name indicates, it is a bridge across the now infant River Usk, which has arrived in twists and turns from its source about 2 miles to the south, up on the moorland flank of Fan Foel. Here it defines the boundary between old Breconshire and Carmarthenshire and is at the threshold of an open hill area of the Black Mountain that is renowned for its upland landscape, ecology and numbers of special archaeological features. Within an area totalling some 15,000 hectares, a great amount is classified as a Site of Special Scientific Interest (SSSI).

After another cattle grid the road descends between hedges to Talsarn and its forlorn, abandoned blue-painted chapel and ahead there is likely to be the first sight of numbers of red kites indulging their exciting aerobatics. The reason for this spectacle becomes clear at the Cross Inn, **Llanddeusant**, where there is a

feeding station, complete with a hide, about 200 yards off to the right down the Myddfai road. It opened in 2002 and already some 50 birds are said to gather daily before feeding times, at 3pm in the summer and 2pm in the winter. (Arrangements to visit should be confirmed at the pub.) Also close to the crossroads to the right is the Black Mountain Caravan and Camping Park, while about a mile up the road to the left overlooking the Sawdde Valley is the former Red Lion inn, dating from 1789. This is now a 3 star self-catering Youth Hostel and a favourite starting point for walks up to the heights of the

Near the source of the Usk

Carmarthen Fans and to the mystical Llyn y Fan Fach. Offering views of some of the finest pieces of mountain scenery in South Wales, the trail shadows the River Sawdde to its source in the lonely Lake of the Little Peak and its deep craggy hollow, below the daunting slopes of Bannau Sir Gaer.

---

7. The Legend of the Lady in the Lake and the Physicians of Myddfai

Llyn y Fan Fach is in a glaciated cwm or hollow scooped out by descending ice during the last Ice Age, while almost 100 years ago it was converted into a reservoir for Llandeilo and to assist with the thirsty needs of heavily industrial Llanelli on the Loughor estuary. In the wild and beautiful mountains some 20 miles away the contrasting solitude and stillness have a magical atmosphere that has sometimes been said to hang in the air — and which could have helped to account for the creation of the legend of the fairy who rose from the lake. Her stunning looks quite bowled over a young farmer from nearby Blaensawdde as he tended his cattle by the enchanted lakeside and after three attempts, for even fairies can play hard to get, he persuaded her to wed him. But her father, who also lived in the lake, laid down an important proviso that meant that she would leave him if he so much as tapped her reprovingly three times. They set up home, farmed at Esgair Laethdy near Myddfai and produced three fine sons, but of course the inevitable happened! Today's rule of 'Three strikes and you're out' clearly applied in medieval times and the lady returned to the depths of the lake, along with her marriage dowry of sheep and cattle. But before disappearing for good she instructed her sons in the art of healing and showed them where to find the medicinal herbs and plants they would need. Here is where folklore can be said to shade into firm fact, for

Myddfai Church

184

historic records mention that a Rhiwallon (the same name as that of the eldest son of the marriage) and his sons Cadwgan, Gruffudd and Einion, were indeed doctors to Rhys Gryg, lord of Dinefwr and Ystrad Tywy, in the mid-13th century, and that they became the first of a long line of Myddfai physicians. A description dating from *c*.1400 in part of the *Red Book of Hergest* details almost 500 medicinal remedies derived from around 175 locally grown plants and great interest is being shown in their properties, effects and potential use in modern life by researchers at the National Botanic Garden of Wales in Llanarthne (pp.61-62). A modern interest in herbal remedies is also being linked with the legend by a co-operative, planning to diversify by growing for the herbal medicine market. Myddfai Herbal Products hopes to generate an alternative source of income as local farming, mainly reliant on milk and sheep, declines to the detriment of the fortunes of the area and the prospects of its young people. Their village has become renowned as the home of a medical dynasty, the Physicians of Myddfai, which survived until the 18th century and the gravestones of the last of their line practising at Myddfai are to be seen in the porch of **St. Michael's Parish Church**, to the left alongside the main door. They are of David Jones (d.1719) and John, his eldest son (d.1739), surgeons, but there have been later Welsh doctors elsewhere, even today, who have claimed direct descent from the Meddygon Myddfai.

In Llanddeusant, turn right at the Cross Inn and follow the narrow road past the red kites, noting all the while the positions of the few passing places in case some reversing is called for, remembering with good grace that local drivers have to do it all the time. The views lower down towards the Tywi valley are all very worth while, but the twists and turns make it important for drivers to concentrate on what they are doing and not be distracted by the scenery before reaching the Plough Inn at Myddfai. The first written reference to a church on the opposite side dates to 1284, although there are indications of a place of Christian worship there at least back to the 8th century. St. Michael's appears to have been constructed in two stages. The original nave and chancel with its barrel ceiling were probably completed in the 13th or 14th centuries while, separated by a five-bay arcade of massive arches, a 15th-century aisle runs along the whole southern side of the church and with an altar and chancel is used for present day services.

The route continues to wind onwards downhill towards Llandovery, crossing the River Bran close to where it is joined by the River Gwydderig at the Waterloo Bridge. Turn left to rejoin the A40 and look for the car park sign pointing left to the pay and display site below the castle ruins.

8. Llandovery. Town on the Dyfri

Straddling the A40 leading to and from the Pembrokeshire and west Wales beaches, an hour or so away, the centre of Llandovery, or Llanymddyfri as it is known to the Welsh, is a regular stopping place for holidaymakers. But, surrounded by mountains, it is also situated at the junction of ancient military and trading routes and river valleys and there are four rivers around the town, the Tywi (or Towy), Bawddwr (now culverted and formerly Dyfri), Gwydderig and Bran.

The remains of the battered D-shaped tower and other traces of stonework, perched on the knoll above the central car park, date from between the late 12th century and the end of the 13th century, after the death and removal in 1282 of Llywelyn ap Gruffudd. The strategic importance of the locality had previously been appreciated by the Norman invaders, for they built a motte and bailey **castle** at the start of the 12th century, and well before them in the middle of the 1st century, the Romans, who were also quick to recognise the value of the location for the control of Towy Valley traffic and trade, established a fort named *Alabvm* below Llanfair Hill, a mile to the north. It was linked by road with Abergavenny (*Gobannivm*) and Brecon (*Cicvitio*) to the west and Carmarthen (*Moridvnvm*) to the east, and also with the Dolaucothi area to the north-west where the Romans mined gold, and the marching

Llandovery Castle (left) and the stainless steel monument to Llywelyn ap Gruffydd Fychan

camps at Y Pigwn to the east. Deep in Wales the entire area was constantly vulnerable to attack and soon after the Norman Richard fitz Pons had completed his timbered castle in *c*.1100 it was overcome by the Welsh and later-built stone fortresses changed hands many times before everything that remained by 1403 deteriorated further after an attack by Owain Glyndwr. A striking reminder of this concluding phase of conflict was placed in part of the former castle bailey in 2001 in the form of a figure fashioned in stainless steel as a **monument to Llywelyn ap Gruffydd Fychan of Caeo**. He was hanged, drawn and quartered in the town in 1401 for refusing to betray Glyndwr to King Henry IV. The main car park occupies much of the area of the former bailey after it recently replaced the long established cattle market, now further down a new access road close to the River Bran.

There is another reminder of the history of Llandovery, as an important drover town and great centre of the cattle trade, near the entrance to the car park and close to the TIC. It is in the form of a realistic **bronze sculpture of a drover** and a plaque records that at one time more than 30,000 store cattle and other livestock for fattening were driven each year from Wales to London, largely to Smithfield and the Barnet Fair. A significant number must have passed through Llandovery, standing as it did at the junction of three main droving routes, from Pembrokeshire, Carmarthenshire and Cardiganshire, and the consequent benefit to the local economy played a significant part in the shaping of the town. The early settlement was essentially based on one main street that ran eastwards from Broad Street, through the Market Square and King's Road and along High Street, almost as far as a ford at the River Bran. Burgages were set out on each side of this main thoroughfare, except for the area of the castle bailey. Off Lower Road, the original **church of St. Dingat** was probably of Celtic origin like many in the region and already

The statue of a drover near the TIC

*The old Market Hall in the main square
at Llandovery*

standing when the Normans invaded, while **St. Mary's** was built just to the north at Llanfair ar y Bryn within the area of the Roman fort. It was equally likely to have been founded during the flourishing of the Celtic Church which followed the Roman withdrawal. Later development near the centre produced island plots and significant buildings such as the **Town Hall**, and the **Market Hall** that has now been converted into a Craft Centre. In a building originating from 1750 the Heritage Centre has many features to illustrate the rich history and legends of Llandovery and the surrounding Towy Valley and it also serves as the National Park and Tourist Information Centre. It was built when the drover trade that provided Llandovery with its main livelihood was by 1822 entering a phase supporting 47 pubs and inns. Today the town's population of around 2,000 and its visitors get by with fewer, but they are still quite well provided for.

Llandovery Station has so far survived as an unmanned halt. Near the station is **Llandovery College**, a co-educational boarding and day school for 4 to 18 year olds founded in 1847, and one of only two recognised public schools in Wales.

The Drovers' Bank of the Black Ox

The wild country to the north and west of Llandovery is physically unsuitable for many forms of agriculture, but has always been more than adequate for the rearing of livestock, especially sheep but also the hardy, adaptable breeds of Welsh Black cattle. These were exported in a flourishing trade that, during the Civil War was described as 'the Spanish Fleet of Wales which brings us what little gold and silver we have' and constituted a vital part of the fragile Welsh economy by the mid-17th century. Conveying the livestock in herds generally of between 100 and 400 to provide 'The Roast Beef of Olde England' were the dealers and drovers. They built up numbers for the drive by purchasing store cattle from local fairs, or taking them 'in trust' from farmers and smallholders — paying for them when they returned from the distant English markets and fairs. The drovers were thus entrusted with the modest wealth of the producers, and they also undertook financial transactions for other people in London or elsewhere on their way — often out of the proceeds of the cattle sales. They produced receipts and cash and also brought news of social, economic and political changes taking place in the outside world.

The sign of the Black Ox

But, always exposed to highwaymen and other robbers in the wild country that they had to cross, they constantly ran the risk of loss, despite the benefit of their numbers. And so the practice began for their money to be looked after for them, including perhaps bullion obtained from the ancient Dolaucothi gold mines. Remarkably this trust fell to a teenaged farmer's son, one David Jones, and this led to the founding in 1799 of the Banc yr Eidion Ddu, the Bank of the Black Ox, existing on the site of the Kings Head Inn until 1848. It produced promissory banknotes bearing an engraving of a black ox, only accepted by the bank from reputable customers and not therefore of any value to thieves or anyone else. Just as happens in the 21st century, the bank made a good profit out of this and David Jones, after marrying well, became very wealthy and prominent in society. After he died in 1839 his business was continued by three of his grandsons at Llandovery, Llandeilo and Lampeter and in 1903 the family moved to the imposing Georgian Prospect House on High Street. After taking over from 1909, Lloyds Bank (now Lloyds TSB) still trades there, and the Black Ox image continued to appear on cheques issued by the Llandovery Branch until just before the First World War.

The Vale of Towy Railway Company and Heart of Wales Line

The days of the drover, which had lasted for more than seven centuries, came to an end with the building of the railways. By 1856 cattle could be driven to Shrewsbury to be loaded on trucks for the rest of their journey to the English sales, which they reached in better condition than before. Then two years later the Vale of Towy Railway Company completed an onward link via Llandeilo to Llandovery from Llanelli and finally in 1868 the Heart of Wales Line from Craven Arms joined up at Llandovery to cover the entire distance of 120 miles from Shrewsbury to Llanelli. It thus linked the industrial north to the south Wales coalfields and ironworks and provided a passenger service that became a prime factor in the social and economic life of much of mid-Wales. There was capacity for the carriage of parcels, luggage, milk, newspapers and mail and stations were laid out with freight loops for coal and agricultural goods and ramps and pens for livestock. But by the 1960s the Motor Age had well set in, the animals were being transported by lorry and in 1964 the line was downgraded to light railway status, with no freight traffic. On at least two occasions it was marked down for complete closure and once reprieved only when George Thomas MP, the Welsh Secretary and later to become the Speaker, is said to have reminded his Cabinet colleagues that the line ran through a number of marginal constituencies. Increased grants were miraculously found and drives to attract more passengers have continued.

To continue with the main tour go to page 193, but a possible side tour from Llandovery is a run of 11 miles deep into the hills up the Towy Valley to the **Llyn Brianne Reservoir**.

To take this side trip, head out of town along the A40 (here called Queensway) and just past the college turn right into New Road to join the A483, signposted to Builth Wells and Llyn Brianne Dam. After a short distance there is a left turn on to an unclassified road with signs in brown to Drovers' Country Tour / Taith Wledig y Porthmyn, Dinas Nature Reserve, 10 miles, Llyn Brianne, 11 miles. On a separate sign there are further pointers to the villages of Rhandirmwyn, 7 miles and Cilycwm, 3 miles.

But at this point there is a rewarding although somewhat longer way of reaching Rhandirmwyn and the dam. By continuing along the A483 following the signing for Builth and Rhayader (A470) there is first an opportunity at the next junction of entering a loop road to visit **Llanfair ar y Bryn church**, which was built on the site of the Roman fort of *Alabvm*, has fragments of what are perhaps Roman red brick below the east window and that is the last resting place of Williams Pantycelyn (p.179). Past the far end of the loop the A483 shadows the River Bran and follows the course of a Roman road for much

Llanfair ar y Bryn Church

of the distance to the village sign for Cynghordy and the Glanbran Arms inn on the left. Continue on the A483 to take the next turning to the left, again signposted for Cynghordy, descending quickly on a country road to cross the River Bran, then proceed past the village school before turning right onto the road that leads to a cattle grid and the viaduct.

The **Cynghordy railway viaduct** is the most spectacular feature of this detour. The largest on the Heart of Wales line, it is a triumph of Victorian civil engineering design. Built in 1868 on a curve that is 283 yards long and carrying trains 102 feet above the River Bran, it has 18 semi-circular arches of 36 feet 6 inches span, supported by elegantly tapered masonry piers. Far below in its shadow is a small Methodist chapel and one can only imagine what the minister and congregation can have felt, 24 years after it had opened in 1844, when they had their services regularly disturbed by the trains — rumbling over 100 feet above them!

Afterwards the single width road continues up into the hills, in some places rather challenging and requiring the use of bottom gear and resolve, but in the wild and lonely country at the top the sweeping views down below and towards the distant Carmarthen Fans are worth the detour on their own. After a mile of this spectacle the road starts to descend into the wide Towy Valley to rejoin the road leading from Llandovery towards the Llyn Brianne reservoir. Turn right on this road,

Cynghordy railway viaduct

which has the luxury of two lanes, and after just over a mile the route reaches Rhandirmwyn, the Pennau General store and Post Office (formerly the Queen's Arms Inn), the Royal Oak Inn, and a signed reminder that it is on part of the Taith Drovers' Tour.

---

9. The lead veins of Rhandirmwyn

For such a remote village in the foothills of the Cambrian Mountains the settlement is quite extensive. Some individual houses are modern but many more date from early in the 19th century and onwards and are in the form of terraces and stone- or brick-built workers' cottages. Until well into the 18th century farming was the main occupation of the community, but by the beginning of the 19th numbers had expanded around a thriving mining industry. The Romans are thought to have realised that the district was rich in lead ore and it seems quite likely that, just as at Tintern Abbey in the Wye Valley, this was not also lost on the Cistercian monks of Strata Florida (pp.238-240), for they had a grange close by. Certainly there is documentary evidence of lead mining by the late 13th century and by *c*.1760 the Cawdors, as local landowners, wished to exploit ore for their Carmarthen lead-works. Quite soon some 400 people were employed in the task and between 1775 and 1797 nearly 30,000 tons of ore (galena) were hauled down the valley. Production afterwards fell, but 42,000 tons of lead and 125 tons of zinc were still extracted over a 64-year period during the 19th century. However yields continued to reduce until production ceased early in the 20th century, leaving a legacy of derelict mines, shafts, adits, crosscuts and 23 miles of levels.

The Towy Valley narrows considerably beyond the village, then at the roadside a mile further on comes the **Nant-y-Bai Mill**. It is believed to have originated in medieval times and, with an overshot timber and cast iron wheel and a corn-drying kiln, has been listed as a Building of Special Architectural or Historic Interest, Grade II. Just across the road, a site and cwm (valley) shown on the map as Nant-y-glo suggest that minerals once found in the parish could have also included coal (glo), as well as all the lead and zinc.

After a further 2-mile drive, the territory becomes increasingly associated with the stories of Twm Siôn Cati, who was commonly known as The Welsh Robin Hood (see p.242). Much has been written about him and not all of it is that credible. One early 19th-century piece of verse refers to his adventures in this area:

> In Ystrad Fecn a mirthful sound
> Pervades the hollow hills around
> The very stones with laughter bound
> At Twm Shon Catty's jovial round

Soon the prominent steep, craggy and wooded Dinas Hill appears over to the left of the road and near the top is the cave that Twm, during his more rollicking days, was said to have used as a hideout and refuge when on the run. Nearly opposite is Ystradffin Farm, the scene in a previous state of a romantic yarn concerning Twm and the lady Johan, or Joan, Williams. Apparently he had been a welcome visitor at the farm after once rescuing her from a robber on the road from Llandovery, and much later, after she was widowed, and by a cunning but not unwelcomed subterfuge, he married her just two years before his death in 1609.

To the left, a short distance further on is the remote small **church of St. Peulin, or St. Paulinus**, who was the head of the renowned college of Whitland during the 5th century. Built on the site of earlier structures dating from 1117, the present building dates from 1821 and it has since been tastefully restored

St. Paulinus' Church

(but as is all too often the case now, can be firmly locked without any chance of borrowing a key). It was closely associated with the Methodist Revival in the 18th century.

Next comes the Royal Society for the Protection of Birds (RSPB) **Dinas and Gwenffrwd Reserve** car park. From here it is possible to follow a lovely walk along a 2-mile nature trail, which passes below the Twm Siôn Catti cave above a turbulent River Towy, and to discover the beauty of the Welsh oakwoods while looking out for buzzards, peregrines, ravens and a great many special smaller species. But especially the red kites, for here was another retreat in the area, one that became a sanctuary against their potential extinction from the UK.

---

10. The Rescue of the Red Kite — Wales' National Bird

A superb master of the sky, the red kite is widely regarded as just about the most beautiful, graceful bird to be seen anywhere in Britain. It has reddish-brown plumage and a pale grey head over a body only about the size of a small chicken but a wingspan that can exceed 6 feet. Its wings, often angled, display white patches from below as the bird soars and glides in wide agile sweeps, steered by a deeply forked tail. Kites are no newcomers to Wales, for their remains from 120,000 years ago have been found in a Gower Peninsula cave. It has not always been a bird of the countryside and during the Middle Ages it was almost as common in towns, where it was welcomed as a scavenger of offal, vermin and general street garbage. Some of this, including rags and bones, was used for nest-building and this practice doubtless lies behind a reference from William Shakespeare's day, when in *The Winter's Tale* the rogue, Autolycus, warns those with washing on clothes lines that 'When the kite builds, look to lesser linens'.

But by the second half of the 19th century the kite and other raptors were starting to fall victim to gamekeepers, then egg-collectors and taxidermists as they became more rare, followed by the sterilising effects of agricultural chemicals and the 1950s myxomatosis disease impact on rabbit prey. Because of all this, Britain's red kite population was driven close to extinction in little more than 50 years — a fact starkly driven home later in a genetic 'fingerprinting' study by the University of Nottingham. This revealed that the entire UK domestic red kite population is descended from just one female bird! It is tempting to think that she had survived here, in this last bastion of the upper Towy Valley. With the help of legislation, recovery started slowly under a concerted programme of conservation, involving the RSPB and many other organisations, agencies and individuals. Even a team of Gurkha soldiers from Brecon Barracks, doubtless complete with their fearsome kukri knives, were called in to help with guard duties at nests as part of their

Sculpture of a red kite at Llanwrtyd Wells

concealment training. By the early 1970s some 20 pairs of birds could be counted in Wales and by 1993 there were 100 pairs — the greatest number for over a century. After another ten years the number had doubled and in 2003 the Welsh Kite Trust was able to report that at least 400 chicks had fledged in Wales that season, accounting for later estimates of 250 pairs in mid-Wales.

In the light of this great success story of the 20th century, when so many other wildlife species have been greatly in decline, it surely followed in 2000 that the red kite, *y barcud goch*, should be dubbed Wales' National Bird.

Until the second half of the 20th century, access from Llandovery to this remote area would have been by little more than cart tracks and the ancient drovers' trail, but this had changed with the inauguration of the **Llyn Brianne Reservoir** by May 1973. A huge barrier of rockfill and clay was built at the narrowest point below two deep mountain gorges, and to appreciate its vastness (and maybe form a view about its appearance in that setting), drive a further ¾ mile beyond the church and then turn left to the first viewpoint and car park.

11. Llyn Brianne Reservoir

Llyn Brianne Reservoir

The dam is 91 metres (300 feet) tall and measures 290 metres (950 feet) from side to side and it impounds 61 million cubic metres of water. This covers an area of 215 hectares, fed by the Rivers Towy, Cawddwr and lesser streams flowing within a catchment area of some 8,800 hectares. With a top water level of 277.8 metres (911 feet) above sea level it must be the highest reservoir in Great Britain, and measures 84 metres (275 feet) at its deepest point. Someone has worked out that this would be enough to submerge all but the cross at the top of St. Paul's Cathedral, and with the steepness of the rocky, tree covered gorge it brings to mind the fjords of Norway. To the east side of the dam a wide lip of concrete allows surplus water to escape down a spillway to the stilling pool at the base. Also there is an 'Industrial Hydropower Station', built in 1997 and capable of producing electricity to supply the annual needs of 6,500 houses. A new road rises to another viewpoint and car park where it is possible to appreciate the great beauty of what, thanks to careful design, seems more of a huge natural mountain lake than a reservoir engineered to supply the needs of the City of Swansea and other parts of West Glamorgan. The water is not delivered all the way there by pipe, as might be thought, for it first flows down the course of the River Towy for about half the distance before entering large diameter pipes and pumps at Nantgaredig, near Carmarthen.

The former old track now lies deep beneath the water until it emerges alongside the River Towy again, 3 miles further on at the northern end of the reservoir — to be met near the end of a new road, built as part of the reservoir scheme. As the wooded slopes down to the water's edge were too steep for it to run from the dam level, this has instead been set out on a winding, undulating course higher up, achieving a design ideal of continually changing vistas across the lake and over the hills rolling north to the Cambrian Mountains.

Afterwards the motorist can continue along a road through the pine forest to connect with the mountain road between Tregaron and Abergwesyn, which is described in Tour 10, page 243. Nearby the River Towy flows down under a bridge from its source in the Cambrian Mountains, a few further miles beyond Nant-ystalwm, to begin its 70-mile journey to the sea.

But returning along the new road, rejoin the Towy below the dam to pass St. Paulinus' Church and Dinas Hill before turning right to cross the river at a sign for Cilycwm, Cwrty Cadno and Pumsaint. Turn left at the Towy Bridge

Dolauhirion Bridge over the River Towy

Inn to make for Cilycwm to enjoy a different perspective of the valley as it broadens again opposite Rhandirmwyn. The Neuadd Fawr Inn appears on the left soon after the village sign for **Cilycwm**, at the centre of a small and scattered community made up mainly of hill farms. Open channels running with water in front of roadside houses have survived from the days when they served to provide for cattle from the hills when this was an important drovers' collecting point. St. Michael's Church dates from the Middle Ages and is especially known for its 18th-century wall paintings. Pressing on, follow the next sign pointing left for Llandovery before again crossing the Towy and turning right at the Give Way sign to join the return road to the town. After about 1½ miles, it is worth stopping to look at the Dolauhirion Bridge, an exceptionally graceful single-arched river crossing with medieval origins reputedly built in 1785 by an amateur, Thomas Edwards of Pontypridd. It is now listed at Grade 1 and safeguarded with a weight restriction.

Afterwards return the final mile to Llandovery to rejoin the route of the main tour and head for the A40 junction with the A4069 to head for Llangadog.

Back to the main tour! A short distance down the road, just before open country, **St. Dingat's Church** appears on the right. It dates from the 14th century, was restored in 1906 and is especially associated with the works of Rhys Pritchard (1579–1633), a former vicar. He wrote *Cannwyll y Cymru — The Welshman's Candle* — a collection of verses and observations on Welsh life still highly regarded by many of his compatriots. The original foundation at St. Dingat's might well be of Celtic origin, but there is no written history for the area before the early 12th century when Llandovery started to form after the arrival of the Normans. In a similar way, the church of Cadog, who was a 5th-century Celtic saint of 'The Age of Saints' which followed the departure of the Romans, has survived to give its name to Llangadog which is 5 miles along the road down the Towy Valley.

The village is quite large but its heyday occurred during the Middle Ages when a charter granted the right to hold a market and several annual fairs, but the settlement has not expanded as much as could have been expected. Visible from the road just south of the village, **Castell Meurig** still shows as an imposing motte and bailey, built by the Welsh and involved in the early 13th-century troubles with the English.

Continue on the A4069 into Dyrful Road heading south towards Brynaman for a short distance and then at Carregsawdde make the first right turn signposted Bethlehem on to a secondary road and bridge across the River Sawdde, now near the end of its descent from Llyn y Fan Fach below the Carmarthen Fans to join the Towy. This is the road to the tiny hamlet of **Bethlehem**, which like others in Wales obtained the biblical name from its 19th-century chapel, but the difference here is that many people visit at Christmas time to have cards and other mail specially franked at the post office (limited open days and hours). On a high ridge above the post office and village school is another feature of interest. Indicated by a sign to the left, this is **Carn Goch**, an Iron Age fort and associated satellite fort, shown on *OS Explorer Map OL12* as Y Gaer Fawr (large) and Y Gaer Fach (small). Covering more than 15 hectares, it is the largest in south Wales and still retains massive defences — comprised of gateways, ditches and many hundreds of metres of huge stone rubble ramparts. It stands out in great contrast with the pastoral landscape laid out below and from the top affords spectacular views of the Vale of Towy and Carmarthenshire hills.

The road continues from Bethlehem for another 4 miles along the boundary of the National Park towards Llandeilo, showing ahead spread out high on a hill (p.54), but just before the railway bridge at Ffairfach, turn left at the green castle sign and head uphill for the village of Trapp and, from there, follow further signs for **Carreg Cennen Castle**. Even in the lush green countryside so far seen on this tour, the car park could hardly be in a more atmospheric spot, below what arguably is the most theatrical of British castle ruins.

Admission tickets, Cadw *Guidebook* and refreshments are available at Castle Farm, where a path leads up to the castle outer ward. It is really not for wheelchairs but, with due regard for levels of fitness and stamina, most people should be able to manage the haul up to the gateway in the ruined wall. The sweeping views up there are certainly worth the effort.

---

12. Carreg Cennen Castle

As the guidebook explains in detail, the outer ward was built during the late 13th century in the third constructional stage of the present castle and it points out the limekiln and quarry used for the building and repair work. Also in the south-east corner there is a 50m-long passage beneath the fortress — partly lighted by loop holes but also calling for torches, which can be hired at the farm. The second building phase produced the barbican — an elaborate ramped outer defence with two drawbridges. But instead of a more usual keep, an inner ward was built as the first and most strongly defended element. Placed on the very summit of the carboniferous limestone crag, it contained the King's Chamber, Hall, Chapel and a range of domestic buildings. As well as acting as a military stronghold, it also served in its time as an administrative centre and seat of justice for the region (when a push over the sheer 300ft precipice has been said to have served as an alternative to the hangman's 'drop' for the execution of

From virtually every angle Carreg Cennen Castle produces an amazing profile

capital sentences). There is mention of probable settlers attracted to the site, from prehistoric and Roman periods to Welsh princes, Norman barons and English kings until the Wars of the Roses, when in 1462 the Yorkists dispossessed the resident Lancastrians by the employment of 500 men equipped with bars, picks, crowbars and other assorted demolition tools. Their 4 months of exertion resulted in the state of ruin which, almost 5½ centuries on has remained to be conserved and protected by Cadw. Perhaps persisting here also is some sense of the romanticism that, in *Faerie Queen,* prompted Edmund Spenser to locate Merlin's cave in wooded Carmarthenshire hills, not very far away.

Before returning to the car, visitors may wish to see the selection of rare breeds of farm animals which are kept at Carreg Cennen, or sample the wholesome Welsh *Cawl Cennen*, (leek broth), which might be on offer at 'Mary's Farmhouse'. Afterwards, well fortified, return down the road to Trapp for a last look at the castle, spectacularly poised high above on the crag to the east, to continue on the next stage of the tour. At the T-junction turn left to cross the bridge leading to the Cennen Arms and then turn right to follow the sign for Llandybie and Glanaman, still alongside the Park boundary. Then make a left turn for Llandyfan, still keeping the Black Mountain in full view to the east and passing further signs to Glanaman, just within the South Wales coalfield and outside the Park. Alongside the A474 here there is a complete transition from deep country to an industrial landscape to the right. After about 3 miles look for a left turn for Brynamman on the A4069. After 1½ miles and in Brynamman turn right on the A4068 towards Ystalfera.

The A4067 appears another 4 miles further on in the upper Tawe valley, where signs show the way left to the **Dan yr Ogof Caves** and Ystradgynlais, at one time one of the most important centres of the Industrial Revolution in the world. Follow this road through Abercraf, close to the River Tawe below on the right, to re-enter the National Park, passing the Ancient Briton inn and signs for Pen-y-Cae to reach the small hamlet of **Craig-y-Nos**, and its **Castle and Country Park** across the road. It stands in a narrow defile, cut between the towering limestone crags of the Cribarth on the left and the steep wooded slopes of Craig-y-Rhiwarth on the right — an impressive southern gateway to the National Park. On the banks of the River Tawe in the Upper Swansea Valley, it was an idyllic site that was adopted in 1841 for the building of Bryn Melin, a grand Gothic style mansion.

Entrance to the Castle car park is through the gateway alongside the A4067 and there is a separate car park (pay and display) for the Country Park, also to the right, just beyond in the former kitchen and fruit garden.

13. Craig-y-Nos and the Queen of Song

Adela Juana Maria Patti was born in Madrid in 1843 to musical Italian parents and emigrated with them to New York when she was about 4. By the time she was 7 years old she had undertaken her first stage singing appearance and, by then calling herself Adelina, made her operatic debut as Donizetti's 'Lucia' when just 16 and was soon to take many leading roles. She performed at Covent Garden Opera House in 1861, moved to London and, for the next 40 years became the most celebrated and highly paid soprano in the world. This was long before the introduction of air and car travel, radio, television, recordings or any form of amplification, relying on her great gifts of 'clarity, quality of tone, range and expression — all under exquisite control', as a devotee has recently put it. But her repertoire was not confined to opera, as when for example in 1862 she sang 'Home Sweet Home' at the White House to Abraham and Mary Lincoln. After that, this song rapidly became her most popular encore piece and when, in 1875 and at the height of her dazzling career, she was charmed by the mansion in the Upper Tawe valley, she determined to make it her home and retreat for the rest of her life. Happily it

Craig-y-Nos

came on the market in 1878 and with her second husband, the tenor Ernesto Nicolini, she set about extending Craig-y-Nos — Rock of the Night. New north and south wings, a glass and wrought iron Winter Garden, a small opera house for an audience of 150 — modelled on that at Bayreuth, a conservatory, clock tower and aviary were among many introductions over a period of 40 years. The surrounding parkland was extended and laid out with terraced lawns leading down to the Tawe, and there were lakes, exotic trees and a walled kitchen garden. For the further pleasure and convenience of the many prominent house guests a special drive was opened to the railway station and lavishly appointed private waiting room at nearby Penwyllt on the Neath and Brecon line.

Before Adelina Patti died in 1919 she decided to present the Winter Garden to Swansea, where it became the Patti Pavilion (p.15) and her third husband, the Swedish Baron Cederstrom, afterwards sold the castle and parkland for it first to become a tuberculosis sanatorium in 1921 and then in 1959 a hospital for the geriatric and chronic sick. In 1976 the neglected grounds were taken in hand as a Country Park by the Brecon Beacons National Park Committee, while the Castle is now in private ownership and in 2005 was being extensively renovated. The castle has been adapted as a function venue for parties and conferences — served by the Patti Bar, and in 2001 the small private theatre was granted a full wedding licence. There is a 'Bridal Suite' and other bed and breakfast accommodation ranging between 'Luxury En-suite' rooms to tri-bunk beds in a dormitory for up to 33 visitors — wedding guests to walkers, cavers and others enjoying the pleasures of the National Park.

This whole area is riddled with caves in the band of limestone bordering the South Wales coalfield. The rock is soluble in the water that has flowed in rivers and streams from the Carmarthenshire Fans to the north, after it has absorbed carbon dioxide from the atmosphere to form a mild carbonic acid. After this has seeped into fissures in the limestone over many tens of thousands of years, a very gradual process of erosion has produced what is regarded as the finest show-cave complex in the British Isles, if not Western Europe.

On the left, about half a mile beyond the Country Park, a steep wooded dingle forms a shallow cleft in the flank of the hill. High above road level is the entrance to **Dan-yr-Ogof** (named after the farm below).

14. The National Showcaves Centre for Wales
The cave was first explored in 1912 by Ashworth and Jeff Morgan from Abercraf. The brothers made their entrance above the limestone arch where the River Llynfell emerges from underground to tumble its way to join the Tawe, just above Craig-y-Nos. Equipped with candles, night-lights and a coracle they cautiously entered a quiet world of tunnels, passageways, chambers, lakes and waterfalls for a

length of almost half a mile. No further exploration occurred until 1937, but then a new entrance was blasted to enable a show-cave complex to be opened for the public to see some of the immense caverns and spectacular, colourful formations. Other discoveries followed and by the end of the century some 200,000 visitors were said to be attracted to Dan yr Ogof each year. By then they were able to walk through three separate systems. These are the original Dan yr Ogof cave; Cathedral Cave — discovered in 1953, opened as a show-cave in the 1970s and first called Davy Price's Hall. It is 70ft high and gets its name from the huge tunnel leading back into the mountainside; Ogof yr Esgyrn (the bone cave), named because of over 42 human skeletons found there, many of them dating from when people lived there over 3,000 years ago. Dinosaurs existed on Earth much earlier than that and there are over 100 life-sized replicas of these prehistoric creatures in one area of the Park, while other features include a replica Iron Age farm, a Shire Horse Centre and a shop.

Back at the A4067 main road there is a choice of two return routes to Brecon.

One entails a left turn for a drive over Fforest Fawr (the Great Forest of Brecknock which was Norman hunting country), past Swansea's Cray Reservoir, below on the left, to the A40 at Sennybridge and thence back to Brecon.

The other, through what is sometimes called '**Waterfall Country**', means a right turn to drive back past Craig-y-Nos to Abercraf to join the A4221, then a left turn towards Glyn Neath. The first waterfall, the Henrhyd Fall (NT), is just inside the Park boundary and can be reached by turning off the A4221 after a mile to head through the village of Coelbren and turning left to enter the National Trust car park. With a single fall of 90 feet it is the highest to be seen in the National Park and, it is thought, south of Devil's Bridge (pp.237-238). Like all the others to be mentioned, it can only be reached carefully on foot, with sound walking boots having good grip to deal with wet and slippery conditions. There can be steep and dangerous drops on the side of narrow paths. Here a steep path descends into a wooded valley to reach a bridge across the little River Llech. Follow this upstream to the pool at the base of the drop, where it is interesting

Top: Sgwd Clyn-gwyn (Waterfall of the White Meadow) and Sgwd Isaf Clyn-gwyn (Lower White Meadow Waterfall). Bottom: Sgwd y Pannwr (The Fuller's Waterfall)

15. Waterfall Country

This is where, from its source high in the Fforest Fawr, the River Neath, or Nedd, is joined on its course to the sea at Swansea Bay by the Pyrddin, Hepste and Melte. There are impressive waterfalls along each of them, the easiest to reach being Sgwd Gwladys on the Pyrddin, which also has Sgwd Einion Gam. On the Neath there are the Horseshoe Falls, the Lower Sgwd Ddwli and Upper Sgwd Ddwli, on the Hepste the Sgwd yr Eira and the Lower Cilhepste and falls on the Melte are Sgwd y Pannwr, Sgwd Isaf Clyn-gwyn and Sgwd Clyn-gwyn. Roughly 1 mile north of this upper fall of the Melte the river has been underground for ¾ mile at Porth yr Ogof (Gateway to the Cave),

Porth yr Ogof on the River Meete, about 1 mile north of Sgwd Clyn-gwyn (pictured on the previous page)

near Ystradfellte. Measuring approximately 60 feet in width at a height of 16 feet, this is surely the largest and most impressive cave entrance in all Wales — only rivalled by the Dan yr Ogof show caves.

to see a thin layer of coal in the rock behind the waterfall. Strictly, Henrhyd is just outside the locality known as Waterfall Country, or Coed y Rhaeadr to the Welsh. This is situated in a triangle formed by the villages of Hirwaun, Ystradfellte and Pontneddfechan.

After passing Coelbren, the A4221 joins the A4109 for Glyn Neath and before reaching the A465 turn left on the B4242 to reach Pontneddfechan in the Vale of Neath, where there is a Tourist Information Centre covering the area. Any directions given here for Waterfall Country may be confusing and those interested in paying the falls a visit ought to invest in the invaluable *OS Explorer Map OL12. Brecon Beacons National Park/West and Central Areas* and also look out at the TIC for leaflets such as *Waterfall Walks in the Ystradfellte Area* or the booklet *Waterfall Walks in the Vale of Neath.*

The most famous of these spectacular waterfalls is Sgwd y Eira (The Waterfall of the Snow), and it has a special appeal because of the path, once used by packhorses carrying produce from the Vale of Neath to industrial Merthyr, which passes behind the curtain of water. A preferred route for walkers begins at Penderyn, which is on the A4059 road back to Brecon.

To get there, continue onwards from the A4109/B4242 junction, join the A465 by turning left and turn left onto the A4059 at the next junction at Hirwaun. The road rises steadily past Penderyn to an upland area displaying much evidence of the local limestone in the form of funnel-like depressions. They are known as swallow holes, sink holes and shake holes and are where the underground rock has been dissolved over a very long period. Turn left where the A4059 joins the A470 from Cardiff and Merthyr Tydfil, just below the Beacons Reservoir, and rise further to a spectacular crest and watershed at 1,440 feet at the Storey Arms, seen on the right. It is not a pub but an Outdoor Education Centre and Mountain Rescue Post and is where many people start their slog up a well trodden path to the summit of Pen y Fan (2907 feet), the highest point in South Wales.

One final spectacle before the return to Brecon comes with the descent of the stunning Tarrell Valley, down the trunk road that has superseded the old coach road showing on the opposite side. This is now followed for some distance from the Storey Arms by the Taff Trail on its way to Brecon, while the A470 passes through Libanus to join the A40 at the edge of Brecon.

Aberystwyth

Generally regarded as the northern gateway to south-west Wales, Aberystwyth lies in between two headlands that are almost at the centre of the long, curved sweep of Cardigan Bay. First built largely on an area of low-lying ground close to where the Rheidol and Ystwyth rivers flow into Bae Ceredigion, as the bay is known to the Welsh, the town is backed by a third hill that provides a setting for some of the town's most notable, if not exactly stylish 20th-century edifices. To the south of the town, the popular viewpoint on the twin summits of Pen Dinas is crowned by one of the largest Iron Age forts in Wales. It was built in two stages about 2,000 years ago and probably occupied for some 300 years until some time during the 1st century BC. Commanding the routes of the two inland river valleys and overlooking the coastal routes to the north and south, it was intended to protect and control the area around present-day Aberystwyth. Now it can be recognised from a distance by the prominent 1850s memorial to the Duke of Wellington and the Battle of Waterloo that has been erected on the southern summit in the form of an upturned cannon of the period (possibly appearing quainter still had permission been granted for a scheme to mount a statue of the Iron Duke on the muzzle!).

The name of the town comes from the first Norman **castle** to be built in the locality, which was almost a mile to the south — to the west of the A487 at Tanybwlch in the estuary (*aber*) of the River Ystwyth. It would have consisted of a mound, or motte, surmounted by a wooden tower and with a courtyard, or bailey, all protected by ditches and timber palisades. Such was the determination of local resistance during the early 13th century that it was continually taken by the Welsh, retaken, then destroyed and rebuilt until in 1231 the Welsh held on. It is believed that there was a second castle at Plas Crug, further north on the north bank of the River Rheidol, but towards the end of the 13th century, Edward I mounted a strenuous campaign to subdue the Welsh by enclosing Gwynedd. And so a formidable castle was placed under construction on a rise close to the harbour at the mouth of the River Rheidol as one of the first of a chain of major fortifications that extended to Rhuddlan, Ruthin, Flint, Hope and Builth at the end of the first war with Llewelyn ap Gruffudd, prince of Wales (d.1282 at Builth — see p.246). By *c*.1330 seventeen castles had been built or refurbished in the greatest and most costly building operation to be seen in Wales in medieval times. Set out on a diamond-shape plan in 1277 and subsequently fortified by Master James of St. George, the genius of military

Aberystwyth as seen from Constitution Hill

Remains of the north-west mural tower at Aberystwyth Castle

engineering who was responsible for most of King Edward's major English castles, Aberystwyth Castle was designed and built on concentric principles comprising an outer curtain with strong towers encircling an inner ring of defences. At the same time a fortified borough was established by charter and protected with a circuit of defensive stone walls joined to the castle. Although no signs of them now remain, the course of their route can still be made out by the present street pattern following King Street, Baker Street, Chalybeate Street, Mill Street and South Road. There were three gates — at the junction of Eastgate Street and Baker Street; at Great Dark Gate Street and North Parade; and at the Trefechan bridge and, typical of planned Edwardian boroughs, two principal streets cross at right angles in the town centre — with minor streets running in parallel.

In 1404 the castle was taken by Owain Glyndwr and was adopted as his headquarters for the next four years, until it was lost to Prince Hal (later to become King Henry V). This was when the castle and town were known as 'Llanbadarn Gaerog' (fortified Llanbadarn), after the important church a mile inland and due to Edward I's defensive works. This meant that Glyndwr sealed at least one document '*in castro nostro de Llanpadarn*' (in our castle of Llanpadarn), but this name was eventually ousted in favour of that given to the earlier Norman Aberystwyth Castle (although it was actually nearer to the Rheidol estuary).

During the Civil War a royal mint was established at the castle to make silver coins from the local ore for Charles I, but when Cromwell's troops assumed control they slighted most of the buildings in 1647. They did however leave scant ruins for some of the original form and extent of this massive fortification to be recognisable 400 years later.

It is taken as a sign of slow, un-prosperous growth in its early days that the borough did not contain a parish church within the walls, but by the early 1700s, the widely travelled Daniel Defoe (1660–1731) found that 'this town is enriched by coals (*sic*) and lead which is found in its neighbourhood and is a populous, but a very dirty black, smoky place and we fancied the people looked as if they lived continually in the coal or lead mines. However they are rich, and the place is very populous'. The number of residents at that time has been put at 1,000 and at the decennial census of 1831, just over 100 years later, the population had risen to 4,128, ranking Aberystwyth as the fourth largest town in Wales. This chiefly resulted from the mining of lead ore and slate quarrying in the Rheidol and Ystwyth valleys and elsewhere and the export of oak bark to the tanneries. The town and port replaced Cardigan as the principal trading centre on the west coast, bolstered by the already prolific Herring Fishery, marked on the Admiralty coastal chart drawn by Lewis Morris in 1748.

Though the port remained busy until the middle of the 19th century, by the 1950s the handling of cargo there had virtually ended. So had the boat building industry with the closure of David Williams and Sons, producers of hundreds of boats from ships' lifeboats to 50ft fishing vessels during the Second World War, and the harbour now acts as a **marina** for pleasure craft.

Almost half the output of the Cardiganshire lead mines had been shipped through the port, but in 1864 the Cambrian Railway reached Aberystwyth through the hills and valleys from Welshpool and a populous north-west England, and in 1867 the Manchester and Milford Railway opened a line from Carmarthen and South Wales via Tregaron and Strata Florida. The new services soon started to take over freight transport at the expense of the port and, where mobility had previously been very restricted, the new rail network offered huge advantages, not only to traditional commerce but also to a tourist industry. A new custom of taking annual holidays was evolving in the late 18th century, and the long curve of the sea front at Aberystwyth attracted numbers of visitors 'of quality', just as other seaside places in Britain, at a time when 'bathing machines' had become

The shoreline south of the castle

popular. Up until then, and afterwards, some local people 'of the lower classes' were not above 'skinny dipping' in the bracing clear waters of Cardigan Bay (maybe to remove some of the grime observed by Defoe). But in one part of Aberystwyth beach between the present Pier and Bandstand, wheeled wood huts with pitched roofs were provided for ladies, and a similar number for the gentlemen in another. Up to 20 or so of these contraptions were rolled into the sea so that the bathers could enter the water without being seen, although little of this delicate process was regarded as pleasurable — the fresh air, salt water and exercise being taken only in small doses by the hut occupants. One such genteel and coy bather was full of praise in 1803 for the way the ladies' and gentlemen's machines were placed 'nearly a quarter of a mile asunder and the indecency of promiscuous dipping, so disgusting at more fashionable resorts, is in consequence avoided'. And so, for a time the town came to be called the 'Cambrian Brighton' — before developing by the 21st century in a markedly different way.

This was not before the arrival of the railway prompted an attempt to promote one of the earliest of all 'package tours'. Keen to encourage visitors to use the new line to the coast and spend time and money in Aberystwyth, the railway contractor Thomas Savin bought a neo-Gothic villa on the promenade and in *c*.1860 converted and extended it to become a grand hotel — with the idea that he would offer special terms there to anyone who was prepared to book a return ticket from London. He is said to have lavished some £80,000 on the luxury **Castle Hotel**, but was disappointed by the response and within a few years was forced at a great loss to put the unfinished hotel up for sale. But bankruptcy in 1866 and failure of his pioneering tourism strategy was to provide an opportunity with huge consequences, not only for the former fishing town and cargo port, but also for the history of education in Wales. This was at a time when elementary education was the province of the churches, chapels, charities or fee-paying schools. It was purposely no concern of the state, and for most of the children merely basic skills were taught, often inexpertly, and only until they were 13. It was not thought to be a good idea to educate the children of the poor and lower middle classes beyond this level for fear that they would develop revolutionary ideas and create trouble (this was not long after the French Revolution). By the time the boys matured and married, barely half of them could sign their names on the register. They could not perform any better in England, where just across the Border the managers of one big school in 1827 not un-typically held a meeting solemnly to consider 'The propriety of teaching the girls to write'. And everywhere intermediate and higher education was generally made available only to middle and upper class children.

But especially in Wales, a tradition of devotion towards all levels of education and teaching was rapidly forming during the second half of the 19th century. Even long before then, Owain Glyndwr had dreamt of a university for Wales and now there were bold ideas for the creation of a first university at Aberystwyth.

The 'Old College', the former Castle Hotel

However without government or local authority funding, everything depended on voluntary contributions. The first big break came when Savin's huge unfinished hotel came on the market at a rock-bottom price and somehow £10,000 was raised and paid over in 1867. Further works of adaptation to the building were carried out by the original architect, the renowned Gothic revivalist J.P. Seddon, and these and subsequent alterations and re-building works account for the varied styles that start with those of John Nash in 1795 at the original Castle House, built for Uvedale Price — a founding father of the Picturesque movement — to arrive at those apparent today.

On 16 October 1872 the first term of the seaside university began with 26 male students (women were accepted 12 years later), two professors, a principal and a registrar. Although the aim was to equip graduates for posts anywhere within or beyond the Principality, in view of the background to the foundation of the university and the extensive voluntary support from all over Wales, it is surprising to find that in what is now one of the Welshest of Welsh towns and universities that the native language had no part in the original curriculum. Despite that, in 1875 some 70,000 Welsh people, many of them from working class families, contributed to the costs — although they were not always able to relieve the college from financial hardship even with extra aid from some industrial concerns. There was to be no state help for a further ten years, and grudgingly only alongside two universities being funded for £4,000 a year each at sites in North and South Wales. Eventually, in November 1893, the charter of the University of Wales, comprising a federation of the colleges of Aberystwyth, Bangor and Cardiff, received Royal Assent and it was able to confer academic degrees of its own rather than through Oxford.

During the second half of the 19th century a general mid-Victorian boom had produced a steep increase in the population of Aberystwyth, encouraged by the arrival of the railway and the associated tourism. In July 1921 the 9.50am restaurant car train commenced a through service from Paddington to Aberystwyth, Barmouth and Pwllheli that was to be the forerunner of the Cambrian Coast Express that followed a year later. By the end of the 1930s this operated to capacity and more as armies of holidaymakers crowded the platforms, eager to get to the seaside. The GWR resumed a normal summer service after the War and in 1951 the Cambrian Coast Express was reborn, departing from Paddington promptly at 10.10am. By 1958 rail business had reached its peak.

By the start of the 21st century, the population of 'Aber', as the town is often called locally, reaches some 20,000 during university term time, bolstered by over 7,000 full time students. Then for the two months of the summer vacation, population figures fluctuate as an important part of the local economy still relies on providing for holiday visitors and day-trippers.

Today it is possible to appreciate some features of what Aberystwyth and its surroundings still have to offer by looking down from the popular viewpoint of **Pen Dinas Hill** above the coastline to the south east of the town, or **Constitution Hill** to the north where there is help to reach the top for those not feeling energetic.

Post Beeching, it is perhaps surprising at a rather isolated Welsh town like Aberystwyth that after more than 140 years, passenger trains may still be seen at the rail station in Alexandra Road. Coming from Welshpool and Shrewsbury, they can also turn off at Dovey Junction to serve Pwllheli, 70 miles along the Cambrian coast on the Lleyn Peninsula. And running alongside the main line for a short distance is the narrow gauge **Vale of Rheidol Steam Railway** of 1902, as it heads for Devil's Bridge.

But it was the sea that provided the town with its livelihood for many years. Three hundred years ago, the 1,000 or so people of Aberystwyth, who were

Looking along the Promenade towards Constitution Hill

still living mainly within the bounds of the medieval wall or at the small suburb of **Trefechan** below Pen Dinas, depended largely for their livelihoods on fishing and agriculture. Fortunately they shared the bounties of the Herring Fishery just offshore: in 1701 they even dispatched a consignment of salted fish as far as the Canary Isles. One night in 1745, when catches were at their peak, the lights of 47 boats would have been sighted from the hill as they entered the harbour with an estimated 1.35 million herring. But from then on, while the shoals began to diminish with a growing shortage of plankton, other ships started to appear that were loaded with lead ore brought from far inland to St. David's Wharf for transport to smelters in Flintshire, South Wales and Bristol. Then shipbuilding began at the northern end of the harbour and between 1778 and 1880, some 278 sailing ships, from 30 ton sloops, schooners of up to 100 tons burden to 300 ton barques were sent to sea. Weather permitting, on 4 April 1848, the Aberystwyth built, two-masted square-rigged brig *Credo* would have been seen setting sail for Quebec carrying emigrants attracted by posters offering cut-rate passages (£3 5s. for adults of 14 and upwards, half price for children and nothing for infants of under 12 months, the rates including the supply of water, fuel and bed places — but not provisions). The largest vessel to be launched and sail from the shipyard was the 1,100 ton *Caroline Spooner* in 1887, but long before then steam had been taking over and as far back as 1831 the first steam powered vessel entered the harbour to pioneer a regular steamship service that lasted until the 1860s. With the arrival of the railway, lead ore was brought from the mines in the hills for onward shipping. The transport of lead ore by sea continued until the early 20th century alongside the export of bark, slates, pit props and other timber products, while imports consisted mainly of material needed for farming and the building industry, notably timber from Canada, Norway and the Baltic. Boat building was to continue at Trefechan until 1959. Fishing still takes place from Aberystwyth and in the 21st century the numbers of pots on the harbour quay indicate good commercial lobster catches, along with boats available for charter. Enthusiasts also travel great distances for sea angling.

The scene of much past industrial activity, the harbour where the fishing boats are berthed saw a transformation in 1985 with the opening of a £9 million **marina** for leisure and recreational use. To the south of the harbour entrance is the long stone jetty which was commenced in 1836 in order to add to the scouring effect of an earlier diversion of the River Ystwyth at its mouth in improving navigation for ships leaving and entering. The road and promenade run alongside South Beach to Castle Point and a rocky shore area that used to be surrounded by castle walls and towers until these were overwhelmed by the sea. Just inland is St. Michael's Church, close to the Georgian Laura Place and the site of Assembly Rooms, the first grammar school, pleasure grounds for the *crachach*, or the local worthies, to disport themselves and the second of the three churches dedicated to St. Michael. The first church opened in 1787 but some time before then the small church of St. Mary's was built on adjacent dry land that, like adjoining parts of the castle was destroyed by sea erosion. This was in front of where, in the 1860s, Thomas Savin came to build what is now the **Old**

The last 300 feet of the original 800ft-long pier after reduction by storms and a wartime mine

College and part of the University of Wales. When the college is open, visitors are invited to see the splendid oval Seddon Room, the unusual internal quadrants and the Old Hall, while facing the sea is a unique public statue of the future King Edward VIII, long before his abdication and crafted in 1920 when as Prince of Wales he was chancellor of the university.

The now far from elegant **Royal Pier Pavilion** was opened in 1896. It had seating for 2,000 and the entertainment ranged from ballet and the piano virtuosity of Paderewski to popular songs and ditties of the day by Maurice Chevalier and George Robey. Moving picture cinema shows inevitably followed and now the chief entertainment is produced by slot machines. The actual **pier** was built in the early 1860s and was 800 feet long until it was shortened by severe storm damage in 1938 and soon afterwards, in 1942, when a drifting sea mine went off as it reached the Pier Rocks below.

Nowadays piers are not as popular as they were and it is unlikely that funds will be forthcoming for new improvements, but much else in Aberystwyth and Ceredigion has been achieved with the aid of substantial European grants. This is because they are in an 'Objective One Area', where the local economy is performing at less than 75% of the European Union average. The wide promenade has thus been completely revamped and tastefully repaved. The seafront buildings date from Regency and Victorian times and these present a colourful picture, mostly as hotels, boarding houses or residences for over 500 university students. The only somewhat un-cheerful looking exception is the magistrates' court in the former women students' hostel at Alexandra Hall, shared with Ceredigion Archives and the Registrar near the junction of Marine Terrace and Victoria Terrace.

Just to the north of Victoria Terrace, **Constitution Hill** rises steeply to a height of 430 feet to overlook the town and, by the use of the world's largest **camera obscura**, it is possible to survey an area of land and sea amounting to about 1,000 square miles and covering 100 miles of coastline and 26 mountain peaks, including Snowdon. The summit has been a challenging viewpoint ever since the first tourists arrived and the name was coined because of the once popular practice of embarking on a 'constitutional'. An easier way was found to reach the top in 1896 when the now famous **Cliff Railway** was opened. Two carriages ran on adjoining tracks and when one was at the summit ready for the descent, the tank it carried was filled with sufficient water to bring up the ascending carriage, which had been emptied of its water. This 'Water Balance System' lasted until 1921, when a 55hp electric motor and winding equipment were substituted. They were sent to the Welsh Heritage Museum in Cardiff in 1978 after being replaced by the present computerised system, but since then the railway has known many vicissitudes. However in recent years great strides have been taken to return it to its former condition and popularity. Former unprofitable attractions at the summit have largely been removed and improved footpaths and wheelchair ramps have instead been installed between the top station and the camera obscura, while heritage grants and European Objective One funding have helped towards the construction of a new café and gift shop. It is also a good starting point for a breezy cliff walk to Clarach Bay.

Visible in the bathing area of the gritty beach between the pier and the bandstand is a recently built boat landing stage. It replaces the former lifeboat slipway and is opposite Terrace Road where the *Aguilla Wren* used to be hauled along on its way from the lifeboat house in Bath Street before it was superseded by the inshore rescue boat. The Tourist Information Centre is open all year and is signposted to the junction of the two roads, where it occupies a ground-floor site that forms part of the Edwardian Coliseum theatre and concert hall of 1904. This striking, elaborately detailed terracotta-faced building is thought to have been one of the oldest music-hall theatres in Wales but it finally closed in 1976 and was converted to become **Amgueddfa Ceredigion, a museum of local history**. This much appreciated new use for the building makes it all the more amazing that the prominent ground-floor shop-front and fascia designs on the Terrace Road frontage have been so crudely and unsympathetically dealt with by the English multiple store owners, and by the local planning authority! However, the museum, which offers free entry, very effectively complements the service provided by the TIC. For any visitor who is interested in the castle ruins, there is for example a reconstruction drawing on display that, based on archaeology and research, shows how huge and formidable the fortress must have looked when it was first built in 1289. The TIC supplies a detailed town map and, on request, a copy of *The Aberystwyth Town Trail* that takes in some of the compact main shopping and commercial centre that contains the cafés, pubs, and shops that are to be expected in a university town. Also it indicates and describes significant features, many of them originating from Georgian and early Victorian times. Maybe it is not altogether surprising that, around the period of the Methodist Revival, there were almost as many chapels here as pubs, and among over 20 places of worship that are listed there are still fine examples of Welsh chapel architecture and buildings for Baptist, Independent, Presbyterian and other denominations with Biblical names such as Bethel, Seion and Ebenezer. Also among the literature at the TIC and elsewhere in the town is *A Fashionable Watering Place*, a very readable and informative local history booklet that was written by W.J. Lewis after he had lived locally for close on 50 years.

Aberystwyth, the largest town in the fourth largest Welsh county of Ceredigion, remains an important administrative, cultural and regional centre serving a hinterland of many hundreds of square miles. Because of its central location in Wales, several national institutions have based themselves here, such as the Welsh Farmers' Union, *Urdd* (The Welsh League of Youth), The Welsh Language Society and the Forestry Commission for Wales. It is also home to one of the great libraries of the world, the National Library of Wales, off the A487 Penglais Road to Borth and Machynlleth, beyond the hospital.

Llyfrgell Genedlaethol Cymru — National Library of Wales

At the 1873 National Eisteddfod in Mold, a year after the opening of the long-awaited University by the Sea, another dream was reborn. It had first occurred more than 100 years before and concerned the establishment of a national library of Welsh literature and archives. It took a further 32 years before financial provision was finally made by the government to provide for both a library and a national museum for Wales — and a whole while longer before locations could be settled. Just a century before, Cardiff had been a small village of only about 2,000 souls, but by the significant Budget Day of 1905 it had become the largest town in Wales, with a population a hundred times greater and with a desire to elevate its profile and prestige. However it was in not the most Welsh-speaking part of the Principality, for this was much further to the north — arguably with Aberystwyth at its heart. There certainly was much argument until a compromise was reached to locate the **National Library** centrally in Aberystwyth and the National Museum down south in Cardiff, where it was later joined by the Museum of Welsh Life at St. Fagans. The case for Aberystwyth had been greatly bolstered by the existence of an already considerable nucleus of great and rare books, especially a collection of 25,000 that had been donated by Sir John Williams (who was incidentally to become medical consultant to Queen Victoria). Among his volumes were three from 1546 and 1547, the first books to

The National Library of Wales

be printed, a *New Testament* in Welsh of 1567 and the most important William Morgan *Bible* of 1588. Other great treasures of the Welsh language are the 12th-century *Llyfr Du Caerfyrddin (The Black Book of Carmarthen)*, the oldest manuscript written in Welsh, *Llyfr Taliesin*, which includes the Welsh mythology, the *Mabinogi,* the *Laws of Hywel Dda*, which dated from the 10th century and codified at Whitland, as well as a famous Hengwrt manuscript of Chaucer's *The Canterbury Tales.* (Many of these priceless books, and others, are to be seen at the permanent exhibition, *A Nation's Heritage,* at the Library.)

Further essential funding was soon raised, land had already been donated by Stuart Rendel, MP, who had become known as 'The Member for Wales', and later Lord Aberystwyth, and with the granting of the Library's Charter in 1907, Sir John Williams was made Charter President.

The first portion of an imposing white building was ready for the opening in 1912 and equally grand additions followed until the whole enterprise was completed in 1955. But soon, even more space was needed and extensions were started in the 1980s, partly because of the effect of the Copyright Act, 1911. This legislation meant that Aberystwyth was, from the start, one of the six major libraries in the British Isles, with Ireland, that were entitled to receive and stock a free copy of every book, periodical, map, pamphlet, item of sheet music, &c. published, said to be some 45,000 items each year. Through this and many other ways, by 2005 there were thought to be altogether over 5 million texts at the Library, including a huge collection of works about Wales and the other Celtic countries. As well as reading material, presented in many forms, there were pictures and photographs, maps, sound recordings and moving images available in the building for all adults to consult. In addition, continually changing exhibitions are arranged and there are various lectures and other events to consider.

Prifysgol Cymru — University of Wales, Aberystwyth

Main public access to the university is along the entrance from the A487, passing the prominent clock tower on the left to enter the car park (free each evening and at weekends), close to the Arts Centre and the heart of the campus. Rapid expansion soon after the Second World War meant that the college building on the Promenade was no longer adequate and a spread began towards Penglais. By the end of the 1960s the student numbers had risen to *c.*2000 and by the end of the century there were almost three and a half times as many, including nearly 900 postgraduates and 250 teaching staff. The Old College on the seafront remains as part of the university and is the administrative base, but except for Education and Welsh, most teaching and research takes place at the Penglais and Llanbadarn campuses, where the portfolio of courses includes Art, Computer Science, Law, International Politics, Rural Studies and Sport and Exercise Science within 18 academic departments. Still retaining a special role and responsibility towards meeting the education needs of Wales, Aberystwyth also now accepts students from most parts of the world — as a recent count of more than 90 countries has confirmed. In the beginning students boarded out in private homes in and around the town but eventually the need arose for college accommodation in halls of residence and building conversions into flats, such as those on the seafront. All are convenient for the lecture theatres, assembly halls, library, laboratories and other college facilities and they include the Student Village on the opposite side of Penglais Road, where 955 students can be accommodated at Pentref Jane Morgan.

The Arts Centre is one department of the University that is open to the general public in such a way that the link between town (and surroundings) and gown is greatly reinforced. It now receives around 500,000 patrons and visitors each year and these are numbers that are bound to increase after a recent £4.3 million redevelopment. An annual programme of some 800 events involves use of **The Great Hall**, built in 1970, which seats an audience of 900 and a smaller theatre for just over 300 people. There are several exhibition galleries, a bookshop, craft and design shops and a restaurant and the Centre houses the University's precious Ceramic Collection.

Below Penglais Hill there are other recreational opportunities for Aber people and visitors at the **Plascrug Leisure Centre**, Llanbadarn Fawr. It is off the A44 that leads to the east and has a heated main and a learner swimming pool, a four court sports hall, squash courts, fitness and health suites, outside courts and a range of other facilities.

Llanbadarn Fawr

Once a town in its own right, Llanbadarn Fawr has now become a suburb of Aberystwyth, but it began as a religious settlement and its monastic church was then a centre of learning and one of the mother churches of Wales. At least part of *Brut y Tywysogion — the Chronicle of the Princes* — a renowned source of early medieval history, was written here. Giraldus Cambrensis records that he stayed and preached at the church of St. Padarn the Great in April 1188 and he wrote an account of its quite exceptional earlier history of murder and malpractice. Built close to the time of his visit, for centuries the present **church of St. Padarn** was the parish church of Aberystwyth, or *Llanbadarn Gaerog* (walled Llanbadarn), its former name. Set on the side of the hill, it has a solid, severe appearance that is accentuated by a low square tower and short spire, placed at the crossing of a cruciform building. The thick walls are mostly pierced with lancets, while the superb design and craftsmanship applied to the south entrance bears comparison with the carved mouldings of the west doorway at Strata Florida Abbey (pp.238-240). The church was restored by J.P. Seddon in 1868 without great harm to its character and ancient origins and inside it is known for its intricately patterned Celtic crosses and several fine monuments, such as those to the landowning Gogerddan Pryse and Nanteos Powell families (pp.235-236), and Lewis Morris (1701–65), of Anglesey literary stock, with whom some of them had been in lively conflict over lead mining ownerships in the nearby hill country. An energetic man of many talents and interests, he was respected for his work as a self-taught hydrographer and land surveyor, especially in producing much needed Admiralty charts of harbours, bars, bays and roads of St. George's Channel, off the Welsh coast. Once even appointed as a customs officer, he became a mining adventurer, an antiquary, philologist and a scholar who has been firmly credited with 'keeping bright the flame of literature in the bleak years of the early 18th century'. He was buried at the church in April 1765 and his memorial tablet is on the floor of the chancel.

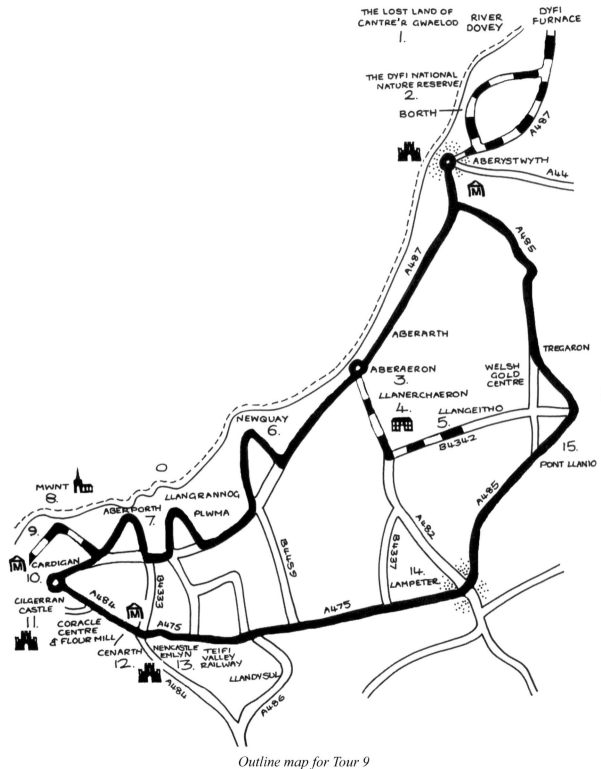

THE LOST LAND OF
CANTRE'R GWAELOD
1.

RIVER
DOVEY

DYFI
FURNACE

THE DYFI NATIONAL
NATURE RESERVE
2.

BORTH

A487

ABERYSTWYTH

A44

A487

A485

ABERARTH

TREGARON

ABERAERON
3.

WELSH
GOLD
CENTRE

LLANERCHAERON
4.

LLANGEITHO
5.

B4342

NEWQUAY
6.

A485

15.

PONT LLANIO

MWNT
8.

LLANGRANNOG

B4459

ABERPORTH
7.

PLWMA

A482

9.

B4337

14.
LAMPETER

CARDIGAN
10.

CILGERRAN
CASTLE
11.

A484

A475

CORACLE
CENTRE
& FLOUR MILL
CENARTH
12.

A475

NENCASTLE
EMLYN
13.

TEIFI
VALLEY
RAILWAY

A484

LLANDYSUL

A486

Outline map for Tour 9
The numbers 1 to 15 relate to the boxed information given within the tour

Tour 9   Skirting South Ceredigion

A largely scenic tour, it uses A roads to head down the coastline as far as Cardigan, branching off onto B and minor roads equipped with passing places to reach dramatic cliff-top scenery along coastal paths, secluded coves, golden sandy beaches and seaside resorts such as Aberaeron and New Quay. After the boundary with Pembrokeshire is reached, further A roads are employed, with similar diversions to places such as Cilgerran Castle, to shadow the River Teifi upstream through Newcastle Emlyn and Lampeter before arriving at a parting of the ways at Tregaron. The final leg of this journey back to Aberystwyth is also on A roads. The distance, without detours, is about 90 miles (OS Landranger maps 135, 145, 146 and 147).

There is an optional mini tour north to Borth and the Dyfi Nature Reserve if you wish. This is described first, the main tour starting on p.212.

One important asset lacking at Aberystwyth as a seaside resort is golden sand, for there is hardly any to be seen with the shingle and grit of either the North or South Beaches. For some small persons this is made up for at low tide by a wealth of interesting rock-pools, but otherwise there are several excellent sandy beaches not far away along Cardigan Bay. One of the most popular is 6 miles to the north of Aberystwyth at Borth.

If you want to quickly sample the golden sands that adorn many of west Wales' beaches, then take the A457 north signposted Machynlleth past the University and turn left at a crossroads to join the B4572. At Llangorwen there is a minor road to the left leading to **Clarach Bay** and its sheltered beach. It is

---

1. The lost land of *Cantre'r Gwaelod*

The story goes that Sarn Gynfelin was one of the dykes or embankments that surrounded a large fertile area of land and forest from the River Teifi to Bardsey Island in what is now Cardigan Bay. There were watchmen to look out for any breaches of the sea defences but during one night of revelry, a man on duty, Seithennyn, defaulted, sluices were left open and all the land was inundated. Medieval storytellers place the catastrophe during the 7th century AD but modern science points to around 3000 BC, during the Neolithic period. Confirming evidence comes through tree ring analysis of the stumps of ancient Scots pines, birches and alders that remain rooted where they grew all that time ago and still to be seen at low Spring tides offshore opposite Borth and further north at Ynyslas in the mouth of the Dovey Estuary. There was a theory that the banks may have been created by tidal action, but it seems more likely that they are side moraines, lines of debris that were left when glaciers retreated with the ice sheet at the end of the last Ice Age as the mountains were shaped and the lakes created further inland. Sea levels are thought to have been lower then by around 200 feet, with the coastline 7½ miles further west, until levels gradually rose down the millennia from a process that nowadays is often called 'global warming' as ice melted. Fertile areas of dry land in the Bristol Channel and Cardigan Bay were among low-lying coastal parts of Northern Europe that were gradually submerged. So too was a zone not far away between Land's End and the Isles of Scilly, the fabled drowned Kingdom of Lyonesse, that is sometimes associated with the lost land of Cantre'r Gwaelod, The Hundred in the Deep.

principally a Holiday Village with large numbers of static caravans, chalets, camp-sites and leisure facilities and it lies on the Ceredigion Coast Path. This leads from Constitution Hill alongside the cliffs, headlands, beaches and coves of one of four sections of designated Heritage Coast between Borth and Cardigan and after a further mile it reaches Wallog and, at very low tide, something of a mystery. Called **Sarn Gynfelin**, a long, shallow bank or reef of stones, silt and sediments extends straight out to sea before disappearing beneath the surface. The Lewis Morris chart of 1748 shows it as about 7 miles long and 6 fathoms deep and it is thought to be one of five *sarnau* (causeways) of up to 21 miles long in the Bay that have long mystified people living and sailing along the coast. Inevitably it has become a source of folklore and legend;

Looking over Borth towards Aberdovey from the road as you enter the town

even of the ballad of the long lost 'Bells of Aberdovey', calling from beneath the waves.

The B4572 continues onward to the straggling former fishing port of Borth, raised on a shingle bank just above a 3-mile length of smooth, almost flat sandy beach, shallow waters and safe bathing. It became one of Ceredigion's most popular seaside resorts soon after the arrival of the railway in the 1860s and now provides mainly for seasonal holidaymakers. Open all year, there is the 'Animalarium', a collection of sometimes abandoned or unwanted animals, many of them interesting and unusual, exotic and endangered species, while revelling in their freedom out in the bay, and with luck even forming part of the stunning views, there are Atlantic grey seals and leaping bottlenose dolphins and porpoise. For visiting golfers, further north towards Ynyslas and straddling the road there is the 18-hole natural links championship course of Borth and Ynyslas Golf Club. It is one of the oldest in Wales and has long been a test for any golfer, especially when there is a breeze blowing in from the Bay. Then beyond that, and the long Ynyslas beach that leads towards the end of the coast road, is the **Dyfi National Nature Reserve** and seasonal Visitor Centre.

2. The Dyfi National Nature Reserve

Aberdovey

Unique in Wales, one of only 11 sites in Great Britain and 243 in the world, the Dyfi National Nature Reserve is recognised as an International Biosphere Reserve for its promotion of wildlife conservation initiatives. The first among its three distinct parts is the **Ynyslas Sand Dunes system** that reaches out into the estuary towards Aberdovey and a backdrop of Snowdonia. By following a recommended trail it is possible to appreciate the wide variety of wildlife, as well as gain some idea of the history. There are places to see dune slack orchids, the uses of marram grass against erosion, the old ferry site for Aberdovey, the wide expanse of Traeth Maelgwyn sands and, far out at low tides, stumps and roots of the ages-old submerged forest of Cantre'r Gwaelod. Although the estuary is not safe for bathing because of the strong and treacherous currents the sands are popular for a variety of outdoor pursuits such as wind-surfing and kite-flying.

The two other parts of the Reserve, the **Dyfi Estuary Mudflats** and the **Cors Fochno Bog**, are not generally appreciated as much, except for the spectacular sight of flocks of feeding wildfowl and shore birds. Some of these refuel with shellfish and worms at the estuary during immigration while in spring they may fly off to breed in the Arctic and return in the autumn on their way to spend the winter in Africa. Not confined to birdwatchers however, these watery and sometimes hazardous places are a source of fascination for a range of ecologists and students on field studies. Perhaps it is difficult to understand how any bog can hold such interest, but Cors Fochno is classed as an 'untouched bog' and is not the more usual waterlogged rushy hollow where all the peat has been cut for fuel or garden composts. A great depth of peat lies intact there and surface peat may still be forming in the ultra-acid conditions at its centre. Borth is regarded as having one of the two most impressive and best preserved lowland raised bogs in Great Britain and the other, also in Ceredigion, is 16 miles to the south at Tregaron (see p.240). The habitat provided by these bogs creates a valuable refuge for diminishing numbers of rare aquatic plants, insects and birds while the preserving action of the peat, laid down layer upon layer with the passing centuries, has received the annual springtime pollen of trees from local Welsh forests of the past several thousand years. Buried and preserved in the order of time, this repository of identifiable grains of pollen can be deeply probed to provide a reliable and intriguing account of past climatic phases. These can determine historic periods of moistness and dryness, warmth and chill, through the presence of the pollen of particular trees such as birch, pine, alder, hazel and oak, and no doubt the bogs will yield many more secrets of the past now that they are protected.

The B4353 continues beyond Ynyslas, crossing the railway from Borth as it heads south of the estuary towards Dovey Junction, providing an alternative way back to Aberystwyth. It skirts what is sometimes called Cors Goch (red) Fochno because of the way the surface of the bog turns colour in the winter. At Tre'r-ddol the B4353 meets the A487 trunk road.

To return to Aberystwyth for the main tour, turn right, but if you have time for a further detour and don't mind travelling 3 miles, only to return on the same road, you might turn left towards Machynlleth. After 2 miles a massive stone building will appear on the right and a car park down a drive to the left. **Dyfi Furnace** was built in *c.*1755 as a blast furnace for the production of iron from Cambrian ore, using charcoal from the local woodland and water power from the stream to drive the bellows. After 50 years production it was converted to become a sawmill and the present huge restored waterwheel dates from that time. Other agricultural uses followed and now it is all cared for by Cadw. Another mile along the road an entrance to the left leads to the **Ynys Hir RSPB reserve** and visitor centre on the south side of the Dyfi estuary. Thought to be best during the autumn and winter, the Welsh oak woodland, wet grassland and salt-marsh areas have much to offer, especially to those remembering to take their binoculars.

The millwheel at Dyfi Furnace

If you turned right towards Aberystwyth — or once you have returned past the junction with the B4353 — another good viewpoint of the Bog can be gained from Tal-y-bont, before the A487 heads beyond the village towards Bow Street and back to cross the River Rheidol at Trefechan Bridge in Aberystwyth for the start of the main tour.

Cardigan Bay

From Bardsey Island at the western tip of Gwynedd across to Strumble Head, just beyond Fishguard in Pembrokeshire, Cardigan Bay is internationally regarded as an outstandingly important marine wildlife area. It shares the warming influence of the Gulf Stream and provides a habitat for some of Britain's rarest species, as well as harbour porpoise and Atlantic grey seals. There can be sightings of some of the 130 resident bottlenose dolphins that have been identified as they leap through and out of the water, but the most spectacular feature of the bay is the coastline. This forms the western boundary of the County of Ceredigion, starting at the Dyfi Estuary and extending south to Cardigan for 60 miles. In 1982, a total length of some 22 miles was officially designated as Heritage Coast and beyond Tanybwlch Bay directly south of Aberystwyth the cliffs between Monk's Cave and Llanrhystyd were included. Added to the section between Borth and Clarach to the north, there are two others — from Gwbert to Pen Peles and between Tresaith and New Quay, which looks out beyond the shoreline and cliff nesting sites to a specially designated corridor of Marine Heritage Coast. This lies within one of two much larger Special Areas of Conservation extending out into the bay, where caution is urged and speed limits imposed on vessels to avoid disturbance to the dolphins and porpoise should they be sighted. Many of the beaches down the coast are being managed to satisfy high standards of water quality and safety, while also respecting the scope and character of the wildlife. During holiday seasons there are regular inspections and in 2005 the annual European Blue Flags, UK Seaside Awards and/or Green Coast Awards were gained by beaches at Aberaeron, Aberporth, Aberystwyth, Borth, Clarach, Cwmtydu, Llangrannog, Llanrhystud, Mwnt, New Quay, Penbryn and Tresaith, and in addition, the National Trust maintained its own standards, not only at Cwmtydu and Mwnt but also Lochtyn and Penbryn.

The main tour starts here!

Take the A487 south from Aberystwyth signposted towards New Quay and Cardigan. Down the coastline from Aberystwyth and Tanybwlch, the first beach is at **Llanrhystud** about 7 miles along the A487 where, just beyond the petrol station south of the village, a narrow road with few passing places leads off to the right for a mile, past the entrance to the Morfa Farm caravan park to a small car parking area above a steep and long storm terrace of rounded pebbles. At low tide the beach below is relatively safe, flat and sandy. A length of designated Heritage Coast cliffs ends just to the north and for the next few miles towards Aberaeron the coastline is low-lying and consists of boulder clay and pebbles.

Above the A487 just to the south of the village, there are steep hills on which are found the Iron Age hillforts of **Castell Bach** and **Castell Mawr**, separated by a gulley gruesomely said to be once called 'The Dell of Slaughter' after a bygone battle. To the east of the village are the earthwork remains of **Caer Penrhos**, a castle built in 1150 and flattened some 50 years later to prevent it from falling into rival hands.

The road continues through the twin hamlets of Llansantffraed and Llanon close to their churches of St. Brigid and St. Non, the mother of St. David (see p.138). Then 5 miles further on, after a drive alongside the coast **Aberaeron** comes into view tucked into its hollow, and some distance beyond it the high bluff of New Quay Head standing out from the harbour.

3. Aberaeron. Picturesque Georgian charm

Just 200 years ago there was no harbour of any size between Aberystwyth and Cardigan and, half way between them the river Aeron reached its shingle-choked estuary (*aber*) after passing through what amounted to no more than a small fishing hamlet. There had been much greater activity about a mile to the north at **Aberarth**, where during the 12th century stone had been unshipped for the building of Strata Florida Abbey (pp.238-240), and where pilgrims subsequently landed. Signs of the *goredi*, curved stone walls placed between high and low water on the beach to trap fish as the tides receded, are said to remain there from the days of the monks. During the 19th century Aberarth was a busy shipbuilding centre and between 1805 and 1851 some 25 vessels were constructed on the beach.

The parish church of St. David overlooking the village was founded some 13 centuries beforehand, and among the graves are those of Susannah and Alban Thomas Jones Gwynne, at rest after a most energetic and creative life in the neighbourhood. The Reverend Alban Thomas Jones had inherited the large Mynachty estate and a substantial fortune from his uncle, Lewis Gwynne, in 1805 on condition that he added the Gwynne surname to his own. In present day terms the legacy could well be compared with a 'Roll-over' win on the National Lottery, while at that time the burden of £100,000 in gold and £50,000 Stock needed to be conveyed under armed escort to his house on a drag cart requiring four horses, so it is said.

A public-spirited man of vision and energy, he saw the great commercial potential of Aberaeron provided that a fine harbour could be built to enable trade to be brought within reach of his tenants in this isolated part of Wales. But even he could not move before obtaining Parliamentary consent and it came through a private Bill that produced the Aberaeron Harbour Act, 1807. This allowed him to proceed with the building of the stone-walled quays and breakwater, to dredge the estuary and divert the river from its former northward course from Pwll Cam so as to scour the obstructing bar away from the harbour mouth. This phase was completed by 1811 and trading vessels began to arrive, soon attracting developers, builders and businessmen. But in applying for leases, they could not proceed without the consent of the Reverend Gwynne, who acted as landlord and planning authority. Through a Master Plan, devised with guidance during one of the best periods of British architecture, he was able to control standards of design and construction in order to produce a town of broad, orderly streets, a spacious open square and dignified buildings. There would be no piecemeal development as use of the harbour grew and one of the first buildings designed for **Quay Parade** was an imposing **harbourmaster's house** — with sweeping views of shipping out in the bay. It became the Red Lion, the first of 20 pubs in the town, and early in the 21st century it is still there — as the Harbourmaster Hotel and deserving a reputation as 'Welsh Hotel of the Year' (despite being near the former mortuary, now TIC!). It is close to other fine dwellings of that era, but unfortunately a row of early houses and a school on the north side of the harbour were swept away during a storm in 1848.

The Harbourmaster Hotel

Alban Gwynne was not to witness the fruition of all his plans, but an open square was formed around Pwll Cam, the inner harbour, to be overlooked by an elegant Town Hall built in brown stone in the design of which Gwynne is said to have had a part. On the opposite side of what is now the A487, and backed by a range of hills, the spacious **Alban Square** enclosing a large playing field and bounded on three sides by tall, dignified buildings was named in his honour in 1840. The dates that the streets, subtly coloured terraces and buildings were constructed are not difficult to establish, for whereas, for example, Waterloo Street and Wellington Street were built soon after 1815, Regent Street, Queen Street, Victoria Street and Albert Street provide ready clues as to the closing phases of Gwynne's pioneering 19th-century new town.

A shipbuilding industry flourished on both sides of the new harbour from the start, at the expense of Aberarth whose shipwrights moved across, and by the time it ended in 1883 nearly 100 sailing vessels had passed down the slipways from the yards, including brigs, schooners — and two-masted brigantines that were much favoured by pirates. About the last ship to enter the sea was the ketch *Cadwgan,* built near the present Harbourmaster hotel in the yard of the Neptune inn and, like a street in the town, named to recall Castell Cadwgan. Now washed away by the sea, this was a castle of the 12th-century Prince Cadwgan ap Bleddyn, within range of the estuary just up the coast towards Aberarth.

Steamships brought an end to sail and negotiated the narrow entrance of the harbour until the 1930s, but coastal trade virtually ceased with the delayed arrival in 1911 at Aberaeron of the Great Western Railway as a means of delivering goods, itself to survive there for just 40 years — closing even before the Beeching Plan. For the rest of the 19th century after completion of Gwynne's plan for Aberaeron, and since, the town extended in accordance with different principles, noticeably to the south of the river. It is one of five modern (not medieval) planned towns in Wales and statutorily designated as 'of Special Architectural Merit'. The central area and part of the riverside are in a Conservation Area and many of the buildings are 'Listed', requiring formal consent before anything else is done to them, inside or out, as well as within their curtilage. All this has helped to maintain the Georgian appearance of Aberaeron, brightened by multi-coloured rows of buildings and the great attraction of a picturesque stone walled harbour and new look-out.

Aberaeron harbour

An Aberaeron street

Between Easter and October at the former Sea Aquarium it is possible to book coastal voyages around the Cardigan Bay Special Area of Conservation in a water jet catamaran, and for boat owners there are good landing and mooring facilities. Aberaeron has its cleanliness awards and there are two stone and pebble beaches, the **South Beach** tending to be preferred because of some sand at low tide and a good view of New Quay, 4 miles away. Inland there are large caravan parks and camping sites, hotels and other accommodation, several restaurants, good shops and various services, including those at the Ceredigion County Council head offices.

The swimming pool at the secondary school campus is open to the public 7 days a week, although reserved for school use some of the time, there is a leisure centre (named after opera star, Sir Geraint Evans, who lived close to the harbour) and, in farm buildings on the south side of the River Aeron, a **Craft Centre** comprising independently run units, shops and a licensed restaurant. Not far away, and still close to the town centre, there is a pleasant footpath running along the bank of the river.

Ideas are being floated for the creation of an outer harbour, probably by extending the south pier with a stone breakwater and the building of a new breakwater to the west, starting near the school playing fields. The intention would be to provide a harbour that could be used in all states of the tide and weather, as well as a level of water inside the existing harbour at all times. But two hundred years after it was built, it is expected that much water will pass through the narrow harbour entrance while this controversial measure is thrashed out, for it could have a considerable bearing on the future character of the town.

It is sometimes held that the English architect and planner, John Nash (1752–1835), had a hand in the planning of Aberaeron, based as he then was at Cardigan. He achieved later fame in London, recreating Buckingham Palace, designing the Marble Arch, laying out Trafalgar Square and St. James's Park and, at Brighton, rebuilding the Royal Pavilion, but earlier on he attracted attention through his design of country houses. One of these was built in *c.*1795 at **Llanerchaeron**, some 2½ miles inland, just off the A482 in the Aeron Valley. If you wish to make a slight detour from the main route to visit this, the A482 can be joined by any one of the three roads leading inland from the A487 in Aberaeron. Repaired after years of neglect it is now open to the public between March and October, except Mondays and Tuesdays (open Bank Holidays), and worth a visit by anyone interested in seeing how Welsh gentry lived 200 years ago.

4. Llanerchaeron (NT). An 18th-century time capsule

Described as a classic small 18th-century Welsh self-contained gentry estate, the centrepiece is the compact villa designed by Nash. In conjunction with an equally well-proportioned service courtyard of farm buildings, including a dairy, laundry, brewery and salting house, it is regarded as the most complete example of his early work. The estate has been landscaped in the spirit of the Picturesque movement (pp.257-258) and there are great views of the surrounding countryside along park and woodland walks. Nowadays it is a working organic farm and there are also two restored walled gardens with a kitchen garden, fruit and flowers that are often available to buy.

Llanerchaeron

It is possible to extend this detour by carrying on along the A482 and then left on the B4342 to reach **Llangeitho**. The B road shadows the River Aeron through a widening valley. The only place of any size along its course, the village, 12 miles from Aberaeron and 4 miles west of Tregaron, is quiet and peaceful now, but not very long ago it could be teeming with thousands of Welsh people who had travelled there over vast distances, across rough terrain or by stormy sea. They had endured great hardships to get there, often to camp out, stand in the open — and then be sometimes terrified out of their wits by powerful accounts of the eternal torments of Hell to be suffered by all sinners, delivered by the village curate, Daniel Rowland.

---

5. Daniel Rowland — and sinners' hopes of Salvation

Daniel Rowland was ordained as an Anglican curate in 1735 at the age of 22 and in the normal course of events could have expected to advance to priest's Orders. But two years later he heard Howell Harris (p.179) preach and as a result joined him and Williams Pantycelyn to become one of the three charismatic stalwarts of the Methodist Revival — said to be the first of the two great forces that created modern Wales. But whereas the others travelled many hundreds of miles on their mission, he tended to remain at Llangeitho and instead thousands of people came to him for his message. He grimly confronted them with their sins, the consequent torments of Hell and he showed them the way to Salvation. Moving his congregations to both terror and exultation, he further shook them towards repentance by dramatically appearing in his pulpit through a rear door, as if directly 'beamed down' from Heaven! (The composer G.F. Handel was taken to one of his prayer meetings and, so it has been locally claimed, obtained the idea for the Hallelujah Chorus from the impassioned 1,000-strong shouts of *Gogoniant!* 'Glory'!). Despite several approaches, his bishop denied Rowland ordination as a priest and after ejection from the Established Church in 1763 he set up in his own chapel. He took most of the congregation with him and the Aeron Valley became an important national religious centre. That chapel has since been replaced by a newer building — not altogether brightened by his somewhat lugubrious statue in the grounds.

The main route continues along the A487 from Aberaeron, climbing a hill and passing Holy Trinity Church and the Craft Centre on the left and routes down to the South Beach and Yacht Club to the right. It soon turns inland and reached **Llanarth**, regarded as one of the oldest settlements in Ceredigion whose **St. David's Church**, of Celtic origin, is associated with many legendary stories about the antics of the Devil. Within there is a font dating from *c.*1200 and a special inscribed stone cross that is named after a 9th-century Irish chieftain, but also thought to have earlier inscriptions in Ogham. This is an ancient British and Irish alphabet of 20 characters that originated in south-west Ireland during the 4th century. A traveller along this way in 1485 might have met with Henry Tudor and an army as they approached from the opposite direction after landing on 7 August at Mill Bay, near Dale in Pembrokeshire (p.120). After being forced to spend some 14 years in France, Henry was now returning from exile with his uncle, Jasper, earl of Pembroke, and was on the way to Bosworth to do battle with Richard III and seize the Crown as King Henry VII. There is a firm tradition that he rested at the home of Einion ap Dafydd Llwyd at Wern Newydd near Llanarth before reaching Aberystwyth and the monastery of Llanbadarn Fawr on 12 August.

Towards the far end of Llanarth, turn right on the B4342, where soon the sea is in sight once more, to reach New Quay. New Quay is certainly quite new by comparison with Llanarth, for the bay was only first charted in 1748 by the Lewis Morris Admiralty survey when it was noted as New Key (*sic*), and repeated as such in 1801 by his son, William.

6. New Quay. 'The cliff-perched town at the far end of Wales'

New Quay harbour

New Quay began as a fishing village and by the mid-18th century had almost 40 small boats of between 4 and 5 tons to help share in the autumn bounty of herring in the Bay. The fish were mostly preserved with salt from Ireland and Cheshire and were in great demand as winter food, especially by poor people who found them cheaper than meat and who transported baskets of them in panniers across the backs of horses to as far away as Hereford. But by the early 19th century the quay within the harbour of refuge created by rocky Pencraig Head and Careg Ina Reef was in far from new condition. Called Penpolion, it simply amounted to a haphazard assembly of poles driven into the sand packed with random boulders. It protected little but the small area below the present Sailing Slip and by the 1820s this was nowhere near enough. There was a pressing need for an extended harbour and there were various proposals, including two from Alban Gwynne of Aberaeron, but it took until 1834 before a scheme for a 456ft-long pier by civil engineer Daniel Beynon was accepted. The New Quay Harbour Act of 1835 authorised the work and the town soon started to grow, with financial help from revenues produced by tariffs on most of the items that were shipped in or exported. By the 1851 national census the population had reached 1,236 and much of this was to do with a burgeoning shipbuilding industry. From early in the 19th century, up to 10 vessels at a time might be seen on the stocks at Traethgwyn, Cei Bach and Dolau Beach and, working on them, some 300 craftsmen and labourers. The prosperity of the town grew to new heights between 1830 and 1860, but in October 1859 a storm struck with unprecedented ferocity. It devastated a wide area of Britain and the Welsh coastline was strewn with the wreckage of sailing ships, the beach at New Quay included and where the end of the new pier was also demolished by massive breakers. In all 133 ships were sunk and another 90 badly damaged during the hurricane, most of them small sailing vessels. Coastal installations were badly hit and, worst of all, some 800 lives were lost, nearly 450 of them men, women and children aboard one ship, the 2,700-ton auxiliary steam clipper, *Royal Charter*. (Because of the enormity of the disaster it is not surprising that it should have become known in history as 'The *Royal Charter* Gale' — long before hurricanes were allotted code names). The Australian Gold Rush had started in *c*.1852 and it was well under way by the time the *Royal Charter*, a veritable treasure ship, cast off at Melbourne on 26 August 1859, to round Cape Horn and head for Liverpool with £322,440 worth of gold bullion in her holds and huge personal fortunes cautiously carried by many of her 390 passengers. By 25 October she had reached Anglesey off the coast of North Wales and was within 50 miles of docking at Liverpool, when she met with winds gusting to full hurricane force at more than 100 mph. With insufficient sea-room to manoeuvre, and attempting to sail against the combined assault of a north-east Force 10 to 12 wind and an adverse tide coming from Liverpool Bay, at 3.30am on 26 October she was driven onto the rocks at Moelfre on the east coast of the island and destroyed — becoming the most disastrous shipwreck in Welsh history.

Launched in 1855 at the Sandycroft Ironworks on the River Dee, the hull of the *Royal Charter* had been constructed of iron, in place of the usual wood, and she was fitted with an auxiliary 200 horse-power steam engine for use when becalmed or in need of extra power. She represented the start of a sea change in techniques of ship construction and propulsion and these were to extend towards the use of steel and highly efficient marine steam engines. At around the time of the disaster, some 40 sailing vessels might be seen in New Quay harbour at a time and another dozen or so under construction (including a small 30-ton smack christened *Royal Charter* in memory of the gale). But by the end of the century shipbuilding had virtually died out and, as at other ports along the coast, there was luckily a new source of employment.

During the 19th century there had been a growing appreciation of the picturesque natural beauty of many parts of Britain, and New Quay, sheltered from prevailing south-west winds by the 300ft Pencraig headland, had the great advantages of golden sandy beaches, safe bathing, boat trips, sailing and fishing — indeed most of the requirements for a nice relaxing holiday. By 1895, the town and close surroundings were catering for some 10,000 visitors a year — some arriving by sea and many others in horse-drawn buses from train stations at Aberystwyth and Llandyssul, New Quay lacking a railway service of its own. Between the wars, one regular visitor to relatives and friends in Ceredigion was Dylan Thomas (pp.7-8), and in September 1944 he rented 'a wood and asbestos shack', named Majoda, for his family at the edge of New Quay.

Dylan Thomas at New Quay

The Thomas family only lived at Majoda until July 1945, but it was during one of Dylan's most fertile periods when he produced masterpieces such as *Poem in October* and *Fern Hill*. One poem, *New Quay*, contained glimpses of characters such as No Good Boyo and Evans the Death who were to appear again much later in *Under Milk Wood*. A radio script for BBC Wales at that time foreshadowed the sleeping town of Llareggub (try spelling it backwards) even more closely. *Quite Early One Morning* was a sketch of life in a small Welsh seaside town 'that was not yet awake' and it portrayed early prototypes of retired and blind Captain Cat of the *S.S. Kidwelly*, the Reverend Eli Jenkins, poet, preacher, and twice-widowed Mrs. Ogmore-Pritchard among characters who were based on some of the local individuals. As the sleepers get up and go about their business there is also much that resembles the pattern and time sequence of the famous 'Play For Voices', first broadcast almost ten years later in January 1954 — shortly after the death of the poet. The 'cliff-perched town at the far end of Wales', where 'the voices moved out of sleep and darkness' in the 1944 script, cannot be anywhere else but New Quay (but this should not be shouted aloud in Brown's Hotel public bar or by 'the heron-priested shore' at Laugharne, pp.78-79). And still the narrow streets of the town climb in terraces as it perches with style on the flank of the headland that shelters the harbour and beaches.

The Beaches

The **Harbour Beach** is close to the sailing centre and also the main pier for seasonal cruises along the Ceredigion coastline and (not guaranteed) to see the bottlenose dolphins, harbour porpoise and Atlantic grey seals in the Special Area of Conservation out in the Bay. A crescent of golden sand provides for safe bathing and boating, and beyond to the east there is **Traethgwyn** — with a great expanse of sand at low tide. Then it is possible to walk across to **Llanina Point**, or perhaps pay a visit to **Llanina Church**, perched close to the cliff edge since 1830. This is at the furthest limit of the 'Dylan Thomas New Quay Trail' of places associated with the poet, starting at the sea front TIC. Beyond the Point, **Little Quay, or Cei Bach**, is also sandy, rather quieter than the others and, like Traethgwyn, a great attraction for the caravanning families holidaying close by. (It requires some stretch of the imagination to picture the

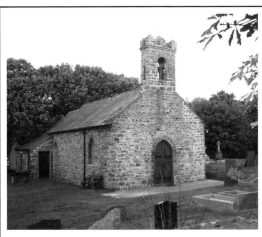

St. Ina's Church, Llanina and New Quay Head

very different scene not so long ago, when large numbers of elegant brigs, schooners and other sailing vessels were being built at both beaches!) The fourth New Quay beach is **Traeth y Dolau**, which is chiefly of stone, backed by shale cliffs and extending northward towards New Quay Head.

Marine Heritage Coast

New Quay Head marks the start of Ceredigion's longest stretch of Heritage Coast and the 9-mile section as far as Tresaith has also recently become the first 'Marine Heritage Coast' to be established in Britain. This recognises the unspoilt nature of this coastline, and it not only includes the shoreline, caves, cliffs and nesting sites of seabirds, but also a wide strip of the adjoining sea area. This is formally regarded as a habitat of European importance, where the abundance of wildlife includes some of Britain's most rare marine species.

From New Quay Head a path climbs steeply to follow the cliffs, and after a short distance it reaches Birds Rock, the largest breeding colony of sea birds in the county. Here, at Craig yr Adar, there are great numbers of guillemots, razorbills, shags, kittiwakes, fulmars and herring gulls crowded along rock terraces — seen (in calm weather) to advantage from offshore from the pleasure boats operating from New Quay and Aberaeron as they visit the caves, Cwmtydu, Seals Bay and Ynys Lochtyn along the coast to the south. An added benefit of these cruises is that the skippers and crew members are well equipped to answer questions about the maritime flora and fauna, geology, geomorphology, archaeology, local history and legends of the coastline. But back on dry land, the coastal path passes tall vertical cliffs towards Cwm Soden and the cliff tops of Cae'r Llan, one of a number of National Trust farms along the coast. Near the river mouth is Castell Bach, the site of an Iron Age promontory fort dating back to around the 3rd century BC. The path then drops steeply to **Cwmtydu**, a small cove with a predominantly shingle beach, about

Ynys Lochtyn on the Marine Heritage Coast

2½ miles down the coast from New Quay. There is some sand at low tide, along with salt water rock pools, a large freshwater pool and caves to explore. Here, as along several other parts of the coast, the cliffs exhibit spectacular folding and faulting of the rocks that tell of the movement in the Earth's crust a long time ago. There is just a short break in the line of tall cliffs at Cwmtydu before they return beneath the slopes of Pen y Parc and continue on down the coastline towards the lower-lying peninsula at Ynys Lochtyn, another 2½ miles away. Half way along, the summit of Penmoelciliau towers 710 feet above the waves and, as the highest point along the Ceredigion coast, offers fine views of the Bay. Just inland from the Lochtyn peninsula (NT), Pen y Badell is the flat-topped site of an Iron Age hillfort that also provides a good viewpoint for many miles around, especially of the scenic small peninsula just below.

In his *'Portrait of Elgar'*, Michael Kennedy tells of a Cardigan Bay holiday taken by the composer at nearby **Llangrannog** in 1901, when he heard a tune 'that drifted across the water' towards the hillside from some singers by Ynys Lochtyn. He sketched it down as his 'Welsh Tune' — to introduce it as a theme in the *Introduction and Allegro for Strings, Op.47*, for its first performance in 1905. Llangrannog was a good choice as a peaceful place for the Elgars to spend their walking holiday over 100 years ago — and it is equally good today with the unchanged dramatic cliff scenery and other natural attractions. They too might have relaxed on the sandy beaches to be found at the foot of the cove or, when the tide was out, at Cilborth just to the north. Six miles down the coast from New Quay, with two pubs — the Pentre Arms and The Ship Inn — it is one of the larger villages in the region, somewhat stretched out from being squeezed into a descending deep and narrow wooded valley. From the late 18th century its sheltered position between the towering cliffs served well as a coastal trading port for the area, and for shipbuilding, and like many other such places there were limekilns for stone shipped in for the production of lime to 'sweeten' the acidic local soil. And because of the secluded position, it is likely that there were secretive imports of desirable duty-bearing commodities as well. All this and other maritime activity took place around the 'Beach Village' near the shore, but Llangrannog was first founded at the top of the valley by Celtic missionaries and the 'Church Village' formed around St. Caranoc's, half a mile away from the sea.

Llangrannog has become well known since 1932 to countless Welsh youngsters through the League of the Youth of Wales — *Urdd Gobaith Cymru* — membership of which now runs to more than 52,000, for not far above the village they have a holiday centre on the slopes overlooking Cardigan Bay. This provides educational courses, and a wide range of activity holidays for up to 350 people at a time that include skiing, snowboarding and sledging. They are fortunate in having a 100m. mist-lubricated ski slope and this is available to the general public at certain times of the day (for a charge).

A further mile down the coast, the small hamlet of Penbryn is set about half a mile inland in a beautiful valley where the National Trust has a car park and other facilities at

Llangrannog

Llanborth. Smuggling probably, herring fishing and curing, shipbuilding and limestone burning have long ceased and the ¾ mile of uncluttered beach, backed by rocks and sand dunes, is now cared for as an Site of Special Scientific Interest (SSSI) by the Trust. The golden sand and shallow water for safe bathing at **Penbryn** are a great attraction, while a further mile away there is more to enjoy at the holiday resort village of **Tresaith**, remembered by many for the way in which the course of the little River Saith ends as a waterfall cascading onto the sandy beach.

The Cardigan Bay Special Area of Conservation continues opposite Aberporth and Cardigan and as far as Ceibwr Bay, but there is a break in the designated Heritage Coast between Tresaith and Mwnt — where a fourth length begins.

From New Quay, take the A486 to Synod Inn and turn right onto the A487. A series of roads off to the right lead to places mentioned in box 6 above — a minor road for Cwmtydu, the B4321 at Pentregat or the B4321 for **Llangrannog** and **Lochtyn** (or the B4334 at Brynhoffnant about 1½ miles further on). Afterwards a tortuous route to **Penbryn** is signposted at Sarnau further on, and then others to **Tresaith**. Yet further on the B4333 leads down to **Aberporth**. Or you can continue on the A487 towards Cardigan.

7. Aberporth. Herrings, Golden Sands — and Missiles

The bay at Aberporth and a dolphin sculpture

Sheltered from prevailing south-west winds, Aberporth has acted as an important port and refuge at least as far back as the 16th century. In far more recent times it has become popular among sailing enthusiasts and canoeists — their pleasures reduced only by bad weather or, on firing days, during operations from the experimental missile range and research centre at DTEO Aberporth when danger from behind the Pencribach headland has extended well out into the Bay.

Dyffryn Beach, the larger of two at Aberporth, served with Penbryn as a subsidiary landing place for the main port of Cardigan/Aberteifi, and from the 16th well into the 19th century the benefits of its sheltered position produced increasing maritime and land-based trade and services for the surrounding area. Unusually for this coastline there is no record of shipbuilding, but along with Aberystwyth, Aberporth became one of the major herring ports in Wales. Unlike fish caught nowadays anywhere closer than Norway, Aberporth herring acquired such a reputation for their impressive size that they are still remembered locally through the rhyme:

> 'Sgadan Aberporth   or   The herring of Aberporth
> *Dau fola ac un corf*   Two bellies and one body
>
> Then in company with other coastal towns, and especially after the railway network extended westwards, Aberporth began to attract large numbers of holidaymakers to its two golden beaches, safe bathing and boating, bracing walks and other amenities and soon a good choice of hotel and boarding accommodation was provided for them, along with serviced sites for mobile homes, caravans and campers.

After passing through the town, the B4333 returns to rejoin the A487 near a small airfield and the adjoining Parc Aberporth, a new industrial development of stylish buildings where one ambition is said to be the design and development of un-manned vehicles.

(Arguably the most enchanting of all Ceredigion bays is **Traeth y Mwnt**, about 4 miles north of Cardigan. Also the most remote, it is best reached with the aid of the OS Explorer 198 map or a good Road Atlas. A minor road to the right leads in that direction from the B4333 just before the Aberporth airfield and others connect with the A487 at Penparc and also the B4548 Gwbert Road that joins the trunk road on the outskirts of Cardigan.)

The A487 continues to Cardigan.

---

8. Mwnt and the Island of 20,000 Saints

The sandy bathing cove of Traeth y Mwnt (NT) is sheltered by low cliffs and by Foel y Mwnt, a pronounced 250ft-high pyramid of bracken, gorse and grass. At its foot, and out of the sight of one-time sea-borne marauders, there is the tiny, whitewashed **Church of the Holy Cross** dating from *c*.1400 AD. It stands on a much earlier Celtic site that would have been familiar during the 6th and 7th centuries to pilgrims from afar on passage for Bardsey Island, Ynys Enlli, 40 miles across the Bay beyond the end of the Lleyn Peninsula. Twenty thousand

Foel y Mwnt with the white speck of the church almost in the bottom of the dip in the slope above the bay

'saints' are said to be buried there, although according to Giraldus Cambrensis in April 1188 (p.91), no-one actually died on the island until they were very old indeed 'because of the pure air ... or through some miracle occasioned by the merits of the holy men who lived there'. In addition, however, it is thought possible that bodies of other deceased faithful may have been taken on their last journey from the beach at Mwnt, across the perilous waters of the Bay to the sacred island.

Another small detour avails itself on the edge of Cardigan. If you turn right onto the B4548 along the southern side of the Teifi Estuary, opposite Poppit Sands and through Gwbert-on-Sea, after 3 miles it is possible to arrive at the **Cardigan Island Coastal Farm Park**. This is on the headland overlooking Cardigan Island — just 200 yards off shore and now a nature reserve of the West Wales Wildlife Trust not accessible by the general public.

9. Cardigan Island Coastal Farm Park

Because of an invasion by rats following a shipwreck some years ago, many sea birds were lost but measures are now hopefully being taken against the vermin to safeguard underground nesting habitats for future shearwaters and puffins. As it is, there are lesser black-backed gulls, herring gulls and a few other sea birds — but also rare choughs nesting on the cliffs, while a flock of the primitive, hardy and very adaptable chocolate-brown Soay horned sheep have been taken over and released to roam the island. Looking down from the heavily fenced cliff-top view point (served during the summer season by a tractor and trailer taxi), it is often possible to see some of the Atlantic grey seals that breed in the caves and, with greater luck, dolphins. And at the Farm and Visitor Centre there are many kinds of friendly farm animals and also wallabies, llamas, emus and rheas.

For those not making this detour, the A487 continues past the B4548 junction, bypassing the old Aberystwyth road, and just before reaching the river bridge a third roundabout exit leads to Pont y Cleifion and into the town centre. Parking spots are scattered about the town.

10. Cardigan. Mouth of the Teifi, and something warm to wear

The anglicised name of the town comes from 'Ceredig's land' and Ceredigion — Ceredig being one of the sons of the famed Cunedda of Gwynedd, while for the Welsh, Aberteifi means 'mouth of the (river) Teifi'. Placed safely some 1½ miles inland from the shores of the Irish Sea up a wide, navigable estuary, and at the threshold of the pastoral Teifi valley, the site of Cardigan possessed a prime military and commercial appeal that was recognised as long ago as Conquest days. In 1093 the Norman Robert Montgomery first installed a motte fortification on the site of a previous fort, opposite St. Dogmaels/Llandudoch on the Pembrokeshire shore, close to the present Castle Farm and Road. This was abandoned during the reign of Henry I (1100–1135). Half a mile downstream on a knoll overlooking the river crossing there followed the first in a succession of new or rebuilt castles that appeared during repeated conflict between the Welsh and Normans.

At a time when the Normans had been driven out, *Brut y Tywysogion*, the medieval Chronicle of the Princes (see above), records that during Christmas 1176, the Lord Rhys ap Gruffudd of Deheubarth (d.1197) held a Court in the castle of Aberteifi that he had just rebuilt in stone, and arranged two kinds

of contests — one for bards and poets, the other for musicians. The festival had been proclaimed throughout the British Isles for a year, chairs and other prizes were awarded, and although it was not named as such, has generally been accepted as the first Welsh national *eisteddfod*.

Most of the present ruins date from *c*.1244 and is the work of Robert Waleron, who had extensively rebuilt the **castle** and added the town wall. Cardigan thenceforth possessed one of the most important castles in Wales and from 1279 it remained substantially intact for a further three centuries. Even though the Tudor historian and cartographer, John Speed, thought it to be 'indifferent

The south wall of Cardigan Castle, near the Teifi Bridge

Cardigan Heritage Centre, in an old warehouse by the Teifi

for repair' in 1610, he nevertheless showed substantial portions on his own plan overshadowing the modest houses that lined the streets. But in 1644, the castle was besieged by Parliamentarian forces, was quickly ruined again and then left largely unoccupied until early in the 19th century. By the time John Wood came to carry out a survey for his 1834 town plan, few traces were left to show, although some remnants of the North Gate had survived long enough for Rebecca anti-toll rioters finally to flatten them in 1843. Today, only the street pattern of the medieval planned town remains to indicate the line of the wall, while the castle ruins that Wood found to be 'inconsiderable'

but 'presenting a venerable appearance' in 1834 presented nothing of the sort in 2005. The south wall facing the Teifi Bridge was heavily shored up with raking steel girders and the remainder were chiefly smothered in scaffolding and 'Health and Safety' measures. However all this seemed positive, for in 2003 Ceredigion Council bought the castle with the intention of gradual restoration, stabilisation and re-opening to the public.

It is thought that a **bridge** has existed since the 13th century, but the present structure dates from 1726, when it had seven arches. It has since been widened and is now closely joined by a footbridge. When standing there now, it is very hard to visualise how the downstream scene could once have been bustling as one of the busiest ports in Wales. After a quiet period, towards the end of the 17th century there was a marked increase in the amount of river traffic and a little over a century later, Cardigan outmatched even Bristol in its level of activity. By 1816, records show that 323 sailing vessels were registered at the port, five shipyards on the north bank accounted for about 200 ships and more than 1,000 men were in employment. The lower stretches of the Mwldan Brook, then wider, had become a hive of industrial activity, much of it related to maritime trades. Huge catches of herring had, since Tudor times, been landed, processed and then shipped out again to England, Ireland, the Continent, and the quays on the north side of the river expanded in both directions to handle a range of merchandise. Limestone was landed at the Mercantile Breakwater opposite for conversion to agricultural lime in the nearby kilns, and closer to the bridge, Teifi Wharf served ocean-going vessels, many of them unloading Canadian and Baltic timber. The tall impressive warehouse on the south quay was built in 1745 and at times was used as a sail loft and granary, but from 1997 has acted as the **Cardigan Heritage Centre**. During visitor seasons this displays a permanent exhibition tracing the history of Cardigan from its earliest days. There are also changing exhibitions and intriguing displays — as well as a gift shop, café, river terrace and picnic area. This wharf could well have been a departure point for many disenchanted Cardi and other emigrants who left for a new, and hopefully better, life in Canada and the USA during the 19th century.

They left behind a town that was undergoing rapid change since the time when Speed had indicated signs of contraction, early in the 17th century. There had then been large areas of open space within the walls, but towards the end of the 17th century the burgeoning of river trade, added to the late-medieval easing of hostility, began to show its effects upon the fabric of the town, both within and increasingly outside the protected area. Ribbon housing development had straggled beyond the North Gate and along the Aberystwyth road, and close to the boundary turnpike gate a new County Gaol was built in 1793 to the design of John Nash. He was based at the time in Cardigan and, during the period of the Howard prison reforms, was also responsible that year for at least one other new County Gaol, at Hereford. The Cardigan gaol was subsequently converted into a police station and then a private house. There was more substantial growth to the east towards St. Mary's Church and in the direction of the Teifi. One special building at the Chancery Lane junction was the late 18th-century Customs House. In its control of all Irish Sea shipping between Fishguard, in the south, and Aberarth, in the north, this affirmed the maritime significance of Cardigan well into the 19th century. This tradition may also be gathered from the many inscriptions on headstones in St. Mary's churchyard, where the church had been built by Benedictine monks during the 12th century and largely rebuilt during the 18th. Next to it on the site of the present hospital, where Nash had also been involved, was the priory. Adding to the growth, gradual infilling occurred within the medieval wall line and along the original street pattern and the combined effect of all the development was to double the population of the town during the first half of the 19th century, from 1,900 residents in 1801 to more than 3,800 by 1851. But such an increase was not sustained and by the end of the century the total had fallen to 3,500 and it would only achieve 3,800 again by the time of the 1971 National Census. Much of the reduction arose because of the decline and eventual loss of maritime trade that resulted from silting that partly blocked the estuary entrance, at a time when larger, steam powered iron and steel ships were replacing the traditional sailing schooners and brigs. Then belatedly in 1885, as a final blow, the GWR opened a branch railway from Whitland, just after the first motor vehicle had appeared on a British road to introduce the new Motor Age. In 1962, even before the Beeching Plan, the line was being taken up again, leaving Fishguard and Carmarthen, 16 and 21 miles away, as the nearest stations to Cardigan.

Cardigan Town Trail

Before any real exploration, it is well worth calling (in season) at the Heritage Centre on the Pembrokeshire side of the river and investing there in a copy of the *Cardigan Town Trail* leaflet.

Well illustrated, and in Welsh and English, it first provides a history of the castle and port and then moves towards the **Shire Hall**. This was built in 1763 to accommodate the Courts and Council when they were transferred from old buildings at the castle, it also served as a corn market and just beyond it was the market cross shown on Speed's 1610 map. High Street and Cardigan's main range of shops, banks, hotels and other market town attributes follow on, but the Trail instead turns left into Quay Street, passes through the site of one of the medieval wall gates to head downstream for Netpool,

Cardigan's Guildhall

which was the main centre of the former ship building industry. Along the way there are the Gorsedd Stones, serving as a reminder of the 1976 National Eisteddfod held in Cardigan to celebrate the 800th anniversary of the great event hosted at the castle by the Lord Rhys. After heading back towards the town to cross the Mwldan brook on the site of the old drawbridge, the route passes alongside the line of the town wall and past the market hall to **Theatr Mwldan**. This comprises an impressive conversion from a former slaughter house that dated from 1858, and as well as its 200-seat auditorium for live entertainment and cinema, it also caters for indoor sports and leisure, has a gallery area, restaurant and also houses the TIC. After reaching the site of the former County Gaol, there is the possibility of heading further up the Aberystwyth road to visit the church of Our Lady of the Taper, the National Shrine of the Catholic Church in Wales, before backtracking to head towards High Street, and **The Guildhall**. With multi-coloured pointed arches and a steep, decorative roof, this edifice was built from 1858, during Cardigan's mercantile heyday, where the old grammar school used to be — just outside the site of St. Bartholomew's Gate. It is an amazing looking building, designed as someone has put it as 'in pseudo-Gothic style with a touch of the Middle East'. The Victorian architect had thrown everything at it, but as if this was not sufficient ornament for the small town, an ornate clock tower was added in 1892. Mounted outside there is a captured Russian field gun from the Crimean War (1854–56).

It was on 25 October 1854 that the 7th earl of Cardigan (d.1868) led the Charge of the Light Brigade. It was also during the Crimean War that some soldiers from the county wore knitted sleeved jackets, buttoned down the front, that have come to be named after their disastrous commander.

There is an arcaded market at the rear of the Guildhall that is worth visiting before continuing back within the medieval walled area down High Street. The trail then turns left through the arch of the Black Lion Hotel, a former coaching inn, and reaches the Customs House to continue along St. Mary Street to the church and hospital, before heading west into the Strand and back to the Teifi bridge and the Heritage Centre.

The route out of Cardigan leads back over the Cardigan Bridge over the bridge and along Pont y Cleifion to join the A484 at a roundabout for Llechryd. In Llechryd a sign indicates Cilgerran Castle, a worthwhile diversion of two miles off to the right from the next stage of the journey that follows, along the A484, the valley of the Teifi.

'Noble Teifi — Queen of Rivers'

Along with mountains, valleys, cliffs, beaches and many other things, Wales does rivers rather well — and one of the finest of these is the Teifi. Giraldus Cambrensis wrote in the 12th century of 'a noble river called the Teifi', and in the 21st the Teifi Trout Association enthused equally about 'the Queen of Rivers'. With letters after its name that include S.S.S.I., S.A.C. and S.L.A. (Site of Special Scientific Interest, Special Area of Conservation and Special Landscape Area) it is certainly well qualified for such plaudits. Some 75 miles from the coast at Gwbert-on-Sea, its source is 1,500 feet up — to the east of Aberystwyth on the western flank of the Cambrian Mountains. After a steep descent from bleak, rocky heights the infant river flows close to 12th-century monastic ruins of Strata Florida that had once been thought of as the 'Westminster Abbey of Wales'. Then shortly joined by waters flowing from Ffair Rhos, once famous for home-knitted garments offered at its annual fair, the river meanders on a low gradient through a 6-mile waste of rushes, peat hags and bottomless swamp before passing more quickly to the west of Tregaron. This is territory that witnessed the escapades and misdeeds of 'The Welsh Robin Hood' of the 16th century, and watered huge droves of black cattle that were being assembled for the long treks to the English markets to provide 'The Roast Beef of Olde England' (see p.187). It closes soon afterwards on the A485 and the former track bed of the Aberystwyth to Carmarthen railway, to be joined by the River Brennig for a sinuous descent past the buried remains of a far western outpost and three-way road intersection of the departed Roman Empire. Then down past wooded hills to skirt the home of the oldest Welsh university at Lampeter, there to be spanned by Pont Steffan carrying the routes for Llandovery and Carmarthen. Forming part of the Welsh name of the town, a 12th-century predecessor was also known to Giraldus Cambrensis as 'Stephen's Bridge', even then without any indication that he or anyone knew who Stephen was! After many twists and turns, and a wide bend at Pencarreg, the Teifi reaches the small market town of Llanybydder on the Carmarthenshire bank, famous for horse sales and fishing. Further downstream and sited largely along the A486, Llandysul and Pont Tyweli around St. Tysul's Church is another small Teifi market town. Famous too for fishing, and also white water canoeing, the Teifi and many of its rapid-flowing tributaries in this area have long been harnessed to drive water mills. All this sustainable energy, combined with lush upland pastures for sheep, produced the two main ingredients for thriving wool and flannel shirt industries. Some 40 mills once operated in the area, and housed now in the former Cambrian Mill at Dre-fach Velindre is the **National Wool Museum**. Other mill buildings in the town have long been converted to different uses, but one 19th-century business that has survived well is the Gomer Press, familiar to readers as the chief Welsh language press in the country as well as for books in English. The river enters a narrow rocky gorge at Henllan before forming a huge, horizontal 'S' bend that created three sides of a natural moat that went some way towards protecting a 13th-century castle. From Newcastle Emlyn the Teifi starts to turn westward towards Cardigan and at Cenarth leaps and thunders down over rocks beside one of the last remaining water-driven flour mills in Wales. Then, close to the A484, it makes a tight 'U' turn round Allt Goch before resuming its heading towards Llechryd Bridge and experience its first effects of the tides. From there it begins to close in on the spectacular, deep wooded gorge far below the castle ruins at Cilgerran, and soon after emerging at the **Welsh Wildlife Centre**, it broadens out for a final run past Aberteifi to be lost in the Bay.

The water is largely unpolluted and the high quality from the catchment is reflected by the presence of otters, even in the tidal reach. There is a very good chance of seeing them at Cilgerran — where in 1188 Giraldus Cambrensis reckoned that the Teifi was the only river nearer than Scotland where there were also beavers. He said too that it was better stocked with the finest salmon than any stream in Wales. Shallow runs, thundering waterfalls and lazy dark pools provide great variety in wild and beautiful scenery and make it one of the most popular, top producing rivers for salmon and sea trout in the UK (despite the otters' share). Although the average weight of a Teifi salmon is c.9lb, rods have accounted for fish of almost 14lb, and 20lb is not unknown. In a good season, such as 2004, numbers can reach 1,000 fish, whereas in a drought year, 400 are more typical. There are also good catches of sea trout (*sewin* to the Welsh), but numbers of brown trout have declined, and there is a catch and release policy in effect. But there are many more fish in the river than salmon and sea trout. Sea bass of 6 to 8lb are caught in the estuary and there are rarities throughout the length that include two different species of lamprey, looking rather like eels, and the bullhead, whose cock fish cares unusually for the eggs until they hatch. A very wide range of rare plants has all added to the case for the very special designation and protection — now formally and firmly provided for river, habitat, flora and fauna.

For the first time since parting at Cardigan, the Teifi reappears close to the A484 at Llechryd and the optional route to Cilgerran crosses over the nine arches of **Llechryd Bridge**, shown on OS Explorer Map 198 in antique lettering to emphasise its great age. Close to the Pembrokeshire bank, on the upstream side, it bears the date of 1695 although there are thoughts that even this might simply be the date of repair to an even older structure. (Immediately to the right after crossing, and worth exploring, a drive leads past a lodge to the stable court and other fine buildings that have been adapted to produce the hotel at Castell Malgwyn.)

11. Cilgerran. Romantic Castle Scenes, Extreme Ardour and Rare Wildlife

The history of Cilgerran is varied and rather obscure, for although it is now just a small village, from burgages appearing on each side of its single through street it reveals signs of a planned settlement and is thought to have once been a borough. During the early 17th century, Speed listed it among the principal towns of Pembrokeshire and it has been the scene of major annual horse, cattle and hiring fairs, and had a gaol, stocks and whipping post to deal with any bad behaviour. As well as farming, another traditional occupation was fishing and much of it was undertaken from coracles that may still be seen at the annual races on the third Saturday in August. Also for over 100 years until 1938, a type of grey slaty stone was quarried at several local sites to be used for roof covering, flagstones, gravestones, window sills and even billiard-table tops. All went down river by barge to Cardigan, where lime and culm fuel were loaded on board for the return journey.

The **parish church of St. Clawddog**, dedicated to the 6th-century Celtic saint, is at the west end of the village. It was visited by Giraldus Cambrensis in 1188, and although mainly rebuilt in the mid-19th century, it may have been at the centre of an earlier settlement. The Pendre Inn dates from the 14th century and Cilgerran also has the Mason's Arms and Cardiff Arms pubs. But what most visitors come to see are the romantically scenic ruins of the 13th-century **castle** (in the care of Cadw) that loom over the village from a high crag above the river opposite the entry of the smaller Plysgog. There was a romance up there that stirred dire consequences throughout Wales during the early 12th century. This was when an infatuated and impetuous son of the prince of Powys attacked and burnt what was a former earth and timber castle on the site in the course of abducting from her abode there the beautiful Nest (d.1136), the 'Helen of Wales'. No less than the daughter of Rhys ap Tewdr, prince of Wales, she had become the wife of the Norman governor of Pembroke Castle, Gerald of Windsor (both of them, incidentally, grandparents of Giraldus Cambrensis).

Despite a daunting cliff-top challenge, during the medieval period the castle often changed hands in action, and was then rebuilt, until it was finally taken by the Norman William Marshal the Younger. The surviving two 4-storey drum towers, curtain walling, main gatehouse and other features date from 1233 until the end of that century, and although they suffered neglect and had to be refurbished by order of Edward III (1327–1377), the castle was occupied until the end of the 16th century. Sometimes compared with Carreg Cennen Castle for its stunning cliff-top siting, it too has been at the focus of countless cameras and long the subject of work by famous landscape artists, such as Joseph Turner and Richard Wilson.

Indicated locally by brown signs, the 270-acre **Welsh Wildlife Centre** further downstream is regarded as the best place in England and Wales to see otters. It comprises seven different habitats that include marsh, reed-bed,

Cilgerran Castle

woodland, mud flat and river bank that are said to support 130 species of bird, 15 of dragon-fly and damsel fly, 25 of butterfly, 250 of moth and 350 kinds of plant. There are herds of Red and Sitka deer and even some water buffalo to help keep down the reeds. With a network of walks, cycle-ways, hides, good disabled access and a car park (daily charge), the **Teifi Marshes Nature Reserve** element of the centre is open all year, and there is a seasonal visitor centre, complete with other attractions for much of the time.

Back at Llechryd the A484 follows the twists and turns of the Teifi until they both reach the old narrow four-arched masonry bridge at Cenarth, where it spans the Cardiganshire and Carmarthenshire county boundary. In order to cross, the road makes a right-angled turn, while ahead there is the 'Cenarth Falls Salmon Leap Car Park' (charge).

12. Cenarth. Salmon Leap and Age-old Coracles

At a major beauty spot, in a village largely designated as a Conservation Area, the *c.*18th-century bridge with its distinctive circular openings is part of a picturesque and exciting scene where the Teifi cascades through a broad rocky gorge over low ledges into turbulent eddying pools. Visitors have for many years waited there expectantly in the hope of seeing salmon leap upstream, while fishermen below have enjoyed good sport—although restrained to catch just one salmon and three *sewin* a day in order to conserve stocks. Probably no such limits applied during past times when Cenarth was a centre for coracle fishermen, or when in 1861 there are said to have been some 300 coracles in use down the river. Because of a severe reduction in netting licences, few remain

The bridge over the Teifi at Cenarth, and the working 17th-century flour mill (below)

now, but there are reminders of past times in the National Coracle Centre at this their traditional highest point of use in the river. Set in the grounds of a working 17th-century flour mill as a private enterprise, in season this contains exhibits of coracles from many parts of the world. All of them are different, often based on local conditions, even those on the generally less turbulent Tywi not far away. The Teifi coracle is almost oval, sits slightly lower in the water and is made with a framework of the plentiful local willow, tied together into a gunwale of intertwined hazel saplings. Early versions used hide as a covering, but from the early 19th century this was changed for calico or flannel waterproofed with hot pitch, and subsequently canvas, the whole treated with linseed oil. Such a vessel had an effective working life of two years. Being a highly manoeuvrable and lightweight boat with a shallow draught of only 3 to 4 inches, they were also easily carried on land over one's head, making the bearer resemble some strange tortoise.

Driving on into Carmarthenshire, the A484 soon reaches the market town of **Newcastle Emlyn**. It has been suggested that a motte at Cenarth, still shown on the OS map, was the 'old castle' of the cantref, or district, of Emlyn that led to the choice of 'new castle' for the name of the town, but there is greater support for Cilgerran as the predecessor.

For exploring the town itself there is a convenient car park on Castle Terrace at the cul-de-sac approach to the castle. The hub of a wide agricultural area, it is especially busy here every Friday market day and, is well provided with good places to eat and drink. The Bunch of Grapes in Bridge Street is very popular, but not to the exclusion of the range of other cafés, restaurants, great pubs and locals. These intermingle with a good selection of independent shops, several displaying antiques, and businesses.

13. Newcastle Emlyn / Castellnewydd Emlyn

Newcastle Emlyn Castle

The Market Hall

The Teifi effectively formed three sides of a natural moat for the **castle** that, exceptionally for the year 1240, was built of stone from the start. But this could not protect it effectively from determined attack and in 1287 it changed hands three times — a process that was to be repeated several times during its lifetime. It was intended to serve as an administrative centre for the district, although it took some 60 years before it became associated with a town. Then rapid growth began to occur after the creation in 1302 of a borough along the axis running parallel with the meander of the river and in 1318 the castle was refurbished and strengthened. A connection was made at right angles with the road leading north to Adport across the river bridge, a bailiff was appointed, the borough held its courts, annual fairs took place and a weekly Friday market was opened which has continued to this day. Then in 1403, Owain Glyndwr mounted an attack that, even for him, was ruthlessly destructive and in 1645 further devastation was caused by Parliamentary forces, just leaving the scant remains of the castle walls and gatehouse that can be seen at the end of Castle Terrace. Somehow the settlement continued in its market role and became a hub of the thriving cattle droving trade, as records of all the inns and pubs show. The rather small-sized **market hall**, with its large clock tower, now houses the Attic Theatre, the Old Library and Hanes Emlyn, the town's historical society, and a seasonal TIC is there to advise about the fishing, walking and relaxing opportunities that make the town so good a base for touring the Teifi Valley.

The route now returns to Cardiganshire over the bridge across the Teifi to Adpar, where a plaque marks the site where Isaac Cook built the first printing press in Wales in 1718. Immediately over the river turn right then drive on upstream where the A475 heads towards a crossroads with the A486 at Horeb, and you go straight across. The A475 eventually arrives in Lampeter.

If you are carrying on through and not stopping, then you turn left on to the A485 at the main intersection in town. Even if stopping here, it is probably best to make this turn and then look for a parking space. The town displays much of its Georgian and Victorian character in its architecture above shop fascia levels, while beneath them there is a good range of local businesses, all rather dominated by the Black Lion, an 18th-century coaching inn complete with old stables and coach house at the rear, although as this is an important market town and seat of learning it is by no means the only place of refreshment.

14. Lampeter. Church of St. Peter by Stephen's Bridge and an early University College

The only evidence of any Norman presence on the north bank of the Teifi is a **castle motte** or mound dating from 1095 that can still be recognised in the grounds of the college. It is thought to have been built by an Anglo Norman named Stephen, and he it is who has also been associated with the Teifi bridge — and remembered in the Welsh name of the town, Lampeter. This is an anglicised version of Llanbedr Pont Steffan — the church of St. Peter by Stephen's Bridge. St. Peter's is built on what could have been the site of one of many small monasteries that were founded in Wales during the early days of Christianity, although often as much involved in farming as in religious devotions. The town grew up around this ecclesiastical core and was chartered as a borough from 1285, entitled to hold a weekly market and an annual fair on the feast day of St. Demus. But there was only modest growth during the

medieval period and afterwards, and even an 1845 map showed little movement beyond the two sides of High Street — even though Lampeter had become an important cattle droving, commercial and business centre for a considerable hinterland. Introduction in 1866 of a station on the projected Manchester and Milford Railway produced changes, not only in the movement of cattle to the English markets but also to the economy of the town and the line survived for just under 100 years until the Beeching measures led to its withdrawal.

As to the Church, by the late 17th century religion of the established church had reached a low pitch throughout Wales while the Methodist Revival was attracting huge, devout congregations to the numerous

Lampeter College

231

chapels that are still to be seen everywhere. Reaction to this decline occurred at Lampeter in 1822 when it became the centre of a counter move in enlivening the Welsh Anglican Church — by first raising the quality of its clergy. Until then, few worthwhile young candidates had the means to attend Oxford or Cambridge, which were then the only universities throughout England or Wales, and so it was decided to lay the foundation stone of a degree-awarding college at Lampeter. Named **St. David's College**, it was founded on donated land at Cae Castell (Castle Field) and opened for students in 1827 to function not just as a seminary but also to provide for study of the classics, history and other subjects. The main building was designed on the lines of the quadrangle of a typical college at Oxford, where a link was formed with the University, and by 1852 Lampeter had progressed by receiving a Charter enabling it to award its own degree of Bachelor of Divinity, and then another in 1865 for the Bachelor of Arts. Since then many more buildings have been added, women have been admitted and the college is no longer confined to the training of the clergy and offers a wide range of subjects. As the third oldest degree-awarding institution after Oxford and Cambridge, it became part of the **University of Wales** and in 2005 there were 1,100 full-time undergraduates and postgraduates — and almost six times as many part-time students who were prepared to study for up to 10 years in order to obtain their degrees.

The A485 passes the university along College Street to enter North Road and soon afterwards it parts from the A482 as the Tregaron Road is followed to the right as it runs alongside the River Dulas making its final descent to join the Teifi, and the route of the defunct Cardigan to Aberystwyth railway close to the former crossing point of the Aberaeron branch line at Pont Silian. Green and wooded hills embrace the route as it passes through Betwys Bledrws and Llangybi and then it re-enters the Teifi valley near Pont Llanio.

15. Roman *Bremia* and Sarn Helen

Archaeological evidence has confirmed that Pont Llanio was close to the site of *Bremia*, one of a chain of Roman forts, during the 1st century AD. *Bremia* was served by a well built road system that extended parallel with Cardigan Bay from *Moridvnvm* (Carmarthen) to *Segontivm* (Caernarvon), with strategic eastward connections to the Severn Valley and West Midlands. Some of these routes have survived to serve modern transport, and one of them has been adopted for the B4578 that leads to the left towards Tyncelyn. From there it is thought to head for a minor Romano-British settlement at Trawscoed, 7½ miles up the course of the River Ystwyth — recently discovered from the air. Like some of the others, this Roman road is known to the Welsh as Sarn Helen — sarn meaning 'causeway', and in one account in *The Mabinogion* collection of tales, Helen is suggested as being a popular Welsh princess who became the wife of the usurper-emperor, Magnus Maximus, until he was killed off. A duller and less imaginative theory is that it is a corruption of sarn y lleng meaning 'the legions' road'. Some of these roads were used for transporting metals from the lead and silver mines and levels in the upper reaches of the Ystwyth and the foothills of the Cambrian Mountains and there was one that left *Bremia* south-eastwards for an auxiliary fort at *Lventivm* (Pumsaint), close to the Dolaucothi Roman gold workings, to *Alabvm* (Llandovery) and on into England. A third road runs in a south-westerly direction to the fort at *Moridvnivm* (Carmarthen).

The B4578 provides for a fairly direct but hilly route towards Aberystwyth, but our route keeps to the A485 for Tregaron.

Another detour is a possibility at Pont Llanio. Here a minor road to the right leads to the small village of **Llanddewi-Brevi**, 'the church of David on the Brefi'. There is a fragment of stone from *Bremia* at the large church, where a long association with Christianity is marked by legends about St. David and five 6th-century Celtic crosses. Maybe because of these credentials the village was proposed in the 19th century for the setting up of an Anglican clergy college — but when suitable land was donated at Lampeter nothing more was heard.

Back on the A485 Tregaron is soon reached. Our route carries on, but the road to the right crosses the River Brennig to reach the Market Square, Kite Centre and a memorable 14-mile drovers' route eastward through the Brennig Valley and high moorland across the remote Mynydd Elenydd Range to Abergwesyn. The B4343 straight ahead almost runs alongside the Cors Caron Nature Reserve, the great bog of Tregaron, towards Strata Florida Abbey and Devils Bridge. With Tregaron, these routes are described under Tour 10, starting at page 235, whereas for now the A485 turns left up a hill to begin the final journey back to the coast and Aberystwyth. After just over a mile it passes over the River Teifi at Pont Einon, ending a sluggish passage through a 4-mile stretch of apparent wilderness known in Welsh as Cors Goch Glanteifi, 'the red bog along the Teifi'.

Meeting the B4578 again at Tyncelyn, the A485 takes a sharp right turn to adopt the course of the Sarn Helen for ¾ mile before veering off to the left for Bronnant and the twists and turns leading down to Lledrod. The road rises there up the valley and reaches Rhos-y-garth, and the chance to see red kites, before dropping down beneath trees to face the squat tower of Llanilar church. A sharp left turn leads the A485 into the Ystwyth Valley — and to join the A487 coast road near Pont Llanchaiarn across the river for the return to Aberystwyth.

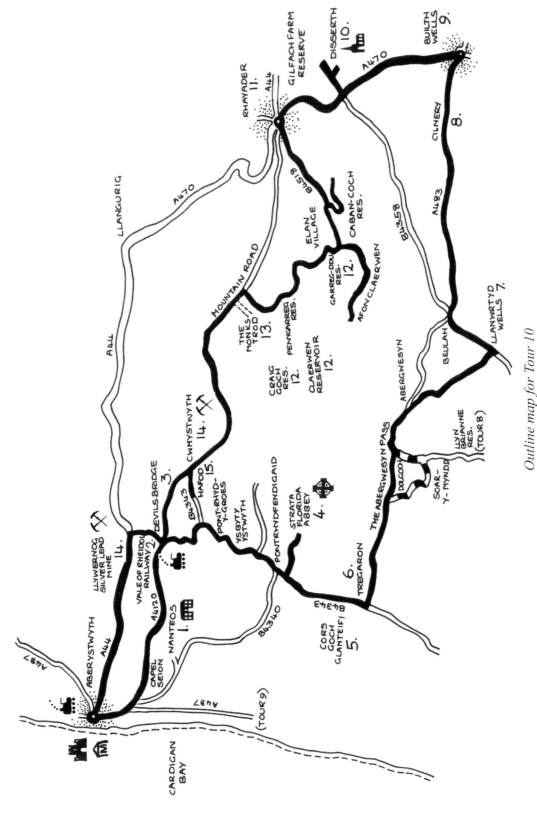

Outline map for Tour 10

The numbers 1 to 15 relate to the boxed information given within the tour

Tour 10   By Mountain and Valley

This route is largely scenic, and on a mixture of A, B and (very) minor roads, some of the latter passing through truly amazing scenery, and takes in Devil's Bridge, the Elan valley dams and lakes and old mineral mines. Side excursions from the main route include the ruins of Strata Florida Abbey and the Hafod Estate with walks through historic parkland in the style of the Picturesque. The distance, without detours, is about 95 miles (OS Landranger 135, 147).

Leave Aberystwyth on the A487 signposted towards Cardigan and cross the River Rheidol at Trefechan. The A487 then makes two junctions with the A4120, and you take the second signposted for 'Devils Bridge'. After making the turn there is an immediate junction with the B4340, on which you turn right if you want to make a detour to Nanteos. After a mile there is a fork leading to the left, signposted for the mansion at a lodge where a drive passes a lake on the right to reach the car park.

If you don't want to make the detour, continue along A4120 which takes a breathtaking course with glorious views across the Rheidol Valley as it heads towards Devils Bridge. At the approach there is a car park to the right and another at the train station the entrance to which is on the left (in 2005 trains ran from late March to the end of October except on some days, but check the timetable at local TICs). There is a third car park on the right across the bridge beyond and close to the turnstiles for those just wishing to visit the Mynach Falls, three bridges and gorge.

---

1. Nanteos and The Holy Grail

Now a hotel the house is a Grade I Listed Building standing squarely and solidly three storeys high in the thickly wooded Paith Valley and enjoying sweeping views over a magical landscape of open green spaces and hills. Although the name 'Nanteos' translates as 'the valley of the nightingale', the estate now lies well outside the range of this elusive songster — but maybe it was heard here much earlier during the long history of the Powell family. They, and the Pryse family of Plas Gogerddan (now housing a crop research centre north-east of Aberystwyth), had vast possessions and influence in the region, the Powells owning lead mines and other property including much of Aberystwyth. They claimed descent from early Welsh royalty and many noble families, and it was in 1738 when Thomas Powell (d.1752) built the present mansion in the Palladian style then so popular with the landed gentry. Extensions followed in the mid-1800s after completion of the now Grade II Listed stable block and huge neo-classical entrance archway. Externally the mansion has been regarded as unpretentious and rather severe, but after passing through the main entrance the interior is quite different. This is at once apparent in the spacious entrance hall and staircase leading to the stained glass of the landing windows. Of the many stately rooms, arguably the finest is the glittering and elegant music room on the first floor — with its gilded plasterwork, marble fireplace and huge mirrors. Now that Nanteos has become a hotel, holding a licence for the conduct of marriages, this is where the ceremonies usually take place but it is actually there as part of a Powell tradition as patrons of the arts. As one of many great writers, artists and musicians, the composer Richard Wagner (1813–1883) is believed to have stayed with them at Nanteos while he was composing his sacred drama, *Parsifal*. This is based on the actions of the Knights of the Holy Grail who guarded the vessel from which Christ drank at the Last Supper, and he could well have gained inspiration from the sight of the famous *Cwpan Nanteos* during his visit. Made of olive wood, this is claimed to be the Holy Grail, brought to England by Joseph of Arimathea to be cared for at Glastonbury. There the monks treasured it until forced during the Reformation to flee with all their precious relics to Strata Florida Abbey. However this abbey was not to be spared for long and the cup was taken by its monks to Nanteos, where it was guarded by the Powells, venerated and used for several centuries by those believing in its healing powers. This has told on its condition and relatively recently it was placed in a bank for safe keeping.

2. The Vale of Rheidol Railway — 'Y Lein Fach'

Activity in the station for the Vale of Rheidol railway

Except in wartime, the railway has operated since 1902 with the intention of serving lead mine, timber and passenger traffic of the Rheidol Valley. This was over a line of 1ft 11¾ins between the rails, an exceptionally narrow gauge adopted in order to cater for all the sharp curves, narrow ledges and steep gradients occurring over the 11¾ mile distance between the termini. Conversely the locomotives are, at 8ft, designed for other practical reasons to be unusually wide. In 1923 the national railway system was regrouped, the GWR took over from the Cambrian Railway and immediately introduced two new and one rebuilt steam tank-engines for what had by then become solely a passenger service. Tourists were appearing in increasing numbers, and in 1938 the original carriages were replaced to provide everyone with greater comfort and much better scope for taking in the spectacular valley scenery. After further changes up to the 1989 'privatisation', British Rail was the owner of this, its last steam railway, which it then handed over to a charitable trust. Now the three locomotives — No 7 *Owain Glyndwr,* No 8 *Llywelyn* and No 9 *Prince of Wales*—take approximately 1 hour each way to haul their coaches over a difference in levels of well over 600ft.

Devil's Bridge Station is 680ft above sea level, and once the train has departed through a rocky cutting it moves steeply down a ledge cut into the wooded hillside at a gradient of 1 in 50 until it leaves the narrow part of the valley and after 4½ miles arrives at Aberffrwyd, 480ft lower down. The descent down the south side of the valley continues as far as Capel Bangor, where the ground levels off for the final run in to the terminus at Aberystwyth main line station. For most of the season there is just half an hour to wait before the train sets off again, whereas there is normally at least a full hour at Devil's Bridge — to allow engine and crew to build up steam again after their far more taxing uphill haul, and for their passengers to explore the locality.

3. The Devil's Bridge, Monks' River and ancient roads to Strata Florida

Mynach Falls at Devil's Bridge

Access to the Rheidol Gorge is through a turnstile where there is an informative *Nature Trail Guide* leaflet that indicates features of interest, starting with a good view of the three famous bridges. The stopping places mentioned in the text are marked by numbered signs along the way—which consists of level and steep paths, steps, 'Jacob's Ladder', and the footbridge over the Afon Mynach (*afon*: river, *mynach*: monk), involving a descent into the gorge of over 300ft. Then there are further steps, paths and stairways back up to the main road, car park, café, Hafod Arms Hotel and the train station. Little of it is 'wheelchair or small person friendly' and anyone else wishing to take on the complete trail described in the leaflet should have due regard for their levels of stamina and fitness.

The top-most bridge seen at the start carries the A4120 Aberystwyth to Ponterwyd road and was built by the County Council early in the 20th century, strengthened in 1971–72 and fitted with authentic new parapets in 1983. The middle bridge, with its fine balustrades, dates from *c.*1708, but it is the lowest of the three that has been given the name of 'Devil's Bridge'.

According to ancient legend, this arises from an occasion when an old lady was unable to retrieve her cow that had wandered over the river to the other side of the gorge. The Devil appeared, with a promise that he would produce a bridge provided that he could have the first living thing that crossed it. The woman agreed, wary enough to realise that it was she who was expected to be the first to cross in order to collect her cow. So instead, she threw a crust of bread across the bridge and her dog chased after it and, as was agreed, had to be claimed by the Devil — while the old lady safely rounded up her cow.

Another more likely story, that might have led to the bridge being called the 'Monks Bridge' instead, comes from the 12th century when a monastery of the Cistercian Order was founded close to the site of the present Strata Florida Abbey. This grew in importance to such an extent that it became known as the 'Westminster Abbey of Wales', and although the White Monks observed strict ascetic standards, they also possessed and managed a vast amount of land and property, spread throughout mid-Wales. Much of it had been donated by the founder, Lord Rhys, but there were gifts from many princelings, nobles and others who wished to secure a measure of salvation for their often wicked souls and, hopefully, the promise of an open door to Paradise. In order to keep in touch with these distant properties and communities it was necessary for the abbot to establish a system of tracks (just as the Romans had done on a larger scale), and these would form the basis of later routes for pilgrims, friars, drovers and lead miners, and even tarmac roads for 21st-century motorists and tourists. And so, for example, the monks pioneered the old coaching road from Aberystwyth to Rhayader via the Ystwyth and Elan valleys (p.253), with a connection a short distance to the south of Ponterwyd leading to Ysbyty Cynfyn on the present A4120. This was a hospice intended for the rest and refreshment of pilgrims, and from there the trail led to the bridge the monks are believed to have built over the River Mynach, now known as Devil's Bridge, and another across the River Ystwyth further along at Pont Rhyd-y-groes ('bridge of the ford of the cross'). Afterwards it reached another travellers' hospice at Ysbyty Ystwyth, before arriving at Pontrhydfendigaid ('bridge of the blessed ones') and the final approach to the abbey.

The route now follows the trail of the medieval cowled monks for part of the way by turning back a short distance past the Hafod Arms and train station, then turning left up the B4343, shortly to meet the B4574 coming from Hafod Uchtryd before dropping down to cross the River Ystwyth at Pont Rhyd-y-groes. This is at a steep gorge that has prompted comparison with an Alpine landscape, and then there is a climb to reach the village past the Miner's Arms Hotel, its name and long history a reminder of the lead mines which once underpinned the economy of the area. The road continues to rise from the Ystwyth Valley past a large quarry on the right to arrive high above open undulating country and a first sight in the far distance of Tregaron Bog. Along the way, Ffair Rhos was once the scene of some of the most famous fairs in Cardiganshire, and at the Teifi Inn a secondary road leads off to the left towards the Teifi Lakes.

In order to visit the remains of **Strata Florida Abbey** turn left at Pontrhydfendigaid towards Tregaron, and opposite the Red Lion Hotel near the far side of the village, turn left again to follow Abbey Road for about a mile to where they can be found, close to the church, the infant River Teifi and the start of the Teifi Pools Walk.

---

4. Strata Florida and 'The Vale of Flowers'

The Cistercians were a dissenting order of French monks who separated from the monastery at Citeaux (Latin: *Cistercium*) in Burgundy, departing towards a 'daughter house' at Clairvaux. Under a strict interpretation of the rule of St. Benedict they flourished and expanded during the early 12th century and reached Whitland in south Wales (p.80) in 1140. In 1164, with support from the Anglo Norman lord, Robert fitzStephen, the community established a daughter foundation on the banks of the Ffleur brook, a tributary of the Teifi, that well satisfied a desire for solitude 'far from the concourse of men' in towns and villages. Because of their habits of unbleached wool they were known as White Monks and followed the Benedictine rule by earning a living through manual labour — although leaving the heavy work to lay brothers, or *conversi*. They became effective in clearing and improving land and were accomplished sheep breeders — but the Welsh population had not accepted French occupation and not long after the monks' arrival, the Lord Rhys ap Gruffudd (d.1197) attacked and captured fitzStephen and overcame foreign control of the region. Nevertheless he greatly valued the practical contribution of the monastery towards the improvement of the land in this part of his kingdom of Deheubarth, and by a charter of 1184 he provided it with substantial grant aid. As a result the community chose to move two miles from the initial site, on land now occupied by Old Abbey Farm on the Tregaron road known as *yr hen fynachlog* (the old monastery), taking with them the name *Ystrad Ffleur* (the Vale of Flowers), latinised as Strata Florida. Support received from Lord Rhys was continued by following generations and this patronage and the cultural standing and influence of the Welsh abbots and communities led to the abbey securing a high reputation as a powerhouse of Welsh scholarship and culture. It is believed that the *Chronicle of Princes* (*Brut y Tywysogion*) may have been annotated at Strata Florida and it is certain that during the late 13th century many of the princes of Deheubarth (south-west Wales) were buried there. Legend also insists that Dafydd ap Gwilym, the greatest of medieval Welsh poets, is buried within the abbey precincts and he is commemorated in the north transept of the church by a slate memorial.

But the monks did not enjoy their solitude and peace for long. Among many tribulations, lightning and fire caused great damage to the buildings, this was added to by Welsh rebels and there was further destruction during the reigns of Edward I and Henry VI. And then in 1539 came Henry VIII, and the Dissolution. Lead was promptly removed from roofs and walling stone 'quarried' for redeployment in other buildings until the abbey must soon have become just piles of overgrown rubble. The site passed to private

The west doorway to the abbey

ownership in 1567 and was partly used for the building of a house. Much later, in 1744, everything went to Thomas Powell of Nanteos, and subsequently to the Church in Wales. Then in 1931, guardianship was passed to the State and Strata Florida is now managed by Cadw. An illustrated Cadw *Guidebook* is available at the old school entrance building when the monument is open and staffed (it is important to check on seasons, dates and times at local TICs). This sets out the detailed historical background, building sequence and a tour of the church, cloister and monastic buildings.

Immediately after leaving the shop and ticket counter the best surviving and certainly most striking feature to be seen is the late 12th-century west doorway of the abbey church. The superb carving consists of five of the original six continuous roll mouldings, with no capitals but divided by 13 cross bands, each terminating with a scroll or spiral ornament. The workmanship is regarded as being without close parallel in Cistercian architecture anywhere in the British Isles, and nowadays it frames the slopes of sheep farming land in the near distance that form part of the foothills of the

Looking towards the north transept and eastern chapels

extensive upland estates that were once managed by the monks. Originally, use of the west door was reserved for ceremonial purposes, especially Sunday rites and processions and, once beyond it, the chief points of interest of the ground plan of what is left of the abbey begin with the nave. This is where the lay brothers attended services, facing inwards and screened from the north and south aisles by partition walls. Their altars were at the *pulpitum* at the east end, a screen placed at the crossing between the nave, monks' choir and the north and south transepts. The monks' choir, reserved for the abbot and ordained choir monks only, opened beyond massive crossing piers to the high altar and before two small chapels that were set up against the east wall of the church. Leading from the choir, and tower above, the north transept had three chapels and on the opposite side the layout and design of the south transept was similar, but there the three chapels have been protected with modern roofing to display the medieval tiled flooring and traces of painted wall plaster. The cloister and monastic buildings were to the south of the abbey church, and here the community prepared and took meals, studied, relaxed and slept. Most important was the large, imposing chapter house where, each morning, the monks gathered on seats around the walls to conduct business and administrative affairs, to hear what the abbot had to say and listen to a chapter being read from the *Rule of St. Benedict* — hence the name of the building. It was here also, as well as to the east of the south transept, that many princes of Deheubarth — descendents of the Lord Rhys — and other notable people including departed abbots were buried. Nothing much else is at present evident of the dormitory, refectory and the customary service buildings that would once have been set around the cloister, but it is quite possible that more remains will be researched and revealed by archaeologists in the fullness of time.

Much of what has been learned so far about Strata Florida Abbey is due to the work of Stephen Williams, an enthusiastic railway engineer who conducted excavations in 1887–90. One incidental outcome was that these prompted the Manchester and Milford Railway to display posters that advertised 'Cheap Day Return Tickets to see the excavations at Strata Florida', where there was a station until 1964. It had been reached with some difficulty a hundred years before, after the line had been forced to encounter much of a 2-mile stretch of deep peat-bog from the direction of Tregaron. This was not exactly railway engineers' dream terrain, and it was fortunate therefore that there were many sheep about to contribute sufficient wool to be used as a load-distributing base for the track bed. Now, 140 years later, the 'Old Railway Walk' is still stable and, at all times, serves as the only means of access to the **Cors Goch Glanteifi bog** and observation tower without a special permit from the Countryside Council for Wales.

5. Cors Goch Glanteifi. The Red Bog along the Teifi

Protected as a National Nature Reserve, this is regarded as the greatest surviving Welsh peat-bog, like many others getting its name from the rich red colour of leaves and stems of the widespread cotton sedge after it has ended its summer display of fluffy white tassels. Botanically, and in most other regards, it is similar to Cors Fochno at Borth (p.211), but this bog is 600 feet above sea level and 10 miles from the coast. It was formed some 20,000 years ago after a large shallow lake was left behind a terminal glacial moraine of stony debris.

This was not impermeable, and the River Teifi seeped through, leaving the lake as a morass of rushes, sedges and sphagnum moss. This has become the great mass of peat that now exists, and is still forming, today. The effect on the Teifi has been to reduce its upstream velocity to a sluggish flow, winding its way from north to south between great peat banks past rare bog plants, insects, amphibians, reptiles, water voles, otters and many other mammals. Some 170 species of bird have been recorded, prominently wild duck, geese and swans, and there are uncommon examples such as reed buntings, sedge warblers and goldcrests, all alert for any sign of predatory hen harriers, kestrels and buzzards or scavenging red kites.

The B4343 heads south-west after leaving Pontrhydfendigaid, crossing the River Ffleur bridge at Old Abbey Farm as hills begin to close in on the left at the approach to Allt Ddu. Until 1964 there was a Halt here and the road now runs close to the route of the railway at the edge of the bog for most of the way to **Tregaron**. Here a left turn across the River Brennig leads to the market square.

6. Tregaron. Cattle Drovers, Black Sheep and the Welsh Robin Hood

The market square and the church dedicated to St. Caron, a mythological 3rd-century Welsh king, comprise the hub of this the most easterly town in Ceredigion. Tregaron dates back to the late 13th century, and to when in 1292 Edward I by Royal Charter granted it a weekly Tuesday market and the right to hold two annual fairs. The Ffair Garon is still held now, but these privileges did not meet early hopes of expansion and prosperity for the town and during several centuries it was confined to the east bank of the River Brennig and a small grouping of cottages around the area known now as Pentref. However one valuable natural resource in this part of Wales was its capacity for cattle and sheep rearing, and as far back as the 14th century large droves of these animals were being driven for great distances well into England. The licenced trade of drover had become established by the 17th century, and Tregaron was one of their main collecting centres for cattle, sheep, ponies, pigs and even geese that were to be driven over the mountains after being purchased from local fairs, farmers or smallholders.

The busiest time came during the first half of the 19th century, and as a result the town began to spread to the east and south and across the Brennig — although only to a limited extent, and this was mostly to do with the services needed by the farmers. There are records of there being some 20 inns at one time, although some of these were simply farms or houses where home brews were on offer. But Tregaron has an important place in the history of banking, for it can boast one of the two earliest Welsh banks. The 'Banc-y-Ddafad' opened at Aberystwyth in 1762 and amalgamated in 1810 to form the 'Aberystwyth & Tregaron Bank', its notes bearing the insignia of black sheep, or a lamb, according to their values. Like the 'Bank of the Black Ox' in Llandovery (pp.187-188) it was strongly supported by the drovers, who played a significant part in the economy of the town and surrounding areas during the first half of the 19th century. By the time George Borrow set off on his long tour of Wales in 1854, Tregaron had reached its heyday, as he was assured when he came upon a retired drover who was making his monthly business visit to the town. 'What kind of place is Tregaron?' he asked. 'Oh very good place, not quite as big as London, but very good place' was the reply! Although the population is still only a little over a thousand, what Tregaron did have was a great reputation for its wool, knitting and other woollen products (not to mention the use of fleeces to help support the railway line to cross the Cors Caron bog), and the many blacksmiths shops and others associated with the drover trade, all of which contributed towards the success of 'The Bank of the Black Sheep'.

Twm Siôn Catti

This however was not the only connection with black sheep, for Tregaron is also famous as the probable birthplace of Twm Siôn Catti, (*c.*1530–1609). A figure of legend and the subject of several books and references, a London play and at least two TV serials, at birth he was given the name Tomas Siôn, plus that of Catherine, his unmarried mother. It amounted in English to Thomas John son of Catherine and he eventually became Thomas Jones (or Johns). Much of what has been written is apocryphal and historically inaccurate but it seems clear that his life was divided into two main phases. Until he was almost 30 he had a reputation as a master of trickery and reckless pranks, producing his nickname of 'The Wild Wag of Wales' because of his practical jokes and raffish ways. He was also guilty of horse and cattle stealing, but was often considerate towards the poor and needy — producing his other nickname of the 'Robin Hood of Wales'. But he too was forced to become a fugitive from the authorities, sometimes hiding in a cave in deep rocky woodland in the upper reaches of the River Towy at Ystradffin. And so he might have continued, but for an amnesty to mark the accession of Good Queen Bess in 1559. Written in Latin, his pardon was addressed to 'Thome Johns, alias Cattye, lately of Tregaron &c.' and it forgave *omnia escapia et cautiones* ('all escapades and obligations'). From then on he largely turned over a new leaf, and the remaining chapters of his life as Thomas Jones were those of a member of the establishment, justice of the peace, mayor and sheriff of Brecon. He was also a significant scholar, poet and genealogist and, acknowledged by his supposed father, eventually became landowner of the Fountaingate estate, east of Tregaron. There he had assumed yet another role, as a resourceful drover of the farm livestock — who at least once had outwitted with inborn cunning and trickery a gullible highwayman who was gunning for the sale proceeds.

Tregaron drovers and the 'Apostle of Peace'

The Talbot Hotel in the market square

One other famous son of Tregaron was Henry Richard (1812–1888), a nonconformist minister who became internationally known as the 'Apostle of Peace'. He founded the Peace Union, forerunner of the League of Nations, and his bronze statue is on a granite pedestal in the market square in front of the Talbot Hotel, overlooking the Welsh Gold Design Centre and the Cambrian Contemporary Art Gallery. The Talbot has long been closely associated with the drovers' trade, as George Borrow discovered when researching for his book *Wild Wales* (1862), and enjoying in the process 'good entertainment, an excellent supper and very comfortable bed' (which may still be possible!). In his day the cattle were gathered and shod in a field behind the inn in preparation for the long trek into England. The most famous of the routes ran immediately to the east for 14 miles across wild mountain moorland that is sometimes known as the 'Desert of Wales', then down through Abergwesyn to Beulah heading towards the Wye and Usk valleys and eventually reaching the west midlands, London and south-east fattening grounds and markets. With the completion of the Central Wales Line in 1868, herds were instead driven to Llanwrtyd to be loaded on wagons for the journey into England, and soon the days of the cattle drovers were over. The movement of sheep on foot, involving ewe and lamb couples and yearling sheep from the end of May, ewes from the end of September and droves of wether lambs at the end of October, continued well into the 1930s until it gave way to lorry transport. The sheep droves followed much the same route from the Talbot Hotel at Tregaron — to the well-known farm at Nant-ystalwyn just north of the mountain road in the upper Tywi valley, and other key assembly points such as the Grouse Inn at Abergwesyn, the Garth Inn on the road to Builth Wells and across the Epynt plateau to the Market Tavern at Brecon, sometimes arriving with 1,200 sheep or more for the sales.

The route follows the trail of the herds from the market square, but now along a tarmac road signposted for Abergwesyn, Beulah and Llanwrtyd Wells rather than rough tracks as before, and it starts a memorable drive that will lead past some of the most spectacular mountain and moorland landscape in Britain. There are views that snatch the breath away — as indeed may some of the driving challenges, for the road is often really narrow, snakelike and short of passing places. But the remote and beautiful scenery of the Elenydd is such that few drivers are inclined to hurry along, even if it were possible.

The Abergwesyn Pass

After the Pentre area of the village there is a steady climb above the rivers Brennig and Berwyn and through the Cwm Berwyn forestry plantation that now totally envelopes Lake Berwyn close to the summit of the pass, then emerging 1,000 feet above Tregaron into the open at over 1,500 feet above sea level. A vast wild and empty plateau of rolling moorland and a seemingly boundless mountain landscape of grassy hills runs north to south along the spine of Wales and it is not difficult to feel 'on top of the world' here. There was an intention in the early 1970s to designate much of the Elenydd Range of the Cambrian Mountains as the fourth National Park of Wales — until opposing interests and some politicians were said to have put a stop to the proposals. But it would have been too late to provide any level of protection against the monotonous spread of conifers that began when the Forestry Commission was created in 1919, transforming huge areas of such mountain scenery and wildlife habitats.

Two views of the Abergwesyn Pass

After some 2 miles of steep descents and climbs the road re-enters forest land at Bwlch Esgair Gelli and winds its way down, past a parking area and lookout on the right, to meet with an upper length of the River Towy, just south of Nant-ystalwyn and not far from its source. After shadowing the river downstream for a mile there is a parting of the ways where the Tywi continues southwards to enter the Llyn Brianne Reservoir, a further 2 miles downstream. As an interesting detour here you can take a new forestry road that branches off to the right to follow it, and connect with another good new portion of road that has been built to replace the now deeply submerged old road — as part of the accommodation works connected with the water supply scheme for Swansea. Below the dam, the old road leads past Ystradffin and Twm Siôn Catti's cave on Dinas Hill, on the way downstream to Llandovery (p.190).

The Beulah Speckled Face sheep have been bred on the hills of Epynt, Llanafan, Abergwesyn and Llanwrtyd Wells for over one hundred years and are known for being easily managed and lambed because of their need of little attention in rugged conditions

Part of the way down this detour, there is another one leading off to the right for 1½ miles towards the isolated, tiny mountain chapel of **Soar-y-mynydd**, still there from the now distant days when there were many more hill farms, and worshippers who must mostly have attended on horseback. From there the road winds its narrow way back to the 'main' mountain pass road where it is necessary to turn right.

If ignoring the detour, or once back on the main route, the road continues uphill and after another 1½ miles of pine forest it arrives at '**The Devil's Staircase**', a formidable 1 in 4 descent of sharp hairpin bends to the Irfon Valley and to the former 'Irish Fords' that have been replaced by simple bridges. From there the road reaches the pass of 'The Wolf's Leap' and runs on a ledge above the River Irfon to a junction of two valleys at Abergwesyn. The Grouse Inn, once a rendezvous of the drovers, is now no more and has reverted to a former use as the Pentwyn farmhouse, while Llanfihangel Abergwesyn, dating from 1871, the survivor of two churches there, suffered collapse and was demolished in 1964.

Turn right at the junction to follow the narrow wooded Irfon glen to cross the river at Pont Newydd below Garn Dwad, close to the hillside church of **St. David, Llanwrtyd**. The circular churchyard suggests an early foundation and an inscribed Celtic pillar stone brought in from another site is thought to date from around the period. The present building is said to date from the 14th/15th centuries, while between 1740 and 1742, Williams Pantycelyn served as curate, along with the parishes of Abergwesyn and Llandewi. He worked under the Reverend Theopilus Evans, vicar of Llangammarch, who in 1732 had unwittingly been responsible for transforming part of his quiet pastoral charge into a hugely popular spa town and holiday resort.

---

7. Llanwrtyd Wells. A frog and the vicar's scurvy

It was not unusual during the early 18th century for many people to suffer from scurvy. It is caused by vitamin deficiencies, especially vitamin C, and the most extreme instances occurred at sea — caused by inadequate diets on long voyages. (A bad example occurred during an expedition round the world between 1740 and 1744, when of 1,955 crew, 997 died of scurvy — added to 320 others who had been

---

ravaged by fevers and dysentery!) It could be just as bad on dry land, and was not confined to the under-privileged, and so it was that the Revd. Evans was a sufferer. He could well have been bleeding painfully into his muscles and joints and from his gums, with loose teeth and other debilitating and even life-threatening symptoms. The story goes that, while walking through Dolycoed Park at Llanwrtyd he noticed a very lively frog in a well that reeked of bad eggs — not for nothing known locally for many years as 'Ffynnon drewllyd' (stinking well). Believing that the sprightliness of the frog came from the water, which could not be poisonous, and willing to try anything, he drank some himself, had more and within a very short while his lost appetite returned, and after two months of drinking and immersing himself in it he is said to have been cured of the disease. (This book is not able to explain how a solution of hydrogen sulphide, lacking as it does any vitamin C, could have had any effect. Maybe it was a matter of Faith, or perhaps the vicar's regained appetite led to him eating up all his greens and fruit — even trying an orange or two?).

This was quite early in the period when 'taking the waters' was starting to be popular and in due course there were four groups of well offering treatments at Llanwrtyd — the Dolycoed (the upgraded Stinking Well), Victoria, Abernant and Henfryn.

That they existed at all was because, in an otherwise geologically sedimentary part of Breconshire, they were in an outcrop region of igneous volcanic rocks. These accounted for mineral springs that issued also at Llangammarch, Builth, Llandrindod and Llandegley, which duly became spas too.

In 1868 the 10-mile Vale of Towy railway extension from Llandeilo to Llandovery, taking in the Sugar Loaf tunnel and Cynghordy Viaduct (p.189), finally linked the south Wales main lines to Llanelli and Swansea with Shrewsbury and the north-west of England. After that, visitors — especially from industrial areas of south Wales — soon started to arrive at the new station, and they came not just for the waters to ease their ailments but also to breathe in the pure and bracing air at above 700 feet and to enjoy the pleasures of the wonderful countryside as holidaymakers. Hotels, boarding houses, pubs and eating places were soon being built to cater for them, and to mark the queen's Golden Jubilee, the Victoria Wells opened in 1897, becoming a base for regular impromptu concerts and eisteddfodau, this being a very Welsh community. There were many steel and tinplate workers from Llanelli (p.51) whose leading products included kitchen equipment, and especially saucepans. So when they heard the song 'Sosban Fach' ('little saucepan') being sung at Llanwrtyd they adopted it for their own and sang it with great gusto at every opportunity. There is now a plaque on Britannia House, next to the post office, which reads in English and Welsh 'The famous Welsh folk song *Sosban Fach* was composed by visitors from industrialised west Wales. Famously sung by tin plate workers from Llanelli. Centenary celebrated 1995'. At Llanelli, the mighty 'Scarlets', Llanelli Rugby Club who have saucepans on top of their goal posts, have adopted it, and many versions, as their team and supporters' anthem.

While most signs of wells, spas and pump rooms have now gone, many of today's hotels, boarding houses and lofty town houses remain from the Victorian and Edwardian heydays, not least Carlton House in Dolycoed Road which in 2006 had a vaunted Michelin Star for its restaurant. And despite Dr. Beeching, there is still a rail service and the **station** has been winning top prizes in 'Wales in Bloom' competitions, thanks largely to a local action group. The liveliness of more than 100 years ago is now matched by an annual calendar of events quite remarkable for a town with a census population in 2001 of just 604, officially 'The smallest town in Britain'. The **Neuadd Arms Hotel** in the main square (official HQ of the 'Monster Raving Looney Party'), serves as the base for well supported, although at times bizarre, entertainments that run throughout the year. There are Saturnalia events in January, a 'Man and Horse' Marathon in June, Bog Snorkelling Championships in July and August, carriage driving in September and pony trekking, walks and festivals at other times. **The Red Kite Activity Centre** and **Red Kite Mountain Bike Centre** are based at the hotel, and on the nearby town green, alongside the main road passing through the town, can be seen a striking steel sculpture of the red kite, created in the late 1990s by Sandy O'Connor. The proximity of the A483, running between Swansea in the south-west, through Llanwrtyd to Chester and the north-west of England, combines with the Shrewsbury to Llanelli and Swansea Heart of Wales railway line to help maintain the long-established appeal and vibrancy of this small town in the beautiful surroundings of the Irfon Valley.

Turning left from the main square onto the A483, the route heads for the upper Wye Valley and after ½ mile reaches the **Cambrian Woollen Mill** on the left. Dating from the 1820s, this was once a corn mill but in 1918 was converted to wool weaving for the benefit of disabled ex-servicemen. Jobs have since been extended to others and tours of the mill and looms are offered, as are opportunities to buy from a wide range of the Welsh tweeds and other woven articles.

Meanwhile the River Irfon has turned away for Llangammarch Wells, second of the spa towns, and is rejoined beyond Beulah, near Garth railway station, and after another 3 miles, road, rail and river reach **Cilmery**, at the approach to Builth Wells.

8. Cilmery and Llewelyn, 'Ein Llyw Olaf' — Our Last Leader

The memorial stone to Llewelyn ap Gruffudd

Near here, Llewelyn ap Gruffudd (1246–1282), the last national prince of Wales and grandson of the legendary Llewelyn the Great (1194–1240), was killed in a chance encounter with a small English force and beheaded. The year 1282 is said to be as familiar to many Welsh school children as 1066 is to their English counterparts, and a site has been chosen on the right-hand side of the A483 for a memorial that has become a focus for Welsh national inspiration. Llewelyn had obtained grudging recognition of Welsh independence from England at the Treaty of Montgomery in 1267, but after the death of Henry III, his authority had been crushed when the formidable Edward I assumed the English throne, and with it his dream for the Welsh people. Edward made his own surviving son, Edward, prince of Wales in 1301 and since then the eldest son of the reigning monarch has usually been created Prince of Wales.

A huge granite standing stone from near Llewelyn's Caernarvonshire birthplace has been erected on an earth mound, replacing an earlier memorial of 1902. Parts of this have been built into the approach steps, and around the site there are 13 oaks, one for each Welsh county — while the stone is rarely without a tribute of flowers. At the entrance from the road there are two stones, in English and in Welsh inscribed: 'Near this spot was killed our Prince Llewelyn. 1282' and 'Ger y fan hwn y lladwyd Llewelyn. Ein llyw olaf. 1282'.

The head was displayed at Rhuddlan Castle before the king, and then at the Tower of London, while there is a local tradition that Llewelyn's headless torso is buried near Cefn y bedd close to here. But there are also stories that his remains were carried the 13 miles to the Cistercian abbey of Cwmhir, where there is now an inscribed stone tablet near the site of the high altar, also a place of pilgrimage.

Leaving Cilmery past the Prince Llewelyn Inn near the station and continuing within sight of the sandstone escarpment of Mynydd Epynt, the A483 soon arrives at Builth Wells, the third spa town along the Irfon — which here enters the River Wye about a mile upstream from the main road bridge. Close by, the car park, recreation ground and new TIC at The Groe can be reached by following the direction signs for through traffic, and looking for the entrance on the left.

9. Builth Wells. A Meeting of the Ways

Looking along the one-way Broad Street

The car park makes a good starting place for a pleasant stroll along the riverside footpath beneath an avenue of trees and beside the tennis courts, swimming pool, putting area and bowling green to where, joined by the Chefri, the River Irfon flows into the Wye. This forms part of the 111 mile-long *Wye Valley Walk* that follows the river from its junction with the Severn at Chepstow — to Rhayader, where this tour is soon to arrive. If you follow the path, it turns left at the confluence and shadows the Irfon as far as the Rhosferig footbridge. This was built in 1984 to replace an earlier crossing that gave access to Park Wells. These, with Glanne Wells, served the many visitors who wished to drink, be immersed in or showered or sprayed with the saline, sulphurous or chalybeate (iron) waters in which they had placed so much faith for the improvement of their health.

Turning right after the bridge, the path returns to the bank of the Wye and continues upstream towards the awesome rapids and deep pools of Pen ddol rocks.

Taking the opposite direction from the car park and passing the TIC, the route of the *Walk* follows The Strand to the southern approach of the Georgian Wye Bridge. According to a commemorative stone

The Wyeside Arts Centre near the bridge over the Wye in Builth

set on the upstream parapet it was built with six three-centred arches by James Parry of Hay on Wye in 1779, cut waters were added in 1820, but by the onset of the Motor Age its width was soon inadequate. It was 1925 before any widening took place, strengthening works followed in 1975 and the width is now 30 feet, over a length from the Breconshire to Radnorshire sides of 275 feet. But despite considerable changes that have included adopting modern structural materials and reinforcement, the bridge still continues to be one of the most elegant in appearance along the whole course of the River Wye.

According to late 13th-century records, this was not the first bridge to appear here, and there was also a ferry, while according to Leland in the 16th century, Builth had the only bridge across the Wye after Hereford — over 50 miles downstream. Other timber bridges followed during the 18th century but they were either destroyed by floodwaters or severely damaged by ice.

It is this river crossing that established the historic significance of Builth. There has not yet been visible sign of any Roman interest, but the strategic importance was not lost on the Norman invaders who appeared in the mid-1090s. There is evidence of a timber motte and bailey castle being sited to protect the crossing by 1168, it had to be refortified early in the 13th century and afterwards was subjected to repeated attack until it was destroyed by Llewelyn ap Gruffudd in 1260. Then in 1277, in a bid to suppress the recalcitrant Welsh, Edward I built a much more formidable stone fortification, at the same time placing castles at Aberystwyth, Rhuddlan and Flint. This was the first phase of a huge and costly building programme that, by the end of the 13th century, produced a total of ten new castles reinforcing an arc around the Snowdonia fastnesses of Welsh resistance, at Harlech, Caernarvon, Beaumaris, Conwy, Ruthin and Hope.

Befitting its role as the hub of a great crown lordship, **Builth Castle** was built to impressive standards in a commanding position over the river and surrounding territory. To a concentric plan, it is thought to have consisted of a tall shell keep placed high on a large mound within a stone curtain wall defended by six towers — a chemise. An outer curtain wall encompassed baileys, a Great Hall, domestic quarters and the chapel, while a drawbridge over the wet moat was flanked by another two towers. This led across to the outer side of a daunting counterscarp bank, and to what could well have been an early settlement. It was as the building work was being completed in 1282 that Llewelyn ap Gruffudd appeared in an attempt to persuade the garrison to support him against the king. He was spurned by John Gifford, the first Governor, not allowed to enter, left to the mercy of his English enemies and killed just outside the town. This act of treachery left the entire local population to share in long-held and undeserved stigma as 'The Traitors of Builth'.

The substantial motte of Builth's castle

The castle fulfilled its intended role during the turbulent 14th century and early in the 1400s stood up to an assault by forces of Owain Glyndwr, remaining effective and not to be taken for the rest of the century. But after that, neglect and dilapidation set in, hastened by 'quarrying' activities of local Elizabethans, who stand accused of removing every last stone for their own building schemes. All that was left of the fine Edwardian fortress was a complex layout of earthworks that quickly became overgrown. This has been largely forgotten during the past 450 years, while even Aberystwyth Castle (pp.199-200) has some vestige of its former royal state, and despite the passing of the centuries, the Edwardian castles at Harlech, Caernarvon, Beaumaris, Conwy and Rhuddlan still offer a formidable presence and great romantic appeal.

But all that is left of Builth Castle may be seen by following the *Wye Valley Walk* southwards as far as the lane beside the Lion Hotel, beyond the foot of the bridge at 2 Broad Street. There is an informative plaque at a right-angled turn to the left, not far before the stile on the boundary of just banks, ditches, the motte and other earthworks.

As well as suffering from violent bouts of warfare during the Middle Ages, the stamina of Builth was badly weakened by plague in 1350, and then on 20 December 1691, the whole town was almost totally destroyed by fire. Consequently, with few exceptions, notably the 14th-century tower of St. Mary's Church, the architecture dates from the 18th century but is mainly of Victorian and Edwardian periods.

There are several so-called planned or 'planted' towns and settlements in Wales and the Marches, extending back from modern times to the days of the Normans and Romans, and often under the protection of a castle. But Builth is not one of them. During the 100 years and more after the 'Great Fire', the surviving remnants of 80 of its former houses are said to have 'mushroomed' to a state that in 1803, with the town population at around 700, was described as 'dilapidated antiquity', the main street 'as fashionless, as miserable and as dirty' as anything the writer had seen. It is evident that during the passing of 200 further years, Builth has not experienced much more in the way of formal town planning, the ancient street pattern continues to be irregular and narrow and it is struggling hard to cope with 21st-century traffic. The first major change to occur was in the middle of the 19th century when Builth became a fashionable spa and holiday resort and there was a further surge when, from the mid 1860s, visitors started to arrive by train on the Cambrian and LNWR lines. It was necessary to augment the limited accommodation provided by the early 19th-century Lion Hotel, the Crown Hotel and other existing hostelries and more shops and service premises were introduced in and around Broad Street and High Street. Then in 1875 a colourful, arcaded Market House (now the **Wyeside Arts Centre**) was built in Castle Street, close to the Wye Bridge, and during the same period St. Mary's Church was rebuilt. Its dedication originates with the Normans and the name forms part of *Llanfair ym Muallt*, as Builth is known by the Welsh, (Builth coming from *Buallt*, which is thought possibly to arise from *Bu* and *Allt* — meaning 'the wild ox of the wooded slope'). There is a large churchyard, and round it are ranged the Alpha Presbyterian Chapel of 1903 and 1747, Horeb Congregational Chapel, 1869, and the Baptist Chapel of 1899.

As well as providing for their spiritual needs, the town went all out in other ways to cater for the visitors, as when the main hotels arranged early in the 20th century for omnibuses to attend train arrivals and departures. But before long, interest in 'taking the waters' started to ebb and holidaymakers were opting more for dipping in sea water at flourishing resorts around the coasts. Soon the economy of Builth came to depend strongly on its traditional position as the market centre for a huge sheep-farming hinterland of Breconshire and Radnorshire, while it also served as a much appreciated rendezvous for farmers, shepherds and their families who at most other times were out in remote and lonely hill-farms. They still add significantly each week to the 2001 population of 2,352 residents, while the opening of the Royal Welsh Showground just across the river at Llanelwedd brings in immeasurably more people, most of all in July each year when it hosts the hugely popular Royal Welsh Agricultural Show.

St. Mary's Church

The tour continues by turning left out of The Groe car park into The Strand (or carry straight on if you have chosen not to stop in Builth). Turn left at the junction by the Wye bridge to cross the bridge, taking note of the heavily scarred landscape to the right, where extensive quarries at Llanelwedd have been blasted, in no small measure between 1893 and 1904 in order to provide masonry to build the Elan dams and water works (p.252). Close to the site of the former Builth Wells Cambrian Railway Station, the tour takes the first exit at the roundabout near the main Showground Entrance to join the A470 for Rhayader.

After a short distance the A470 parts company with the Wye for a few miles then crosses the River Ithon. At Newbridge-on-Wye it might be worth making a short detour on the B4358 towards Llandrindod, breaking off right at the signpost for **Disserth** to see the tiny 13th- century, mainly whitewashed church of St. Cewydd.

---

10. Disserth, and laying an evil spirit

The charm of St. Cewydd's embraces its setting close to the River Ithon, despite a neighbouring caravan site. It is one of a number of churches to be found in a circular churchyard, which indicates that it was founded as an early Christian site in the Dark Ages. One of the bells has been calling the faithful to worship since about 1300 and inside, the 17th-century high-backed box pews are painted with names of owners and their dates from between 1666 and 1714. They also identify more recent proprietors, who include James Watt the Scottish engineer (see below), who was a member of the congregation in the early 19th century. From 1687 sermons would have been delivered from the distinctive three level pulpit, installed that year, while more could perhaps have been made by the inattentive of the wall paintings, which can still be recognised in their fragmented state.

But it has not always been serene and peaceful at Disserth, for according to local folklore there was an evil spirit about, requiring for its subjugation an assembly of parsons at the church, complete with books and candles. During his lifetime, Charles Lewis had been a tanner from nearby Henllys and had earned a reputation as a dishonest scoundrel for the way he juggled his weights — according to whether he was buying or selling. After his death he was buried in the churchyard at Disserth, but his spirit was said to persist in accosting anyone who passed Henllys at night. So the evil tormentor was summoned to appear before the spirit-laying assembly, and by prayer, solemn anathema, and with no small difficulty, was reduced to the size of a bluebottle fly, popped into a snuff box and dropped into a well, or other safe place, never to re-emerge.

After Newbridge the A470 and River Wye converge and remain close companions all the way to Rhayader (and beyond), parting slightly at Doldowlod. Here the dismantled railway station and yard have been laid out as an unobtrusive Caravan Club site. Rightly said to enjoy 'glorious views of the surrounding hills', it is part of the estate created by the son of James Watt. His work in the improvement of the steam engine played a crucial part during the Industrial Revolution and his descendents have continued to live at Doldowlod House. The whole area contains a variety of unfamiliar wildlife, and at **Dyffryn Wood**, ¾ mile short of Rhayader, the Royal Society for the Protection of Birds has a nature reserve and lay-by parking on the opposite side of the A470. Just 300 yards south of Rhayader town centre the farmer at **Gigrin Farm** has provided several bird hides, suitable for wheelchair access, where it is possible to 'watch breathtaking feats of aerial piracy as 60 or more red kites swoop down to feed to within 25 yards, competing with opportunistic buzzards and ravens for choice pickings!'. The birds are fed each day at 2pm from October to March and 3pm during the summer, and the 198-acre farm also contains an interpretive centre, nature trail, bird reserve, picnic site, children's play area and badger viewing via CCTV.

11. Rhayader. Waterfall on the Wye

The Wye at Rhayader

The town's earliest days date from the 5th century and it has known much warfare and lawlessness. A **castle** was built by the Welsh in *c*.1177; a much mutilated motte which is mainly on private property and can be seen from the Elan Valley road near the church. There is another, south of the church on part of a public playground, which followed in around 1200. Years later a sitting Assize judge was murdered here by bandits, and in the 1840s the Rebecca rioters — farmers dressed as women and with blackened faces — violently assaulted the toll-gates and gatherers at the town approaches. The name of the town is a curiously Anglicised version of Rhaeadr Gwy, Welsh for 'Waterfall on the Wye'.

The Clock Tower junction at Rhayader

The head of the Elan valley reservoirs, near the junction of roads at Pont ar Elen

At **Rhayader** the road becomes South Street and passes the former Victorian Workhouses, more recently the Brynavon Country House Hotel and Workhouse Restaurant, and arrives at the War Memorial Town Clock Tower at the main crossroads. It is at the starting, or finishing, point of the official *Wye Valley Walk* between there and Chepstow, 111 miles downstream.

The tour continues to the 'Lakeland' of mid-Wales by turning left at the war memorial and along West Street and over the river bridge of 1780. The river channel, which had produced a truly spectacular cataract until then, especially in times of flood, was widened at the same time but even the present waterfall can be quite impressive (but do not be tempted to emulate local youths who have been known to jump from the bridge parapet into the pool below!).

The B4518 soon shadows the River Elan appearing to its left and then passes by Elan Village down below, originally built for the first Elan Estate employees, and a side road to the left leads to the **visitor centre**.

The road continues through vast open moorland, much of which may eventually be submerged if the new dam at **Craig Coch** receives the go ahead, to connect with the ancient Rhayader to Devil's Bridge mountain road at Pont ar Elen.

12. The Elan and Claerwen Valleys. Lakeland of mid Wales

The Visitor Centre, open each day from Easter until the end of October, offers a wide range of maps, books, fact-sheets, as well as mounting exhibitions and audio-visual presentations. Countryside Rangers encourage nature conservation and help the public to enjoy the area — leading more than 100 free events each year, including guided walks and bird-watching trips on the 70 square miles estate. The Elan Valley Dams were built after Birmingham Corporation compulsorily acquired land in 1892 in order to provide clean water for its ever-growing population. In the process houses, farms, meadows, woods and other features were submerged under 100 feet of water and a community of some 400 people was dispersed, with little or no recompense. The epic work of James Mansergh, who had begun with his search for a site as far back as 1861, the three Elan dams were commissioned in 1904. The first looms to a height of 122 feet just above the Visitor Centre. It contains a submerged dam about a mile upstream to ensure sufficient head of water at **Garreg ddu**, so as to feed the aqueduct at the Foel Tower to carry water by gravity for the 73 miles to the Frankley Reservoir in Birmingham. Just visible above the reservoir are remains of the redundant **Nant-y-Gro dam** that was used for underwater explosion tests during planning of the Dambuster raid of May 1943. The **Claerwen**, largest of the present reservoirs, reached on a detour across the Garreg ddu viaduct to the left, was constructed between 1936 and 1952 and, holding 10,626 million gallons, impounds almost more water than all the others combined. It was opened by Queen Elizabeth II at one of her earliest ceremonies as sovereign — just under half a century after her great-grandfather, King Edward VII, fulfilled a similar role at Elan. **Pen-y-Garreg** has an island and, as at the others, there is a small parking area for soaking in the view. The top dam is **Craig Coch** and it is some 120 feet high. In a catchment area receiving an average rainfall of 65 inches a year, the Water Supply Scheme supplies enough water to keep the Rivers Elan and Wye flowing, sufficient to serve Birmingham and parts of Staffordshire and Radnorshire and, in times of drought, areas of south Wales through a downstream transfer from the Wye to the Usk.

Proposals have recently been announced for a new dam at Craig Coch, which at 320 feet will be three times the height of the present dam. If it proceeds, it will contain 55 billion gallons, becoming Europe's largest man-made reservoir. For future days of climate change and major water shortages it is being seen as the centrepiece of a new national water grid which will convey water from Wales to taps in London or Suffolk. There will be many years of planning ahead, involving land incorporating 12 Sites of Special Scientific Interest, ranging from ancient pasture and meadows to woodland and rare upland marshes—and with special protection under the EC directive on wild birds. The Welsh community, not least dispossessed long-serving farmers who were unhappy about aspects of the Elan scheme, might also have much to contribute.

Water coming over the cill of the Pen-y-Garreg dam in the Elan valley

The route turns left onto the mountain road, signposted to Cwmystwyth, and quickly reaches a long feature entering from the left, shown on the 1999 OS Explorer 200 map as a 'Byway open to all traffic' (see box no.13).

The route moves onwards up the valley alongside the Elan, now little more than a mountain stream as it snakes its way in the opposite direction towards the reservoir. Sheep are everywhere over the wild open mountain and a wind farm can be seen on the horizon beyond isolated farms. But for the driver it is best to concentrate on the road, for although it is generally wide enough for two passing cars, it is necessary to keep clear of the edge of the tarmac as the road ahead winds almost as much as does the river just below. When the watershed at Blaen-y-cwm is reached, it is worth pulling over to the parking area on the opposite side of the road to take in the mountain air, the immense views far across the mountains and the instructive contents of an Information Board.

Upon returning to the road, a small bridge is crossed on reaching the Powys/Ceredigion border to enter the Ystwyth Valley. There are soon steep twists and turns alongside the infant river, and during the narrow descent it pays to note passing places and also watch out for drainage ditches just beyond the white edge-of-carriageway marking. After the reappearance of roadside boundary fences there is one more steep descent to a sharp left turn at the approach to **Cwmystwyth**, just by a prominent well-executed farmhouse and barn conversion, named after Esgair Wen, below which it stands. This towering ridge rises to *c*.1650 feet and lies just to the east of Bryn Copa, or Copa Hill, which, along with the Great Orme at Llandudno,

---

13. The Monks Trod or Sarn Elenydd

This 'byway' is along a part of the 25 mile 'Monks Trod' over the Cambrian Mountains between the 12th-century monasteries of Ystrad Fflur (Strata Florida, see pp.238-240) and Abbey Cwmhir. It reaches its highest point at nearly 1,800 feet above sea level and provides walkers with stunning panoramic views of the upland plateaux of central Wales. Also known as Sarn Elenydd, the path follows a much earlier, possibly prehistoric, one (there are the remains of prehistoric hut circles on some of the nearby hills) and over time it has acquired historical, cultural, spiritual and, not least, ecological meaning. It therefore became a matter of great and widespread concern when the authorities gave approval for the 5-mile length between Pont ar Elen and Claerwen to become open for use by 4 x 4 vehicles and off-the-road motor-cycles. Widespread damage soon resulted, not only to the path but also adjacent areas of land — as well as to the peace and quiet of the mountains and farms. Eventually the abuses were stopped, in the hope that the damaged areas would in time regenerate, and it remains to be seen what will happen there next.

The Rhayader to Devil's Bridge Mountain Road

This route, being narrower and with stiffer gradients than modern A roads, was, until early in the 19th century, part of the important coaching route linking London and Aberystwyth. There are no clues as to its actual age, but it was first mapped at 1 inch to 1 mile in John Ogilby's *Britannia Road Book* towards the end of the 17th century. A two-man survey team had travelled from London, along a route corresponding very much to today's A44, and had started the task at the then wooden bridge that spanned the Wye at Rhayader. One member of the team rode a horse and the other pushed a wheeled distance-measuring device, and distances from London were plotted at every mile-point on the strip-form map. Their first 14 miles took them through really wild and mountainous territory, and across countless watercourses, and after the first 4 miles they had reached *c*.1,600 feet above sea level. They then followed a descent to the upper Elan valley and a fairly level section until climbing again to 1,320 feet at the Elan/Ystwyth watershed. After that it was a steady drop to 'Ecomistwith' (Cwmystwyth), followed soon by another climb to a 1,240 feet crest above Devil's Bridge, before eventually reaching 'Aberistwith' — 199 miles and 2 furlongs away from Cornhill in London.

The present A44 route opened in the early 1830s, with only one summit of 1,358 feet above sea level, at Eisteddfa Gurig, and for the next century the mountain road was almost abandoned and it rapidly crumbled. But in the mid-1930s major restoration works were undertaken, fords were bridged, surface water drains were laid and the track formation was rebuilt and surfaced with tarmacadam. So now, and especially since the building of the spectacular Elan dams and reservoirs and the growth of tourism, this ancient highway has become busier (but far from excessively) than it ever was before.

has an important place in the history of mining in Wales — not for coal, but copper (although Copa is not named after the metal but is the Welsh word for top, crest or summit). Recent research has shown that working took place at the top of a copper lode here during a period lasting for up to 600 years, starting at *c*.2000 BC and was concluded during the early Bronze Age. Radio-carbon dating of charcoal remains on the hill confirmed that this was the earliest mine to be worked at Cwmystwyth, and as the road proceeds towards the village there is soon bleak evidence of a quest for metals that continued there for periods during another 4,000 years, until early in the 20th century. It lies at the south-east corner of a large metallic ore field between the hills of the Ystwyth, Rheidol, Levi, Dyfi and Mynach rivers, bounded by the western coastline and the heights of Plynlimon to the east, that has yielded copper, lead, silver, zinc, nickel and even a little gold.

On this final stretch of the return to Aberystwyth, which was once the port for much of the lead ore that was being sent to the smelteries, and had a Licensed Royal Mint for coining the silver, this tour will pass three of a great number of mines that were once active in the region: Cwmystwyth, Llywernog and Goginan.

14. Northern Ceredigion lead and silver mining

Cwmystwyth

The Early Mines Research Group of archaeologists and mining engineers discovered signs that lead veins were worked in later stages of Bronze Age activity, high above the road at Bryn Copa. The Cwmystwyth workings extend for a mile down the valley towards the village and mostly occupy the north side, although extending in places across the road closer to the River Ystwyth to the south. The argentiferous galena converted to *c*.80% of lead metal, making this mine one of the richest and most important in Britain. It was known to the Romans, who extracted the lead for roofing, lining baths and conveying water back in Rome, while the Normans in their turn used it in the many castles and other buildings in Wales. But later regimes were more interested in the silver impurity that was present in the ore and minted it into coinage to pay and equip their armies. The boom years for the industry came between the 1840s and late 1870s, with a peak in 1856 when 8,560 tons of lead ore are said to have been produced, yielding 38,751 ounces of silver. But not long afterwards a decline set in, largely because of severe competition from cheap imported ore from newly discovered sources in Australia and the USA. After a brief attempt to convert to zinc production in 1899, operations at Cwmystwyth ended in 1916.

Some of the mining remains at Cwmystwyth

Almost 100 years later, much of the valley beside the road is still left with the dangerous remnants of disused and unprotected mine shafts, tunnels, adits and levels, vast spoil heaps and derelict, collapsing buildings. One feeling is that the entire area should have been 'tidied up and landscaped' many years ago, but another view is that it should be made safe and conserved as an important heritage site — to represent an industry that was vital to the economy of the region and the whole of Britain until the early 20th century. To some extent, this is what has been done through a private enterprise scheme at the Llywernog silver/lead mine alongside the A44 at Ponterwyd.

Llywernog

Shallow veins were discovered here in the early 1740s and ore was first extracted by opencast or shallow mining until greater depths were reached later in the century by the use of hand drills and gunpowder charges. The name 'Gwaith Poole', or 'Poole's Mine' after an early 19th-century tenant, has been remembered by local people — whose forbears may have worked there to depths of 180 feet at the 'old mine' and eventually 432 feet in the main shaft. By the 1850s the outlook for the mine was good with a boom in lead prices, but fortunes fluctuated greatly over the years, sometimes even in a single year as in 1869. This started as the year of 'The Great Bonanza' when record amounts of silver/lead ore were raised during the spring, and until the driest summer on record. An absence of rain, thought to have been for 6 weeks or more, dried the water courses, brought the great water-pumping wheel to a halt and placed the rich sources of ore out of reach beneath several feet of water. A steam operated engine and pump was belatedly installed the following year and for the first time all the men were able to continue working. But it was nearly too late and after periods of bad weather, sporadic activity, reduced demand and foreign competition, the mine closed completely in 1910. The area soon became overgrown, buildings started to crumble and in 1953 the landmark 50ft-diameter waterwheel, so often seen by travellers on the main road, was scrapped.

But that did not mark the end of 'Poole's Mine', for just over 10 years later it was revived as '**a museum to the past mining industry**'. Evidence of the activity from the 1740s at this typical small lead/silver mine can be seen by following a 'Miners' Trail' along a self-guide footpath system linking the various natural and man-made features. Part of the way around the 7-acre site leads deep underground, but starts with the huge pit of the overshot waterwheel that drove the pumps in the main 'engine shaft' and

Llywernog silver-lead mine museum

turned the rollers in the rock crusher. Other surface features along the Trail include a replica of a horse-whim used for winding ore from underground workings, the rock crusher house, jigger shed and waterwheels, while there is also a panning shed where it is possible to work the mine material for silver/lead ore and iron pyrites which you can keep. There are also exhibitions on Welsh gold mining and panning techniques, a souvenir shop and tea room, and the site in 2006 was open, with set admission times, from April until October (not Saturdays).

Goginan

This mine is thought to have been worked from Roman times and was one of the largest in the region until it finally closed in 1886. It reached a depth of 130 fathoms, or 780 feet, and was predominantly worked for silver, from 1837 producing ½ million ounces of the metal along with 25,000 tons of lead ore. The power mainly came from up to 12 large waterwheels fed by long leats and streams and reservoirs in the mountains, later supplemented by a steam engine. There is now little to see of this famous mine but the results of 'quarrying' of the stonework for other purposes and more recent 'landscaping'.

After crossing a cattle grid and still following the Ystwyth, the road makes a more leafy descent towards the village of Pentre, and where John Paterson's Road Book of around the turn of the 19th century showed a small inn that had probably been a haunt of thirsty lead miners. The B4574 appears as a sharp turn just beyond, the right hand section leading towards Devil's Bridge — which is the one taken by the main tour.

However, for an interesting detour, the left one continues in the direction of the Ystwyth to join the B4343 for Pont-rhyd-y-groes. After 1 mile the road reaches **Eglwys Newydd**, down on the left, and then a Forestry Commission car park on what many know as *Peacocks in Paradise* territory.

St. Michael's church, or Eglwys Newydd

This is a reference to a work that amounts to a biography by Elizabeth Inglis-Jones of an extraordinary estate — as the sub-title puts it: *The Story of a House – its Owners and the Elysium they established there, in the mountains of Wales, in the 18th century*.

15. Hafod. Thomas Johnes and the 'Picturesque'

There had been a house of some interest on the site from Elizabethan times, until the sorry relics of a very grand mansion had to be blown up in 1959 on public safety grounds. The estate changed hands many times, until finally the ruins and surrounding land were bought in 1950 by the Forestry Commission. But Hafod is associated almost exclusively with one man: Thomas Johnes (1748–1816) and his vision. His grandfather, also Thomas Johnes, married well into the wealthy Knight ironmaster family of Downton in Herefordshire and moved into their nearby Croft Castle home. Born at Ludlow in the family town house, the young Thomas was brought up at Croft, and after schooling in Shrewsbury then Eton, Edinburgh and two years abroad, he visited the family estates in Wales, which included Hafod, in a remote part of Ceredigion. He immediately knew he had found 'Paradise' — 'amidst bleak hills, boggy hollows, steep slopes and narrow valleys', all of which, and much more, he inherited in 1780 upon the death of his father. His first wife died two years later and the following year, he moved to Hafod with Jane, his second wife. In 1784 their only child to survive, Martha Anne, who became known as Mariamne, was born. Johnes quickly set about building a splendid mansion to the design of Thomas Baldwin, city architect of Bath, and by early 1788 it was mainly completed, except for elegant wings that were added soon after by the then almost unknown John Nash. It was shaped in classical style, but enhanced in detail with pseudo-Gothic elements such as pointed windows and pinnacles and was said perfectly to complement its wild surroundings. The interior was lavish, and Johnes' most treasured possessions — a very fine collection of books, much of it priceless rich Welsh literature — was housed in a splendid octagonal-shaped library with a prominent copper-covered domed roof. A Member of Parliament and the Lord Lieutenant, he owned a vast acreage in the county and indulged passions for model farming and forestry, judicious stock breeding and planting literally millions of trees from his tree nurseries. But there were also many rare species from afar that he introduced as part of a consuming passion for landscape gardening, which he shared with his cousin, Richard Payne-Knight at Downton Castle and Sir Uvedale Price of nearby Foxley in Herefordshire. They were two leading exponents of the concept of '**the Picturesque**' of the day, whereby a landscape was meant to have the qualities of a fine painting. This had evolved to a great extent from writings about 'the principles of picturesque beauty' by the Reverend William Gilpin, contained in *Observations on the River Wye and Several Parts of South Wales ...* (1782) and Hafod possessed all the essential components — of a wild mountain background, caverns, rocks and crags, old woodland, rushing streams and waterfalls. By 1788, with collaboration from his cousin and Uvedale Price, Thomas Johnes converted one of the wildest and lawless parts of 18th-century Ceredigion into a spectacular Welsh meeting place for illustrious visitors and romantics as one of the finest examples of 'the Picturesque'. An idea of the scene is shown in the watercolour by William Turner, who visited in 1798, and students of works by the poet S.T. Coleridge, who passed through on a walking tour in 1793, do not discount the possibility that he remembered Hafod when he wrote *Kubla Khan*:

> In Xanadu did Kubla Khan
> A stately pleasure-dome decree
> Where Alph, the sacred river, ran
> Through caverns measureless to man
> Down to a sunless sea ...
> And there were gardens bright with sinuous rill
> Where blossomed many an incense-bearing tree;
> And here were forests ancient as the hills,
> Enfolding sunny spots of greenery ...

The Johnes family graves in the churchyard
at Eglwys Newydd

But in 1807, the Picturesque scene at Hafod changed into one of utter devastation, when a relentless blaze destroyed the work of 30 years in just three hours. The losses included the collection of priceless manuscripts and books that were reduced to ashes, along with much else, leaving only the outer walls of the mansion. However Johnes decided to rebuild, again engaging Thomas Baldwin, but this time, now that he was almost 60, it would all be for Mariamne. The builders dragged out the rebuilding work for three years until late in 1810, and the family had hardly moved back in before Fate delivered another bitter blow. Just four days after her 27th birthday, Mariamne, their adored only heir, died on 4 July 1811. Thomas Johnes survived her by just five years, Jane, his wife, died in 1833 and they and Mariamne are buried in a family vault in the churchyard of Eglwys Newydd, not far from the poignant marble memorial within the church featuring all three in a moving group, famously sculpted by Francis Chantrey.

In 1932, disaster struck once more at Hafod, and this time the church was gutted by fire. Fortunately the outward appearance of the building remained much as James Wyatt had designed it for Thomas Johnes in 1801 and restoration was sympathetically managed by W.D. Caröe, St. Davids diocesan architect, who displayed the calcined monument behind an open screen.

In 1994 the Hafod Trust, in partnership with the Forestry Commission (Wales), embarked on long-term objectives: 'to continue the restructuring of the historic landscape as a working wooded parkland in the style of the Picturesque, and with enhanced biodiversity; to improve and sustain standards of conservation and maintenance of the estate and its historical features, appropriate to its grade I ranking and other designations, and to develop community participation together with training, education and interpretation for visitors, consistent with best practice nationally'. In an illustrated history and guide, *The Hafod Landscape*, the Trust describes a variety of walks extending over 8 to 9 miles of paths within the estate and these are also covered by guides in a programme running between March and September. In 'The Lady's Walk', 'The Garden Walk and Flower Garden', 'The Gentleman's Walk', 'The Ystwyth Gorge Walk', 'Coed Hafod Walk' and 'Bedford Memorial Walk' they take in diverse landscapes and dramatic scenery from open parkland to woodland, Peiran Cascade and Falls, the chain bridge, 'Tunnel', 'Cavern Cascade' and a route around the mansion fields and paths along the River Ystwyth.

To continue with the tour, turn right from the car park and back track to the sharp bend on the B4574 at Cwmystwyth and then turn left towards Devil's Bridge, rising as far as the rough stone **Hafod Arch** spanning the road at the highest point of the estate. This was constructed in 1810 by Thomas Johnes to mark the Jubilee of George III, 'Farmer George', and more recently restored by the Forestry Commission, whose adjacent car park provides a base for walks and trails to suit all tastes and physical states. These are

The Hafod Arch

waymarked through 200-year-old beech trees and spacious larch woodland and one, The Pwllpeiran Trail, is associated with a name, once part of the estate and now an ADAS Research Centre, that has long been concerned with experimental husbandry and change and development in the Welsh uplands. This was activity close to the heart of Thomas Johnes, and on its way the trail rather fittingly passes through Gelmast, the site of his original experimental farm.

The B4574 descends from the arch to the A4120 at Devil's Bridge, turning right to shadow the Rheidol in passing through Ysbyty Cynfyn, eventually crossing over the river after turning left onto the A44 at Ponterwyd. The George Borrow Hotel is on the left, and after just over a mile, the **lead/silver mine museum** is up a drive to the right at Llywernog (see above). Less than a mile further on to the right comes the Forestry Commission Wales Centre at **Bwlch Nant yr Arian**. This was opened in June 2005 and it offers '*Rhywbeth i Bawb*' — 'Something for Everyone', all the year round. Close to the Visitor Centre and restaurant there are children's playgrounds and picnic sites, kite feeding takes place at the nearby lake at 2pm (winter) and 3pm (summer), there are mountain bike trails and walks through woodland and along ridge-tops — and stunning views are all around. From the lookout point above the car park (pay and display), the finest of these is to the west, down the valley towards Goginan (see above) and thence Capel Bangor, which is where the A44 now heads, soon to meet with the Rheidol again as they both then head finally through Llanbadarn Fawr for Aberystwyth and the Bay.

Near the Visitor Centre at Bwlch Nant yr Arian ...

and view from the car park towards the coast

Glossary of some of the words occurring in Welsh place names

Welsh is a phonetic language with no J, K, Q, V, X or Z. The initial letter of some words changes according to the rules of mutation. Accent should be pronounced on the penultimate syllable.

Aber: confluence of a river or stream
Afon: a river
Allt: hillside or wood
Amroth: near the mound or fort
Ap, Ab: son of
Aran: mountain ridge
Arth: hill
Bach, fach: small
Ban, fan: mountain or lofty
Bedd: a grave
Barcud: a kite
Blaen: source of river; heart of valley
Bod: dwelling
Bont, pont: a bridge
Borth: a gateway or harbour; landing place
Bras: prominent rounded hill
Bron: a hillside
Bryn: a hill
Bugail: a shepherd
Builth, buallt: a cow pasture
Bwlch: a pass
Bychan: small
Byr: short
Cabon: a hut
Cadair, cader: a chair, stronghold
Cae: a field
Caer, Gaer: a fort, stronghold
Cam, gam: crooked
Camddwr: a winding stream
Canol: middle
Capel: a chapel
Carn, carnedd: a heap of stones; a cairn
Castell; castle
Cefn: ridge
Cerrig: rocky stones
Cemaes: river bends
Claerwen: bright sunny water
Clarach: flat land
Clas: a religious community

Clawdd: bank, hedge, hillside
Coch, goch: red
Coed: woodland
Cors, gors: bog
Craig, graig: rock or crag
Crib: ridge
Croes: cross, crossroad
Crug: mound, cairn, tump
Cul: narrow
Cwm: shallow valley
Cwrt: court or mansion
Cymer: meeting of river
Cynghordy: a house of meeting
Dan: below, under
Darren: a hill
Deg: fair
Dinas: a fort, camp
Dol: a meadow
Domen: mound
Draws: across
Dre, dref: town, hamlet, home
Drum: ridge
Du, ddu: black
Dwr, ddwr: water
Dyffryn: a valley
Eglwys: a church
Epynt: haunt of the pony, horse track
Esgair: a mountain ridge
Esgob: a bishop
Felin: a mill
Foel: a bare topped hill
Fron: a hillside
Ffridd: mountain pasture
Ffrwd: a stream, waterfall
Ffynnon: a well or spring
Gallt: hillside
Glas: green, blue
Gwaelod: bottom
Gwastad: flat, plain

Gwaun: moor, meadow
Gwylfa: viewpoint
Gwyn: white
Gwynt: wind
Hafod: a summer dwelling or pasture
Hen: old
Hendre: winter dwelling, main home
Heol: a road
Hepste: a river that dries up
Hir: long
Is: below
Isaf: lower
Llan: originally a sanctified burial enclosure
        and later containing a church
Llech: a flat stone, slate
Llwyn: a bush or grove
Llyn: a lake or pool
Llys: a court or mansion
Maen: a rock, stone
Maes: an open field
Mawr, fawr: big, great
Melyn: yellow
Moel, moelfre: bare topped hill
Mor: sea
Morfa: salt marsh
Mwnt: mound or hill
Myddfai: meadow of the round hollow
Mynach, fynach: a monk
Mynachdy, mynachlog: a monastery
Mynydd, fynydd: a mountain
Nant: a stream or small valley and stream
Neuadd: a hall or mansion
Newydd: new
Odyn: kiln
Ogof: cave
Pandy: fulling mill
Pant: a hollow or valley
Parc: a park
Pellaf: farthest
Pembrey: top of the hill
Pen: top
Pendine, pentywyn: end of sand dunes

Penrhyn: rocky promontory
Pentre, pentref: a village
Pistyll: a waterfall
Plas: a mansion
Poeth: warm
Pwll: a pit or pool
Rhandirmwyn: land of minerals
Rhayader, Rhaeadr: a waterfall
Rhiw: a hillside
Rhos: moorland
Rhyd: a ford or stream
Saeth: an arrow
Sarn: a paved way
Scwd: a waterfall
Sgethrog: rocky
Sir: shire
Sych: dry
Tan: under
Teg: fair
Tenby (Dinbych): small fort
Tir: land
Towyn: place of sand, beach
Traeth: shore, strand
Traws: across
Tre: a homestead, home, town
Troed: fort
Tros: over
Twll: a hole
Twmp: a mound
Ty: a house
Tyn: a small farm or cottage
Uchaf: highest
Uwch: above
Van, Fan: a peak
Vron, fron: a hillside
Waun: moorland or meadow
Wen, wyn: white
Wylfa: viewpoint
Y: the (before consonants)
Ynys: river meadow or island
Yr: the (before vowels)
Ysbyty: hospice

General Glossary

Age of the Saints: The 400-year-long period of the Dark Ages after the end of the Roman Empire, also when Christianity established a hold in Wales.

Anticline: An upfold in the rocks produced by bending of the beds under pressure from the sides.

Anthracite: Shiny coal with over 88% carbon content.

Arcade: A series of arches supported by piers or columns

Ascetic: Indicates an austere life of systematic and strict spiritual self-discipline.

Ashlar: Large masonry blocks cut to even faces and square edges

Austin Canons (also **Black Canons):** Augustinians living in a community bound by religious views and under a rule of creative pastoral ministry. Distinct from monks (below)

Bailey : Defended outer courtyard of a motte or castle.

Barbican: Outwork defence of a castle entrance.

Barrow: Earth or earth and stone burial mound. Mainly Bronze Age.

Bronze Age: From *c.*2000 to 600BC, divided at 1400 and 900BC into Early, Middle and Late

Burgage plots: Generally long, narrow property units in a medieval borough.

Burial Chamber (so **cromlech** or **dolmen):** Neolithic communal grave of upright stones supporting a capstone, usually once but generally no longer, covered by an earth or stone mound.

Cairn: A stone mound covering a Neolithic or Bronze Age burial, or simply stones gathered from field clearance for agriculture.

Cambrian: The oldest system of fossil-bearing rock formed between *c.*500 and 400 million years ago.

Cantref: A hundred townships, a unit of land division from pre-Norman times.

Carboniferous: The geological system formed between *c.*280 and 219 million years ago. The coal measures and most Welsh lime-stones come from this system.

Celts: Migrants from southern Germany of *c.*500 BC. They are associated with the beginning of the Iron Age and are originators of the Welsh, Gaelic and Breton languages.

Cist: A stone-lined or slab-built grave.

Clas: A Celtic monastic community.

Commote: A subdivision of a cantref (above).

Conglomerate: Rock formed of pebbles and rounded boulders in a matrix of fine material.

Corbel: A projecting stone for the support of floor or roof timbers.

Cup Marks: Mysterious man-made depressions in rock of Neolithic/Early Bronze Age period.

Curtain Wall: Courtyard enclosure, often reinforced by towers.

Dark Ages: Period from the fall of the Roman Empire in Britain until *c.*1000 AD

Decorated: English Gothic architecture dated *c.*1290 to *c.*1350.

Deheubarth: Early Welsh kingdom created by Hywel Dda *c.*950. Most of south Wales west of Powys, Brycheinog and Morgannwy.

Early English: English Gothic architecture roughly covering the 13th century.

Early medieval period: Between AD 410 and 1066.

Erosion: The natural wearing of surfaces by running water, glaciers, avalanches, wind &c.

Erratic: A boulder carried from its original bed, generally by the action of glacial ice.

Fold: Flexure in rocks caused by compression of the earth's crust.

Friar: Member of an order that combines significant elements of monastic life with an active ministry 'in the world'. The principal orders are Franciscans, Grey Friars, Dominicans, Black Friars, Carmelites, White Friars, and known as 'mendicant orders'. Distinct from monks.

Gothic: A period of medieval architecture characterised by the use of the pointed arch.

Subdivided into Early English, Decorated and Perpendicular.

Hatchment: A tablet displaying the armorial bearings of the named deceased.

Hillfort: Late Bronze Age and Iron Age embankment of earth or stone built to defend hill-tops and coastal promontories.

Ice Age: The present ice age began approximately 40 million years ago and Earth is now in an interglacial period after the last retreat by glaciers ended about 10,000 years ago.

Igneous rock: Formed by the solidification of molten material from the earth's interior.

Iron Age: The period from *c*.600 BC to AD 43

Lancet: A plain slender window with a pointed arch

Lordship: An area ruled by a lord under the supremacy of the king.

Limestone: Mostly calcium carbonate and of organic origin as sea shells or coral

Mabinogion: The collection of traditional past Welsh tales set down from the 12th century.

Medieval period, or Middle Ages: From AD 1066 to 1485.

Megalith: A large stone structure, for example a Neolithic tomb made of large slabs.

Mesolithic: Middle Stone Age of *c*.12,000 to 3,000 BC.

Monk: A man living under vows of poverty, celibacy and obedience for life in a monastic community. Either an ordained priest or choir monk, or a lay Brother, and different from a friar.

Motte: The mound of a castle supporting a tower and palisade. A Norman introduction.

Mudstone: A fine-grained sedimentary rock usually of silt and clay, laid down in deep water.

Neolithic: New Stone Age from *c*.3,000 BC to, 1,800 BC

Ogham: A 4th-century Irish system of writing with 20 characters formed on stone with notches and parallel lines.

Old Red Sandstone: Formed between *c*.400 to 350 million years ago.

Peel or Pele tower: A small defensive tower, such as that at Angle.

Perpendicular: English Gothic Architecture of *c*.1335-50 to *c*.1530

Pillow Mound: A man-made rabbit warren, dating from the Middle Ages

Post medieval period: From 1485.

Postern: A small gateway, subsidiary to the main castle entrance.

Pre Cambrian: A very long geological period of 570 million to 5,000 million years ago.

Promontory fort: Usually of the Iron Age on a coastal promontory or hill spur, defended on one side by at least one bank.

Putlog holes: Small square holes left in a wall face for scaffolding supports

Ringwork: Early castle made of an earth bank with an external ditch

Roman period: From AD 43 to AD 410.

Romanesque: Of a 12th century architectural style with round arches and thick walls. Often called Norman.

Saint: Formerly a well earned title of honour and respect of a person for his or her Christian devotion and accredited public veneration. Churches came to be dedicated in their honour.

Sandstone: Sedimentary rock of quartz grains forming a compacted bed of sand.

Slate: A dense and fine-grained metamorphic rock that readily splits into thin smooth plates.

Slight: Render a castle or other defence ineffective by demolition of stonework.

Stone Age: See Mesolithic and Neolithic.

Syncline: A downwarp in rock generally produced by the buckling of strata on its flanks.

Transitional: Architectural style generally regarded as between Romanesque and Early English

Tympanum: The triangular wall space between a lintel and the arch above.

Wheel Cross: A cross with an inset wheel joining the arms.

Further Reading

The titles of some published works, with their authors, that have been valued sources of factual information for this book have been included in the text. This further selection should also be useful for anyone who wishes to find out more about south-west Wales.

Pembrokeshire Coast Path. The Official National Park Guide. Alf Alderson. 2001

Pembrokeshire Coast Path. John H. Barrett. 1974; Dennis Kelsall. 2003; Brian John. 2004

Swansea and its Region. W.G.V. Balchin (ed). 1971

Wild Wales. George Borrow. 1862, 1955.

Exploring Wales. W.T. Barber. 1982

Pigs and Ingots. The lead/silver mines of Cardiganshire. Carr and Schone. 1993

Exploring the Pembrokeshire Coast. Phil Carradice. 2002

The Neolithic Sites of Carmarthenshire, Cardiganshire and Pembrokeshire. Children and Nash. 1997

Exploring Wales. William Condry 1970

The National Trust. Wales. William Condry 1991

Historic Gower. Paul Davis. 1997

A Company of Forts. Paul Davis. 2000.

A History of Wales. John Davies. 1990. 1993

The Making of Wales. John Davies. 1996

A Tour through the Whole Island of Great Britain. Daniel Defoe. 1724-6, abridged 1971

A History of Gower. Derek Draisey. 2002

The Story of the Milford Haven Waterway. Sybil Edwards. 2001

Ancient Monuments. South Wales and Monmouthshire. Sir Cyril Fox. 1950

Introducing West Wales. Maxwell Fraser. 1956

The Life and Times of the Swansea and Mumbles Railway. Gerald Gabb. 1987

The Journey through Wales / The Description of Wales. Gerald of Wales. 1188

The Mabinogion. Original introduction and translation. Charlotte Guest. 1849

Wales. South and West. John B. Hilling. 1976

Castles and Bishops Palaces of Pembrokeshire. Lise Hull. 2005

Cardiganshire. Interpreting an ancient County. J. Geraint Jenkins. 2005

The Geology of Pembrokeshire. Brian S. John. 1979

The Itinerary in Wales in and through the years 1536-9. John Leland. Toulmin-Smith (ed). 1994

Born on a Perilous Rock. Aberystwyth Past and Present. W.J. Lewis. 1980

Wales. R.M. Lockley. 1966

The Island. R.M. Lockley. 1969

The Golden Wreck. Alexander McKee, 1986

The Architecture of Death: *The Neolithic Chambered Tombs of Wales.* George Nash. 2006

The Brecon and Abergavenny Canal. John Norris. 1998

Rhandirmwyn: A Brief History. David Owen. 1993

Twm Siôn Cati: Life and Legend. David Owen. 2004

Description of Penbrockeshire in Generall. George Owen. 1603. Dillwyn Miles (ed). 1994

The Buildings of Wales. Pevsner Architectural Guides. Powys 1979; *Pembrokeshire* 2004; *Carmarthenshire and Ceredigion* 2006

Military Airfields. Wales. Alan Phillips. 2006

The Physicians of Myddfai. Facsimile reprint of the English translation by John Pughe. 1861
The Castles of Wales. Alan Reid. 1998
Wales. History of a Nation. David Ross. 2005
Castles of South West Wales. Mike Salter. 1996
Portrait of South Wales. Michael Senior. 1974
St. Davids Peninsula. Jacki Sime. 1999
The Towns of Medieval Wales. Ian Soulsby. 1983
South Wales. Ward Lock Guide. 1950
South Wales. Black's Guide Books. 1910
South Wales. British Regional Geology. 1970
Drovers Roads of Wales II. Toulson and Forbes. 1992
The Shell Guide to Wales. W. Vaughan-Thomas and A. Llewellyn. 1969
Wales. Wynford Vaughan-Thomas. 1981
The New Shell Guide. South and West Wales. Wynford Vaughan-Thomas. 1987
South Wales. G.W. and J.H. Wade. 1913
Birds of the Welsh Coast. T.G. Walker. 1956
The Secret Waterway. Milford Haven and Daugleddau. Theodore Whalley (ed) and others. 1988

Index

Pembrokeshire: a year and a day

144 pages, 125 photographs, full colour.
Hardback (ISBN 978 1904396 73 4) £20;
Paperback (ISBN 978 190396 72 7) £12.95

Eleven photographers have come together to provide a mix of images that show Pembrokeshire in its stunning beauty in a range of light and across the seasons. Portrayed are numerous of the county's bays, stretches of the coastline, several historic sites, occasional remnants of the industrial past, sporting activities, the Preselis, the Gwaun valley and much flora. Some of the photographs are taken from the air, and one dangling from a rope. The quality of images is undeniable and several will cause pause for thought.

Fishguard Fiasco

by John S. Kinross, 128 pages paperback, 40 illustrations, (ISBN 978 1904396 68 0) £9.95
(A revamp and resetting of the book first published in 1974)

Why choose to land an invading force at Fishguard and then surrender with hardly a shot being fired on either side? The range of possible options given to the commander of this force from Revolutionary France, the American William Tate, suggest that it was seen more as a chance to offload a prison population on the English. If they should happen to burn Bristol, or raise the Welsh in revolt, or act as a flying column up the Welsh border to join with French and Irish forces landing in Liverpool, having successfully freed Ireland, then so much the better.

As it was, the force landed at Fishguard, the ill-fed French troops feasted on all the food they could find to hand and washed it down with copious amounts of alcohol. Coupled with lack of decisiveness by Tate to make the most of his surprise appearance, this left them in no fit state to face the hastily assembled bands of Yeomanry and Militia, backed up, at least in the popular imagination, by scythe wielding Welsh women in their national costume, which the inebriated French supposedly took for additional regular army units.

Also from Logaston Press

Castles and Bishops Palaces of Pembrokeshire
Volume X in the Monuments in the landscape Series
by Lise Hull, 240 pages, over 100 illustrations, (ISBN 978 1904396 31 4) Price £7.95

It was with the Norman arrival in the area around 1093 that castle building commences. It was then that Arnulf de Montgomery founded Pembroke Castle as the centre of his *castellarium* which later grew into the seat of the earldom of Pembroke. Within 50 years of their arrival, the invaders had built a line of castles on the southern side of the Preselis that was to become the Landsker line, with a second clutch to the north of the Preselis. Pembrokeshire has a rich heritage of still standing castles: massive Pembroke, Manorbier on the south coast, the towering remnants of Haverfordwest, the bishops castle at Llawhaden, Cilgerran and the much upgraded Carew, along with those still occupied such as Roch, Picton and Upton. Often clustered around these are the remains of an assortment of mottes or ringworks, sometimes with a bailey, which may have formed part of the early Norman encroachment and presence, or perhaps served as bases for knights who owed allegiance to the nearby lord. Also covered are the bishops palaces that form part of Pembrokeshire's rich heritage. A series of chapters give an overview of the county's military history from 905 to the Civil War of the 1640s, after which each site is given its own entry detailing its construction and history, together with a note about specific location and access arrangements.

Castles of Glamorgan
Volume XII in the Monuments in the Landscape Series
by Lise Hull, 256 pages, close to 100 illustrations, (ISBN 978 1904396 75 8) Price £7.95

With the penetration of the Normans into the fertile plains of Glamorgan, castle building began in earnest. Some of the early earth and timber structures were gradually replaced in stone, others seemed to have progressed no further and perhaps were either always seen as temporary structures, or once destroyed by the Welsh were never rebuilt. In the uplands of the county some of the castles were built by the Welsh in reaction to the Norman arrival.

Introductory chapters set the historical scene for the construction and subsequent development of the castles. The grandest surviving example is that at Caerphilly. Cardiff Castle is now probably best known for the palatial house it became under the Marquesses of Bute, but the medieval castle remains in the grounds. Gower has a plethora of stone castle remains, amongst them Loughor, Oystermouth, Oxwich, Penrice, Pennard, and Weobley, along with more fragmentary remains of that at Swansea. Elsewhere there is the very scenic hill-top site of Morlais above Merthyr Tydfil, extensive remains at Coity, Newcastle Bridgend and Ogmore; a cluster of stone and earthwork remains to the east of Cowbridge; the remains of Kenfig half-buried in sand dunes; and a bevy of much less known (and known-about) earthwork remains scattered across the county, from the suburbs of Cardiff to the coastline of Gower. For all of these and more, Lise Hull sets out what there is to see (and arrangements for access) and provides a history of the site.